Decolonisation in Universities

Decolonisation in Universities

The Politics of Knowledge

EDITED BY Jonathan D. Jansen

WITS UNIVERSITY PRESS

Published in South Africa by:
Wits University Press
1 Jan Smuts Avenue
Johannesburg 2001

www.witspress.co.za

First published 2019

http://dx.doi.org.10.18772/22019083351

978-1-77614-335-1 (Paperback)
978-1-77614-336-8 (Web PDF)
978-1-77614-337-5 (EPUB)
978-1-77614-338-2 (Mobi)

Project manager: Elaine Williams
Copyeditor: Colin Bundy
Proofreader: Alison Lockhart
Indexer: Elaine Williams
Cover design: Hothouse South Africa
Typesetter: Newgen
Typeset in 10.5 point Minion Pro

Contents

List of Figures

Acronyms and Abbreviations

ANC	African National Congress
ASC	Africas Core
CAPRISA	Centre for the AIDS Programme of Research in South Africa
CAS	Centre for African Studies
CHE	Council on Higher Education
CPUT	Cape Peninsula University of Technology
DE	Development Education
EASE	East African Society and Environment
EFF	Economic Freedom Fighters
HBU	historically black university
HEI	higher education institution
HRE	human rights education
HWU	historically white university
IDS	Institute of Development Studies
IKS	indigenous knowledge systems
IMF	International Monetary Fund
ISA	Income Sharing Agreement
ITE	initial teacher education
NQF	National Qualifications Framework
NRF	National Research Foundation
OBE	outcomes-based education
PEZ	Political Economy of Zimbabwe
RAU	Rand Afrikaans University
#RMF	Rhodes Must Fall
SACE	South African Council for Educators
SACHED	South African Committee for Higher Education
SAQA	South African Qualifications Authority
SARChI	South African Research Chairs Initiative
UCT	University of Cape Town
UFH	University of Fort Hare
UFS	University of the Free State
UJ	University of Johannesburg
UNISA	University of South Africa
UP	University of Pretoria
UWC	University of the Western Cape
Wits	University of the Witwatersrand

Making Sense of Decolonisation in Universities

Jonathan D. Jansen
Stellenbosch University

The student protests starting in 2015 added a new term to the lexicon of South African universities – decolonisation. It is of course a word with a long history dating back to the anti-colonial struggles of the 1950s and extending to the postcolonial period to signal ongoing efforts to 'undo' the legacies of colonialism. But decolonisation had never been a prominent or sustained component of the struggle discourse under or after apartheid. The discursive terminologies of the struggle included terms like anti-apartheid education, liberation pedagogy, reconstruction and development education, and of course that ubiquitous referent, transformation. Literally overnight, the word decolonisation rolled off the lips of activists, bannered everyday protests and initiated across mainly the formerly white campuses seminars, conferences and committees to determine meanings and methods for changing universities – their complexions, cultures and curricula.

This book brings together the best curriculum minds in South Africa to make sense of decolonisation as a signal moment in the century-old history of higher education in South Africa. What does the word even mean? Why does it emerge at this moment, more than 20 years into democracy? Where does the press for decolonisation come from – intellectually, socially, culturally and politically? How does it relate to associated concepts such as Africanisation or indigenous education or postcolonial education? Is decolonisation the appropriate response, substantively and strategically, to the complex of problems gripping the education system in South Africa? Does the term decolonisation carry much validity in a country last formally colonised more than 100 years ago? Or is decolonisation simply a byword for proxy discontents in education and society? And what does decolonisation imply for the nature, purposes and politics of curriculum?

THE CONCEPTUAL ORIENTATION OF THE BOOK

In the literature, decolonisation is a concept that has been applied broadly to various things, from changes to the artworks of a university to the social transformation of entire nations. The specific focus of this book, however, is primarily on decolonisation as applied to the university curriculum; that is, as a *knowledge* project.

The question of knowledge as framed in this book is a political subject and therefore the decolonisation thesis is interrogated from the viewpoint of *The Politics of Knowledge*, as reflected in the subtitle of this volume. There is in fact a long and continuing tradition of scholarship on the politics of knowledge in political studies more broadly (Neave 2006; Dominguez Rubio and Baert 2012) and in curriculum studies more specifically (Apple 1979; Lim and Apple 2016).

The starting point of this tradition is that knowledge is never neutral. Who produces knowledge, what knowledge is produced and what knowledge is 'left out' are central questions of inquiry within the politics of knowledge. This is what Michael Apple (1993) calls 'the selective tradition' or what Elliot Eisner (1985) once referenced as 'the null curriculum' – that what is 'left out' in the choice of knowledge is consequential for both social and disciplinary learning. Those knowledge choices, critical theorists would argue, are political decisions vested in authorities like the government in power, commercial textbook publishers and international funding agencies (Littoz-Monnet 2017).

Knowledge and power are therefore inextricably linked, whether in global interstate relations or in curriculum decision-making affecting schools. This intriguing relationship between knowledge and power is co-dependent, leading to what Hans Weiler calls 'reciprocal legitimation' (Weiler and Jansen 2019). Knowledge draws its authority from power, which in turn legitimates itself through the authority of knowledge.

Decolonial theorists would argue that the regnant knowledge in the former colonies draws its authority from the West and, in particular, from the former colonial powers. What is 'left over' is a legacy in which established knowledge retains its authority in the curriculum of once-subjugated territories in the form of a Eurocentric curriculum or traditional modes of assessment (such as the Cambridge O- and A-level examinations) or hierarchical relationships in the pedagogic relationship between the teacher and the students (Jansen 2017).

This book does not, however, take the politics of knowledge to be static over time or linear in its operations in the postcolonial period. Rather than taking this framing of Western knowledge authority as retentive and dominant within nations once colonised, the chapter contributions interrogate the politics of knowledge transactions in the relationship between the Global North and the Global South. Rather than assume passivity and dependence on hegemonic knowledge from the West, the book examines ways in which African leadership in knowledge production emerges *inside* these historical constraints so that the question of 'whose knowledge matters' is made complex by the flattening of relationships in knowledge partnerships between rich countries in the North and poorer nations in the South.

THE ARGUMENTS FOR DECOLONISATION

The first section of the book presents the arguments for decolonisation. Mahmood Mamdani starts by making the important point that the institutional form, and content, of the African university lies in colonial Europe. This is significant, for while precolonial institutions did exist (Timbuktu and Alexandria, for example) – a point of pride in African debates on knowledge – the institutional and curricular implications of European origins has a direct bearing on the change project, as Lis Lange and Jonathan Jansen, separately, discuss in later chapters. In other words, knowledge itself has become institutionalised and therefore simple declaratory statements about the need to decolonise curricula involve a much more complex subject than bold political manifestos or hastily assembled curriculum committees would suggest.

The uniqueness of Mamdani's contribution – first presented in the form of the 2017 T.B. Davie Memorial Lecture at the University of Cape Town – is that he is able to trace these debates on the knowledge project to the East African universities of Dar es Salaam (known by its shorthand, Dar, 'the flagbearer of anti-colonial nationalism') and Makerere ('the paradigmatic colonial university') in the 1960s and 1970s. What should the African university be for?

These debates flowing between Dar and Makerere were, respectively, between relevance and excellence; place versus ideas; justice against academic freedom; and anti-colonial nationalism as opposed to the accommodation of the universal scholar. Mamdani gives embodiment to these rival ideas through the compelling voices of two of Africa's most prodigious scholars at the time – Walter Rodney and Ali Mazrui. This location of the debates in East Africa is vital for understanding the emergence of decolonisation in South Africa as late as 2015, for it points to a richness of intellectual exchange on the subject that must be taken account of in how the knowledge project is pursued after apartheid. What can we learn from the experiences of these two iconic universities? What did happen to the knowledge project in those contexts? What were the internal and external forces that gave shape to the curriculum after independence? And could Africa's universities really upend the deeper epistemological dilemmas of knowledge – what Mazrui called 'modes of reasoning' – in radical attempts at changing curricula? What Mamdani does is to force South African scholars and activists alike to avoid the trap of exceptionalism by tracing the long path of these debates on knowledge, the colony and decolonisation – and to examine critically the prospects for change.

Whereas Mamdani situates the debate on decolonisation within African historical perspective, Lesley Le Grange places the subject in broader comparative relief. His work among indigenous peoples of New Zealand and Australia casts fresh light on the South African struggles for decolonisation. Le Grange's arguments are cogent, drawing on a range of concepts in curriculum theory to make the case for decolonisation. This is what has been absent from national deliberations on the decolonisation of knowledge – the work of curriculum theorists who are well placed to examine the discursive meanings of the subject within the literature of this exciting field of inquiry called curriculum theory.

Were curriculum concerns in fact neglected in the euphoria of South Africa's political transition, as Le Grange contends? Did matters of access, equity and mergers of universities really dominate policymaking and planning to the exclusion of the knowledge project? Is the adoption of outcomes-based education (OBE) in fact a factory model of education or, as the OBE advocates claim, an attempt to make knowledge explicit and accessible to the disadvantaged? These are important questions that again place the other chapters in conversation with this one – such as Lange's contention that curriculum was in fact a matter of policy deliberation, but concerned with the externalities of knowledge (such as qualification standards) rather than the content of curricula. Which in turn raises other concerns, such as whether the state in fact *should* have a determining role in the knowledge question, as far as autonomous institutions are concerned.

Crain Soudien and Jonathan Jansen, in their respective chapters, argue that there have, in fact, been significant changes to university curricula since 1994 and that the failure to acknowledge this fact undermines the new momentum for re-examining settled knowledges.

Le Grange is not, however, an uncritical advocate of decolonisation. He is aware of the experiences of scholars and activists in Australasia where, even though indigenous knowledge is officially recognised, adding a module to the university curriculum or offering separate streams that include local content hardly qualifies as the kind of transformative move that gives due recognition to decolonisation struggles at the *institutional* level. This is a timely warning, since there is some evidence that South African universities are doing exactly that – tinkering with modules and courses in some humanities disciplines without the deep interrogation of what counts as knowledge in the institutional curriculum; André Keet, in his chapter, takes on this problem of 'the intellectual hair spraying' of the disciplines with intent.

Nor does Le Grange fall into the trap of discarding Western knowledge in favour of indigenous knowledge. He recognises the value of both even as he criticises the universal claims to truth presumed in the colonial legacy with respect to knowledge. This author is also practical in this strong conceptual chapter by proposing the kinds of actions that could systematically lead to a rethinking of inherited knowledges. In this respect Le Grange's knowledge of curriculum theory is invaluable for giving conceptual clarity to a complex debate. Nevertheless, one question that will always be asked of his very rational approach to curriculum change is whether it would have any *institutional* purchase given the power of settled knowledges.

THE POLITICS AND PROBLEMS OF DECOLONISATION

That is exactly the kind of question taken on in a set of three chapters questioning in different ways the uncritical adoption of the language of decolonisation 20 years into South Africa's democratic transition. Jansen's starting point is that decolonisation is simply one of the many discursive terms emerging from a society in which political slogans often carry important concepts, which then come to assume common-sense meanings in everyday use on campuses and in communities: concepts such as 'white monopoly capital' or 'radical economic transformation'. The role of the social scientist is to interrogate such concepts as they emerge in society by asking questions like: Why does the particular slogan/concept emerge now? Who are its advocates? And whose purposes does it serve?

The reduction of complex curriculum problems, argues Jansen, to one particular kind of regime, colonialism, is to deny the many ways in which knowledge has been propagated, contested, nullified, subverted and transformed across more than three centuries stretching from the precolonial society to post-apartheid governance. These episodes in governance Jansen calls knowledge regimes – specifically referring to the relationship between the state and knowledge in each period of history. While Jansen points to continuities across knowledge regimes, he also describes knowledge emphases that differ from, say, colonial rule to apartheid to democracy. To understand what happens to curricula in these respective periods of history is to recognise the complexity of the knowledge problem over time and the danger of reducing all such dilemmas to 'colonialism'.

Nor does it help to insist on framing the knowledge problem in terms derived from the 1960s when the overlay of world system theory and, in particular, dependency theory posed the problem of an all-powerful (and epistemologically homogenous) West imposing its will on vulnerable, weak and powerless colonies or former colonies. A sense of the world in which knowledge is increasingly co-produced through powerful partnerships in those two parts of the world system is a pervasive reality that defies an earlier but persistent notion that theory is developed in the West and applied in Africa and other parts of the formerly colonised world. Jansen draws attention to such complexity through specific examples in the South African university system of international knowledge leadership in fields as diverse as immunology, southern African history and cardiovascular disease.

Lange situates the problem of decolonisation within the politics of recognition. Black students not only feel alienated within the dominant white culture and authority of the English liberal universities, but also feel they are not recognised in their full humanity in these strange environments. Such recognition should therefore be reflected in, inter alia, the curriculum, which centres white/European knowledge to the exclusion of African knowledges. In other words, one way of being recognised is in *what* is being taught. This is important terrain and yet, as Lange asks, what are the limits of identitarian politics?

Warnings about a narrow view of knowledge and identity are not new to curriculum theory. As Le Grange points out, it was William Pinar, the eminent curriculum theorist, whose warning about the narcissism of identity politics went something like this: If I don't see myself in the curriculum, it is not mine and I reject it. In an interconnected age when knowledge is increasingly produced from across the planet and in collaboration between institutions and individuals across the world system, a broader perspective on curriculum is required, one that pursues a more cosmopolitan knowledge rather than narrow nationalist ends. And yet this must be done in ways that take account of the quest for justice in curriculum through, for example, the recognition of black presence in former white institutions.

What makes Lange's contribution particularly powerful is her distinction between the academic curriculum (the everyday practices of teaching, learning and assessment) and the institutional curriculum (the routines, rules and regulations that constitute particular ways of thinking about knowledge, authority and change). The former is relatively easy to alter but the latter is where change becomes difficult and, as Lange warns, a new line of research is required to determine whether, over time, the energy and enthusiasm around decolonisation in fact leads to deeper transformations in the institutional curriculum.

The third contribution in this section on the politics and problems of decolonisation comes from Ursula Hoadley and Jaamia Galant. What counts as knowledge? What are the rules for determining disciplinary knowledge in fields such as mathematics? How is membership of the academy decided and what criteria are used to validate knowledge? These are important questions for this book because they bring to attention something not talked about in decolonisation forums – the question of evaluation.

The two authors bring to their analysis the complex but important work of the English sociologist Basil Bernstein on the framing, selection and evaluation of knowledge. And while the decolonisation moment has addressed the first two elements, little is said about the grounds for deciding what knowledge counts within the disciplines. The selection of knowledge cannot simply be informed by political calculation, whether in physics or sociology or anatomy, but has to derive from evaluative rules that have to do with the deep knowledge of the disciplines.

To make this point, Hoadley and Galant provide an insightful discussion on a controversial lecture by a visiting Indian mathematician to the University of Cape Town at the height of the decolonisation debates, one C.K. Raju. What if, as in Raju's case, the arguments for decolonisation are based on caricature, derision and the misrepresentation of knowledge – its nature, origins and constitution in the disciplines? What if personal slight and non-recognition across fields is at stake rather than concerns about knowledge and curriculum? And what if such non-recognition of the individual is based on not having satisfied the evaluative criteria for admission to membership of a discipline?

These are crucial questions because the simplistic notion that content can be added or removed from established disciplinary knowledge on the whim of recognition politics is of course highly problematic, especially when one moves beyond the core humanities fields. Such caution also speaks to the facile positions of recent curriculum committees on university campuses where demonstrating new content has become more important than establishing the intellectual validity of what passes as decolonised knowledge. Several chapter contributors speak to this issue, including Achille Mbembe and Piet Naudé.

DOING DECOLONISATION

More than one author in this book points to the absence of theory and in particular curriculum theory for making sense of decolonisation. They also point to the considerable gap between high theory in decolonisation writings and the practicalities of 'making decolonisation work' on the ground. This section of the book presents the work of academics who engage in the practice of the decolonisation of knowledge and they reveal some powerful insights for curriculum theory as well as the prospects for curriculum change in South African universities.

On the Indian Ocean island of Mauritius a higher education entrepreneur was in the process of establishing an ambitious leadership institution that would train entrepreneurship leaders across the African continent. This highly innovative programme attracted with its inspiring vision scores of young lecturers eager to participate in the establishment of the new university. A core group decided to create a radical new 'Africa Studies' curriculum that would represent the best social science programme on the continent. For the creators of this curriculum, it was to be 'innovative, engaging, pedagogically cutting edge ... and decolonial'. With great energy and commitment the designers set about giving content to the curriculum they recognised as 'our decolonial elephant'. Conscious of movements like #RhodesMustFall in South Africa and #BlackLivesMatter in the USA, the group mobilised students to engage with leaders and literatures on decolonisation.

There was however a major problem. The decolonised curriculum was being offered in the context of a corporate university whose leaders would come to define the new mission in business terms – scale and impact mattered; making donors feel comfortable was more important than disruptive knowledge; and aligning the leadership institution with a European university was required by the government, even if that 'curriculum [was] firmly rooted in the epistemologies and needs of the Global North'. While initially supportive of the African Studies curriculum, leadership would gradually discourage this bold innovation for 'in a corporate environment ... brand loyalty is absolutely crucial'.

In this Mauritian case study there are two critical lessons for efforts that seek to decolonise curricula. First, institutional power and leadership authority matter. When a curriculum innovation emerges from junior faculty without the support and funding of senior leadership, its chances of success are slim. Second, the institutional environment functions to regulate discordant initiatives out of business, so to speak. This is the case in the corporate environment of this Mauritian institution where profits come before the politics of knowledge, and donors ahead of epistemological discord.

Crain Soudien presents for critical analysis another case study, this time of a major South African initiative to change curriculum, the South African Research Chairs Initiative (SARChI) in Development Studies at the University of South Africa (UNISA). Since the Chair was established in 2008, it is not surprising that the term decolonisation does not appear in the founding documents; as indicated earlier, this particular language is new in education struggles in South Africa. However, the core ideas associated with decolonisation form part of the rationale for the Chair in Development Education – critiquing the presumed superiority of Western knowledge and, in the process, recovering and restoring indigenous knowledges at the centre of the curriculum.

The signal contribution of this Chair, occupied by Professor Catherine Odora Hoppers, was to make a strong conceptual case for 'transformation by enlargement'. The notion of knowledge becoming more inclusive is rather different from the 'recall and replace' demands of some of the more urgent advocates of decolonisation. Such 'hospitality to all knowledge forms' is not, however, uncritical of standards of validation and the quest for cognitive justice in bringing to the epistemological table those knowledges left out in deliberations inside, between and across the disciplines.

But then the hosting institution, UNISA, despite earlier suggestions of continued support, decided not to continue funding the project and it came to an abrupt end just as it was poised to make a major contribution to an emergent politics of decolonisation. Soudien asks the pertinent question – 'Why was it so difficult for the university to sustain the initiative?' This query, I would like to propose, has little to do with practicalities of the immediate – not enough budget or uncommitted university leaders. What is really in question here is a much larger institutional question, as in the case of the Mauritian institution. Here Soudien draws on writings about homeostatic systems 'that respond to certain kinds of change with built-in mechanisms that restore certain aspects of the status quo'. At UNISA, as at the Mauritian university, institutional curricula remain powerful by keeping discordant change at the margins.

The third and final example of 'doing decolonisation' is offered by Yusuf Sayed, Shireen Motala and Tarryn de Kock, whose specific focus is on the teacher education curriculum. What these authors tackle is the neglected subject of 'who teaches' the presumed decolonised curriculum. The assumptions about the teachers in the push for decolonisation have always been highly problematic. The curriculum change assumption in South Africa has been that there are willing, committed and transformed teachers simply waiting to take the decolonised curriculum and 'implement' it in receptive classrooms for change to happen.

It is one thing decolonising knowledge but what does it even mean to shift the mindsets of the teachers (or in this case, teacher educators) in line with the political and epistemological demands of the new curriculum? A curriculum does not teach itself. It is interpreted through the personal and professional biographies of those who teach. This is what Sayed, Motala and De Kock found in their small but insightful sample of teachers and it extends, of course, to university lecturers. It should not surprise, therefore, that 'no single interviewee planned to change her or his curriculum in response to student activism'. If teachers in schools cannot be instructed to adopt a decolonised curriculum, then professors in universities are certainly not going to give up their autonomy to follow a radical script for teaching their students. This is where the rhetoric of decolonisation so often outstrips the realities of 'doing decolonisation' in school classrooms and university seminar rooms. And yet 'doing decolonisation' as a radical act means thinking differently about the university and what is taught beyond the formal curriculum.

REIMAGINING COLONIAL INHERITANCES

This is precisely where Brenda Schmahmann brings into focus the ways in which campus monuments and sculptures 'constitute a type of "curriculum" with the capacity to elicit enriched knowledge and understanding on the part of the viewers'. In other words, whether it is the statue of British imperialist Cecil John Rhodes on the University of Cape Town (UCT) campus or that of King George V at the University of Kwa-Zulu-Natal, these structures 'teach' important lessons about inclusion and exclusion as well as recognition and disregard. In this sense it is useful to think about curriculum not only as *content* in the narrow sense of meaning but also as *symbolism* – in other words, as standing in for something else.

But is the purging of statues from public spaces like the university campus a transformative act? Put differently, is replacing one kind of curriculum with another an educative experience? This is what the continent's leading scholar of campus commemorations addresses in this important chapter on 'Public Art and/as Curricula'. Schmahmann's thesis is provocative: that removal of offending structures like campus monuments is more a project of those on the political right than a progressive act that challenges understandings of the past and present. More than one university has grappled with how to engage with these commemorations – such as the Pink President's Project, the act of repurposing the prominent statue of Marthinus Theunis Steyn (last president of the Orange Free State republic) on the Bloemfontein campus of the University of the Free State (UFS).

It is striking that critical voices in the decolonisation debates can imagine with respect to formal knowledge an enlarged curriculum (Soudien, Le Grange, Jansen in their respective chapters) that does not replace Western knowledge with African knowledge but brings both into conversation, (re)centred on new and inclusive understandings of humanity. However, when it comes to public art as curricula, there is little appetite for such generosity, perhaps because of the particular representational form – single, visible, prominent and tangible. As was the case with Rhodes at UCT and more recently Steyn at the UFS, these statues are candidates for acts of erasure, suggesting that they cannot teach even with a critical repurposing of such commemorations. What activism has given us, instead, is a rather crude replacement of whatever stands in prominence on campuses, leading, as we now know, to attacks on the creative works of black artists such as Willie Bester at the UFS and artworks representing campaigners for black freedoms, such as the collages commemorating Molly Blackburn at UCT. Perhaps that is the point – by not knowing what these images/symbols in fact represent, the act of taking down what we do not know is a failure of curriculum to teach how to recognise and value affirming representations of ourselves and others. How we deal with the past represented in concrete memory matters. But there is another memory that carries so powerfully South African understandings of that past into the present – the concept of Ubuntu.

In the search for an Africa-centred knowledge, Ubuntu is often represented in popular discourses as an obvious referent for indigeneity. But what is Ubuntu, a term that has come to assume many meanings, not only scholarly but also political and commercial, over the long and troubled history of ideas in South Africa? Piet Naudé offers one of the most thorough treatments yet of the complex meanings of Ubuntu, its misrepresentations in academic usage ('something uniquely African') and its inescapable ties to Western trains of thought.

There are some very important contributions in Naudé's chapter that enrich the debates on the decolonisation of knowledge. For example, there is the frequent misrepresentation of Western knowledge as unitary when, in fact, the West itself has experienced considerable epistemological turmoil over more than a century that belies the descriptions of European science as positivist, universal and exclusionary; this is simply false. Then there is the important distinction between tacit knowledge (the everyday) and scientific knowledge for which standards of validity apply – a point also made by Hoadley and Galant in this book about the evaluative function in the determination of knowledge. And Naudé rightly warns of the dangers of any kind of centring of knowledge where an African centre simply creates another kind of asymmetry in dealing with curriculum dilemmas.

Naudé's approach is not to dismiss Ubuntu but to ask how this important concept can become Africa-centred knowledge. He evaluates three ways of doing this in the specific context of business ethics – via transfer, translation or re-contextualisation of Western knowledge in African contexts. It is the third approach, re-contextualisation, he argues, that provides 'a de-centring of Eurocentric views and consequently a tempering of coloniality'. But Naudé stops there, for an actual epistemic decolonisation with respect to Western knowledge is simply not possible, given the existing rules of validation for knowledge and, as Mbembe might add, in the absence of a theory of knowledge that infuses the academic project. A rather pessimistic view of knowledge transformations, one might conclude.

André Keet, by contrast, is among the more optimistic of the contributors to this volume about the essential 'transformability' of institutions. His notion of plasticity – with its own rich intellectual history – and therefore of 'the plastic university' suggests that institutions are much more flexible, malleable and adaptable than some of the curriculum theorists hold. Keet's novel thesis is that we are 'disciplined by our disciplines' and therefore that the intellectual restraints we encounter are in fact imposed by ourselves. Whereas Hoadley and Galant bring to attention the criterial rules that validate disciplinary knowledge, Keet argues that the point of decolonisation is 'to dislodge the rules that generate the existing patterns of rewards and sanctions' with respect to the disciplines. In other words, the rules of validation are themselves up for grabs. Which raises the inevitable question – what comes after Keet's disruption and how do we know the resultant knowledge is valid?

The power of Keet's contribution is to warn of interventionist strategies that turn decolonisation into a metaphor and therefore justify superficial attempts at changing curriculum through, for example, the altering of modules here and there. There is something embedded within the deep structures of knowledge in the disciplines that must be excavated in order for meaningful changes to emerge in the university curriculum. Keet calls out the 'Eurocentric coding' of knowledge; Odora Hoppers (in Soudien's chapter) mentions the colonial pin codes that still determine valid knowledge; and the late Ali Mazrui referred to 'modes of reasoning' that kept scholars within Western frames of thought. For Keet, unlike Mazrui, there is a way out of these dilemmas through 'patience and [the] deep reflexive work required for the decolonisation of knowledge'.

DECOLONISATION AND THE FUTURE

What then does it mean to do such reflexive labour with regards to decolonisation in a world where knowledge is unbounded, learning is digital and algorithmic reasoning has become a new form of thinking? Achille Mbembe once again shifts the now circular debates on what/whose knowledge into the future – does it even matter when digital economies have fundamentally altered how we think about the disciplines? This after all is a world in which old antagonisms between the sciences and humanities, or nature and society, have all but dissolved, and time has been reconfigured on a planetary scale.

This plasticity (compare Keet) of digital forms is also evident in what Mbembe calls Afro-computation, in which 'boundaries of perception are being outstretched … and Africans are projected from one temporal regime to another'. His example is the mobile phone as a technology that allows for the extension of ourselves and changes our relationship with data/knowledge in significant ways. We can, in other words, imagine ourselves differently as a result of these new technologies.

What Mbembe might be pointing to is the staleness of our categories of thinking. Such thought is trapped in a time warp that recycles old language and conventions of decolonisation that work inside unchallenged hierarchies of knowledge, Western loci of control, hard boundaries between disciplines and 'them/us' understandings of content that are increasingly tenuous in a world experiencing 'the geological recasting of historical time'. We are in a different place, in other words, than the ideologies and technologies of the 1970s allowed us to see when the colonies were first being dismantled. What, in other words, does decolonisation look like in this world of Afro-computation, which has challenged and even changed the distribution of knowledge/power? That is an open question in need of exploration – looking towards the future.

It falls to Grant Parker, a scholar from Cape Town, now at the Department of Classics at Stanford University in California, to engage in a final act of sense-making of decolonisation as represented in this volume. Parker stands with a foot in both worlds – South Africa, and its concerns with decolonisation, and the USA, where struggles over the Western canon have for some time energised student politics on university campuses and

Stanford University in particular. A comparative perspective takes care of the simplistic notion of a Western consensus on what counts as valid knowledge amidst struggles over curriculum among marginalised groups in advanced capitalist societies. As a classicist Parker makes another key contribution in his synthesis chapter by pointing to the loss of subtlety and nuance in how South Africans deal with the 'sites of memory' where an unthinking displacement of prominent symbols often comes at the cost of a deeper transformation of the colonial legacy. This critical observation is related to another warning, and that is of the dangers of race essentialism in campus discourses that again threatens to derail a more critical politics of knowledge.

CONCLUSION

It was the explicit goal of this book to bring together social and curriculum theorists with different perspectives on the purposes, prospects and politics of decolonisation. The idea was to draw attention to the intellectual ferment within the South African academy and society about decolonisation, especially as it applies to knowledge codified in the university curriculum. The authors are, by discipline, historians, sociologists, educationists, comparativists, philosophers and anthropologists, and they all share a lifelong professional and scholarly interest in curriculum theory and practice. This synthetic, opening section has sought to introduce some of the connections across the chapters, the controversies among them and the coherence of the volume as a whole as a signal contribution to the contemporary literature on the politics of curriculum.

REFERENCES

Apple, Michael. 1979. *Ideology and Curriculum*. London: Routledge.

Apple, Michael. 1993. 'The Politics of Official Knowledge: Does a National Curriculum Make Sense?' *Discourse* 14 (1): 1–16. DOI: 10.1080/0159630930140101.

Dominguez Rubio, Fernando and Patrick Baert. 2012. *The Politics of Knowledge*. London: Routledge.

Eisner, Elliot. 1985. *The Educational Imagination*. New York: Macmillan.

Jansen, Jonathan D. 2017. *As by Fire: The End of the South African University*. Cape Town: Tafelberg.

Lim, Leonel and Michael Apple. 2016. *The Strong State and Curriculum Reform: Assessing the Politics and Possibilities of Educational Change in Asia*. New York: Routledge.

Littoz-Monet, Annabelle. 2017. *The Politics of Expertise in International Organizations: How International Bureaucracies Produce and Mobilize Knowledge*. New York: Routledge.

Neave, Guy. 2006. 'Mapping the Knowledge Society Back into Higher Education'. In *Knowledge, Power and Dissent: Critical Perspectives on Higher Education and Research in Knowledge Society*, edited by Guy Neave, 13–24. Paris: UNESCO.

Weiler, Hans and Jonathan Jansen D. 2019. 'Whose Knowledge Matters? The Politics of Knowledge and the Dynamics of Change in Higher Education'. Paper prepared for the Comparative and International Education Society (CIES) Conference, San Francisco, 14–18 April.

THE ARGUMENTS FOR DECOLONISATION

1

Decolonising Universities

Mahmood Mamdani
Makerere University and Columbia University

Institutions of higher education originated in different parts of the world in the premodern era[1], but it is only one particular historical experience, the Western, that became globalised during the modern colonial era. The modern university, as the name suggests, claims a universal significance as a site for the study of the human. Its graduates claim 'excellence' globally. This chapter draws on the experience of two universities, Makerere University and the University of Dar es Salaam, and the contribution of two intellectual figures, Ali Mazrui and Walter Rodney, to flesh out some key post-independence debates regarding the role of the university and the scholar. The first debate arises from the nationalist demand that the university be a site of 'relevance', and not just 'excellence'. This demand informed debates over curriculum, leading to a second debate over the relationship between two different roles: those of the public intellectual and the scholar, articulated as the difference between 'ideological orientation' (Rodney) and 'mode of reasoning' (Mazrui). The chapter closes with a discussion on language. In a context where colonial languages were given official status, developing them into dynamic languages of popular culture and higher learning and scientific reasoning, the tendency was to freeze languages of the colonised into a folkloric condition due to a lack of recognition and resources. Two experiences in particular – those of Afrikaans and Kiswahili – pointed a way forward to social inclusion, creating internal institutional capacities and translation work to support African languages. The chapter claims that the cases it discusses are important not because they are representative, but because the questions they raise are of wider and general significance. The challenge in higher education, in Africa and elsewhere, is to be both responsive to the local and engaged with the global.

THE IMPORTANCE OF THEORY

Theory is born of comparison. Comparison is older than colonialism, but it matures to its fullest in the colonial period. The Greeks made modest comparisons, first between cities like Athens and Sparta. Later, they turned to larger contexts, Greece, Persia and Egypt. Then came Arabs and Berbers. The great Berber historian, Ibn Khaldun, and the Arab traveller, Ibn Battuta, compared the North African and the West African worlds. Others compared Arabia and lands to the east. But the most comprehensive comparative work was carried out during the European colonial project. It is this work that is of concern to us today as we seek to define the problem of decolonisation.

With the European colonial project, classification became global. In the heyday of European expansion, the eighteenth and nineteenth centuries, European intellectuals – as far apart as Hegel, Marx, Weber, Durkheim and others – began comparing the European and the non-European worlds, asking: What was and is so distinctive about the West?

The production of knowledge begins with ordering phenomena. Comparing requires classifying and mapping. Durkheim looked to chemistry as the master classificatory science. Marx looked to biology and its most elementary unit of analysis, the cell form. Comparison requires a standard, the familiar, through which the not-so-familiar is understood, sometimes as not-quite-yet, at other times as an outright deviation. All ordering has a reference point. For those who did the classifying and ordering of everything around the world, the reference point was the West, the reality they knew and considered natural. The problem is unavoidable: Since we are part of that which we compare, how does one avoid the problem of being evaluative and subjective? You cannot avoid it; you can only be conscious of it, and thus limit your claims.[2]

Take the example of Jesuit priests who went to China looking for 'religion'. Non-Buddhist China has no scriptures, but plenty of ritual. But religion for Europeans had a particular definition – there could be no religion without sacred texts. So, they concluded that China had no religion. In later years, they reached a similar conclusion in Africa, that it had no religion, only magic and superstition – practised by witches and witchdoctors.[3]

COLONIALISM AND THE UNIVERSITY

The *institutional form* of the modern African university did not derive from precolonial institutions; the inspiration was the colonial modern. The model was a discipline-based, gated community with a distinction between clearly defined groups (administrators, academics and degree-seeking students). The model traces its origin to the Humboldt

University in Berlin, a new type of university designed in the aftermath of Germany's defeat by France in 1810. Over the next century, this innovation spread to much of Europe and from there to the rest of the world.

Not only the institutional form but also the *intellectual content* of modern social sciences and humanities is a product of the Enlightenment experience in Europe. The European experience was the raw material from which was forged the *category 'human'*. However abstract the category, it drew meaning from the actual struggles on the ground, both within and outside Europe. Internally, the notion of the human was an alternative to that of the Christian. It was a Renaissance response to Church orthodoxy. The intellectuals of Renaissance Europe looked to anchor their vision in a history older than that of Christianity. They found this in pagan Greece and imperial Rome, and self-consciously crafted these into a foundational legacy for Europe. Externally, it was a response to an entirely different set of circumstances – not the changing vision of a self-reflexive and self-revolutionising Europe, but of a self-assertive Europe, reaching out, expanding, in a move that sought first to conquer the world, starting with the New World, then Asia, and finally Africa, and then to transform and to 'civilise' this world in its own image. This dual origin made for a contradictory legacy. The modern European university was a site for the study of the human. In their universal reach for the human, the humanities and the social sciences both proclaimed the oneness of humanity and defined that oneness as sameness – from a very European vantage point.

My point is that the modern university in Africa has very little to do with what existed on this continent before colonialism, and everything to do with what was created in modern Europe. We may find and study great examples of institutions of learning in the African world before European conquest – in Timbuktu, Cairo, Tunis, Alexandria – but these did not shape the contemporary African university, whether colonial or post-colonial. The decisive influence was the European university.

THE PROBLEM

The African university began as a colonial project – a top-down modernist project whose ambition was the conquest of society. The university was in the front line of the colonial 'civilising mission'. Properly understood, this 'civilising mission' was the precursor, the original edition of the 'one-size-fits-all' project that we associate with the structural adjustment programmes designed by the International Monetary Fund (IMF) and the World Bank in the 1980s. Its ambition was to create universal scholars, men and women who stood for excellence, regardless of context, who would serve as the vanguard of the 'civilising mission' without reservation or remorse. For those of us who are inmates of the modern university, prisoners in an ongoing colonising project, at least in a metaphorical sense, I suggest we think of our task as one of subverting the project from within, through a series of acts that sift through the historical legacy, discarding some parts, and adapting others to a new-found purpose.

The first critical reflection on this colonial project took place in the nationalist movement. From the ranks of the nationalist movement emerged a different kind of intellectual, the public intellectual. If the hallmark of the global scholar was *excellence*, that of the public intellectual was *relevance*. Excellence was said to be universal, measured without regard to context; relevance, however, was necessarily contextual, place-specific. The contest between the two unfolded on two very different campuses in East Africa. Makerere University, established in 1922, was the paradigmatic colonial university. The University of Dar es Salaam (widely referred to simply as 'Dar'), established at independence in 1963, would soon emerge as the flag-bearer of anti-colonial nationalism. The two universities stood for two contrasting projects: the colonial university as the turf of the universal scholar and the nationalist university as home of the public intellectual.

The different visions were articulated by two academics from the two universities: Ali Mazrui and Walter Rodney. Mazrui called for a university true to its classical vision, as the home of the scholar 'fascinated by ideas' (Mazrui 2005, 56); Rodney saw the university as the home of the public intellectual, a committed intellectual located in his or her time and place, and deeply engaged with the wider society (Karioki 1974).[4] One moral of the story I want to tell is that we should resist the temptation to dismiss one side and embrace the other. However compelling, these contrasting visions were anchored in two equally one-sided notions of higher education: relevance and excellence. At the same time, each contained something of value. Rather than choose between them, I suggest we identify the kernel of value in each through a dialectical approach.

Does place matter, as Rodney claimed? Or do ideas matter, regardless of place, as Mazrui insisted? Obviously, place matters. If universities could be divorced from politics, if knowledge production could be immune from power relations, then place would not matter. But we know that is not the case. At the same time, ideas also matter. If they did not, why have a university at all? This is to say that politics is not all.

The debate began at Makerere University in the early 1960s, on the eve of state independence. The two sides to the debate lined up on familiar ground – one side mobilised in defence of academic freedom, the other called for justice. The first round of change produced resounding victories for the broad nationalist camp, which called for limiting the autonomy of the university, and of the faculty in particular, so as to put an end to racial privilege. They said the university should be national not only in name but also in appearance. To undermine the disciplinary nationalism and institutional autonomy that propped up the authority of the expatriate staff would not be possible without a strong role for the independent state in higher education. Dismissing academic freedom as a codeword in defence of the status quo, they called for state intervention in the name of justice. It did not take long for the terms of the debate to change, and dramatically so. With the emergence of the single-party regime in Uganda, the university turned into an oasis where the practice of academic freedom allowed free political speech for those who disagreed with the ruling power. Instead of a defence of racial privilege, as at independence, many began to rethink academic freedom as the cutting edge of a critique of nationalist power.

It was in this context that Rajat Neogy founded *Transition*,[5] a cross between a journal and a magazine, in which public intellectuals wrote for a public that included both the gown and the town. Those who wrote for it included writers like James Baldwin, Langston Hughes, Nadine Gordimer and Chinua Achebe, and politicians like Julius Nyerere and Tom Mboya. *Transition* made possible a conversation that was simultaneously national, regional and global. Paul Theroux (1967) wrote 'Tarzan Is an Expatriate', an understanding of Tarzan and Jane as the first expatriates. Ali Mazrui (1966, 1967) wrote 'Nkrumah The Leninist Czar', an essay on authoritarianism with a socialist tilt and 'Tanzaphilia', of which I will have more to say.

In the decade that followed the launch of the Arusha Declaration in 1967, the debate on Tanzania was framed by two critics. If Ali Mazrui was the most important liberal critic of nationalism in power, Issa Shivji (1973, 1975) was its most important critic from the left. Two of his books, *The Silent Class Struggle* and *Class Struggles in Tanzania* proposed that nationalisation and socialism should really be understood as the language masking accumulation by a new state-based class.

Despite this intellectual *brassage*, the two institutions – Makerere and Dar – continued along their distinctive paths. The main issue for reformers at Makerere was the deracialisation of the teaching body, whose leading lights were predominantly white. Newly qualified young academics were promoted under pressure from government-appointed senior administrators. Among these was the young Mazrui: freshly graduated with a doctorate from Oxford, he rose from lecturer to professor like a helicopter in the space of a few years. At Dar, by contrast, the relevance of the curriculum itself was being called into question; there was also a growing demand for interdisciplinarity, especially by faculty who thought disciplinary nationalism was at the root of the university's being increasingly irrelevant to the larger discussion on social and political ills in the country. The developments at Makerere and Dar did not take place sequentially, one after another. They took place side by side, generating a strong and spirited exchange between two scholars at these institutions: Mazrui at Makerere and Rodney at Dar.

DAR: THE QUESTION OF RELEVANCE

Whereas the main issue at Makerere was deracialisation of academic staff, the mobilising concerns at the University of Dar es Salaam were the relevance of the curriculum and the demand for inter-disciplinarity. The Dar discussion unfolded in the context of rapid political change, triggered by a student demonstration on 22 October 1966 protesting a government decision to introduce compulsory national service for all secondary-school graduates. The government's response was drastic: accusing students of betraying the nation, the government withdrew fellowships from all 334 students and sent them home. A few months later, on 5 February 1967, President Nyerere issued the Arusha Declaration, a clarion call for building a socialist society. Then followed a programme of nationalisation of key sectors of the economy. The university responded with a conference on the 'role of the University College, Dar es Salaam in a socialist Tanzania'. Held from 11 to 13 March 1967, the conference noted that 'various disciplines and related subjects [were not studied] in the context of East Africa's and particularly Tanzania's socio-economic development aspirations, concerns and problems'. It ended with a call for *relevance*, including a recommendation for a 'continuous "curriculum review"' (Kimambo 2008 107–132).

The conference triggered vigorous debates among the academic staff and students on campus. Accounts of these discussions identify three different points of view. *Radicals*, mostly non-Tanzanian, wanted a complete transformation, of both curriculum and administrative structure; above all, they wanted to abolish discipline-based departments. *Moderates*, who were the majority and included most Tanzanian members of staff, agreed that there should be a radical review of the curriculum but not an abolition of departments. *Conservatives*, then a minority, resisted any radical change in either curriculum or the discipline-based organisation of the university.

There followed two rounds of reform. The first round began with the introduction of an interdisciplinary programme in 'development studies'. But changes were Ad hoc and contradictory: interdisciplinary streams were introduced; at the same time, however, departments remained. The response was mixed, and opposition was pronounced. A professor in the Law Faculty (Kanywanyi 1989) recalled 'political-rally like classes' where 'speakers were drawn mainly from outside the college' including 'Government Ministers and other public figures of various calling'. The course 'became unpopular among students' – indeed, students rejected the new curriculum in 1969 (Kanywanyi 1989 and 2008: Kimambo 2008 120). Perhaps the most acute observation came from a subcommittee of the University Council, appointed in November 1970 to review the programme (Kimambo, Mapunda and Lawi 2008 118, 124–125). It began by noting that the compromise that had introduced streams but retained departments was contradictory: 'some departments have departed drastically from the sub-stream structure in their attempt to respond to the market situation'. The resulting tension 'proved right the fears of those who were opposing co-existence of streams and departments which has enabled disciplines to reassert themselves at the expense of the interdisciplinary programme'. More importantly, the subcommittee asked whether a problem-solving focus was likely to reduce the scholarly content of higher education, producing 'technocrats' rather than 'reasoning graduates' (Kimambo 2003: 5, 7). The academic staff opposed to the changes either voted with their feet or were booted out of the university. Between June and November 1971, 28 academic staff resigned, and 46 academic contracts were not renewed. Of 86 academics in established posts, 42 per cent departed. In light of this, the Council subcommittee called for 'careful preparation' and recruitment of new staff. Those who think of interdisciplinarity as the key to a new world may want to remind themselves that both World Bank teams and the various centres for area study – as for African Studies – have been interdisciplinary from the start. Given the history of the development of the social sciences and humanities, disciplines have been the predominant site for the development of method. Like the call for relevance, that for an interdisciplinary approach to university education may also prove one-sided.[6]

Round two began with a two-track institutional reorganisation. The Faculty of Arts and Social Sciences set up its own interdisciplinary core to be taught by its own faculty. The Institute of Development Studies (IDS) was formed to teach an interdisciplinary core in all other faculties, including the sciences and the professions. IDS hired over 30 academic staff between 1973 and 1990. Departments remained, but so did career streams and sub-streams. The curriculum was revised, and a compulsory interdisciplinary curriculum was introduced at all levels. The interdisciplinary core in the Faculty of Arts and Social Sciences, known as EASE (East African Society and Environment), focused on the teaching of history, ecology and politics in the first year, taking 40 per cent of student class time (two of five courses). In the second and third years, the time devoted to the interdisciplinary core course was reduced to one course out of five, focusing on the history of science and technology in year two and development planning in year three.

The reform process at the University of Dar es Salaam was sustained over years because the process was not confined to formal processes at the university. Those who wanted change built their own structures: student activists launched key publications, first *Che Che*, and, when it was banned, *Maji Maji*. Activist students and academic staff came together in regular discussion groups. The formal one, known as the 'ideological class', deliberately met at 10 am every Sunday. Its stated aim was to provide students and staff with an alternative to church attendance. The second was less formal but also organised. This comprised a range of after-class study groups that proliferated over the years. In 1975, I recall belonging to five university-based study groups, each with between two and eight members. Meeting once a week, each required a background reading of around 100 pages. These groups focused on five different themes: Marx's *Capital*; the three Internationals; the Russian Revolution; the Chinese Revolution; and the agrarian question.

We were looking to glimpse the outlines of a new world outside our own reality. This was a period of tremendous intellectual ferment, marked by two different trajectories, each represented by a different work. The first was Rodney's (1972) *How Europe Underdeveloped Africa*. Written in the vein of dependency theory, its mode of reasoning was very much in line with that of the Arusha Declaration. The second contrasted the language and promise of the Arusha Declaration with the reality of internal social and political developments in the country. Two books authored by Shivji (1973, 1975), *The Silent Class Struggle*, and *Class Struggles in Tanzania*, reflected the accent on internal processes. The publication of Shivji's books triggered a debate among academics at Dar; that debate focused on imperialism and the state.[7]

This is the context in which a series of memorable debates were held between Rodney and Mazrui, first in Kampala, and then in Dar. Rodney called on intellectuals to join the struggle to consolidate national independence in an era when, though colonialism had ended, imperialism reigned supreme. If Rodney focused on the outside of nationalism, Mazrui called attention to its inside. If Rodney called on intellectuals to realise the unfinished agenda of anti-imperialism, Mazrui called attention to the authoritarian tendencies of nationalism in power. The debate between the two mirrored larger societal processes, the tension between nationalism and democracy on the one hand, and state and popular sovereignty on the other. It also reflected a growing tension within the academy, between the 'nationalist' public intellectual and the 'universalist' scholar. From this latter group emerged the most important critics of nationalism in power: Mazrui from among the liberal critics, and Shivji from the left.

Tanzaphilia

Mazrui's critique soon extended beyond nationalism in power to left intellectuals seduced by radical state nationalism. Among the memorable essays Mazrui wrote in *Transition* was one titled 'Tanzaphilia: A Diagnosis' (Mazrui 1967). Mazrui defined Tanzaphilia as 'a political phenomenon ... an opium of Afrophiles ... the romantic spell which Tanzania casts on so many of those who have been closely associated with her', a condition 'particularly marked among Western intellectuals' (Mazrui 1967: 20). Mazrui chided left intellectuals, liberals and socialists, expatriates and locals, for having succumbed to this disease. He claimed that, seduced by the language of 'socialism', they were caught in the drift to single-party rule, approaching power with timidity and soft hands: 'Many of the most prosaic Western pragmatists have been known to acquire that dreamy look under the spell of Tanzania.'

Mazrui had his eye on simple facts like the 'Committee of Nine' at the University of Dar es Salaam, which he termed the 'super-left' (Tordoff and Mazrui 1972). Citing the pressure from the 'super-left' to turn the University of Dar es Salaam into 'an ideological college', Mazrui suggested that 'a genuine university should not be monopolistic'. He argued that the university should be 'multi-ideological rather than uni-ideological ... permit[ting] maximum interplay between different interpretations of reality'. Mazrui cited Colin Leys, a left-wing British intellectual who had earlier been principal of the party ideology school in Dar es Salaam, Kivukoni College. Leys had famously lamented that besides the three conventionally listed social ills – poverty, ignorance and disease – Tanzania was also suffering from a fourth: empiricism.[8]

To those like Leys – and presumably Rodney – who thought of ideological orientation as everything, Mazrui, in 'Tanzaphilia' (1967: 21), pointed to a deeper epistemological reality that he called 'style of reasoning'. Compared to intellectual acculturation, ideological orientation is both superficial and changeable: 'To be in favour of this country or that, to be attracted by this system of values rather than that, all are forms of ideological conversion. And under a strong impulse one can change one's creed. But it is much more difficult to change the process of reasoning which one acquires from one's total educational background.' As proof, he gave the following example: 'No amount of radicalism in a Western-trained person can eliminate the Western style of analysis which he acquires. After all, French Marxists are still French in their intellectual style. Ideologically, they may have a lot in common with Communist Chinese or Communist North Koreans. But in style of reasoning and the idiom of his thought, a French Marxist has more in common with a French liberal than with fellow Communists in China and Korea. And that is why a French intellectual who is a Marxist can more easily cease to be a Marxist than he can cease to be a French intellectual'. To bring the point home, he distinguished between a 'pro-Western' attitude and a 'Western' mode of thinking: 'Applying this to Julius Nyerere, we find that someone like him can more easily cease to be "pro-Western" than he can cease to be "Westernised" in his basic intellectual style and mental processes. And it is the latter quality which has often captivated Afrophile Western intellectuals.'

Was Mazrui implying that his interlocuters from the left – this time not just Nyerere but also Rodney – needed to go beyond changing phrases, beyond a mere ideological facelift to an epistemological shift? Mazrui called for a shift of focus, to use his own language in 'Tanzaphilia', from 'ideological orientation' to 'mode of reasoning', or 'intellectual acculturation' and 'style of analysis'. The year was 1967. If Mazrui evokes Michel Foucault for the reader, let us keep in mind that Foucault would write about 'discursive formations' in *The Archaeology of Knowledge* two years later, in 1969.

The development of higher education in Africa is basically a post-independence phenomenon. Except in South and North Africa, the number of universities founded in the colonial period can be counted on two hands. There was only one university in Nigeria with 1 000 students at the end of the colonial period; by 1990, Nigeria would boast 31 universities with 141 000 students (Bako 1994). East Africa had a single institution of higher learning, Makerere, during the colonial period. Today, it has over 30. Having a national university was considered as much a hallmark of national independence as having a flag, an anthem, a central bank and a currency.

If Makerere was the quintessential colonial university, Dar es Salaam stood as the hallmark of nationalist assertion. The fortunes of the African university dipped with the fiscal crisis of the African state and the entry of the Bretton Woods institutions, which claimed to bail out countries in financial trouble in return for subjecting their public budgets to a strict disciplinary regime. In this era of structural adjustment, too, Makerere was the model university.

The World Bank took hold of Makerere's planning in the late 1980s, around the same time the IMF took charge of the Ugandan treasury. The Bank proposed a three-fold reform premised on the assumption that higher education is a private good. First, it argued that since the benefit from higher education accrues to an individual, individuals should pay for it by way of fees. Today, nearly 90 per cent of students at Makerere are fee-paying. Second, the Bank argued that the university should be run by autonomous departments and not by a centralised administration. This was done by a simple formula: by requiring that 80 per cent of student fees should go to the student's disciplinary department or faculty, the Bank managed to starve the central administration of funds. Third, the Bank said that the curriculum should be revised and made market-friendly and more professional. To give two examples of the changes ushered in at this time: The Department of Geography began to offer a BA. in Tourism, and the Institute of Linguistics began offering a BA. in Secretarial Studies, through which a student would be equipped with secretarial skills in more than one language. The Makerere model was exported to other universities in the region and around the continent over the next decade. So, it was not a surprise that fees were rising around the same time as 'independence' – transition to majority rule – in

South Africa. Nor was it a surprise that expanded entry of black students into 'white' universities was followed by an expanded exit of more and more of the same students, either because they were failing to pay fees or to maintain good academic standing. When more and more of these students looked for explanations for their predicament, the discussion pointed to rising fees and a curriculum that bore little relationship to their life experiences, or family and community histories.

To the distinction Mazrui drew, between ideological orientation and style of reasoning, Rodney had no answer. Mazrui's point was, of course, that though Rodney (like Nyerere) might have an ideological critique of the West, he was speaking from inside that same Western tradition. Mazrui was right, but then Rodney was not alone in this insider-outsider position. Frantz Fanon was also in a similar position. To stay with Mazrui's distinction between 'mode of reasoning' and 'ideological orientation', we may pose a question: Is there an intellectual mode of reasoning we can term 'African', the way Mazrui spoke of a 'French' or a 'Western' mode of reasoning? And by this, I mean not a mode of reasoning genetically or ancestrally African, but a discursive tradition constituted by a set of engagements and debates communicated in a common language, weaving a coherent intellectual community into a long-term historical formation.

Most of us who have come out of colonialism speak more than one language. One of these is the language of colonialism, inevitably a language of science, scholarship and global affairs. The other is a colonised language, a home language whose growth was truncated because colonialism cut short the possibility of the development of an intellectual tradition in the languages of the colonised. As a result, our home languages remain folkloric, shut out of the world of science and learning, high culture, law and government. There are of course exceptions, as always. In East Africa, the exception is Kiswahili, today a language of both popular interaction and culture, and a language of official discourse. Kiswahili is a language of primary and secondary education, but not of university education. At the university level, Kiswahili functions more like a foreign language, with its own department of Kiswahili Studies, Idara Ya Taasisi Ya Kiswahili. Not surprisingly, Kiswahili is not the bearer of either a scientific or a scholarly tradition.

The difference would become clear if we look at the example of Afrikaans. One needs to recall that Afrikaans, once disparaged as 'kitchen Dutch', developed from a folkloric language to be the bearer of an intellectual tradition in less than half a century. That development would not have been possible without a vast institutional network – ranging from schools and universities to newspapers, magazines and publishing houses, and more, all resourced through public funds. This vast affirmative action programme lifted Afrikaans from a folkloric language to a language of science and scholarship, high culture and legal discourse in the short span of a half century. It is no exaggeration to say that Afrikaans represents the most successful decolonising initiative on the African continent. Not only did this happen under apartheid, the great irony is that it was not emulated by the government of independent South Africa.

Many think that the Afrikaans experience is not relevant when it comes to the plurality of African languages. Why? Because it is said that this continent is plagued by extreme linguistic heterogeneity. Numerous studies claim this: from Lord Hailey's (1938) tally of over 700 languages in Africa, to Barbara F. Grimes's (1996) more recent count that upped the number to over 2 000! The point, however, is that the count depended on the definition used to distinguish a language from a dialect.

Let us scan the horizon for some examples. Is Arabic a single written language, *Fusha*, or a federation of multiple spoken dialects? Is Chinese a single written language or also a federation of different spoken dialects? Of course, Arabic is both a single written language and a family of a large number of spoken dialects. And the same goes for Chinese. Jacob Nhlapo, the editor of the *Bantu World* in the 1940s and 1950s, led an untiring campaign to develop two core languages out of the cluster of spoken vernaculars in Nguni- and Sotho-group spoken vernaculars. Nhlapo was a pioneer who inspired others in the decades that followed. Among these were Neville Alexander of the University of Cape Town and Kwesi Prah of the Centre for Advanced Studies of African Societies in Cape Town.

Ngũgĩ wa Thiong'o (1986), who talks of the importance of decolonising history, memory and language, has argued that the starting point of decolonisation is language, not geo-politics. Let us return to the problem as I defined it at the beginning: the African university began as a colonial project – a top-down modernist project – its ambition being to transform society in its own image. Add to this the fact that this project was unilingual, it was an English or French or Portuguese language project, and it acknowledged a single intellectual tradition, the Western tradition. At the same time, it aimed to create an apartheid society, one that shut the vast majority of the colonised out of the common discourse of humanity. What would it mean to decolonise such a project?

The East African experience suggests the following: *One*, socialising the cost of university education, so as to make it more inclusive. In every African country that I know, independence was followed by attempts to socialise spending on health, education, housing and so on. South Africa is the exception. In practical terms, this means reducing fees – indeed, fees must fall, as demanded by the South African student movement in recent years. I was at the University of Cape Town from 1996 to 1999, what I thought of as the post-independence era, and was amazed that fees were rising! *Two*, the decolonising project has necessarily to be a multilingual project whose purpose should be not only to provide Westernised education in multiple languages but also to provide the resources to nurture and develop non-Western intellectual traditions as living traditions with the capacity to sustain public and scholarly discourse.

The challenge is one of inclusion on every level. This is to acknowledge that affordable higher education must become a reality if the end of apartheid is to have meaning for the youth. In a university context, this calls for the establishment of a centre for the study of Nguni and Sotho languages and life traditions, and of associated translation units, which will translate the best of the literature – global, African and South African – into these languages. To broaden our referential world, we need to stop looking to only the West and start getting to know our neighbourhood by investing resources in developing academic units that can study and teach non-Western intellectual traditions. But that study should not be a superficial gloss, an homage to some new fashion. It needs to begin with the understanding that if you want to access a different intellectual tradition, you have to learn the language in which the tradition has been historically forged.

Theory cannot be developed without reference points – and our objective must be to develop new and multiple reference points. Give up the obsession of comparing with the West – the world is larger than we have known. The Sanskrit scholar Sheldon Pollock (2009, 2015), of Columbia University, has fruitfully compared Indian and Chinese worlds. The Chinese scholar Kuan-Hsing Chen (2010) has written a book, *Asia as Method*, calling for comparative studies across Asia. The Senegalese scholar Souleymane Bachir Diagne (2011) wrote a book on the Urdu poet and philosopher Muhammad Iqbal. Perhaps the best example of intellectual labours that have gone into rethinking received categories of thought and formulating new categories adequate to understanding and valorising particular histories and experiences is the work of Nigerian historians of the University of Ibadan and Ahmado Bello University. I am thinking of the work on the oral archive for the writing of a history of the premodern, and that on the historicity of ethnic identity by historians from Dike to Abdullahi Smith and, above all, Yusufu Bala Usman.[9]

Colonialism brought not only theory from the Western academy but also the assumption that theory is produced in the West and the aim of the academy outside the West is limited to applying that theory. Its implication was radical: If the making of theory was a truly creative act in the West, its application in the colonies became the reverse, a turnkey project that did no more than operationalise theory. This was true on the left as well as on the right, whether student effort was going into the study of Marx and Foucault or of Weber and Huntington. One student after another learned theory as if learning a new language – some remarkably well, others not so well. As they stutter in translation, these others give us an idea of what is wrong with the notion that to be a student is to be a technician, whose learning stops with applying a theory produced elsewhere. The unfortunate outcome of such an endeavour is to produce high-cost caricatures, yet another group of mimic men and women for a new era. The alternative is to rethink our aspiration, not just to import theory from outside as another developmental initiative, but to aim differently and not just higher: to theorise our own reality.

The process of knowledge production is based on two distinct but related conversations, local and global. The scholar needs to balance two relationships in the process of knowledge production: one with the society at large, and the other with the scholarly community globally. The local conversation is with different social forces: their needs, their demands, their capacities and their visions. The global conversation is the product of an ongoing global debate within and between disciplines, a debate where geo-politics is of little obvious relevance. The local conversation makes for a public intellectual who is very mindful of political boundaries, the global conversation calls for a scholar who transgresses boundaries. Our challenge is to acknowledge that the public intellectual and the scholar are not two different personas but two sides of a single quest for knowledge. To pursue this quest is to bridge and close the gap between the public intellectual and the scholar.

NOTES

1   This chapter is a development of the T.B. Davie Memorial Lecture delivered at the University of Cape Town on 22 August 2017.

2   The point was made generally by Bala Usman with reference to the relation between the subjectivity of the writer in relation to the 'objective' reality the writer seeks to understand; see Bala Usman (2006a, 2006b).

3   For a fuller discussion, see Pollock (2009, 2015).

4   For Ali Mazrui's response, see Mazrui (1974).

5   Rajat Neogy was jailed by Milton Obote on sedition charges in 1968. *Transition* was revived in Ghana in 1971, and its editorship was taken over by Wole Soyinka in 1973. It folded in 1976 for financial reasons, and was then revived in 1991 by Henry Louis Gates, Jr., who brought it to the W.E.B. Du Bois Institute for African and African-American Research at Harvard University where it continues to be based, dislocated both in terms of its vision and its place.

6   The interdisciplinary PhD programme in Social Studies, introduced at the Makerere Institute of Social Research (Makerere University), required students to combine a set of interdisciplinary core courses with a major and a minor in two disciplinary specialisations: political economy, political studies, historical studies and cultural studies; see Mamdani (2013b).

7   The 'debate' began with a set of critical comments on the writings of Nabudere and Shivji, but soon turned acerbic with a series of interventions. Led by Karim Hirji, they turned the 'debate' into a sharply political exchange devoid of any significant scholarly or even political merit; see Nabudere (1976) and Tandon (1979).

8   In an earlier version of this chapter (Mamdani 2018), I had mistakenly assumed that Colin Leys had been the principal of Kivukoni College at the time Mazrui wrote Tanzaphilia. Leys (2018) wrote a letter to the editor of *London Review of Books* pointing out that he had been principal from 1961 to 1962, a year before the University of Dar es Salaam opened its doors. Leys also claims that Kivukoni was not 'the ruling party's ideological school' as I had characterised it but 'a local version of Ruskin College, created by a Ruskin graduate, Joan Wicken'. Leys forgot to add that Wicken was then also Nyerere's principal private secretary. Leys also complained that my article focused on the part and ignored the whole: 'the Cold War context, which conditioned Nyerere's efforts to chart a path out of neocolonialism and avert the risks of the kind of civil conflict that would later cause devastation in so many African countries, including Uganda (it was this, not an abstract idea of what an African university should be that preoccupied most of the left academics at Dar.)' I do not disagree. The article I wrote was admittedly about the university ('the part') and not about Nyerere's rule ('the whole'). Leys accurately describes the frame of mind of the 'left academics at Dar' (among whom I was one). In defining the vocation of the intellectual as exclusively political, they ran the risk of divorcing the public intellectual from the scholar and turning the university into the left wing of the party state.

9   For a brief discussion, see Mamdani (2013a, chap. 3).

REFERENCES

Bako, Sabo 1994. 'Education and Adjustment in Nigeria: Conditionality and Resistance'. In *Academic Freedom in Africa*, edited by Mahmood Mamdani and Mamadou Diouf, 150–175. Dakar: CODESRIA.

Bala Usman, Yusufu. 2006a. 'History, Tradition and Reaction'. In *Beyond Fairy Tales: Selected Historical Writing of Yusufu Bala Usman*. Zaria, Nigeria: Abdullahi Smith Centre for Historical Research.

Bala Usman, Yusufu. 2006b. 'The Problem of Ethnic Categories in the Study of the Historical Development of the Central Sudan: A Critique of M.G. Smith and Others'. In *Beyond Fairy Tales: Selected Historical Writing of Yusufu Bala Usman*. Zaria, Nigeria: Abdullahi Smith Centre for Historical Research.

Chen, Kuan-Hsing. 2010. *Asia as Method: Toward Deimperialization*. Durham, NC: Duke University Press.

Diagne, Souleymane Bachir. 2011. *Islam and the Open Society: Fidelity and Movement in the Philosophy of Muhammad Iqbal*. Dakar: CODESRIA.

Gubara, Dahlia El-Tayeb M. 2013. 'Al Azhar and the Orders of Knowledge'. PhD diss., Columbia University.

Hailey, William Malcolm. 1938. *An African Survey: A Study of Problems Arising in Africa South of the Sahara*. Oxford: Oxford University Press.

Kanywanyi, J. L. 1989. 'The Struggle to Decolonise and Demystify University Education: Dar's 25 Years' Experience Focused on the Faculty of Law (October 1961–October 1986)'. *Eastern African Law Review* 16 (1): 1-70.

Karioki, James N. 1974. 'African Scholars versus Ali Mazrui'. *Transition* 45: 55–63.

Kimambo, Isaria N. 2003. 'Introduction'. In *Humanities and Social Sciences in East and Central Africa: Theory and Practice*, edited by Isaria N. Kimambo, 5–7. Dar es Salaam: Dar es Salaam University Press.

Kimambo, Isaria N. 2008. 'Establishment of Teaching Programmes'. In *In Search of Relevance: A History of the University of Dar es Salaam*, edited by Isaria N. Kimambo, Bertram B.B. Mapunda and Yusufu Q. Lawi, 107–132. Dar es Salaam: Dar es Salaam University Press.

Kimambo, Isaria N., Bertram B.B. Mapunda, and Yusufu Q. Lawi, eds. 2008. *In Search of Relevance: A History of the University of Dar es Salaam*. Dar es Salaam: Dar es Salaam University Press.

Leys, Colin. 2018. 'Letters: The African University'. *London Review of Books* 40 (15) (2 August).

Mamdani, Mahmood. 2013a. *Define and Rule: Native as Political Identity*. Johannesburg: Wits University Press.

Mamdani, Mahmood. 2013b. *Getting the Question Right: Interdisciplinary Explorations at Makerere University*. MISR Book Series 1. Kampala: Makerere Institute of Social Research.

Mamdani, Mahmood. 2018. 'The African University'. *London Review of Books* 40 (14) (19 July): 29–32.

Mazrui, Ali. 1966. 'Nkrumah: The Leninist Czar'. *Transition* 26: 8–17.

Mazrui, Ali. 1967. 'Tanzaphilia: A Diagnosis'. *Transition* 31 (June–July): 20–26.

Mazrui, Ali. 1974. 'Africa, My Conscience and I'. *Transition* 46: 67–71.

Mazrui, Ali. 2005. 'Pan-Africanism and the Intellectuals: Rise, Decline and Revival'. In *African Intellectuals: Rethinking Politics, Language, Gender and Development*, edited by Thandika Mkandawire, 56–77. London: Zed Books.

Nabudere, D. Wadada. 1976. *Imperialism Today*. Dar es Salaam: Tanzania Publishing House.

Ngũgĩ wa Thiong'o. 1986. *Decolonising the Mind: The Politics of Language in African Literature*. London: James Currey.

Pollock, Sheldon. 2009. *The Language of the Gods in the World of Men: Sanskrit, Culture, and Power in Premodern India*. Oakland, CA: University of California Press.

Pollock, Sheldon. 2015. 'Big Comparisons: China, India and Methodological Cosmopolitanism'. Lecture presented at Brown University, Providence, Rhode Island, 24 February.

Rodney, Walter. 1972. *How Europe Underdeveloped Africa*. Dar es Salaam: Tanzania Publishing House.

Shivji, Issa G. 1973. *The Silent Class Struggle*. Dar es Salaam: Tanzania Publishing House.

Shivji, Issa G. 1975. *Class Struggles in Tanzania*. Dar es Salaam: Tanzania Publishing House.

Tandon, Yashpal. 1979. *Imperialism and the State in Tanzania*. Dar es Salaam: Tanzania Publishing House.

Theroux, Paul. 1967. 'Tarzan Is an Expatriate'. *Transition* 32 (Aug.–Sept.): 13–19.

Tordoff, William and Ali A. Marzrui. 1972. 'The Left and the Super-Left in Tanzania'. *Journal of Modern African Studies* 10 (3): 427–445.

CHAPTER 2

The Curriculum Case for Decolonisation

Lesley Le Grange
Stellenbosch University

—·—

After vowing never to return to the University of Cape Town (UCT), decolonial scholar Mahmood Mamdani revisited UCT in 2017 to deliver the T.B. Davie Memorial Lecture on academic freedom. When he was asked by someone why he returned, he said, 'Because Rhodes fell' (Omar 2017). The #RhodesMustFall and #FeesMustFall campaigns have been the impulse for a renewed interest in the decolonisation of the university curriculum in South Africa. The multi-natured #FeesMustFall campaign is cogently captured by University of Witwatersrand PhD student Katlego Disemelo (2015):

> It is, firstly about access to equal and quality education. It is about teasing out the ever-so-confusing intricacies of class relations in post-apartheid South Africa. It is about eradicating the painful exclusion and daily micro aggressions which go-hand-in-hand with institutional racism within these spaces. And it is also about laying bare the failures of the heterosexual, patriarchal, neoliberal capitalist values which have become so characteristic of the country's universities.

Mamdani's response to being asked why he returned to UCT after a 16-year absence signifies his view that there now is a space in South African universities to have public conversations about issues (un)intentionally silenced in post-apartheid South Africa, which the #RhodesMustFall and the #FeesMustFall campaigns have laid bare. The matters raised by Disemelo, as well as curriculum issues, have largely been put on the back burner in post-apartheid South Africa. This is because higher education transformation post-apartheid has mainly been characterised by a proliferation of policies (focusing mainly on governance, funding, quality assurance and student access and success); the merging of institutions; and institutional changes such as the introduction of strategic plans, quality assurance directorates, equity plans, and so. (Le Grange 2011).

The neglect of conversations on matters curricular is not unique to higher education, in South Africa as Ronald Barnett and Kelly Coate (2005: 1) write:

> All around the world, higher education is expanding rapidly, governments are mounting inquiries into higher education, more institutions are involved in running courses of study and more money is being spent on higher education, not least by students themselves. Higher education is ever more important to increasing numbers of people. And yet, despite the growth and debate, there is very little talk about the curriculum. What students should be experiencing is barely a topic for debate. What the building blocks of their courses might be and how they should be put together are even more absent from the general discussion. The very idea of curriculum is pretty well missing all together.

There are multiple reasons for the neglect of matters curricular in the contemporary university, which include the massification of higher education, the (re)ascendency of neoliberalism and the technology of performativity (Le Grange 2006; Peters 2007). And in South Africa, one might add pressures on a 'new' state to legitimate itself both inside and outside the country, which saw matters of curriculum in higher education relegated to the margins. As we see cracks in the pillars of the modern Western university (Lyotard 1984; Readings 1996; Le Grange 2009b) generally, we are transversally witnessing the crumbling walls of the South African university as a consequence of modernism (unquestioning beliefs in the ideals of modernity), its delinquent cousins of colonialism and apartheid, and the particular priorities of a neoliberal state in post-apartheid South Africa, which have led to declining subsidies paid to universities.

Bill Readings (1996) views the transformation of the modern university as a crisis,[1] driven by performativity and the hollow idea of excellence.[2] As his title indicates, Readings (1996) speaks of 'the university in ruins'. Lesley le Grange (2009b) notes that the word 'ruin' has at least three meanings, which suggest subtle differences. First, it could refer to something that has been damaged or destroyed. Second, it could refer to something that is on the decline or decaying. Third, it could refer to the remains of what was – what has already been destroyed. These different meanings enable us to gain a more nuanced understanding of the state of the contemporary university, including the South African university. The first meaning suggests that earlier incarnations of the university have passed and will not return. The second meaning suggests that the pillars of the university are cracking, but that there is the possibility of restoring the university – winning back what was valued in earlier incarnations. The third meaning helps us to understand that in practice, even when transformation occurs, there are always the remains of what had existed before, which could be harnessed in a new era.

I aver that the South African university in ruins (what remains of it) should be imagined differently – that 'lines of flight' could be invigorated,[3] so that what 'remains' becomes something other than what it is/was. I wish to suggest that the current ferment around decolonisation (of the curriculum) presents opportunities for reimagining the South African university and that the focus of our conversations should not only be on what decolonisation is, but on what it might become. The impetus given by the student protests and conversations currently occurring within universities, at conferences and in scholarly publications provide fertile ground for the germination of a different South African university. Moreover, the decolonisation conversations have once again brought to the fore the perennial curriculum question that was first articulated by Herbert Spencer (1884): 'What knowledge is of most worth?' And, I would add, whose knowledge is of most worth?

Against this backdrop, I discuss what is meant by decolonisation and the need to decolonise the South African university curriculum, and present ideas on an expanded notion of curriculum. The latter is necessary because dominant views on curriculum evident in decolonisation debates in South Africa are circumscribed to the idea that curriculum concerns subject-matter knowledge learned by students. This idea is evident in some students' erroneous critiques of Western science and in critical responses to these critiques (see Jansen 2017: 155).

WHAT IS MEANT BY DECOLONISATION?

Decolonisation has received much attention over the years by historians, philosophers, sociologists of knowledge, postcolonialists, postmodernists, literary scholars, Indigenous scholars, and so forth. What decolonisation entails has been well rehearsed in the literature and I shall not repeat much of it here. For detailed discussions on decolonisation, see Dane Keith Kennedy (2016), Nelson Maldonado-Torres (2007, 2016), Walter D. Mignolo (2007, 2009) and Achille Mbembe (2001, 2015). My interest lies not so much in what decolonisation is, but in what it could become. Decolonisation, as Noel Gough (1999: 73) writes about globalisation, 'is not a subject and/or object to be constrained by definition, but a focus for speculation – for generating meanings'. But let me say a few things about decolonisation for the sake of advancing the discussion.

First, there is no single meaning to decolonisation. Second, decolonisation does not have to mean or involve destruction. Third, decolonisation is a process, not an event – what has been decolonised has the potential to produce colonising effects and vice versa. Fourth, decolonisation does not necessarily mean turning back the clock to a time when the world was a different place – it needs to speak to challenges faced in a contemporary world.

The insights on decolonisation from scholars representing the world's indigenous peoples are worth noting. Drawing on the work of Poka Laenui, Bagele Chilisa (2012) suggests five phases in the process of decolonisation: *rediscovery and recovery*; *mourning*; *dreaming*; *commitment* and *action*. *Rediscovery and recovery* is the process whereby colonised peoples rediscover and recover their own history, culture, language and identity. *Mourning* refers to the process of lamenting the continued assault on the world's colonised/oppressed peoples' identities and social realities. It is an important part of healing and leads to dreaming. *Dreaming* occurs when colonised peoples invoke their histories, worldviews, and indigenous knowledge systems to theorise and imagine alternative possibilities – in this instance, a different curriculum. *Commitment* sees academics/students become political activists who demonstrate the commitment to include the voices of the colonised, in this case, in the university curriculum. *Action* is the phase where dreams and commitments translate into strategies for social transformation. In other words, the transformation of the university curriculum is both a microcosm of and impetus for broader societal transformation.

Linda Tuhiwai Smith (1999) identifies the following elements of decolonisation: *deconstruction and reconstruction*; *self-determination and social justice*; *ethics*; *language*; *internationalisation of indigenous experiences*; *history*; and *critique*. *Deconstruction and reconstruction* constitutes discarding what has been wrongly written, and 'interrogating distortions of people's life experiences, negative labelling, deficit theorizing, genetically deficient or culturally deficient models that pathologized the colonised … and retelling the stories of the past and envisioning the future' (Chilisa 2012: 17). *Self-determination and social justice* relates to the struggle by those who have been marginalised by the Western academy, who are seeking legitimacy for knowledge embedded in their own histories, experiences and ways of viewing reality. *Ethics* concerns the formulation, legislation and dissemination of ethical issues related to the protection of indigenous knowledge systems. *Language* invokes the importance of teaching/learning in indigenous languages as part of the anti-imperialist struggle. *Internationalisation of indigenous experiences* relates to international scholars sharing common experiences, issues and struggles of colonised peoples in global and local spaces. *History*, in this instance, involves a study of the past to recover the history, culture and languages of colonised people and to use it to inform the present. *Critique* amounts to a critical appraisal of the imperial model of the academy that 'continues to deny the colonised and historically marginalised other space to communicate from their own frames of reference' (Chilisa 2012: 19).

WHY THE NEED TO DECOLONISE THE CURRICULUM?

I suggest that the decolonisation of the university curriculum is necessary for at least the following mutually inclusive reasons:

- colonisation resulted in the decimation of the knowledges of the colonised and therefore cognitive justice should be sought;
- the illusion that Eurocentric knowledge is universal needs to be debunked;
- colonisation reduced the knowledges of the Global South to culture and this needs to be corrected;
- the need for psychosocial transformation of the colonised;
- South African universities are based on Western models of academic organisation.

Decolonisation is a necessary response to first- and second-generation colonialism and neo-colonialism. Catherine Odora Hoppers and Howard Richards (2012: 7) remind us that first-generation colonialism was the conquering of the physical spaces and bodies of the colonised, and second-generation colonialism was the colonisation of the mind through disciplines, such as education, science, economics and law. 'Neo-colonialism' was coined by the first president of independent Ghana, Kwame Nkrumah. It relates to the nominal independence of a country that is still under the influence of ex-colonial or newly developed superpowers. Such superpowers could be international monetary bodies, multinational corporations and cartels, as well as education and cultural institutions (Ashcroft, Griffiths and Tiffin 2000). Nkrumah (1965) argued that neo-colonialism is a more insidious form of colonialism because it is more difficult to detect. It also involves new elites who were trained by colonialists that take on the roles of colonialists in countries after independence.

First- and second-generation colonialism resulted in the denigration and decimation of indigenous knowledges. Boaventura de Sousa Santos (2013: 92) refers to the decimation of knowledge as 'the murder of knowledge', which he designates *epistemicide*. He writes:

> Unequal exchanges among cultures have always implied the death of the knowledge of the subordinated culture, hence the death of the social groups that possessed it. In most extreme cases, such as that of European expansion, epistemicide was one of the conditions of genocide. The loss of epistemological confidence that currently afflicts modern science has facilitated the identification of the scope and gravity of the epistemicides perpetrated by hegemonic Eurocentric modernity.

It is because of epistemicide that cognitive justice should be sought. Cognitive justice refers to the decentring of all knowledges so that they can coexist and be equitably compared – hierarchies are effaced so that no knowledge system is subjugated by another. It also gives legitimacy to knowledges of the Global South that have been reduced to culture by Eurocentric scholars. Cognitive justice also involves what Mignolo (2009, 160) terms 'epistemic disobedience'. Epistemic disobedience is the act of detaching from the zero point epistemology.[4] Mignolo points out that this act/process of epistemic disobedience marks a shift away from clichéd notions that all knowledge is situated and constructed, to asking critical questions such as 'Why did Eurocentric epistemology conceal its own geo-historical and bio-graphical locations and succeed in creating the idea of universal knowledge as if the knowing subjects are universal?' And of course, 'Why does this remain pervasive today in the humanities, social sciences, natural sciences and professional fields?' Gough (1998: 508) points out that it was because of European imperialism, aided and abetted by the exercise of military power, that Western knowledge has the 'appearance of universal truth and rationality, and [is] often assumed to be a form of knowledge that lacked [the] cultural fingerprints' that appear to be much more conspicuous in other knowledge systems. This brings me to the importance of self-(re)discovery of the colonised subject as central to decolonisation.

When Frantz Fanon ([1961]1965) wrote *The Wretched of the Earth*, Ngũgĩ wa Thiong'o (1986) wrote *Decolonising the Mind*, and Mignolo (2009) called for *epistemic disobedience*, they did so with reference to the colonised. Fanon writes about the psychiatric and psychological dehumanisation of colonised peoples and nations and about what a social movement of decolonisation might entail for both the individual and society. For Ngũgĩ, it is the mind of the colonised (the African writer) that must be decolonised and for Mignolo (2009), it is the colonised that must engage in epistemic disobedience.

Decolonisation in colonial times meant the removal of the colonial state; in a contemporary world it might mean resistance to being subjugated by global superpowers, the dismantling of systems and symbols of colonialism and neo-colonialism, and so forth. But it necessarily involves the psychosocial transformation of the colonised – a transformation of self and society that is integral to, but more than, the targeting of that which is external. I shall return to this discussion when discussing the autobiographical method of curriculum, *currere*, which William Pinar (1975) first coined. Before that, it is instructive to consider the Western models of academic organisation that characterise South African universities.

Since inception, all South African universities adopted Western models of academic organisation, which largely excluded and decimated the knowledges of colonised people.[5] The colonial model of academic organisation of the university, based on Western disciplinary knowledge, was entrenched during apartheid and has not been redressed in post-apartheid South Africa in any serious way. According to Anim van Wyk (2014), 73 per cent of professors and associate professors are white (mostly men), more than two decades into South Africa's democracy. Furthermore, although student demographics at South African universities (particularly historically white universities) changed significantly in post-apartheid South Africa, staff demographics have not changed accordingly. This has ensured the preservation of colonial academic organisation (including curricula) within universities, akin to Nkrumah's (1965) neo-colonialism. The preservation of colonial academic organisation was also done under the guise of academic freedom and institutional autonomy. The adoption of neoliberal policies in South Africa has resulted in public universities becoming state-aided universities rather than state-funded universities. At Stellenbosch University, for example, the state subsidy comprises less than one-third of the institution's consolidated budget. This situation in part explains rising student fees and undesirable practices, such as the outsourcing of workers, and provides the context in which student protests and calls for the decolonisation of universities might be understood.

It is imperative to decolonise South African universities and by association the university curriculum, for the reasons advanced above. However, a few qualifications are necessary. First, as mentioned, decolonisation does not mean that we simply turn back the clock – we cannot begin on a clean slate. Félix Guattari (2000) argues that we cannot create new ways of living by reversing technological advancement and going back to old formulas, which were pertinent when the planet was less densely populated and when social relations were much stronger than they are today. New ways of living are to be found in responding to events (associated with colonisation) as potential carriers of new possibilities. As Ian Pindar and Paul Sutton (2000: 9) write:

> It isn't a question of exchanging one model or way of life for another, but of responding to the event as the potential bearer of new constellations of Universes of reference. The paradox is this: although these Universes are not pre-established reference points or models, with their discovery one realizes they were always already there, but only a singular event could activate them.

Second, as George J. Sefa Dei (2000: 113) points out, indigenous knowledge (knowledges of the colonised) does not reside in 'pristine fashion' outside of the influences of other knowledges. He argues that bodies of knowledge continually influence each other, demonstrating the dynamism of all knowledge systems. Rendering a false dichotomy or 'moral evaluation between good [Indigenous] and bad [conventional/Western] knowledges' is therefore not useful. However, Dei importantly emphasises the need to challenge imperial ideologies and colonial relations of production, which continually characterise and shape academic practices. Moreover, the exclusion of indigenous knowledges from the academy leaves unchallenged space for the (re)colonisation of knowledges and cultures in local environments and contexts.

Furthermore, as noted, decolonisation of the university is not an easy task, as my visits to both New Zealand and Canada attest. It would be fair to say that New Zealand is moving into what might be called a post-settlement society. Maori tribes are empowered economically to the extent that some tribes would be considered wealthy by any standards. I was excited to hear upon visiting the University of Waikato that the university pays rent to a Maori tribe and was encouraged to hear that Maori education is offered up to doctoral level. Yet, incorporating one module on Maori studies in all its undergraduate programmes remains a challenge for the university. On a visit to Canada I discovered that at the University of Saskatchewan three different initial teacher education programmes were offered: one for First Nations students; one for Métis students; and one for Canadian students. This arrangement is based on the principle of self-determination and social justice that I described as a key element of decolonisation. But the arrangement could also foster segregation and leave unchallenged what is offered in the mainstream Canadian programme in particular.[6] There are no simple solutions for the decolonisation of the curriculum and therefore the process should be embarked upon thoughtfully but also be open to experimentation, from which much could be learned.

Discussing the decolonisation of the curriculum, I suggest that it involves a process of change that does not necessarily mean destroying Western knowledge but rather decentring it or perhaps deterritorialising it (making it something other than what it is). My approach to the decolonisation of the curriculum incorporates rethinking the term 'curriculum' itself (or how it is conventionally understood).

RETHINKING/DECOLONISING THE CURRICULUM

As the canonical curriculum question: 'What knowledge is of most worth learning?' suggests, knowledge is a central element of any conversation on curriculum. Following student protests of 2015 and 2016, we have witnessed task teams and curriculum transformation committees put in place at South African universities to explore ways in which university curricula could be decolonised. Changing content knowledge of teaching/learning programmes is essential to the decolonising process. But decolonisation of the university curriculum needs to involve more than just changing the content of programmes (the knowledge included in programmes). It also requires changing the dominant approach to curriculum, which is based on the factory model of curriculum first articulated by Frederick Winslow Taylor (1911). As Gough (2011: 4) writes:

> Taylor's emphasis on designing industrial systems to achieve specified products is reproduced in the objectives-driven curriculum models of Franklin Bobbitt (1918, 1924) and Ralph Tyler (1950), and more recently manifested in outcomes-based approaches to … education curriculum …. Bobbitt, Tyler and Biggs represent curriculum as a simple, tightly coupled system in which it is both possible and desirable to closely align what students do in order to learn with intended learning outcomes and how they are assessed.

Alternative ways of viewing curriculum to the current outcomes-based approach used in South African higher education (and elsewhere) are therefore necessary. The curriculum literature on schooling reflects a rich body of knowledge that presents alternative ways of viewing curriculum. Although well established in relation to schooling, many of these ideas have not migrated into discourses on higher education. I shall therefore draw on alternative views of curriculum produced over the past 40 years in relation to schooling so as to generate insights into and open up pathways for decolonising university curricula. I describe some of the different perspectives on curriculum and relate these to the theme of decolonisation.

Almost 40 years ago, Madeleine Grumet (1981) defined curriculum as the stories that we tell students about their past, present and future. This view of curriculum enables us to ask what the stories are that students are told, and who tells the stories. One way to respond to this question, in an effort to decolonise, is to ask students to:

- choose a text of the Western canon;
- examine what the text says of the 'other';
- analyse and describe the author's assumptions in deciding what knowledge to include in the text;
- and use the same information to construct a different narrative to that of the author.

This approach is akin to that suggested by Mamdani (2017). Another is for teacher and student to 'walk in both worlds' or follow a 'two way approach' to teaching/learning – Indigenous and Eurocentric ways of knowing (Le Grange and Aikenhead 2017: 33). Glen Aikenhead and Herman Michell (2011: 142) point out that the latter is analogous to what some elders in Canada's Mi'kmaw Nation refer to as 'two-eyed seeing', that is, using the strengths of both knowledge systems or exposing the learners to both systems and leaving them to choose which aspect of the knowledge systems they wish to personally appropriate. An example of the latter could be 'string theory' in physics, first studied by Western scientists as recently as the late 1960s, but understood by indigenous peoples for centuries through their own ways of knowing. Dorothea Frances Bleek (1936: 134) states that the /Xam Bushmen (San) in southern Africa spoke of 'ringing strings that vibrated inside them and connected them to the physical and cosmological world'. The understandings of string theory from the two knowledge systems could be studied by students, points of resonance could be harnessed to bridge knowledge cultures, and points of dissonance could be respected in the sense that students are left to decide how they will appropriate aspects of the different knowledge cultures.

Another understanding of curriculum is that of Japanese-Canadian Ted Aoki (1999) who argues that curriculum should not focus only on the planned (the curriculum-as-plan) but also on how it is lived (the curriculum-as-lived), in this instance by lecturers and students. Legitimating the curriculum-as-lived will take seriously how students are experiencing the current university curriculum and use this as a basis for its decolonisation. Aoki importantly points out that legitimating the curriculum-as-lived does not discard the curriculum-as-plan, but legitimating the former produces a tensioned space in between the two that is a space of struggle, creativity and transformation. If understood/recognised, this transformative space could become a decolonising one where the assemblage of lecturer, student and knowledge becomes transformed into 'something altogether different and unknown' (Kawash 1999: 238).

Curriculum scholars have also distinguished between three broad perspectives on curriculum that have not received much attention in relation to universities: the *explicit, hidden* and *null* curriculum. The explicit curriculum is what students are provided with such as module frameworks, prescribed readings, assessment guidelines, and so on. The hidden curriculum is what students learn about the dominant culture of a university and what values it reproduces. For example, at Stellenbosch University, where I work, students and staff may learn that the molar identity (homogenisation of identity into an ideal form) of the university is white, male, Afrikaans, Christian, heterosexual and 'abled', which is the screen against which difference ('otherness') is constructed. They may learn that the probability of a black person who is not Christian, not Afrikaans, and a member of the LGBTQ community becoming the rector of the university is close to zero. The null curriculum is what universities leave out – what is not taught and learned in a university. And here we might ask what the null curriculum of the University of Cape Town is, for example. The invocation of the term 'null curriculum' invites critical questions, such as why indigenous knowledge systems do not have legitimacy in many South African universities, or as Mignolo (2009: 152) puts it, why 'the first world has knowledge, the third world has culture; Native Americans have wisdom, Anglo Americans have science'?

More than 40 years ago, Pinar (1975) first invoked the etymological root of curriculum, the Latin *currere*, which means 'to run the course'. He did so to refocus curriculum on the significance of individual experience, 'whatever the course content or alignment with society or the economy' (Pinar 2011: xii). *Currere* privileges the individual, and Pinar (2011: 2) argues that it is a complicated concept, because each of us is different: in our genetic make-up; our upbringings; our families; and more broadly our race, gender, class, and so on. Put simply, *currere* shifts the attention away from the concept of a predetermined course to run to focusing on how the course is run by each individual, given each one's unique make-up, context, hopes, aspirations and interactions with other human beings and the more-than-human world. In other words, each individual has her or his own life story, and the understanding of one's own story through academic study is at the heart of curriculum. Pinar develops *currere* as an autobiographical method with four steps or moments – regressive, progressive, analytical and synthetical – that depict both temporal and reflective moments for autobiographical research of educational experience (Pinar et al. 1995):

- The **regressive step** focuses on the past, a moment in which one re-enters the past so as to enlarge and/or transform one's memory. This would involve remembering all influences on one's life in the past, be they environmental, cultural, religious, educational, political, and so on., and how these impact one's present.
- The **progressive moment or step** focuses on the future. Pinar avers that in this step one looks forward to what is not yet present; one meditatively imagines possible futures and also how the future inhabits the present (2004: 36). This step might focus on personal aspirations but also future possibilities, such as inhabiting a planet that is more sustainable or a world that is more just.
- The **analytical step** involves a distancing from one's past and future to create a space of freedom in which one analyses how the future is present in the past, the past in the future and the present in both (Pinar 2004: 36–37).
- The **synthetical step** brings about a sense of wholeness as one re-enters the lived present and asks what the meaning of this present is. It is also involves a process

of awareness of what flows within us, what drives us to do and be, what gives meaning to our lives. Mary Aswell Doll (2000: xii) notes: 'Curriculum is also … a coursing, as in an electric current. The work of the curriculum theorist should tap this intense current within, that which courses through the inner person, that which electrifies or gives life to a person's energy source.'

Pinar's autobiographical method, *currere*, resonates with the project of decolonisation in that a fundamental concern for both is the (re)construction of the subject. Pinar (2011) argues that subjective reconstruction, a central concern of *currere*, is one form of decolonisation. Decolonial revolutionary Fanon (1967) emphasises the primacy of the liberation of the individual in the process of decolonisation. And Terry Goldie (1999: 79) goes so far as to say that for Fanon, 'true liberation is the achievement of subjectivity'. Pinar (2011: 40) neatly captures the role of *currere* in the psychosocial transformation of the colonised subject:

> Autobiography – the regressive-progressive-analytic-synthetic method of *currere* – can be political when it disables, through remembrance and reconstruction, colonisation through interpellation. By affirming the capacity to restructure one's subjectivity, autobiography disentangles us from absorption into collectives – even when presumably these are self-affirming cultural identities.

Importantly, however, Pinar (2011) does point to the danger of the narcissism of identity politics and therefore advocates invoking *currere* to perform a collective autobiography as an impetus for political mobilisation. The regressive step of *currere* enables the individual to re-enter the past and to focus on colonial influences on his/her life, and in particular how the individual has actively taken up colonial discourses. This step is also a moment in self-criticism and marks the beginning of the individual's efforts to rid the self of the fetters of colonial thought. The progressive step focuses on the future and the individual imagines a future that is more just, more democratic, for example. In the analytic step, the individual distances himself/herself (akin to bracketing in phenomenology) from the past and future and analyses how the past, future and the present imbricate one another. By distancing himself/herself from the past and future the individual is able to experience a moment of freedom from the present – free from colonising thoughts. In the synthetic moment the individual re-enters the present with a renewed sense of self, able to see the wholeness of past, present and future, and asks 'What does this mean?' and 'What can I do?' This is the moment when the individual is able to join others or mobilise others in collective action to alter the present that will make possible a different future. Questions that could be raised in this moment of *currere* are: 'What shall I/we do about: the land issue; ongoing racism; homophobia; the content of the university curriculum; access (physical and epistemological) to the university for those on the margins of society?' and so forth. In this moment/step the individual is driven by that which is within, by a power that is productive, that connects, affirms and is joyous – a form of power that several philosophers call *potentia*. This form of power is contrary to power as *potestas*, a power that is hierarchical, transcendent and colonising. The reference to *potentia* and *potestas* is an appropriate juncture to turn to a discussion on the active force of *currere*.

Canadian scholar Jason Wallin (2010) has revisited the notion of *currere* – he rethinks the idea with Gilles Deleuze and Félix Guattari (1994) and their contention that a concept is not a name attached to something but a way of approaching the world. Deleuze and Guattari's (1994) interest is not in what a concept is but what it does or what it could become. Wallin (2010) draws attention to the paradoxical character of *currere*'s etymology: its active and reactive forces. On the one hand, curriculum can be thought of as an active conceptual force. Thinking of curriculum as an active conceptual force means that the concept does not have fixity or closure – that the term does not convey an a priori image of a pedagogical life. It instead relates to the immanent potential of the becoming of a pedagogical life – the multiple coursings of a pedagogical life that exist prior to thought. As Wallin (2010: 2) elaborates:

> To *run* implies that the conceptual power of *currere* is intimate to its productive capacity to create flows, offshoots, and multiplicitous movements. For example, the 'running' roots of rhizomatic bulbs and tubers extend to create new interfaces with other organic and nonorganic bodies, extending the experience of what a body can become. … Running flows of volcanic magma create new courses along and through the ostensible stability of the Earth's mantle, articulating the immanent geomorphic potential of territories to deterritorialise. … A musical 'run' creates lines of flight potentially incongruous with the codes that structure it, overflowing, extending, and traversing tonal registers in producing new affects.

The conceptual power of *currere* implies newness, creation of things unforeseen, experimentation, expanding of difference and movement. This notion of curriculum opens up multiple pathways for the becoming of pedagogical lives and therefore the basis for decolonisation – difference is valued for its intrinsic worth. In its reactive form, on the other hand, *currere* colonises, as one way of knowing becomes *the* way of knowing. The reactive power of *currere* severs currere from its immanent potential to become other. But it is the active force of *currere* that is of interest here. The active force of *currere* is decolonising in that it opens up (not closes) what a body (a concept, a person, an organisation, and so on) can do/become. Through its movement *currere* creates new connections, new assemblages, and unlikely fidelities. *Currere* calls us to a life of experimentation, through the release of immanent flows rather than constructing transcendent ideas that are imposed. In recent works, Le Grange (2018a, 2018c) performs decolonising experiments of a conceptual nature, invigorating vectors that connect Ubuntu and theories emerging in response to a (post)human condition.[7] Le Grange explores connections between emerging (post)human theories, Ubuntu and *currere* to create a new concept *Ubuntu-currere*: (2018a)

> *Ubuntu-currere* shifts our registers of reference away from the individual human being to an assemblage of human-human-nature. In other words, subjectivity is ecological. Moreover, the subject is always in-becoming and the becoming of a pedagogical life is relational – the subject becomes in relation to other humans and the more-than-human-world. The notion of in-becoming ensures that the human cannot be defined nor have fixity and therefore *Ubuntu-currere* is anti-humanist. Put differently, *Ubuntu-currere* negates the construction of a molar identity that is a screen against which anything different is othered in a negative sense. … *Ubuntu-currere* opens up multiple coursings for developing post-human sensibilities driven by the positive power of *potentia* that connects, expresses desire and sustains life. … But, it also makes possible conversations with the more-than-human so that we can listen to the rhythm and heartbeat of the earth – so that our conversations do not happen on the earth but are bent by the earth … *Potentia* promises to counteract the manifestations of the crisis of humanism such as racism, sexism, homophobia, xenophobia, environmental destruction, centrally controlled and standardized education systems, and so on. These crises are manifestations of a negative power, *potestas*, the same form of power that produces *currere's* reactive force. Counteracting *postestas* (criticism of and resistance to it) and the releasing of *potentia* is at the heart of living hopefully and that make possible [a decolonised curriculum]. (Le Grange 2018a: 291–292)

Informed by the active force of *currere*, pedagogy is akin to improvisational jazz rather than the classical orchestra. In improvisational jazz every musician (student) is a composer. A 'mistake' could be a line of flight that produces something new. In the context of the university classroom, although the lecturer 'may be more experienced and "knowledgeable", the educative performance, as in the case with improvisational jazz, is a meshwork of interactions that does not enable one to identify actions of teacher/lecturer that causes learning' (Le Grange 2014: 1292). Through the educative performance both lecturer and student become other, become decolonised.

My discussion of different ways in which the university curriculum could be decolonised points to the need for an expanded notion of curriculum. By this I mean that curriculum should not simply be viewed as a planned activity that is designed with a tightly coupled alignment between elements such as outcomes, teaching/learning and assessment, and as something that is delivered in university lecture venues. Needless to say, academics cannot simply efface the planned dimensions of curriculum because these will necessarily exist as long as institutions exist. However, what they can do is to make room for unplanned activities in teaching/learning spaces, to give legitimacy to students' lived experiences and to experiment with new ways of doing that open up pathways for students to become, instead of colonising students' desires and potential to create newness in the world, through privileging a predetermined curriculum.

SOME PARTING THOUGHTS IN LIEU OF A CONCLUSION

In this chapter, I have discussed what decolonisation might entail and why there is a need to decolonise the university curriculum. I further argued that we cannot speak about the decolonisation of the university curriculum without rethinking the concept curriculum itself. I therefore explored different ways of rethinking the curriculum that enable me to infer that decolonisation should be driven by the positive power of *potentia* and not the negative power of *potestas*. This is because all forms of colonisation are based on transcendent thought (that change is effected by an external idea/force to life itself). Any decolonial project that is also framed by transcendent thinking will in all likelihood itself become colonising. Decolonisation is not something that should be imposed because then it would be driven by *potestas*.

Decolonisation/decoloniality should involve resistance to all manifestations of *potestas*; it should involve stripping the humanist subject from its ontological privilege and Western science from its epistemological privilege.[8] This does not mean that humans do not (should not) have the capacity to care for others (human and more-than-human) or that Western science does not work – much of it is efficacious.[9] Placing the human being on an immanent plane (re)inscribes the human's relationality to everything in the cosmos – its embeddedness in all of life. Placing Western science on an immanent plane means that it can then be equitably compared with other ways of knowing, and that its coexistence with other ways of knowing can be explored, along with the ways it can productively work together with seemingly disparate knowledges.

Decolonisation could mean invigorating lines of connection between different knowledge systems (Western and indigenous), which could give birth to something new or unforeseen. In the world of music, blues as well as jazz emerged from the intersection of the struggles of marginalised communities in the United States and the use of Western musical instruments to create new musical genres. In relation to knowledge production, Aborigines in Australia's Northern Territory have for many years through their own performative modes mapped their country by identifying every tree and every significant feature of their territory. Today some Aborigines are doing the same using the latest in satellites, remote sensing and geographical information systems (GIS). By representing their local knowledge on digital maps they are able to make their ways of knowing visible in Western terms – 'a new knowledge space which will have transformative effects for all Australians' (Turnbull 1997: 560). Similarly, in South Africa, San trackers are being equipped with digital devices (as part of the CyberTracker programme) to record animal sightings, a local example of traditional African ways of knowing working together with sophisticated Western technologies (Le Grange 2009a, 2015). I am suggesting that decolonisation/decoloniality occurs through the decentring/deterritorialisation of dominant knowledge systems and the creation of new knowledge spaces in which 'disparate' knowledge can work together.

Moreover, decolonisation is not an imposition, but a becoming – an unfolding. The process of becoming/unfolding may require the psychosocial transformation of colonised and coloniser, and Pinar's (1975) autobiographical method *currere* provides the steps for navigating this process. But to live hopefully in an unequal world and on a planet that is on the brink of ecological disaster requires a connection to the life force within (our *potentia*) that connects us to all of life. Education driven by *potentia* means a lifelong affair of experimentation with the real (Le Grange 2018b) – an individual and collective becoming. Decolonisation involves a releasing of that which is within, so that it connects and creates (new concepts, new knowledge, new subjectivities). This idea manifests in the active force of *curerre*. The time is now ripe for generating (new) meanings of decolonisation and decolonising the university curriculum in South Africa, through the power of *potentia*.

In Susanne Kappelar's (1986: 212) words: 'I do not really wish to conclude and sum up, rounding off the arguments so as to dump it in a nutshell for the reader. A lot more could be said about any of the topics I have touched upon. … I have meant to ask questions, to break out of the frame. … The point is not a set of answers, but making possible a different practice' – a decolonised university curriculum.

NOTES

1   Jean-François Lyotard (1984) argues that the status of knowledge is changing as societies enter a post-industrial age, and cultures a postmodern age. The key change is that knowledge is no longer produced in pursuit of truth but of performativity – 'that is, the best input/output equation' (Lyotard 1984: 46). Since this usage of the term by Lyotard, performativity has been widely invoked in the criticism of contemporary education practice. As Ronald Barnett and Paul Standish (2003: 216) write: 'The term aptly exposes the jargon and practices of efficiency and effectiveness, quality assurance and control, inspection and accountability that have become so prominent a feature of contemporary educational regimes. Whatever is undertaken must be justified in terms of an increase in productivity measured in terms of a gain in time.'

2   Readings (1996) characterises the modern university in terms of the idea of excellence so as to emphasise the dominance of the institution of performativity. He also contrasts it with earlier incarnations: the Kantian University of Reason (for which the founding discipline is philosophy) and the Humboldtian University (in which philosophy was replaced with literature). But, unlike its predecessors, the ideal of excellence conceals a kind of vacuity. As Barnett and Standish (2003) elaborate: 'Globalisation and the decline of the nation state create conditions where the currency of excellence can function ideally for a knowledge economy. Homogenised systems of transferability and commensurability enable the free flow of cultural capital, and these are realised through a down grading in importance of content and a weakening of cultural attachments. The modern university is dominated by procedural reasoning in its emphasis on skills and on management systems, and in an incipient reduction of knowledge to information (all accelerated by computerisation).'

3   For Deleuze and Guattari (1987) a line of flight is our desire to escape the status quo that enables us to innovate – be creative.

4   Colombian philosopher Santiago Castro-Gómez (2007) described the detached and neutral point of observation of the knowing subject as the *hubris of the zero point*. This subject maps the world, classifies peoples and zooms into what is good for him/her.

5   The decimation or at least marginalisation of knowledges of the colonised holds largely true for South African universities. In relation to schooling, interestingly, Bantu education denied Africans access to Western knowledge during apartheid, which speaks to the uniqueness of coloniality in different contexts. Importantly, however, during apartheid Africans could of course not self-determine what knowledge was of most worth for their children and in this sense their knowledges were marginalised.

6   In this chapter I draw on scholarship from different countries, acknowledging that histories and lived experiences of colonisation have been different in different localities. However, my interest is not to emphasise difference, which is privileged in Western thought, but to highlight common histories of experiences of colonised peoples.

7   Rosi Braidotti (2013) argues that (post)humanism is the historical moment that marks the end of the opposition between humanism and anti-humanism and affirmatively charts new alternatives. She identifies three major strands in contemporary (post)human thought; the first derives from moral philosophy and develops a reactive form of the (post)human; the second derives from science and technology studies and takes an analytic from of the (post)human; and the third derives from anti-humanist philosophies and proposes a critical (post)humanism.

8   Decolonisation and decoloniality have distinct meanings when decolonisation is understood as the removal of the colonial state and decoloniality as an analytic of coloniality (the colonial matrix of power that remains after independence). The reason for conflating decolonisation and decoloniality in this chapter is because the notion of decolonisation expressed by Smith (1999) and Chilisa (2012) aligns with the notion of decoloniality. It relates to resistance and critique of colonial vestiges.

9   Efficacy should, however, not be confused with truth. The fact that science works does not mean that there is a correspondence between ... between the world and representations produced by science.

REFERENCES

Aikenhead, Glen and Herman Michell. 2011. *Bridging Cultures: Scientific and Indigenous Ways of Knowing Nature*. Toronto: Pearson Education Canada.

Aoki, Ted. 1999. 'Interview: Rethinking Curriculum and Pedagogy'. *Kappa Delta Pi Record* 35 (4): 180–181. doi: 10.1080/00228958.1999.10518454.

Ashcroft, Bill, Gareth Griffiths and Helen Tiffin, eds. 2000. *Post-colonial Studies: The Key Concepts*. London: Routledge.

Barnett, Ronald, and Kelly Coate. 2005. *Engaging the Curriculum in Higher Education*. Maidenhead: Society for Research into Higher Education & Open University Press.

Barnett, Ronald and Paul Standish. 2003. 'Higher Education and the University'. In *The Blackwell Guide to the Philosophy of Education*, edited by Nigel Blake, Paul Smeyers, Richard Smith and Paul Standish, 213–233. Oxford: Blackwell Publishing.

Bleek, Dorothea Frances. 1936. 'Beliefs and Customs of the /Xam Bushmen, from Material Collected by Dr. W.H.I. Bleek and Miss L.C. Lloyd between 1870 and 1880, Part 8: More about Sorcerors'. *Bantu Studies* 10 (1): 131–162. doi: 10.1080/02561751.1936.9676027.

Bobbitt, John Franklin. 1918. *The Curriculum*. Boston: Houghton Mifflin.

Bobbitt, John Franklin. 1924. *How to Make a Curriculum*. Boston: Houghton Mifflin.

Braidotti, Rosi. 2013. *The Posthuman*. Malden, MA: Polity Press.

Castro-Gómez, Santiago. 2007. 'The Missing Chapter of Empire: Postmodern Reorganization of Coloniality and Post-Fordist Capitalism'. *Cultural Studies* 21 (2–3): 428–448. doi: 10.1080/0950238060116263.

Chilisa, Bagele. 2012. *Indigenous Research Methodologies*. Thousand Oaks, CA: SAGE Publications.

Dei, George J. Sefa. 2000. 'Rethinking the Role of Indigenous Knowledges in the Academy'. *International Journal of Inclusive Education* 4 (2): 111–132. doi: 10.1080/136031100284849.

Deleuze, Gilles and Félix Guattari. 1987. *A Thousand Plateaus: Capitalism and Schizophrenia*. Minneapolis: University of Minnesota Press.

Deleuze, Gilles and Félix Guattari. 1994. *What is Philosophy?* New York: Columbia University Press.

Disemelo, Katlego. 2015. 'Student Protests Are about Much More Than Just #Feesmustfall'. *Mail & Guardian Online*, 29 October 2015. https://mg.co.za/article/2015-10-29-student-protests-are-about-much-more-than-just-feesmustfall.

Doll, Mary Aswell. 2000. *Like Letters in Running Water: A Mythopoetics of Curriculum*. Mahwah, NJ: L. Erlbaum Associates.

Fanon, Frantz. [1961] 1965. *The Wretched of the Earth*. New York: Grove Press.

Fanon, Frantz. 1967. *Toward the African Revolution: Political Essays*. New York: Monthly Review Press.

Goldie, Terry. 1999. 'Saint Fanon and Homosexual Territory'. In *Frantz Fanon: Critical Perspectives*, edited by Anthony Alessandrini, 75–86. London: Routledge.

Gough, Noel. 1998. 'All around the World: Science Education, Constructivism, and Globalization'. *Educational Policy* 12 (5): 507–524. doi: 10.1177/0895904898012005003.

Gough, Noel. 1999. 'Globalization and School Curriculum Change: Locating a Transnational Imaginary'. *Journal of Education Policy* 14 (1): 73–84. doi: 10.1080/026809399286503.

Gough, Noel. 2011. 'A Complexivist View of Higher Education: Implications for Curriculum Design and Research on Teaching and Learning'. Keynote address at the 5th Annual University Teaching and Learning Conference, Durban, 26–28 September. https://www.researchgate.net/publication/274375252_A_complexivist_view_of_higher_education_implications_for_curriculum_design_and_research_on_teaching_and_learning.

Grumet, Madeleine R. 1981. 'Restitution and Reconstruction of Educational Experience: An Autobiographical Method for Curriculum Theory'. In *Rethinking Curriculum Studies: A Radical Approach*, edited by Martin Lawn and Len Barton, 115–130. London: Croom Helm.

Guattari, Félix. 2000. *The Three Ecologies*. London: Athlone Press.

Jansen, Jonathan D. 2017. *As by Fire: The End of the South African University*. Cape Town: Tafelberg.

Kappeler, Susanne. 1986. *The Pornography of Representation*. Cambridge, UK: Polity Press.

Kawash, Samira. 1999. 'Terrorists and Vampires: Fanon's Spectral Violence of Decolonization'. In *Frantz Fanon: Critical Perspectives*, edited by Anthony Alessandrini, 235–237. London: Routledge.

Kennedy, Dane Keith. 2016. *Decolonization: A Very Short Introduction*. New York: Oxford University Press.

Le Grange, Lesley. 2006. 'Quality Assurance in South Africa: A Reply to John Mammon'. *South African Journal of Higher Education* 20 (6): 903–909.

Le Grange, Lesley. 2007. 'Integrating Western and Indigenous Knowledge Systems: The Basis for Effective Science Education in South Africa?' *International Review of Education* 53 (5): 577–591. doi: 10.1007/s11159-007-9056-x.

Le Grange, Lesley. 2009a. 'Are There Distinctive Indigenous Methods of Inquiry? IKS Community Development and Resilience'. *Indilinga: African Journal of Indigenous Knowledge Systems* 8 (2): 189–198.

Le Grange, Lesley. 2009b. 'The University in a Contemporary Era: Reflections on Epistemological Shifts'. In *Higher Education Studies in South Africa: A Scholarly Look Behind the Scenes*, edited by Eli Bitzer, 103–120. Stellenbosch: Sun Media.

Le Grange, Lesley. 2011. 'Challenges for Curriculum in a Contemporary South Africa'. In *Curriculum Inquiry in South African Higher Education: Some Scholarly Affirmations and Challenges*, edited by Eli Bitzer and Nonnie Botha, 67–78. Stellenbosch: Sun Media.

Le Grange, Lesley. 2014. 'Currere's Active Force and the Africanisation of the University Curriculum'. *South African Journal of Higher Education* 28 (4): 1283–1294.

Le Grange, Lesley. 2015. 'Indigenous Students' Learning of School Science: A Philosophical Interpretation'. In *International Handbook of Interpretation in Educational Research*, edited by Paul Smeyers, David Bridges, Nicholas C. Burbules and Morwenna Griffiths, 1037–1055. Dordrecht, Netherlands: Springer.

Le Grange, Lesley. 2018a. 'Currere's Active Force and the Concept of Ubuntu'. In *Internationalizing Curriculum Studies: Histories, Environments, and Critiques*, edited by Cristyne Hébert, Nicholas Ng-A-Fook, Awad Ibrahim and Bryan Smith. New York: Palgrave Macmillan.

Le Grange, Lesley. 2018b. 'Spinoza, Deep Ecology and Education Informed by a (Post)Human Sensibility'. *Educational Philosophy and Theory* 50 (9): 878–887. doi: 10.1080/00131857.2017.1384723.

Le Grange, Lesley. 2018c. 'The Notion of Ubuntu and the (Post)Humanist Condition'. In *Indigenous Philosophies of Education around the World*, edited by Roxanne M. Mitchell and John Petrovic, 40–60. New York: Routledge.

Le Grange, Lesley and Glen Aikenhead. 2017. 'Rethinking the "Western Tradition": A Response to Enslin and Horsthemke'. *Educational Philosophy and Theory* 49 (1): 31–37. doi: 10.1080/00131857.2016.1167656.

Lyotard, Jean-François. 1984. *The Postmodern Condition: A Report on Knowledge*. Minneapolis: University of Minnesota Press.

Maldonado-Torres, Nelson. 2007. 'On the Coloniality of Being: Contributions to the Development of a Concept'. *Cultural Studies* 21 (2–3): 240–270. doi: 10.1080/09502380601162548.

Maldonado-Torres, Nelson. 2016. 'Outline of Ten Theses on Coloniality and Decoloniality'. Fondation Frantz Fanon. http://frantzfanonfoundation-fondationfrantzfanon.com/IMG/pdf/maldonado-torres_outline_of_ten_theses-10.23.16_.pdf.

Mamdani, Mahmood. 2017. 'Decolonising the Post-colonial University'. T.B. Davie Memorial Lecture. Cape Town, 22 August.

Mbembe, Achille. 2001. *On the Postcolony*. Berkeley: University of California Press.

Mbembe, Achille. 2015. 'Decolonizing Knowledge and the Question of the Archive'. Presentation at the University of the Witwatersrand, Johannesburg, 22 April. https://wiser.wits.ac.za/system/files/Achille%20Mbembe%20-%20Decolonizing%20Knowledge%20and%20the%20Question%20of%20the%20Archive.pdf.

Mignolo, Walter D. 2007. 'Delinking: The Rhetoric of Modernity, the Logic of Coloniality and the Grammar of De-coloniality'. *Cultural Studies* 21 (2–3): 449–514. doi: 10.1080/09502380601162647.

Mignolo, Walter D. 2009. 'Epistemic Disobedience, Independent Thought and Decolonial Freedom'. *Theory, Culture & Society* 26 (7–8): 159–181. doi: 10.1177/0263276409349275.

Ngũgĩ wa Thiong'o. 1986. *Decolonising the Mind: The Politics of Language in African Literature*. London: James Currey.

Nkrumah, Kwame. 1965. *Neo-Colonialism: The Last Stage of Imperialism*. London: Nelson.

Odora Hoppers, Catherine A. and Howard Richards. 2012. *Rethinking Thinking: Modernity's "Other" and the Transformation of the University*. Pretoria: UNISA Press.

Omar, Yusuf. 2017. 'Mamdani Returns Cos "Rhodes Fell"'. *Africa Daily*, 25 August. http://www.africadaily.co.za/index.php?option=com_k2&view=item&id=1027:decolonial-professor-mahmood-mamdani-returns-to-uct.

Peters, Michael. 2007. *Knowledge Economy, Development and the Future of Higher Education*. Rotterdam: Sense Publishers.

Pinar, William. 1975. *Curriculum Theorizing: The Reconceptualists*. Berkeley, CA: McCutchan.

Pinar, William. 2004. *What Is Curriculum Theory?* Mahwah, NJ: L. Erlbaum Associates.

Pinar, William. 2011. *The Character of Curriculum Studies: Bildung, Currere, and the Recurring Question of the Subject*. New York: Palgrave Macmillan.

Pinar, William, William M. Reynolds, Patrick Slattery and Peter M. Taubman. 1995. *Understanding Curriculum: An Introduction to the Study of Historical and Contemporary Curriculum Discourses*. New York: Peter Lang.

Pindar, Ian and Paul Sutton. 2000. 'Translators' Introduction'. In *The Three Ecologies*, by Félix Guattari. London: Athlone Press.

Readings, Bill. 1996. *The University in Ruins*. Cambridge, MA: Harvard University Press.

Santos, Boaventura de Sousa. 2013. *Epistemologies of the South: Justice against Epistemicide*. Boulder: Paradigm Publishers.

Smith, Linda Tuhiwai. 1999. *Decolonizing Methodologies: Research and Indigenous Peoples*. London: Zed Books.

Spencer, Herbert. 1884. *What Knowledge Is of Most Worth*. New York: J.B. Alden.

Taylor, Frederick Winslow. 1911. *The Principles of Scientific Management*. New York: Harper & Brothers.

Turnbull, David. 1997. 'Reframing Science and Other Local Knowledge Traditions'. *Futures* 29 (6): 551–562. doi: 10.1016/S0016-3287(97)00030-X.

Tyler, Ralph W. 1950. *Basic Principles of Curriculum and Instruction*. Chicago: University of Chicago Press.

Van Wyk, Anim. 2014. 'How Many Professors Are There in SA?'. *Africa Check*, 18 August. https://africacheck.org/reports/how-many-professors-are-there-in-sa/.

Wallin, Jason J. 2010. *A Deleuzian Approach to Curriculum: Essays on a Pedagogical Life*. New York: Palgrave Macmillan.

THE POLITICS AND PROBLEMS OF DECOLONISATION

2

On the Politics of Decolonisation: Knowledge, Authority and the Settled Curriculum

Jonathan D. Jansen
Stellenbosch University

The fatalistic logic of *the unassailable position of English* in our literature leaves me more cold now than it did when I first spoke about it. ... And yet, I am unable to see a significantly different or a more emotionally comfortable resolution of that problem.

    – Chinua Achebe, *Morning Yet on Creation Day*

One of the critical roles of the social scientist, especially in times of high change, is the scrutiny of important concepts as they emerge from time to time in the public arena (Lee 2009). In South Africa, political slogans frequently serve as the currency carrying important concepts in social discourse. Those slogans become the rallying point for political competition among rival parties but they are also taken up in everyday conversations among citizens, often without closer examination. In recent years, those slogans include 'radical economic transformation', 'white monopoly capital' and 'land expropriation without compensation'.

It is not that these 'concepts as slogans' (Head 1988) have no substantive merit in a massively unequal society harbouring deep grievances in the present about an unresolved past.[1] Nor should this criticism be read as a dismissal of political slogans, for they have always been 'significant symbols of society' (Raj 2007), with the power to suggest actions, evoke emotions and persuade publics (Denton 2009). It is, rather, that these crisp and simple descriptions of complex problems – such as the urgent need for land reform – are seldom subjected to critical reflection and quickly attain the status of 'empty signifiers' (Long 2018: 20). We now know, for example, that concepts like 'white monopoly capital' were conjured up by the disgraced British public relations firm Bell Pottinger to deflect attention from the charges of state capture and corruption by President Zuma and his cronies (Chutel 2017).

The task of the social scientist when 'concepts as slogans' emerge is to subject them to critical analysis with questions such as: What does the concept mean? Why now? Where does it come from? And whose purposes does it serve? Social scientists fail in their responsibilities when they merely parrot popular terms and rush towards uncritical usage in academic work, without much reflection on the social and intellectual validity of key concepts.[2] Critical review is therefore both political – examining the interests behind each sloganeering claim on public attention – and educational, enriching public engagement with important concepts whether propagated from above (government policy) or from below (democratic struggles).

The goal of this chapter, then, is to lay bare *the politics of knowledge* represented in the decolonisation moment, as it emerged in the historic student protests of 2015–2016. It identifies various approaches and theories of decolonisation, and then outlines a conceptual framework called *knowledge regimes* for making sense of the changing relationship between knowledge and authority from precolonial times into the democratic present. The chapter then presents three empirical cases that challenge, if not overturn, conventional views of knowledge and authority, the so-called centre-periphery thesis. And it concludes with an assessment of the likely futures of decolonisation, given the institutionalisation of knowledge within universities.

THE EMERGENCE OF DECOLONISATION AS A POLITICAL SLOGAN ON UNIVERSITY CAMPUSES

In the course of 2015, major South African universities experienced an unprecedented level of campus protests focused initially on what would become known as 'the decolonisation moment' (Jansen 2017c) and more ambitiously as 'the decolonial turn' (Badat 2017) in struggles for institutional transformation. The second protest moment, from September 2015 onwards, was focused on the exclusionary costs of higher education and was carried by a different slogan, #FeesMustFall.

The most visible symbol of the earlier moment was the toppling of the massive bronze statue of the British imperialist Cecil John Rhodes on the upper campus of the University of Cape Town (UCT) in April 2015. Subsequently, the #RhodesMustFall moment was borne by the concept of 'decolonisation', which referred generally to the quest for racially and culturally inclusive campuses and more specifically to the transformation of campus symbolism, the university curriculum, institutional cultures and the professoriate. The charges were clear: campus symbolism celebrated colonial conquest; the curriculum remained centred on Western knowledge; institutional cultures were racially exclusive and the professoriate remained white and male-dominated. In everyday speech and on protest banners, the solution was equally clear – formerly white institutions needed to be *decolonised*.

Very soon universities across South Africa – though less so on traditionally black campuses – convened seminars, workshops and conferences on 'decolonisation'. The term was attached to every discipline from the social sciences to the natural sciences and engineering. How could these fields be 'decolonised'? Professional bodies, science councils and non-governmental organizations flagged their concerns with 'decolonisation'. A major US funder, the Mellon Foundation, set aside millions of dollars to fund research into 'the decolonial turn' at seven selected universities. Some of the most affected universities convened elaborate curriculum committees to implement the decolonisation project.

With little critical engagement with the concept itself, decolonisation was often taken by students to be a catch-all description of, and solution for, the lack of transformation on university campuses. The meaning of decolonisation was often assumed rather than explicated, and any challenge to what had clearly become a political slogan was met with an intensity of response that painted the questioner as the enemy. Decolonisation very rapidly became the litmus test of political commitment to changes in universities, with important consequences for both critical analysis and informed activism.

DECOLONISATION – ANOTHER LOOK AT A TROUBLED CONCEPT

In the spirit of critical review, what are the meanings of *decolonisation* as the concept came to occupy prominence on university campuses in the historic protests of 2015–2016?

To begin with, the word 'decolonisation' has a rich intellectual ancestry that emerged within particular contexts over time. The term first gained prominence in the anti-colonial struggle, in which the straightforward goal was the removal of the European colonial authority from the occupied territories. That anti-colonial struggle had its own landmark texts such as Aimé Césaire's ([1950] 2000) *Discourse on Colonialism*, Albert Memmi's ([1957] 2016) *The Colonizer and the Colonized*, and of course Frantz Fanon's ([1961] 1965) *The Wretched of the Earth*. All these works describe in painful detail the devastating effects of colonisation on the colonised.

With colonial rule toppled, *decolonisation* was extended to mean dealing with the legacies of colonialism that remained even after the colonial authorities withdrew, including the continued dominance of European or Western knowledge in the curriculum of the former colonies. As the human rights education scholar André Keet put it, decolonisation today means dealing with 'what colonialism left undone' (Keet 2014).

The dense and complex movement broadly called decolonisation has many intellectual strands and traditions. One tradition is *postcolonialism*, in part a cultural analysis of colonial legacies, and it has a rich literature, including Edward Said's *Orientalism* (1978), Homi Bhaba's *The Location of Culture* (1994) and Gayatri Spivak's famous essay 'Can the Subaltern Speak?' (1988). Another tradition is *decoloniality*, in part an epistemological analysis of colonial legacies, which draws its literatures from Latin American writings on the colonial aftermath, as in the work of Aníbal Quijano (2007), Nelson Maldonado-Torres (2007) and Walter Mignolo (2011).

This chapter will not, however, deal with the full range of concerns raised by the advocates of decolonisation, but will focus specifically on the curriculum as arguably the most durable and tangible of colonial effects – the matter of *what counts as knowledge* (curriculum) once the colonial authorities have left.

THE KNOWLEDGE PROBLEM IN DECOLONISATION

What specifically is *the knowledge problem* in decolonisation? As already suggested, the criticism of the curriculum after colonialism expresses itself very differently in different regions of the world.

In the Latin American critique of the colonial legacy, the problem is that knowledge is represented as universal, rational and scientific to the exclusion of other ways of knowing. It is atomistic, breaking knowledge into small parts rather than offering a 'total' view of society that includes those who are left out. It separates reason from emotion, subject from object, and body from mind. This cold, clinical and scientific view of the world therefore denies inter-subjectivity, for surely the objects of study (such as subjugated people, the colonised) are simultaneously human subjects with feelings, emotions and desires that cannot be neatly separated from methods of inquiry. Such legacy knowledge is also hierarchical in nature, presenting as authority those who know (colonials) and those who do not (the colonised) as in the pedagogical situation (Germana 2014).[3]

In the classroom situation, therefore, the exchange of knowledge happens inside a power relationship between the knower (white authority) and the known (native subject).[4] In the research situation, the white, colonial authority is understood as human subjects that study native cultures merely as 'ironical parodies' (oddities, in other words) as was the case with fields like ethnology and anthropology (Quijano 2007).

The rather ambitious decolonisation task, from this perspective, is not only 'to liberate the production of knowledge … from the pitfalls of human rationality' but also 'to clear the way for an interchange of experiences and meanings' that are truly universal, and ultimately secure 'the liberation from all power organised as inequality, discrimination, exploitation, and as domination' (Quijano 2007: 177–178).

In the African/South African meanings of decolonisation, on the other hand, the critique has emphasised matters of knowledge and identity rather than simply the epistemological legacies of colonial rule. That is, the question of *whose knowledge* is at the centre of the continental contestation over the curriculum. The intellectual leadership for this position can be traced to scholars like Ngũgĩ wa Thiong'o, as in his famous criticism of the centring of European knowledge in the teaching of English in early postcolonial Kenya (Jansen 2017c). Since then, numerous African scholars have expanded on the ways in which Eurocentricity continues to characterise education customs and curricula in the postcolonial period, whether in schools (Christie and McKinney 2017) or universities (Grant, Quinn, and Vorster 2018).

Against this background, during the South African protests of 2015–2016 decolonisation was often presented by students in the form of an emphatic Afrocentrism delivered in charged language:

> The current curriculum dehumanises black students. We study all these dead white men who presided over our oppression and we are made to use their thinking as a standard and as a point of departure. Our own thinking as Africans has been undermined. We must have our own education from our own continent. We cannot be decolonised by white people who colonised us. Decolonisation advances the interests of Africans, instead of advancing Eurocentric interests (Evans 2016; see also Sebidi and Morreira 2017).

But how valid is this criticism – both in its Latin American and African variations – in the context of South Africa? This requires some attention to the source of the problem that the decolonial critics are responding to – that is, the colonial project. In this respect, it is important to take a longer view of South African history than one that reduces a complex three or more centuries to the colonial regime.

I will invoke the term *knowledge regimes* to describe the relationship between state and knowledge at distinct moments (eras) in South African history. I am not therefore using the term narrowly in relation to the generative sources of ideas, such as policy research organizations, and how they affect economic policies and performance (Campbell and Pedersen 2015).[5] My focus is more broadly on the state and the kind of knowledge it authorises as official knowledge within a particular period in history.

KNOWLEDGE REGIMES

South Africa's history was not only or always one of colonial occupation. Colonialism was preceded by precolonial authority, followed from 1910 by segregation and then apartheid, and then by 25 years of post-apartheid government. It is therefore useful to characterise the relationship between the state and knowledge in these different periods (precolonial society, colonialism, segregation/apartheid and democracy) in South African history as *knowledge regimes*.

Knowledge regimes are described here as the dominant and authoritative form(s) of knowledge, often originating in the state, which determine what counts as official knowledge (curriculum) in a nation's educational institutions. Each knowledge regime:
- stakes its claim on being different;
- changes within its own period;
- is contested within its own period;

- leaves a trace in practice;
- owes its authority to power;
- seeks to embed itself in institutional life;
- eventually falls to a successor regime and;
- resists pressure for change from below.

Figure 3.1: Curriculum as knowledge regime

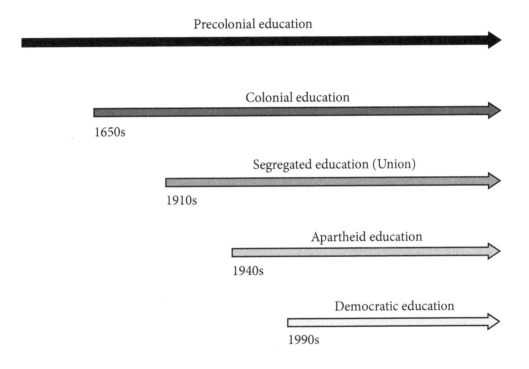

CURRICULUM as knowledge regimes

Precolonial education

Colonial education

1650s

Segregated education (Union)

1910s

Apartheid education

1940s

Democratic education

1990s

The first knowledge regime precedes colonial rule. In this pre-seventeenth–century period, education was offered by traditional authorities, including tribal chiefs. In other words, the knowledge regime was the tribal authority. The curriculum was of course relevant to local conditions and indigenous in content in this precolonial period. And yet scholarly accounts of the precolonial curriculum (and there are too few) refer to authoritarian relations of teaching and learning; of hierarchy and obedience; of telling and repeating as the dominant forms of pedagogy. Teaching was transmission and learning was imitative (Seroto 2011; see also Booyse et al. 2011). These deeply embedded patterns of pedagogy continue to this day (Tabulawa 2013; Hoadley 2018: 153–168).

The second knowledge regime, and certainly the most enduring, was the colonial authority. In this respect, the education of black South Africans was not highly organised by the state, whether under Dutch or British rule. It was not a priority for the Dutch, so that outside of the Slave Lodge, the 1778 Census found that only 11.1 per cent of free children and 5.3 per cent of enslaved children received formal education. In curriculum terms, slave education was about containment and control, with the focus on religious education as well as reading and writing in Dutch.[6]

During the British colonial period, missionaries from various European countries ventured into southern Africa with their ambivalent agendas of both education and 'civilisation' (see Holmes ([1967] 2007), of the simulatenous freeing of the mind and its colonisation (Woeber 2000). In the course of time churches came to dominate the formal education of black youth in South Africa even though the numbers remained small; in fact, by 1939 two-thirds of black children had no school education and by 1950 only 2.6 per cent had advanced beyond primary schooling (Giliomee 2012: 75). Mission schools (including a handful of famous ones) produced an African elite of well-schooled Christians.

The post-war settlement between Brit and Boer permitted the use of both English and Dutch (later Afrikaans) in schools, and after Union in 1910, education was more rigidly and systematically segregated. In this third knowledge regime, the formal curriculum contained both academic and vocational subjects; whites and blacks wrote the same examinations. But beyond the curriculum as subjects, there was a much more contentious educational experience for black students that the historian Linda Chisholm (2017) calls 'the invisible beliefs, pedagogies and practices that constructed internal regimes of schooling'. These included contestations about authority, discipline, manual labour and respect – the curriculum-as-experienced, in other words.

In the interwar years there started to emerge within white South African politics a more audible concern with African education – that it was too liberal and presented blacks with a sense of freedom and expectation of careers for which they were not destined. With the rising tide of Afrikaner nationalism, stifling the ambitions of missionary education became a political rallying point and led the Minister of Native Affairs, Hendrik Verwoerd, to make the notorious charge about the uselessness of mathematics as a curriculum subject for black children.

The fourth knowledge regime, apartheid, was the most emphatic when it came to stipulating the curriculum appropriate for black South Africans and led to the closing down of most church schools. It established what would become known as Bantu Education under the control of the white government. It is apartheid, and not colonialism, that comes to leave its most enduring legacy in the post-apartheid curriculum in that it created vastly different resourcing infrastructures for education, which showed in the unequal learning outcomes for black and white students. Unlike colonialism, apartheid education emerged in the broader context of anti-imperialism (anti-British, specifically) and a virulent Afrikaner nationalism at the very time in history that independence came to African states to the north and the colonial authorities left their so-called possessions. The otherwise progressive precepts of Dutch philosophies of education were crudely transplanted in the form of the Afrikaner's Christian National Education with its pretence of scientism (neutral knowledge) and its propagation of racism (white supremacy) (Suransky-Dekker 1998).

The fifth knowledge regime was ushered in during the early 1990s as the first democratic government was elected and found itself confronted with these legacies of past curricular ideologies of successive authorities. For more than two decades the current knowledge regime has worked to establish its own authority on the curriculum as it struggled with a complex legacy that simply would not go away. It started with a commissioned 'cleansing' of the apartheid syllabuses to eliminate racist, sexist and 'generally offensive' knowledge from the curriculum (Jansen 1999). Then followed the installation of a massive new knowledge infrastructure on the curriculum of schools and universities that sought to orient teaching and learning away from content coverage to essential learning outcomes. The instruments for achieving this were the National Qualifications Framework (NQF) and in schools a system called outcomes-based education (OBE). The NQF persists as a governing structure for curriculum but OBE would eventually be replaced with a scripted curriculum for schools that returned to the principle of coverage (teachers were again required to 'cover' the full curriculum in pressed time) as a primary concern (Jansen 2019).

CHARACTERISTICS OF KNOWLEDGE REGIMES

Eight important features of knowledge regimes, the dominant authority governing curriculum at a particular moment in history, need to be accounted for in estimating the prospects for change.

1. *Each Knowledge Regime Stakes Its Claim on Being Different.* This should be self-evident. The state at any particular point in time is an outcome of social struggles for political dominance and therefore seeks to impress its authority on institutions, including the curriculum. The apartheid curriculum is not the colonial curriculum and the curriculum of democracy is certainly not the apartheid curriculum. The curriculum formally reflects the resident power of the state. The state determines in each era what knowledge counts as worthwhile for children in public schools and, as far as the public curriculum is concerned, what is represented in symbolic representations such as museums, artworks and monuments (Tietze 2017).[7]

2. *Each Knowledge Regime Changes within Its Own Period.* Curricular knowledge is never static. The heavily ideological curriculum of apartheid, invested with notions of white supremacy, gradually changed to become a largely technicist curriculum by the 1980s, concerned with skills and competences (Buckland 1984). The OBE project of the democratic government, with its emphasis on teacher autonomy and learner exploration, was eventually scrapped and further deformed into a heavily scripted content-heavy curriculum, with the emphasis on coverage (Spaull and Jansen 2019).

3. *Each Knowledge Regime Is Contested within Its Own Period.* Curriculum knowledge is never at rest. The state's attempt at prescription is challenged by rival knowledge. Apartheid's knowledge regime was constantly challenged from below – think of any number of alternative education projects, from People's Education (Mathebula 2013) to SACHED (South African Committee for Higher Education) (Nonyongo and Ngengebulu 1993) – and from outside the state, as in the case of mission education. Even the relatively autonomous university curricula are constantly challenged by alternative visions of knowledge, such as 'the great curriculum debate' sparked by Mahmood Mamdani at UCT (Mamdani 1998; Hall 1998) or, more recently, the decolonisation moment at several institutions of higher learning (Jansen 2017b). While such regimes are dominant, they are contested by alternative or rival visions of what should constitute official knowledge.

4. *Each Knowledge Regime Leaves a Trace in Practice.* Despite the radical change of political authority – from colonial education to segregation/apartheid education to democratic education – the knowledge from previous regimes leaves a trace in teaching and learning practice (Buenfil-Burgos 2000). Governmental authority might change, but its curriculum imprint changes far more slowly. For example, successive attempts across the African continent and the developing world to change from an authoritarian pedagogy towards much more egalitarian forms of curriculum interaction and exchange have failed because of the embeddedness of previous knowledge regimes (Tabulawa 2013). And even though it has been discarded, South African education still reflects the imprint of OBE in its curriculum as the dominant knowledge regime for schools. There is no such thing as a pure knowledge regime; the newly dominant order always reflects in the curriculum, as codification of knowledge, vestiges from previous or alternative authorities.

5. *Each Knowledge Regime Owes Its Authority to Power.* What gives knowledge its stamp of authority in the public school curriculum or in the university curriculum is official power. In the case of public schools, directly, that power is the government. In the case of public universities, that power is the Senate. A complex of laws, rules and regulations govern what counts as knowledge. The *Government Gazette* issues policy for schools; the Senate rules govern curriculum policy in universities. No teacher or professor makes their own curricular arrangements without approval from above. And it is the sense of authorising power that partly explains why it is so difficult to simply change the knowledge arrangements within institutions.

6. *Each Knowledge Regime Seeks to Embed Itself in Institutional Life.* Knowledge does not only exist as examinable content in the official curriculum. It is also institutionalised within the day-to-day practices of schools and universities. A knowledge regime therefore not only represents formal knowledge codified in the curriculum, but also its expression in methods of teaching, patterns of learning and modalities of assessment. These activities (teaching, learning and

assessment) convey, process and evaluate knowledge formally codified in what might otherwise be described as content. All these expressions of knowledge are not only authorised by authority; over time they assume common sense within institutional life. This is what has been called the institutional curriculum (Lange 2017; Jansen 2009).

7. *Each Knowledge Regime Eventually Falls to a Successor Regime.* What this conception thus implies is that no knowledge regime is ever permanent, for it changes either more dramatically (as during radical social change, such as at the end of colonial rule) or less dramatically (as during a major shift in education policy under an existing social order). The change from one political regime to the next (colonial rule, apartheid, democracy) means a new knowledge regime is established under a new authorising power to change the curriculum.

8. *Each Knowledge Regime Resists Pressure for Change from Below.* Under centralised governments, as in developing countries, knowledge regimes seldom yield to activist pressures for change outside the state. This is as true of People's Education in the anti-apartheid struggle as it is of 'decolonised education' in the democratic period. It is also the case that in autonomous institutions, such as universities, knowledge regimes seldom change at their core how knowledge is received and transacted over time; curriculum change in response to activist pressures within universities is ephemeral and tends to happen at the margins of institutional life, if at all. Curriculum committees will be assembled, topics might change here and there, and new modules introduced in parts of the Organization, but what counts as knowledge seldom yields to external challenges from below. Even radical proposals for knowledge shifts within the state seldom find traction within institutions, as in the case of the defunct OBE model for curriculum in South Africa.

THE IDENTITY PROBLEM OF DECOLONISATION

This review of knowledge regimes means, first of all, that to speak about decolonisation requires one to be precise with respect to the context of usage – 'where', 'when' and 'what' questions are required. Colonialism was only one influence on knowledge and curriculum. It follows that to label every institutional problem as in need of decolonisation is to render the word impotent whether for purposes of analysis (what is going on?) or progressive action (what is to be done?). It is, moreover, to deny the complexity of power and authority that shaped, and continues to shape, what counts as knowledge in the post-apartheid period.

This does not mean that there are not vestiges of colonial thought and knowledge in our institutions – the prominent bronze statue of Cecil John Rhodes was perhaps the most visible case – nor that all such vestiges are necessarily negative – university education in English is a prime example. But it does mean that when we speak of colonial knowledge – and what to do about it – this requires the critic to be specific about the relevant knowledge regime and its consequences in the present.

In this respect, it is important to restate that colonial knowledge is not the same thing as apartheid knowledge: the latter's referential framework was not Empire but Afrikaner nationalism; its political and curriculum struggles were defined in Afrikaans not English; it was not foreigners imposing their will on black people, but fellow South African citizens. Nor is it the same as democratic knowledge since 1994, a project largely anti-apartheid in character. It is therefore impossible to pin South Africa's curriculum legacy to a particular knowledge regime. This means that the blanket, accusatory statement that university curricula are colonial artefacts and therefore in need of decolonisation is, at best, misleading.

THE INSTITUTIONAL REFRACTION OF DECOLONISATION DILEMMAS

It is also not helpful to speak about decolonisation as if all institutions are similarly affected by a complex, multi-regime past. The curriculum is more afflicted by colonial legacies in some institutions and more by apartheid legacies in others. South Africa's premier research institution, UCT, bears the fingerprints of its colonial legacy more prominently in its culture and curriculum than is the case with the University of Stellenbosch, which carries the apartheid legacy emphatically in its curriculum.

The University of the Western Cape (UWC), a product of the apartheid imaginary for so-called Coloured students, has much more in common with Stellenbosch than with UCT. That said, UWC boasts a proud record of resistance against the apartheid project, which reflects in its curriculum.

One scholar demonstrated these differential refractions of the past through institutions (Papier 2006), presenting systematic evidence of how authorship and knowledge in the field of teacher education mirrored almost perfectly these different ideologies. Joy Papier found that 'institutional histories and traditions feature prominently as "shapers" of academic responses to change, factors that … government policies have not taken into account'. The British/European theorists in UCT's education curriculum (Bernstein, Young, Bourdieu) contrasted with the Afrikaner nationalist theorists of Stellenbosch University and the liberation pedagogy authors of UWC (Annala, Liden and Mäkinen 2016). There is a reason, therefore, that the decolonial charge is so emphatically made at the old English universities (UCT, Wits, Rhodes) while decolonisation finds little traction in student struggles at the historically black universities, where funding often animates protest.

'WHO IS THE TOLSTOY OF THE ZULUS?'

What then does it mean to say the university curriculum is 'colonial'? As reviewed elsewhere, the dominant meaning associated with the decolonial charge in public and scholarly usage is that of the *centring* of Western or European knowledge (Jansen 2017b). In this limited frame, the charge is of course true. Most of what constitutes curriculum knowledge in universities throughout the world and across disciplines is derived from the West. The major theories and theorists, methods and methodologists, are disproportionately situated outside of the developing world.

The reasons are well established and can be found in the history of conquest and domination – politically, economically and also intellectually. The inflammatory question therefore posed by the Canadian-American novelist, Saul Bellow – 'Who is the Tolstoy of the Zulus? The Proust of the Papuans?' – not only ignores the colonial legacy but is also ignorant of the significant contributions of Africans (including Nobel Laureates in literature) to the stock of world knowledge.

Recognising both the knowledge legacy and the knowledge contributions from Africa/South Africa, what is to be done? The ideal of course is to infuse curricula in psychology, chemistry, teacher education and medicine with knowledge from Africa, Asia and Latin America; and to do this, as reasonable critics would concede, alongside knowledge from the West.

But how to proceed, given the uneven state of knowledge production in the South? Take the field of curriculum theory, relevant to the thesis pursued in this chapter on the relationship between the state and knowledge. There cannot be more than one or two powerful instances of curriculum theory, touching schools alone, that have emerged from the African continent before or since the end of colonialism. Rather than spawn local theory in the field of curriculum, since 1994 almost all of South Africa's major curriculum policy positions have their origins elsewhere, such as OBE (Australia) or standards-based qualifications (the UK) or learner-centred instruction (the USA).

In the absence of vibrant, original and creative knowledge production systems in (South) Africa, where will African-centred or African-led curriculum theory come from? It would of course have to come from well-qualified and experienced scholars, who are rooted in the study of education and endowed with a critical independence of thought. It is unclear for the African continent where such curriculum theorists are and might come from, given the deteriorating state of public universities characterised by underfunding, chronic instability and the weight of compensatory education cultures.

This dearth of inventive curriculum theory from South Africa alone has had four principal effects.

First, that the knowledge debates in the field are led not by education scholars but by academics from disciplines of political science, psychology, history and even the natural sciences; scholars not grounded in the sociology or politics or anthropology of school and university knowledge.

Second, that the attack on the decolonised curriculum has been reduced to 'a language of critique' because there is little expertise or substance within movements with which to replace the settled curriculum, thereby pointing the way for 'a language of possibility' (Giroux 2013). South African students, academics and activists are masters of criticism, fluent in the discipline of 'unpacking' what is wrong with society and eloquent in our articulation of social problems. The 'language of critique' is often a substitute for intellectual depth and scholarly production.

Third, this poverty of national (or, for that matter, continental) curriculum theory has led to the fact that the knowledge producers are overwhelmingly progressive white scholars inside, and more often outside, South Africa; this has implications for one of the major lines of criticism in the decolonisation moment, that the knowledge producers are themselves a racially privileged class. The question therefore remains: who produces curriculum knowledge in the aftermath of apartheid. There is a serious problem – the knowledge producers remain overwhelmingly white in part because of the narrowing pipeline of black scholars from school (where more than half of learners leave the system before completion), to the first degree, to the PhD, to the postdoctoral student, to the academic lecturer, to the leading professor in a discipline; but also in part because of the lack of intellectual inventiveness, boldness and prominence even among the slim group of black professors in South Africa.

Fourth, the poverty of inventive theory has resulted in *a retreat into indigenisation*. Major funding has been reserved for this escape into indigeneity, as if there exists a treasure trove of as yet undiscovered knowledge buried – or suppressed, in the language of scholars of the indigenous – and waiting to be excavated and brought to light as a challenge to a regnant coloniality in resident knowledge systems.

No doubt there is great value in investments in local (indigenous) knowledge and especially the study of neglected problems from the vantage point of the subaltern or those on the underside of history. There are concerns, however, that the return to the indigenous in South Africa often suggests a narrow Africanism bordering on racial essentialism (Naudé 2017) rather than a broader intellectual quest for the diversity of knowledges un- or under-explored in the local academy; for example, the question of slave Afrikaans in the Cape.[8]

The discussion so far demonstrates that the legacy of colonialism includes its negative effects on knowledge production in the former colonies, curriculum theory being a case in point. It is, however, also true that some scholars in the South have made significant progress in challenging and overcoming their marginalisation in the knowledge enterprise and their intellectual dependency on knowledge from elsewhere. But to understand this point it is important to revisit the model that still determines how African (or for that matter, Southern) scholars are framed in the decolonisation debates.

KNOWLEDGE AT THE CENTRE AND ON THE PERIPHERY

The heart of the decolonisation argument is the notion of Europe at the centre and Africa on the margins of knowledge. It is worth retelling the terms of the centre-periphery argument in relation to knowledge production. The basic thesis is that the knowledge transaction between the centre and periphery corresponds to the economic transaction between those at the centre and those on the margins of production (see figures 3.2 and 3.3).

Figure 3.2: The economic transaction

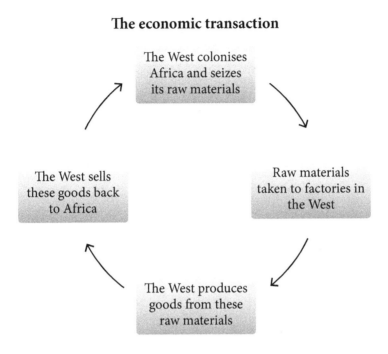

The economic transaction

The West colonises Africa and seizes its raw materials

Raw materials taken to factories in the West

The West produces goods from these raw materials

The West sells these goods back to Africa

Source: Walter Rodney, *How Europe Underdeveloped Africa* (1972)

In these schemas, knowledge is produced in the North (Europe and America – the developed world, also called 'the West') and consumed in the South (Africa, Latin America, Asia – the developing world). Africa, for example, produces the 'raw materials' for knowledge production when Western scientists descend on poor countries and extract knowledge from local sources through fieldwork in which African scientists are the junior partners. These Western scientists bring with them conceptual frameworks and methodological tools compromised by Eurocentric biases and procedures. They then proceed to excavate knowledge of the local, which is taken back to Europe, for example, and processed there, once again using Western analytical frames and tools, away from the original sites of knowledge collection (data gathering). The knowledge so produced appears in scholarly journals under Western authorship. Such knowledge published in learned journals is out of reach (too expensive, too shrouded in abstract language, too irrelevant to local conditions) for African scholars and communities. Their role remains giving access to external actors to repeat the vicious cycle. In other words, research knowledge is generated in the same way that manufactured goods are produced, through cycles of dependency in which the centre gains and the periphery remains marginalised.

Figure 3.3: The knowledge transaction

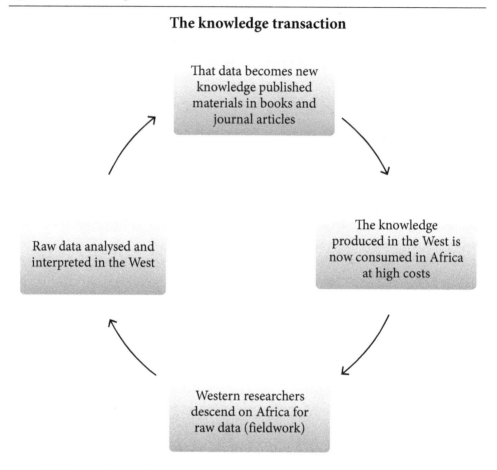

The knowledge transaction

That data becomes new knowledge published materials in books and journal articles

The knowledge produced in the West is now consumed in Africa at high costs

Raw data analysed and interpreted in the West

Western researchers descend on Africa for raw data (fieldwork)

Source: Schiebinger and Swan, *Colonial Botany* (2005)

THE CRITICS RETHINK THE CENTRE-PERIPHERY FRAMING OF (DE)COLONISATION

It is clear that in recent years some of the most prominent articulators of the centre-periphery problem are rethinking such a crude framing of the postcolonial condition. Guy Neave (2006) speaks of 'the inhuman tidiness of a binary world' while Peggy Ochoa (1996) holds that 'the antithetical pairs advanced by colonial discourse do not allow for a record of alternative thinking because one of the most powerful distinctions between coloniser and colonised is the emphatic difference between a speaker with agency and the figure of the silent or silenced subaltern.'

Paulin Hountondji (2006) concedes that older descriptions of the centre-periphery problem were 'exceedingly pessimistic' and that 'today the "Third World" features structures of scientific and intellectual production where extremely important work is done [with] resounding world-wide impact'.

Raewyn Connell and her colleagues concur: 'It is a serious conceptual mistake to equate global marginality with passivity' and relationships between North and South reveal 'a pattern of agency … not a position of powerlessness' (Connell et al. 2017). And Edward Said (1991: 80) famously claimed that

> a single over-mastering identity at the core of the academic enterprise, whether the identity be Western, African, or Asian, is a confinement, a deprivation. The world we live in is made up of numerous identities interacting, sometimes harmoniously, sometimes antithetically. Not to deal with the whole … is not to have academic freedom.

These tired binaries, then, so easily become 'essentialising binaries' that carry within them the very structure of colonial thinking that spawned the criticism in the first place (Ochoa 1996: 225, 228). For what *globalisation* has done in social and economic terms is to shrink the world, creating new relations and new authorities within the realm of production (think of Singapore in the world economy); what *technology* has done is to flatten access to knowledge with the potential for greater participation in knowledge production (think of Indian software engineers in Silicon Valley); and what *democracy* has done is to open up opportunities for Southern scholars to lead major research programmes with a global imprint (think of South African scholars in the global academy).

TURNING THE DECOLONISATION PROJECT ON ITS HEAD

I have selected three major research programmes in South Africa that turn the centre-periphery argument of knowledge in the decolonisation project on its head. Consider these high-profile 'Southern projects' led by South African scholars across three different disciplines – cardiology, infectious diseases and history. What follows are excerpts from my interviews with Bongani Mayosi at UCT; Quarraisha Abdood Karim at the University of KwaZulu-Natal, and Ian Phimister at the University of the Free State. While not verbatim transcripts, they are reported in the first person.

Bongani Mayosi, Poverty and Cardiovascular Disease

The research project that I'm engaged with is about dealing with heart disease among poor people. These forms of heart diseases occur before middle age and they are usually related to infections. And in addition to using a genetic approach I also took an approach of involving colleagues from multiple centres. We created some of the first African-initiated studies in multiple African countries of these particular neglected conditions.

The countries participating in our studies include Namibia, Mozambique, Zambia, Zimbabwe, Malawi, Kenya, Cameroon, Sudan, Ethiopia and Egypt. So our studies have tended to be pan-African in nature and really the collaborations have been borne out of just an enthusiasm of investigators. We started most of these consortia with absolutely no money but an interest in shining a spotlight on these heart conditions that are still highly prevalent in Africa but neglected because they are heart diseases of poor people.

Collaborations outside Africa have been vital in moving the African agenda forward. So through the networks that I established in Oxford, in North America and in Europe, I have had collaborators and indeed mentors who are pillars in my work.

In North America, I've been fortunate to work with one of the leading cardiovascular researchers in the world today, Salim Yusuf (an Indian-born Canadian physician, author of *Evidence Based Cardiology*) who is based at McMaster University. And then in Europe, in Italy in particular, I've collaborated with Peter Schwartz, who is also a giant in cardiology. So to some extent it has been vital to have collaborators outside Africa who share their support and expertise and help us to focus the spotlight on the problems that are relevant to our continent. But those collaborations must be premised on the idea that we need to illuminate African problems and *the agenda has to be set by our own conditions*, by our own predicament. And that's a very important balance to strike as we move forward. So there is *huge mutual benefit* from this research.

We have also attracted some students from North America in particular who've come and studied in our groups and have gone back home and some of them now are leaders in their particular area. So we've had that experience as well.

You'll find that in some topics, because we are the only group working on that in the world, we're quoting ourselves. But it has been hugely advantageous to collaborate with colleagues, bring the best science to localised problems.

The Abdool Karims, HIV/AIDS Infections among Rural Women

Both Slim and I (Quarrisha) earned our Master's degrees at the School of Public Health at Columbia University. At the time there were few opportunities in South Africa to study epidemiology. This opportunity was created by Mervyn Susser and Zena Stein, two exiled South African clinicians who had worked with Sydney and Emily Kark, who had developed models of primary health care under the apartheid system. In 1985 they created an opportunity for South Africans to train at Columbia University through funding from the Rockefeller Foundation.

After one year of training at Columbia University, Slim and I returned to South Africa and asked what we could do as scientists. As anti-apartheid activists in the 1970s and 1980s, we interacted with many vulnerable communities and our research approach in these communities was to respect and work in partnership with them. In fact even as we were in the process of establishing CAPRISA (Centre for the AIDS Programme of Research in South Africa), an *inkosi* (chief) from one of the highest-burden districts in

KwaZulu-Natal called us to a meeting with him and said, 'My people are dying of AIDS. What can you as researchers do to help us?'

I observed how the HIV epidemic was evolving in the USA and in Africa. We knew the factors causing the epidemic. We found that women were more infected than men as a result of unequal power in terms of gender in relationships. It was also clear that all interventions available at the time required the cooperation of men, for example, the use of condoms, and this created problems for women who were unable to negotiate condom use with their partner. We therefore needed to address the gap with respect to women in terms of developing women-initiated technology. In this way our understanding of the local epidemic evolved and yet had global relevance for those studying HIV/AIDS.

In 2004 we had an idea derived from providing anti-retroviral treatment to AIDS patients. Having witnessed the benefits of anti-retrovirals and learning how we had virtually eradicated mother-to-child transmission through their use, we decided to try and put a drug called Tenofovir into a gel. We tested whether putting this gel into the genital tract of uninfected women would prevent HIV infection. This was the CAPRISA 004 trial that demonstrated for the first time that anti-retrovirals used by uninfected women can prevent HIV infection. We had a bonus finding in this particular study in that we also established that Tenofovir prevented herpes simplex virus 2. HSV-2 is one of the most common sexually transmitted infections and we were able to show a 51 per cent reduction in HSV-2 incidence with the same product.

These results were presented at the International AIDS Conference in Vienna and simultaneously published in the journal *Science* and this marked a new era of optimism in HIV prevention. It was voted one of the top papers in the journal *Lancet* and one of the top ten scientific breakthroughs in that year. So many other studies followed and in 2015 the World Health Organization included in their guidelines the inclusion of daily use of Tenofovir-containing agents as prophylaxis as part of combination prevention.

These problems could only be solved with local knowledge. In multi-centre studies protocols are often written in the USA and then implemented in Africa. But what we wanted required a different approach. We had to ask, 'How can we solve these unique challenges?' For example, we had to decide when to start anti-retroviral treatment in HIV-TB co-infected patients. This is not a challenge for industrialised countries but was a major gap in our knowledge in South Africa as well as in the rest of Africa and Latin America.

Yet though these independent studies initiated in South Africa we never compromised on excellence. We tend to ask questions that are of importance locally and where we have a strategic advantage. We realise of course that we cannot compete with MIT and Harvard in terms of resources so our studies are locally relevant and unique. We start by asking if anybody else is working on this because it takes ten years to answer fundamental questions, and those questions have to be game-changing and long-lasting even if we end up with negative results.

And so while our research has local origins and impacts, we make a point of publishing in the highest-impact journals, such as *Science, Nature, Lancet* and the *New England Journal of Medicine*. In addition, because of the stature of our local science we find ourselves active in global decision-making bodies, such as UNAIDS, the Global Fund, The President's Emergency Plan for AIDS Relief and the World Health Organization. We also serve on several policymaking and research bodies in South Africa and on the African continent. We have not shied away from joining social movements and advocacy efforts to ensure evidence-based decision-making.

Scientists around the world see us as epitomising what twenty-first century science and knowledge generation should look like; CAPRISA is a very popular centre for students from the North and from the South. Capacity building and training is central to our core business. We have trained more than 600 scientists and developed the science base in southern Africa, investing in staff and the future generation of scientists through the Columbia University–Southern African Fogarty AIDS International Training and Research Programme. We annually accept about 100 medical students from first year to final year into the CAPRISA Clinical Research Placement Programme. CAPRISA implements collaborative training programmes in Africa and in other countries. Several of the CAPRISA staff who joined us with Master's degrees now have PhDs and as postdocs are initiating and independently managing their own research programmes.

CAPRISA also hosts graduate and postgraduate students from Harvard, Columbia, MIT, Johns Hopkins and Yale universities, to name but a few. At any given time we host between three to five students from the US, who are either self-funded or receive training grants from their institutions or the National Institute of Health. We also host students and scientists from African, Asian and European countries. They come to CAPRISA to find out how we undertake our research. Even though we lead most of our research at CAPRISA, we are part of the global research community and collaborations and partnerships are critical for fast-tracking knowledge generation.

We have learnt through this African-led research centre that in your relationship with the North, you cannot go in just asking for funds – you must go in as a partner and define the research agenda with clarity. In this way you earn respect for your expertise, for your research agenda and for your priorities. This is an imperative for mutually rewarding and sustained partnerships.

Ian Phimister, Central and Southern African Histories

The research of the International Studies Group, which I lead, is making the local engage critically with the global from start to finish, trying to draw PhD researchers away from formulating research topics that are parochial; anthropologists use the slightly derogatory phrase 'work on my village' to refer to this, for what that encapsulates all too often is inward-looking research. In a nutshell it is to have them engage the work of a wider literature. Why would somebody in, say, Brazil want to read about labour migration in Malawi, for example? The way to locate that research is to look at the international literature on the narrowing or widening of citizenship, on the construction of identity or on economic opportunity and so on. That could be the broad framing exercise, making your work relevant to a wider audience, reaching a global audience.

Our focus is broadly on central and southern African history and the timeframe is from the late eighteenth century through to as close to the present day as historical inquiry would work. There is a significant interdisciplinary dimension because the historical tools we use draw on sociology, anthropology, economics, politics and so on. We find economic history making a disciplinary comeback in much of the world and particularly in Africa; and the thematic focus of our work is economic and social history. But along the way there are cultural historical studies, a marked gender focus, work with an imperial remit and even identity studies in Ghana.

We have been very lucky in that the first tranche of people coming from Britain and the USA was partly done on personal contact, people whose PhDs I had supervised, keen to experience postdoctoral work with, I suppose, a familiar face. Since then this has turned into something of a virtuous circle for, as our reputation has grown, astonishingly you might think, we have never had any difficulty attracting people from the very best North American, European and British universities. At present we have on our books postdocs who did their PhDs in Wisconsin, Chicago, Cambridge and Oxford; and as the reputation of the group has grown and networks have been developed they have facilitated traffic in the other direction. We have had people from here going to take up fellowships at Humboldt, Basel, Leiden and Cambridge. So this is very good – people from the University of the Free State going to Cambridge, and people from there coming here.

Once we reached a certain size, about three years into the programme, we were then capable of running two or three major seminars in the course of the year as well as hosting occasional seminars. We have now lots of requests from individuals from Europe and America visiting South Africa who would like to present their research in front of us because of the quality of the feedback and comment we can give, as well as traffic in the other direction.

How does an African research centre arrive at such a position? When things start up you need someone initially in charge who has an established track record so that career scholars would think 'I can actually learn something here'. The individual should also be research active so that there is a strong element of leading by example. What is also important is having a network inside southern Africa; an individual needs to be known and have a track record of having engaged respectfully and also critically with people over long periods of time. So, you need a network, you need to be research active and there has to be an element of trust and some achievement because people are not going to move halfway around the world to come in from Europe if they do not learn anything new.

How does achieving such a position actually happen? The goal is to publish in leading journals, to aim for the best; to challenge yourself and to find ways of placing your work before an international audience. That said, as they start up, sometimes as early as the second year, I encourage new PhD students to write book reviews. That illustrates the importance of a network, for with a doctoral student whose name is not widely known, it would fall on me or another senior scholar to contact the book reviews editor of this or that journal and ask, 'Would you be prepared to take a book review from a PhD student of mine so they get that experience?' By the second year they might be ready to write a historiographical essay review; by the third year as they are writing the chapters for their theses based on empirical research, as well as the secondary literature, then more often than one would think a chapter could be sent off to a journal, certainly a national journal, and some of them are good enough to go off to middle-ranking international journals with a recognisable impact score and so on.

The postdocs get a contract to turn their thesis into a single-authored monograph and recently we could demonstrate to the university that we had 11 book contracts or people who had passed through the first stage of review with some really good publishing options from major university presses. There is a lot of pressure on them to do this. All the postdocs must publish one book over the three-year contract period and when they get the full subsidy income they have more than paid for themselves. They have to publish and they get sick of hearing this but I do say to them that if you are serious about an academic career, a PhD is not enough. It gets you out of the starting blocks but in the North and more and more in the wider world, you need your first book and you most certainly need two or three articles in recognisable journals. And they listen and they get the message. They are all intrinsically competing against each other, and you can see this in the research seminars; competition, but not in a nasty way, as they sharpen themselves and measure themselves against each other. It works.

Initially, as we were developing, I would encourage person A at Oxford and say this is what we are trying to do here, and our reputation opened lots of doors and this was particularly true through our connection with you [Jonathan Jansen] in America. Then as the group started to deliver and some of these young people started to attend conferences, we were approached more often than we approached others, to come up with collaborative agreements or memoranda of understanding. Not too long into the life of the International Studies Group we developed relationships with the University of Dundee and the University of Kent and with both of them we now have our students who have gone there and members of their staff have come here. Staff members at British universities outside of the global triangle of Oxford, Cambridge and London have far greater opportunities to burnish their own skills in acting as supervisors or giving workshops or tutorials with African students than they would in Britain. They would be lucky at Dundee, say, if they had two or three PhDs working on Africa or Empire over a ten-year period; they come to us and immediately there's this group – by the time you left [2016] more than 40 students made up the PhD and postdoc group, and the visitors love it. So we enhanced the capacity of people coming from Dundee and Kent; we had similar arrangements with Leiden and with Basel and most recently with Bologna. We have recently hosted two professors in African Studies from the University of Bologna. It was really great for our inspiration and hugely beneficial for them; we could see them enjoying the seminars, and conducting more one-to-one tutorials than they would have experienced in the past decade.

RETHINKING THE CENTRE-PERIPHERY THESIS IN KNOWLEDGE PRODUCTION

These high-profile African research projects (and there are scores of such examples across South African higher education in almost every major discipline of the sciences and the humanities) have five defining characteristics:

1. *Their Projects Are Led Intellectually by South African Scholars.* The decolonisation argument that knowledge from Europe (knowers) is imposed on African implementers (doers) is clearly undermined in these and other case studies. In these casesleadership is South African in every aspect of knowledge projects from design to execution, so that the 1960s' arguments about imposition and dependency simply does not hold. These are exceptionally competent and well-trained leaders whose authority in science and scholarship is undisputed.

2. *Their Content Is Decidedly African in Terms of Subjects of Study.* The decolonisation position that knowledge content is European or centred on Europe and European problems again finds no support in these case examples. The African researchers cited consciously 'design out' local problems that require specific kinds of designs and interventions not necessarily applicable or pursued in wealthier parts of the world system.

3. *Their Work Reflects a Rich and Reciprocal Collaboration with Scholars in the West.* The uni-directional flow of knowledge, whether in terms of production or consumption, is disproved in these and other cases of international exchange. The postcolonial world under globalisation is less hierarchical than in the 1960s and 1970s and flatter in critical parts of the knowledge economy. Knowledge in these examples from the sciences and humanities is not 'theirs' and 'ours' but subject to joint investigation, whether in terms of solving problems of infection or understanding dilemmas of empire. The defensive posture of a decolonisation against an imposing knowledge from outside the Southern world is unnecessary and anachronistic in the twenty-first century.

4. *Their Research Attracts Postgraduate Scholars and Students from the West.* The quality, reach and impact of Southern research is such that academics and students from leading universities in the world visit these research centres to access new knowledge rather than to extract knowledge for use elsewhere. International academics come to learn and to improve their own status as scholars in the community of South African scholars. In the same way, the flow of students and academics to premier institutions abroad in turn strengthens local scholarship in the disciplines. This bi-directional flow of research knowledge and knowledge workers fundamentally changes the frame posited in the decolonisation moment.

5. *Their Research Increasingly Affects Curriculum Transformation across Other University Departments.* The cases mentioned are not isolated examples or exceptions within large institutions. In each case the multidisciplinary nature of

the research means that knowledge circulates and impacts on the broader university itself (Phimister's history group now works increasingly with the traditional history department; the Abdool Karims attract into their research group students from the medical school and other fields; and the Mayosi research has a broader public health disciplinary reach beyond medicine alone). The benefits of African-led research in partnership with international collaborators therefore changes significantly the decolonial complaint within universities.

In short, what we have seen is an ongoing shift in the locus of authority for knowledge production, particularly among the leading universities in South Africa, that defies simple polarities of thinking that in times past were first described by economic dependency (Amin 1972) or scientific imperialism (Ake 1979).

THE KNOWLEDGE PROBLEM IN COLONIALISM – A MUCH MORE SUBDUED CLAIM

The fact that there have been massive strides in the reconfiguration of knowledge after colonialism and apartheid does not mean that knowledge itself has been transformed evenly or completely within the South African university system. Nor do these three cases suggest a complete collapse of a transnational division of labour when it comes to the distribution and consumption of knowledge (Weiler 2011: 211).

But it does mean acknowledging the significant breaks with colonial/apartheid knowledge in many of our universities and that continuing knowledge dilemmas have less to do with 'what colonialism left undone' and more to do with a complex of problems faced by higher education institutions around the world – such as the poor academic preparation of students as they grapple with disciplinary knowledge or a curriculum that is not sufficiently responsive to the demands of changing technological revolutions in the world of work.

Is the arrival of a decolonisation moment perhaps a consequence of South Africa's inability to change these deeper impediments to knowledge and access within higher education? Or is the pressure for the decolonisation of curriculum a necessary step towards a broader transformation of the knowledge enterprise? If so, will the curriculum change under such pressure?

WILL THE INSTITUTIONAL CURRICULUM CHANGE IN RESPONSE TO DEMANDS FOR DECOLONISATION?

To answer this question, one place to start is with powerful curriculum moments in the past when there was a real ferment for change among activists, and ask what this history reveals about the chances of social movements or politically driven movements for altering the curriculum.

In South Africa, there was a popular curriculum moment called People's Education which, like decolonisation, carried considerable sentiment and support among students in the internal struggle against apartheid education. This was 'alternative education' in the best sense of the term and rich textual materials were developed alongside 'awareness campaigns' to topple the state curriculum. That never happened (Motala and Vally 2002; Chisholm and Fuller 1996).

In Zimbabwe, the most radical curriculum invention since settler colonialism was called Political Economy of Zimbabwe (PEZ). The curriculum, modelled on Marxist-Leninist principles, was underwritten by the new government of Robert Mugabe to challenge the colonial curriculum and its straight-from-colonial-England O- and A-level examinations. The curriculum never made it out of the government safe in Harare despite elaborate plans for its implementation organised by curriculum committees.

In both cases, these promising curriculum moments ran headlong into what was referred to earlier as 'the institutional curriculum' – those rules, routines and regulations that continue to frame what counts as knowledge within institutions, including what counts as teaching or learning or assessment.

People's Education and PEZ are cautionary tales which suggest that despite its political momentum on some campuses, *decolonisation as a moment* will have little to no effect on the institutional curriculum – for three main reasons.

The demand for decolonisation offers an incomplete response to a real set of curriculum problems faced by the majority of schools and universities in South Africa. In schools there are complex legacies that embed and sustain inequalities inside a dysfunctional school system. Very few students make it to university and fewer succeed within them. The status quo has to do with a destructive politics in the present (routine disruptions of poor schools by the largest teachers' union) and disabling policies (such as OBE) that undermined teaching and learning. In universities the few students that make it through the school system (the participation rate in higher education is only 19 per cent) are ill-prepared academically and enter institutions that themselves are often disrupted by protests and engulfed in maladministration. These are choices made in the present, not just consequences of a colonial or apartheid past.

The decolonisation moment will fizzle out also because it ignores those significant, transformative changes already made within universities – and that could have been launching pads for meaningful change within the South African academy. By overstating the curriculum crisis in the post-apartheid university for political ends and not recognising African leadership across the disciplines, the arguments for change deflate the very projects that require strategic support for the advancement of a deeply transformed curriculum across institutions of higher education.

And finally, the decolonisation moment is destined to pass because it underestimates the power of a settled curriculum within established institutions that, in terms of their core knowledge commitments, remain impervious to the politics of protest. It should not surprise therefore that in reaction to the pressure for curriculum change, some universities have responded with crude notions of replacing some poorly defined 'Western content' with 'African content' in the name of decolonisation. Other institutions require their academics to complete on a regular basis a standardised form that essentially asks, 'What did you do to decolonise your curriculum this month?'[9] Yet others are required to submit one or two courses in a faculty that would be candidates for decolonisation. It is not argued here that universities are unresponsive to the demands for decolonisation, but that the superficial ways in which they respond do little to unsettle the institutional curriculum.

In a memorable turn of phrase, that brilliant observer of everyday life in universities, Sara Ahmed (2017), refers to the deadweight of internal routines and repertoires as 'institutional as usual'. She includes in rich descriptions of institutional practices how change initiatives led by university committees function to normalise progressive or radical thought despite the veneer of participation in joint decision-making. These practices, she argues, serve the purpose of 'damage limitation' for they ensure that the change proposed – decolonisation, in the South African case – *takes institutional form.*

CONCLUSION

The starting contention in this chapter was that decolonisation served as an important but limiting political moment that conveyed a broader concern about the lack of transformation at formerly white universities. Activists who took up the challenge of transformation in knowledge terms had not made any strategic calculations about how to deal with the institutional curriculum. That is why decolonisation is likely to fade into insignificance as a promising but ultimately flawed concept.

In the end, the university curriculum will always contain legacies of the past, urgencies from the present and aspirations for the future. There can be no clean break with a complex past. This is what Chinua Achebe so eloquently describes in the epigraph that introduces this chapter. His example of English is illustrative of the broader curriculum argument made in this chapter – of a colonial language that has come to both distribute and reshuffle power and access in a world where global partnerships in knowledge production can no longer assume rigid hierarchies premised on the existence of a dominant North and a compliant South.

In other words, the relationship between knowledge and power in the twenty-first century is much more complex than can be captured in a latter-day restoration of the project of decolonisation.

NOTES

1   For an insightful analysis of how slogans as concepts work, albeit in another field (advertising), see David Head (1988).

2   See the special issue of *Perspectives in Education* of November 2017 (35, no. 2) for uncritical and unhelpful use of the term 'decolonisation'. No less an authority than the Council on Higher

Education falls into the same trap of accepting the new language without a hint of criticality of received concepts; see CHE (2017).

3   With respect to this literature on 'the coloniality of power', the Peruvian sociologist Aníbal Quijano (2007), is a very prominent scholar.

4   This can be extrapolated from Cesar Germana's (2014) piece on epistemological decolonisation.

5   The original coining of the term *knowledge regimes* was to address a gap in research on political economy – where national policy ideas come from and their impacts on economic performance. The main authors in this enterprise are John Campbell and Ove Pedersen (2011, 2015).

6   For a rare and concise description of early slave education, see 'The Slave Lodge School', Iziko Museums of South Africa at https://slavery.iziko.org.za/slavelodgeschool.

7   For a fascinating insight into the control and contestation over public memory through museums and memorials, see Tietze (2017).

8   This I illustrate in my review article; see Jansen (2017b).

9   This anecdote was shared with me by a senior curriculum leader at a Gauteng university.

REFERENCES

Achebe, Chinua. 1975. *Morning Yet on Creation Day: Essays*. London: Heinemann.

Ahmed, Sara. 2017. 'The Institutional as Usual: Diversity Work as Data Collection'. Lecture presented at Barnard College, New York, New York, 16 October, and at Princeton University, Princeton, New Jersey, 17 October. https://feministkilljoys.com/2017/10/24/institutional-as-usual/.

Ake, Claude. 1979. *Social Science as Imperialism: The Theory of Political Development*. Ibadan: Ibadan University Press.

Amin, Samir. 1972. 'Underdevelopment and Dependence in Black Africa – Origins and Contemporary Forms'. *Journal of Modern African Studies* 10 (4): 503–524.

Annala, Johanna, Jyri Liden and Marita Mäkinen. 2016. 'Curriculum in Higher Education Research'. In *Researching Higher Education: International Perspectives on Theory, Politics and Practice*, edited by Jennifer M. Case and Jeroen Huisman, 171–189. New York: Routledge.

Badat, Saleem. 2017. 'Trepidation, Longing, and Belonging: Liberating the Curriculum at Universities in South Africa'. Lecture presented at the Public Lecture Series on Curriculum Transformation Matters: The Decolonial Turn, University of Pretoria, 10 April.

Bhaba, Homi K. 1994. *The Location of Culture*. London: Routledge.

Booyse, Johan, Cheryl le Roux, Johannes Seroto and Charl Wolhuter. 2011. *A History of Schooling in South Africa: Method and Concept*. Pretoria: Van Schaik.

Buckland, Peter. 1984. 'Technicism and De Lange: Reflections on the Process of the HSRC Investigation'. In *Apartheid and Education: The Education of Black South Africans,* edited by Peter Kallaway, 371–386. Johannesburg: Ravan Press.

Buenfil-Burgos, Rosa Nidia. 2000. 'Globalization, Education and Discourse Political Analysis: Ambiguity and Accountability in Research'. *International Journal of Qualitative Studies in Education* 13 (1): 1–24.

Campbell, John L. and Ove K. Pedersen. 2011. 'Knowledge Regimes and Comparative Political Economy'. In *Ideas and Politics in Social Science Research,* edited by Daniel Beland and Robert Henry Cox, 167–190. Oxford: Oxford University Press.

Campbell, John L. and Ove K. Pedersen. 2015. 'Policy Ideas, Knowledge Regimes and Comparative Political Economy'. *Socio-Economic Review* 13 (4): 679–701.

Césaire, Aimé. (1950) 2000. *Discourse on Colonialism*. New York: Monthly Review Press.

CHE (Council on Higher Education). 2017. 'Decolonising the Curriculum: Stimulating Debate'. *BrieflySpeaking*, no. 3 (Nov.). http://www.che.ac.za/media_and_publications/monitoring-and-evaluation/brieflyspeaking-3-curriculum-decolonisation.

Chisholm, Linda. 2017. '"Fate Comes to the Mission Schools": Fire at Bethel, 1953'. *South African Historical Journal* 69 (1): 121–137.

Chisholm, Linda and Bruce Fuller. 1996. 'Remember People's Education? Shifting Alliances, State-Building and South Africa's Narrowing Policy Agenda'. *Journal of Education Policy* 11 (6): 693–716.

Christie, Pam and Carolyn McKinney. 2017. 'Decoloniality and "Model C Schools": Ethos, Language and the Protests of 2016'. *Education as Change* 21 (3): 1–21.

Chutel, Lensey. 2017. 'A British PR Firm Spread "White Monopoly Capital" to Distract South Africans from Mounting Corruption'. *MR Online*, 10 July. https://mronline.org/2017/07/10/a-british-pr-firm-spread-white-monopoly-capital-to-distract-south-africans-from-mounting-corruption/.

Connell, Raewyn, Rebecca Pearse, Fran Collyer, Joao Marcelo Maia and Robert Morrell. 2017. 'Negotiating with the North: How Southern-Tier Intellectual Workers Deal with the Global Economy of Knowledge'. *Sociological Review* 66 (1): 41–57.

Denton, Robert E., Jr. 2009. 'The Rhetorical Functions of Slogans: Classifications and Characteristics'. *Communication Quarterly* 28 (2): 10–18. DOI:10.1080/01463378009369362.

Evans, Jenni. 2016. 'What Is Decolonised Education?'. *News24*, 25 September. https://www.news24.com/SouthAfrica/News/what-is-decolonised-education-20160925.

Fanon, Frantz. [1961] 1965. *The Wretched of the Earth*. New York: Grove Press.

Germana, Cesar. 2014. 'The Coloniality of Power: A Perspective from Peru'. *Global Dialogue* 4, no. 2 (June). http://globaldialogue.isa-sociology.org/the-coloniality-of-power-a-perspective-from-peru/.

Giliomee, Herman. 2012. 'Bantu Education: Destructive Intervention or Part Reform?' *New Contree* 65 (Dec.): 67–86.

Giroux, Henry. 2013. 'A Critical Interview with Henry Giroux'. *Global Education Magazine*, 30 January. http://www.globaleducationmagazine.com/critical-interview-henry-giroux/.

Grant, Callie, Lynn Quinn and Jo-Anne Vorster. 2018. 'An Exploratory Study of Heads of Departments' Responses to Student Calls for Decolonised Higher Education'. *Journal of Education* 72: 73–88.

Hall, Martin. 1998. '"Bantu Education?" A Reply to Mahmood Mamdani'. *Social Dynamics* 24 (2): 86–92. doi: 10.1080/02533959808458651.

Head, David. 1988. 'Advertising Slogans and the "Made-in" Concept'. *International Journal of Advertising* 7 (3): 237–252. doi: 10.1080/02650487.1988.11107063.

Hoadley, Ursula. 2018. *Pedagogy in Poverty: Lessons from Twenty Years of Curriculum Reform in South Africa*. New York: Routledge.

Holmes, Brian, ed. [1967] 2007. *Educational Policy and the Mission Schools: Case Studies from the British Empire*. Oxford: Routledge.

Hountondji, Paulin J. 2006. 'Global Knowledge: Imbalances and Current Tasks'. In *Knowledge, Power and Dissent: Critical Perspectives on Higher Education and Research in Knowledge Society*, edited by Guy Neave, 41–60. Paris: UNESCO.

Jansen, Jonathan D. 1999. 'The School Curriculum since Apartheid: Intersections of Politics and Policy in the South African Transition'. *Journal of Curriculum Studies* 31 (1): 57–67.

Jansen, Jonathan D. 2009. *Knowledge in the Blood: Confronting Race and the Apartheid Past*. Stanford: Stanford University Press.

Jansen, Jonathan D. 2017a. *As by Fire: The End of the South African University*. Cape Town: Tafelberg.

Jansen, Jonathan D. 2017b. 'The Lost Scholarship of Changing Curricula'. *South African Journal of Science* 113 (5–6): 1–2.

Jansen, Jonathan D. 2017c. 'Sense and Non-sense in the Decolonisation of Curriculum'. In *As by Fire: The End of the South African University*, by Jonathan Jansen, 153–171. Cape Town: Tafelberg.

Jansen, Jonathan D. 2019. 'What Is to be Done? Knowledge, Action and the Inequality Dilemma in South African Education'. In *South African Schooling: The Enigma of Inequality*, edited by Nic Spaull and Jonathan D. Jansen. Dordrecht: Springer.

Keet, André. 2014. 'Epistemic Othering and the Decolonisation of Knowledge'. *Africa Insight* 44 (1): 23–37.

Lange, Lis. 2017. 'Twenty Years of Higher Education Curriculum Policy in South Africa'. *Journal of Education* 68, 31–57. https://journals.ukzn.ac.za/index.php/joe/article/view/379/819.

Lee, Wen Shu. 2009. 'Social Scientists as Ideological Critics'. *Western Journal of Communication* 75 (2): 221–232. DOI:10.1080/10570319309374445.

Long, Wahbie. 2018. 'Decolonising Higher Education: Postcolonial Theory and the Invisible Hand of Student Politics'. *New Agenda: Journal of Social and Economic Policy* 69: 20–25.

Maldonado-Torres, Nelson. 2007. 'On the Coloniality of Being: Contributions to the Development of a Concept'. *Cultural Studies* 21 (2–3): 240–270. doi: 10.1080/09502380601162548.

Mamdani, Mahmood. 1998. 'Is African Studies to be Turned into a New Home for Bantu Education at UCT?' *Social Dynamics* 24 (2): 63–75. doi: 10.1080/02533959808458649.

Mathebula, Thokozani. 2013. 'People's Education for People's Power: A Promise Unfulfilled'. *South African Journal of Education* 33 (1). http://www.scielo.org.za/pdf/saje/v33n1/02.pdf.

Memmi, Albert. [1957] 2016. *The Colonizer and the Colonized*. London: Souvenir Press.

Mignolo, Walter. 2011. *The Darker Side of Western Modernity: Global Futures, Decolonial Options*. Durham: Duke University Press. https://doi.org/10.1215/9780822394501.

Motala, Shireen and Salim Vally. 2002. 'People's Education: From People's Power to Tirisano'. In *The History of Education under Apartheid* edited by Peter Kallaway, 174–191. Cape Town: Maskew Miller Longman.

Naudé, Piet. 2017. 'Decolonising Knowledge: In What Sense Is an "African" Ethic Possible?'. Inaugural Lecture, University of Stellenbosch.

Neave, Guy. 2006. 'Mapping the Knowledge Society back into Higher Education'. In *Knowledge, Power and Dissent: Critical Perspectives on Higher Education and Research in Knowledge Society*, edited by Guy Neave, 13–24. Paris: UNESCO.

Nonyongo, Evelyn and Thandiwe Ngengebulu. 1993. 'The SACHED Distance Education Students' Support Programme'. *Open Learning: The Journal of Open, Distance and e-Learning* 8 (2): 40–45.

Ochoa, Peggy. 1996. 'The Historical Moments of Postcolonial Writing: Beyond Colonialism's Binary'. *Tulsa Studies in Women's Literature* 15 (2): 221–229.

Papier, Joy. 2006. 'How Faculties of Education Respond to New Knowledge Requirements in Teacher Education Policies: Stepping through the Looking Glass'. PhD thesis, University of Pretoria.

Quijano, Aníbal. 2007. 'Coloniality and Modernity/Rationality'. *Cultural Studies* 21 (2–3): 168–178.

Raj, Sony J. 2007. 'The Slogans of Indian Independence Struggle: A Study in Communication and Representation'. PhD diss., Mahatma Gandhi University. http://shodhganga.inflibnet.ac.in/handle/10603/22528.

Rodney, Walter. 1972. *How Europe Underdeveloped Africa*. London: Bogle-L'Ouverture Publications.

Said, Edward W. 1978. *Orientalism*. New York: Pantheon.

Said, Edward W. 1991. 'Identity, Authority and Freedom: The Potentate and the Traveller'. *Pretexts: Studies in Writing and Culture* 3 (1–2): 67–81.

Schiebinger, Londa and Claudia Swan, eds. 2005. *Colonial Botany: Science, Commerce and Politics in the Early Modern World*. Philadelphia: University of Philadelphia Press.

Sebidi, Kgaugelo and Shannon Morreira. 2017. 'Accessing Power Knowledge: A Comparative Study of Two First Year Sociology Courses in a South African University'. *Critical Studies in Teaching & Learning (CriSTaL)* 5(2): 33–50

Seroto, Johannes. 2011. 'Indigenous Education during the Pre-colonial Period in Southern Africa'. *Indilinga* 10 (1): 77–88.

Spaull, Nic and Jonathan Jansen, eds. 2019. *South African Schooling: The Enigma of Inequality*. Dordrecht: Springer Press.

Spivak, Gayatri Chakravorty. 1988. 'Can the Subaltern Speak?'. In *Marxism and the Interpretation of Culture,* edited by C. Nelson and L. Grossberg, 271–313. Basingstoke: Macmillan Education.

Suransky-Dekker, Carolina. 1998. '"A Liberating Breeze of Western Civilization?": A Political History of Fundamental Pedagogics as an Expression of Dutch-Afrikaner Relationships'. PhD thesis, University of Durban-Westville.

Tabulawa, Richard. 2013. *Teaching and Learning in Context: Why Pedagogical Reforms Fail in Sub-Saharan Africa*. Dakar: CODESRIA.

Tietze, Anna. 2017. *A History of the Iziko South African National Gallery: Reflections on Art and National Identity*. Cape Town: UCT Press.

Weiler, Hans. 2011. 'Knowledge and Power: The New Politics of Higher Education'. *Journal of Educational Planning and Administration* 25(3): 205–221.

Woeber, Catherine Anne. 2000. '"A Good Education Sets up a Divine Discontent": The Contribution of St Peter's School to Black South African Autobiography'. PhD thesis, University of the Witwatersrand.

CHAPTER 4

The Institutional Curriculum, Pedagogy and the Decolonisation of the South African University

Lis Lange
University of Cape Town

Of all the imagery that accompanied the student protest in the period 2015–2017, a photograph of a black woman student during the #RhodesMustFall (#RMF) moment holding a placard with the inscription 'Look at me, I am here', constitutes for me one of the most revealing statements of the issues that the protest movement attempted to address.

'Look at me, I am here' is a call for recognition and acknowledgement that encompasses the physical, socio-cultural, economic, and curricular aspects of life at historically white South African universities (HWUs). This chapter engages with the theme of this book, the politics of curriculum, using the concepts of recognition and misrecognition (Honneth 1995; Fraser and Honneth 2003) implicit in the demand 'Look at me, I am here', to explore the 'problem' of black students' identity at HWUs and its relationship with the meanings of the decolonisation of the curriculum.

LOCALISATION AND CONTEXT

Before I start to develop my argument, I think it is important to situate the place from where I am writing. In the last eight years I have been part of the executive of two very different historically white universities, the University of the Free State (UFS) from 2011 to 2017 and the University of Cape Town (UCT) since 2018, holding the portfolio on teaching and learning. From Bloemfontein I watched #RMF unfolding, hoping it would ignite a similar conversation at UFS. It did not happen. By the time the protest reached UFS the idea of free, decolonised, quality education was squarely focused on the struggle for free education and indirectly on the insourcing of workers, but curriculum and definitions of quality were not a central piece of the protest. At UFS, decolonised, quality education was a political slogan that had little real traction in the debate or even in the protest.[1] What students at UFS retained in their protest was the critique of the pervasiveness of a white Afrikaans university culture they saw embodied in the events that took place at the Shimla Park Stadium in February 2016.[2]

There are not enough empirical studies of the student protest on the different university campuses to have a sense of how they differed and why. However, in the cases of UFS and UCT, one element emerges with clarity even now. While at UFS students were alone in their protest – that is, no academic staff, especially no black academics, directly supported the movement – at UCT many staff, especially black academics, supported the students in a variety of ways, but specifically through teach-ins. This suggests two things: UCT had a sufficient critical mass of black academics for them to be visible and reckoned with during #RMF; and these academics were already steeped in the 'decolonial turn' discourse and could be of help to the students. This was not the case at UFS.

This notwithstanding, there is one point of confluence in the protests of both groups of students: the call, even if by a small group at UFS, for the Africanisation of the curriculum, in particular, the call to have a history of Africa syllabus that dealt with Africa before colonisation. I find it telling that the convergence between the UCT and UFS student demands about decolonisation of the curriculum did not take place in the intellectual space of debates about competing theories and schools of thought in the decolonial academy; it happened in the emotional space of personal recognition embedded in the history of Africa before colonisation. Students were asking for a curriculum that somehow reflected them, that reflected their identity, their history before it was interpreted by the white colonisers. What does this mean? Are there pedagogic limits to an 'identitarian' approach to curriculum? How does this coexist with the need to teach 'global knowledge'?[3] And what is the role that institutional cultures/contexts play in mediating these tensions? These are some of the questions I explore here.

My analytical focus is on HWUs. This does not mean that at historically black universities the issues of knowledge and identity are solved by the mere fact of their demographic composition. Neither does it mean that it is not necessary and important to research the manifestation of the #MustFall movement at historically black universities. On the contrary, it is necessary to demystify the notion that anything that matters in higher education happens at HWUs, or that for issues to be taken seriously nationally, they have to come from these universities. To have a complete view of the system and what #MustFall has meant it is necessary to look at the totality of the higher education system. This is, fortunately, a work in progress.[4]

TWENTY YEARS OF HIGHER EDUCATION CURRICULUM POLICY

As far as South African higher education policy after 1994 dealt with curriculum, it focused on its external organisation and seldom paid attention to the knowledge embedded in the curriculum.[5] This does not mean that a government directive was necessary or desirable in relation to the higher education curriculum. It rather means that the direction of government policy – or statutory bodies like the Council on Higher Education (CHE) – did not encourage serious engagement by academics with whether or not, and to what extent, the knowledge privileged in the university curriculum was the kind of knowledge necessary and appropriate to support South Africa's democratic transition.[6] By this I mean the exploration not only of the extent to which higher education graduates had the required skills set for economic competitiveness but also the investigation of whether and to what extent the post-1994 curriculum was reproducing the racist, patriarchal and monolithic ways of thinking that characterised apartheid curriculum.[7]

Policymaking in South African higher education can be divided into two broad periods: 1990 to 2001 (this includes policy making by the African National Congress (ANC) government-in-waiting) and 2001–2016. The first period had as its focus access, equity and redress. Many important policy frames were produced during this period.[8] Among the most important instruments designed to realise the goals of access, equity and redress, the National Qualifications Framework (NQF), created by the South African Qualifications Authority (SAQA) Act of 1995, is by far the most significant and influential on curriculum issues. As Paula Ensor has indicated, the democratisation of knowledge that informed the creation of the NQF required the breaking of three sets of boundaries 'between education and training, between academia and everyday knowledge, and between different knowledges, subjects or disciplines within the academic domain' (Ensor 2004: 340).

The NQF was the chosen tool to achieve the articulation between professional, formative and vocational knowledge. It was designed to respond to the need for skills development among the majority of South Africa's population. Thus, the discussion about knowledge generated by the NQF revolved around the structure of knowledge in the professional, formative and vocational bands of the framework and the obstacles and objections to the realisation of the 'from sweeper to engineer' dream.

The focus of the National Commission on Higher Education (1996) and the White Paper 3 on Higher Education (DoE 1997) on teaching and learning and on curriculum was shaped by the need to increase South Africa's ability to compete internationally. The two most important conceptual elements in this regard were: growing the number of 'knowledge workers', and the practice of lifelong learning that would allow students vertical and horizontal mobility across the NQF. Both documents stressed the need for higher education programmes to be responsive to local and regional development challenges including labour market needs. The introduction of programmes, as different from qualifications with one or two majors, translated into a conceptualisation of knowledge acquisition and 'transmission' that had different impacts at different institutions depending on a variety of elements from resources to the characteristics of the student body (Ensor 2003). This policy did not result in a focus on knowledge and curriculum transformation but rather on a new structure for the curriculum, which largely left knowledge untouched.

The policy frame did not close off debate about curriculum and knowledge. Debate about knowledge has been constant over two decades but, with few exceptions (development of the foundation and extended programmes), it did not influence policy. The topics of debate during the early period were knowledge, identity and curriculum transformation in Africa, introduced by the Centre for Higher Education Transformation (Cloete, Makgoba and Ekong 1997), and the critiques of mode two knowledge presented in the work published by the Human Sciences Research Council in 2000.

Topics of extensive debate were social constructivism, Bernstein's notions of knowledge, the role of language in knowledge acquisition and even at times what/whose knowledge was being prioritised (Davies, Muller and Morais 2004; Ensor 2003; Griesel 2004; Hall 2009; Moore and Muller 1999; Young 2008). These debates remained within the circle of the academics dedicated to the sociology of education and, from the point of view of curriculum transformation, it operated above the disciplines themselves. In this sense the debate did not filter down sufficiently to disciplines other than education. Academics did not lead a discussion about curriculum transformation. Much less was this discussion focused on non-Western epistemologies of the kind suggested in the decolonial debate. Voices such as that of Catherine Odora Hoppers were circumscribed to the budding and not sufficiently debated field of indigenous knowledge systems.

The second period of policy development, which extends from 2001 to 2016, saw, especially during the first eight years, a growing preoccupation with the effectiveness and efficiency of the higher education system. Newly available data on student performance showed that student success rates, especially African students', were poor and that extra support was needed for students to be successful in bridging the articulation gap between schooling and higher education (Scott, Yeld and Hendry 2007). The solution for this conundrum was sought in the domain of teaching and learning, where extended programmes were introduced and where improved teaching practices were regarded as the answer to the failure of large numbers of students.

These interventions dealt with knowledge through structure, that is, a different organisation of the programme (foundation and extended programmes) was designed for those students who were identified as not ready to negotiate the mainstream curriculum. The new structure provided extra scaffolding, especially in the areas of language and academic literacy, for students to be in a better position to master successfully university knowledge.

Epistemological access was the fundamental concept around which the effort of the extended programmes was built. This concept had its roots in the academic development movement of the 1980s and its application in subsequent years is the closest approximation that the higher education institutions (HEIs) were to have to knowledge and the curriculum in terms of how university knowledge is constructed. However, epistemological access does not engage directly with the knowledge embedded in the curriculum, as it focuses on building student capabilities to access and make meaning of that knowledge (Ballim 2015).

In 2013 a task team set up by the CHE (Ndebele 2013) to advise on the feasibility of a flexible curriculum produced its report. The recommendation basically consisted of restructuring of the existing undergraduate three-year curriculum into a four-year curriculum for all students. Once again structure trumped the knowledge contained in the curriculum. Both government and several higher education institutions rejected the proposal on different grounds, and once again curriculum came off the table.

The closest that South African higher education came to tackling the curriculum as a problem during this period was the 2008 Report of the Ministerial Committee on Transformation and Social Cohesion and the Elimination of Discrimination in Public Higher Education Institutions (known as the Soudien report). The report unequivocally raised the importance of curriculum transformation:

> It could be argued, given that the primary function of higher education is the production and transmission of knowledge, that epistemological transformation is at the heart of the transformation agenda. And at the centre of epistemological transformation is curriculum reform – a reorientation away from the apartheid knowledge system, in which curriculum was used as a tool of exclusion, to a democratic curriculum that is inclusive of all human thought. (Soudien 2008: 90)

Yet, even after the Soudien report, there has been no systematic engagement at institutional level with knowledge as epistemology, with knowledge as different frames of understanding, with knowledge as a necessary critique of knowledge, and with knowledge as creator of identity (Lange 2014). This inevitably created an 'epistemological vicious circle' in which the lack of examination of curricula supported a lack of examination of institutional cultures, especially in relation to academic and student identity.

And then seven years after the Soudien report, out of nowhere, or so it seemed at the time, student protests started at UCT, Rhodes University and the University of the Witwatersrand (Wits). The protests took over the open spaces of the universities and spilled off the campuses into the streets of the cities in which the universities were located. Angry student voices expressed themselves through social media and made use of a variety of modalities of representation of their message outside the 'academic code'. The student revolt focused initially on the dissonance between a changing student population and universities stuck in a colonial frame both intellectually and aesthetically. It demanded the recognition of black students as black and the decolonisation of the institutional space, of pedagogies and curriculum (Godsell and Chikane 2016). Soon enough the material reality of most black students gained pride of place in the movement and the call for free education became a rallying cry that galvanised the movement nationally (Bond 2016; Pillay 2016).

The student protest opened the space for a re-introduction of the curriculum conversation in higher education, forcing institutions to grapple with the conceptual nuances between transformation, decolonisation and Africanisation, and with concepts such as epistemological justice and the examination of accepted epistemologies.

Since the student protest started, two important things have happened. A number of specialists in curriculum and higher education have entered the new conversation about the decolonisation of the curriculum from a variety of perspectives. Some, like Chrissie Boughey and Sioux Mckenna (2016), by re-radicalising existing concepts in order to engage with students' demands; others, to flesh out the possible meanings of decolonisation and its disciplinary incarnations (Luckett 2016; Luckett and Naicker 2016; Le Grange 2016; Leibowitz 2017); some, to flesh out its political and philosophical implications (Mbembe 2015, 2016); and yet others to warn about the historical limitations of 'turns' in education and the weaknesses in the construction of the notion of colonial knowledge in a global world (Jansen 2017). Political activists and students in the trenches (Brian Kamanzi; Leigh-Anne Naidoo) as well as academics (Booysen 2016; Nyamnjoh 2016), and university leaders (Jonathan Jansen, Adam Habib, Max Price) also added their voices to the meanings of student protest and to rethinking curricula and the university itself through a number of books, articles and pieces published in online media such as *The Conversation, The Daily Maverick* and *The Times Online* as well as printed media like the *Mail & Guardian* and *Business Day*. Of particular significance is the collective publication by activists at most South Africa universities released in PDF format that provides perspective of the student movement across the country (Johannesburg Salon 2015).

Out of the student protest universities had to develop different ways of engaging with students' demands. The University of Pretoria (UP) set up an institutional process involving students and academics to develop a framework for the decolonisation of the curriculum (Graham 2016); UCT set up a Curriculum Change Working Group led by black academics and students that worked with faculties on the decolonisation of pedagogy and curriculum (UCT 2015). At UFS, the concept of decoloniality was introduced late in 2017 by management to think about a curricular review across all faculties as part of its integrated transformation plan. In most cases these activities were accompanied by public events where a range of local and international academics were invited to speak. Particularly publicised were the series organised by the University of Pretoria during 2016–2017, and the lectures by Nelson Maldonado-Torres and Mahmood Mamdani's T.B. Davie lecture, all at UCT in 2017. Rhodes University, in its Thinking Africa space, organised two seminar series, one on rethinking curriculum (2015) and the other, together with UFS, on the #MustFall moment (2016). Funders like the Andrew W. Mellon Foundation made available resources to a collective of South African universities to develop a decolonised humanities curriculum; the Department of Higher Education and Training earmarked a portion of the newly established University Capacity Development Grant for curriculum development.

New research is needed to see the fate of these initiatives, and the extent of their penetration into the institutional being; the reaction of the academic body across the disciplines to the explosion of the decolonial turn at different South Africa universities; the various understandings of decolonisation that were at play in the debate; and the extent to which the protest has been successful in achieving curriculum change and with what consequences.

So far, I have argued that South African higher education policy did not encourage institutions to engage with the content of the academic curriculum to test whether the knowledge embedded in it responded to the need for recognition of the new citizens of South Africa's democracy. Instead, policy was especially preoccupied with the structure of the curriculum and the articulation between different levels and bands of the NQF in order to achieve a more skilled population. Thus, by 2015, at the time of the student protest, no systematic critical engagement with curriculum had taken place at institutional level.

In providing the historical context of the student protest, I argue that the demand for the decolonisation of the curriculum was the most intense at HWUs, where tensions arising from marked demographic change in the student body since the 1990s, without concomitant change in institutional practices, played a crucial role in the build-up of the protest.

INSTITUTIONAL CURRICULUM: KNOWLEDGE AND IDENTITY

In 20 years of democratic rule, the South African higher education system has changed substantially. Not only has it almost doubled in numbers, from nearly one million students in 1993 to close to 1,000,000 in 2015, but its demographic profile has changed dramatically. In 1993 African students constituted 52 per cent of the total enrolments (Cloete et al. 2006: 104); in 2015 they constituted 70 per cent (CHE 2015: 4). Nowhere has this change been more remarkable than at HWUs. In 1996 UCT and UFS had respectively 26 per cent (CHE 2004: 5) and 9.86 per cent (CHE 2008: 33) African students in their total enrolments.[9] In 2015, at the time of #RMF, figures had changed to 23 per cent South African African students at UCT (Higher Education Management Information System data), while UFS had reached close to 70 per cent black students (60 per cent African). Reaching a demographic tipping point, whether by becoming majority or by ceasing to be a minority[10] in the student body at HWUs, must be seen as a necessary condition for identity-based movements for change to take sufficient root and force the obvious, yet unseen, problem to be raised: that despite their numbers, the space that black students inhabit at the university is culturally alien and alienating.

As a response to these changes most HWUs have gone through processes of transformation in relation to governance structures, student participation and the renaming of buildings. At many universities there have been attempts at democratising the composition of the senates to give voice to senior black academic staff who were not full professors, and to have greater representation of students. However, not a lot has changed in institutional cultures to accommodate black students and staff in terms other than assimilation. More colourful, newly designed academic gowns and less European-based graduation ceremony choreographies, a countrywide phenomenon, have not necessarily been accompanied by structural changes at institutions. Beneath these essentially surface changes, according to students' complaints about and studies on institutional culture published in the last ten years (Higgins 2007; Kessi and Cornell 2015; Nyamnjoh 2016; Tabensky Alexis and Matthews 2015; Van der Merwe and Van Reenen 2016), universities continued their administrative and academic operations without substantial modifications or restructuring.

Moreover, the renaming of public spaces on HWU campuses has not always been accompanied by a sensitivity to the meaning and symbolism that certain monuments have for black students and staff at these institutions. The Rhodes statue at UCT and the statue of Charles Robberts Swart at UFS are cases in point.[11] However, #RMF was not about the statue per se, as was made clear in the collective's manifesto:

> We want to be clear that this movement is not just concerned with the removal of a statue. The statue has great symbolic power; it glorifies a mass-murderer who exploited black labour and stole land from indigenous people. Its presence erases black history and is an act of violence against black students, workers and staff – by 'black' we refer to all people of colour. The statue was therefore the natural starting point of this movement. Its removal will not mark the end but the beginning of the long overdue process of decolonising this university. (RMF 2015)

As this quote suggests, and indeed the rest of the manifesto confirms, from the very beginning the movement operated at the intersection between knowledge and identity. It pronounced itself against colonial knowledge that fixes/freezes black identity, and determines the position of black people in relation to the university.

In this sense, it is possible to argue that #RMF was about the lack of an unequivocal acknowledgement and repudiation by UCT of its colonial heritage and its implications for the daily life of black people, especially academics and students, on campus. At UFS in 2016, the events unleashed by the Shimla Park protest, and, later, the defacement of the C.R. Swart statue were students' way of confronting what they saw as the continuation of white privilege, mostly through the language policy that supported a parallel medium of instruction in Afrikaans and English, and their sense that the university had not done enough to curb this privilege.

It is against this backdrop that the question of the curriculum needs to be understood as a two-dimensional process of interrogation: an interrogation of the academic curriculum and an interrogation of the institutional curriculum. By 'academic curriculum', I mean the process of engagement of students and staff with knowledge, behaviour and identity in different disciplinary contexts. Here, knowledge refers to the specialist professional or disciplinary knowledge that universities offer in a variety of combinations. It includes conflicting traditions, research, approaches, notions of method, focus, boundaries, and so on, and more than anything else, contains the rules of making knowledge and sense in that particular discipline (Barnett and Coate 2005).

By institutional curriculum I understand, following Jansen (2009: 178), 'the knowledge encoded in the dominant beliefs, values and behaviours deeply embedded in all aspects of institutional life'. This curriculum is tacit in the sense that one is socialised into it; it is not taught in the syllabus but in the classroom behaviour, in the relationship between students and lecturers, in the tea rooms, in the values transmitted implicitly through names, symbols, habits and mores. The tacit and implicit character of the institutional curriculum means that outsiders (culturally, linguistically or socially) can easily feel 'out of place'. While Jansen's (2009) work in *Knowledge in the Blood* focused on the notion of institutional curriculum to analyse Afrikaans universities, and opposed the closed culture of UP to the open culture of UCT, this does not mean that the institutional curriculum is a phenomenon exclusive to historically Afrikaans universities. At traditional English-speaking universities the institutional curriculum has a different character but, as has been shown by research at UCT (Steyn and Van Zyl 2001; Kessi and Cornell 2015), Rhodes (Tabensky and Matthews 2015) and Wits (Cross and Johnson 2008), it is just as active in its ability to make students and academics feel welcome or otherwise. Changing the academic curriculum is equally difficult in both settings because of the force of the institutional curriculum and the lack of critical self-examination that characterise old institutions like universities (Lange 2014).

If 'Look at me, I am here' was a far-reaching call for recognition and acknowledgement, the institutional curriculum played an important role in the misrecognition of black students at HWUs. The concept of recognition belongs to a philosophical tradition that starts with Georg Hegel's early writings on the dialectic between master and slave in the struggle for recognition. This tradition has been analysed in detail by the German philosopher Axel Honneth (1995), who combines Hegel's notion of struggle for recognition and the role that law, love relations and ethical life have in forging a viable society, with George Herbert Mead's social anthropology studies 'to identify the intersubjective conditions for individual self-realisation' (Honneth 1995: xi). According to Honneth, the very possibility of the development of personal identity depends on the development of self-confidence, self-respect and self-esteem, all of which, in turn, depend on the recognition by others who are themselves recognised. At a historical sociological level, struggles against disrespect and for recognition are constitutive of a moral grammar that defines the ethical society (life).

Under systems of oppression and racial discrimination such as colonialism and apartheid, the possibilities for a black individual to develop a personal identity in the sense of Honneth were socially non-existent. Every element of the legal system and privileged culture and sociability that makes possible self-confidence, self-esteem and self-respect in a society of equals conspired against black people's intersubjective recognition in white South Africa. Not only was the law defined in such terms as to deny basic legal and human rights to black people, but the whole social infrastructure was designed to keep black people outside white South Africa in a limbo of personhood (Biko [1978] 2004; Fanon [1952] 2008), while ensuring that their labour was put at the service of capitalist development. Particularly in relation to the access to resources, Honneth's theory of recognition needs to be augmented by Nancy Fraser's perspective on distributive justice. For Fraser (Fraser and Honneth 2003; Fraser 2009) the recognition of subordinated groups cannot fully take place unless a politics of distribution confronts the inequality and hierarchy on which lack of recognition is based. Put differently, recognition based on distributive justice requires the acknowledgement and the redress of privilege, in this case white privilege. However, this process is much bigger than any university. While the university can acknowledge its own roots in white privilege, even its complicity with it, and while it can put in place measures to redress aspects of the life of its black staff and students at the university, it cannot address directly the structural question of white privilege in South African society.

Against this conceptual frame let the lens zoom in on South Africa in 1994. The new democratic settlement can be characterised as the outcome of a struggle for recognition; notionally, the very change of the law and the system of rights made it possible for black people to participate in intersubjective relationships that support the development of self-confidence, self-respect and self-esteem. However, in relation to access to the material resources (from jobs and decent wages to basic amenities) and 'culture', (especially, education) there is no actual fit between rights-based personhood and the material conditions of possibility for the emergence of self-confidence, self-respect and self-esteem. This lack of fitting becomes particularly concrete when it takes place in specific institutions like universities. There is abundant research produced in the last decade on the devastating impact that students' material conditions of existence and institutional culture have on black students' sense of self at universities and yet there is sufficient evidence that universities have been unable to see the signs (Kerr and Luescher, forthcoming).

The colonial university was built on 'scientific' notions of disrespect for the colonial subject that were carried over and refined under the apartheid regime, even at the English-medium so-called open universities. The colonial university was built – it was complacently assumed – on white genius and ingenuity; it conformed to a set pattern of development to modernity that started and culminated with Western history. A hundred years later, in the context of an unsatisfactory and incomplete transition to democracy, the question about black recognition and white privilege in the academic space is being reopened. But this question is asked simultaneously across the domain of knowledge and that of identity for the colonial edifice. This is so because the colonial edifice was not built only on the assumption of the inferiority and incompleteness of its subjects, but also on the mastery and superiority of colonial knowledge, which 'scientifically' demonstrated the inferiority of the colonised. Interestingly, the conflation of epistemology and ontology so ably presented by Mbembe in *Critique of Black Reason* (2017) re-emerges under the guise of the decolonisation of the university during the student movement. Can the roots of the identity question be explained politically and sociologically without dismissing its epistemological and affective dimensions?

Kathy Luckett (2016: 422) has persuasively used Mamdani's seminal *Citizen and Subject* (1996) analysis of the impact of colonial rule on post-independence arrangements in Africa to argue that as a consequence of the South African democratic transition's inability to deracialise civil society and the consequent restriction of the enjoyment of civil rights to urban elites, universities post-1994 have enrolled three categories of students: first, 'state-funded students, admitted to the university as subjects of the political society based on policies of equity and redress'. These students must manage simultaneously material and cultural gaps that impede their belonging to the university. Second, fee-paying black students who enter universities as 'new citizens of the elite civil society'. While these students might fit the university financially, they struggle with it culturally. Finally, the third category of students are fee-paying white students who have both the economic and the cultural capital that allows them to fit into the university. According to Luckett, it is possible to argue that the presence of the urban black elite at universities defines the terms of the 2015 struggle around student black identity and not around class. I would like to take Luckett's argument further to say that the coalescence of the student movement around black identity, in a manner reminiscent of the Black Consciousness Movement, overtook and to some extent obfuscated the demand for the decolonisation of knowledge, by making it equivalent to the Africanisation of knowledge.

Among the areas of contradiction between African students' access to universities and their feeling misrecognised and out of place there, language is possibly one of the most powerful examples. In what follows I use the language of instruction at HWUs to show how misrecognition of African students takes place in different contexts.

Despite its origins as an English-medium college in the 1900s, UFS became an Afrikaans medium university under apartheid and in the 1990s a parallel medium (English/Afrikaans) university. By the end of the first decade of the twenty-first century most (black) students were choosing to study in English and were so taught by mostly white Afrikaans-home-language academics. In 2014 as part of renewed efforts to review language development at the university, a visiting American second-language education specialist conducted a series of interviews to establish academic staff's needs and their willingness to develop their ability to teach in English (Shaugnessy 2015). Among other findings, more to the purpose of the research, the researcher found that white Afrikaans-speaking staff tended to refer to their students studying in English as 'my English class'. The assumptions underpinning a seemingly innocent and obvious descriptor were several and were important: a group of majority black students, Sesotho- and possibly isiZulu- and isiXhosa-speaking, were attributed (white) Englishness; the fact that English was their third or fourth language and certainly not their home language, was also erased by the description; finally the idea of 'my English class' closed off any thought about the difficulties derived from studying university subjects in a foreign language. In this example black students are attributed an identity that replaces, for the length of their university life, who they themselves think or feel they are. The misrecognition does not end here. At UFS Afrikaans has been for many decades not only the preferred intellectual language but also the language of communication for the administration and the language of sociability among most staff. The contemporary occasional use of Afrikaans by the lecturer or a fellow white student in class, by administrative staff in relation to fees, records, and so on, by academics talking to each other in front of a student, constitute moments in which the self-confidence, the self-esteem and self-respect of the student were shattered through lack of identification and erasure of her presence (as academics talk as if she were not there) and through the more immediate problem of not understanding what was being said.

The sense of exclusion and institutionally sanctioned disadvantage were amplified by the belief held by most black UFS students that Afrikaans-medium students had better lectures, were provided with better explanations of exam 'scopes' and had more access to lecturers. Thus, in this context the initial problem of misrecognition, otherness and insecurity becomes one of discrimination (Gqola 2017: 91–110). Although the issue of language as identity and as a tool for exclusion is especially strong at historically Afrikaans-medium universities, language is no less of an issue at traditionally English universities.

Over 30 years academics involved in academic development have researched and theorised the issue of literacy, developing a rich corpus to understand how academic discourse can act as yet another instance of both misrecognition and disrespect, in Honneth's terms, of black students. In an article written during the #RMF protest cycle, Boughey and Mckenna (2016) looked at the relationship between students' demand for decolonisation and the 'language problem'. Their argument is that in the 1980s explaining black students' failure in higher education as a 'language problem' was a politically progressive way out of apartheid's cognitive difference explanation of the academic performance of black and white students. Despite this, they argue, this interpretation is underpinned by problematic conceptualisations of both language and academic literacy. During the 1980s the solution to the language problem was to teach black students skills to write and read English. This approach was oblivious to the fact that reading and writing are socially embedded practices and that therefore there are different literacies that need to be entered as distinct from the ability to speak a language. Boughey and Mckenna suggest that teaching black students writing and reading skills kept them out of language understood as discourse. According to James Paul Gee, discourse is 'composed of distinctive ways of speaking/listening and often, too, writing/reading coupled with distinctive ways of acting, interacting, valuing, feeling, dressing, thinking, believing, with other people and with various objects, tools, and technologies, so as to enact specific socially recognizable identities engaged in specific socially recognized activities. (Gee 2012; discussed in Boughey and Mckenna 2016: 4)'.

When an individual primary discourse is aligned with academic discourse, as is most often the case for white middle-class students, the transition into university discourse is easy. When this is not the case, as happens with many black students, whether middle-class, working-class or rural students, then language becomes another area of misrecognition and disrespect. Students simply do not fit and are made to feel unfit either through bad outcomes, or worse, by disparaging comments. This problem is made all the more complex by the fairly prevalent conception, especially at top research universities, of students as autonomous, self-sufficient agents divorced from their context and history. When, often, as success and throughput rate indicate, these 'decontextualised students' (Boughey and Mckenna 2016) fail to fulfil the expectations of the self-sufficient student model, they are deemed unable to meet the standards demanded by university-level study.

I would like to argue, following on Boughey and Mckenna's explanation, that discourse, as defined by Gee, brings to the fore the role of language in the constitution of the institutional curriculum. The lack of transparency in university discourse and the technical unpreparedness of most academics to deal with language in their teaching exclude students and make the development of intersubjective relationships very difficult, setting once again the stage for misrecognition.

To summarise, in this section I have argued: first, that student protests about their misrecognition at HWUs becomes possible when the number of black students has reached a tipping point – black students constitute a majority or have stopped being a minority; second, that in the context of the university the call for recognition operates simultaneously at the ontological and epistemological level and that the conflation between knowledge and identity tends to focus the discussion about curriculum on the Africanisation of the curriculum; and third, that the institutional curriculum plays a fundamental role in aiding the obfuscation between curriculum and identity.

Misrecognition at the level of language and discourse, as discussed above, constitute one dimension of the institutional curriculum that is implicit in the call, 'Look at me, I am here'. The other, the call for the decolonisation of the knowledge embedded in the curriculum, is the subject of the next section.

ACADEMIC CURRICULUM MEETS INSTITUTIONAL CURRICULUM

As indicated earlier, the notion of the decolonial turn and the politico-philosophical theorisation that supports it, started almost two decades ago, especially among Latin American intellectuals working in US universities (Maldonado-Torres 2007, 2011), without forgetting the work of Boaventura de Sousa Santos (2013, Santos and Monedero 2015) in Portugal and the contributions made by the Indian school of subaltern studies to the understanding of knowledge of the oppressed (Chaturvedi 2000). South Africa has entered this field relatively recently, mostly through the student movement that started in 2015. However, #RMF was not the beginning of the questioning of academic knowledge at South African universities. Several controversies and field-specific debates have taken place over the years, highlighting epistemological tensions that run along political fractures in the South African academy. One such controversy took place 20 years ago at UCT; its virulence, its publicity and the academics as well as the university involved, make it an unavoidable example of the struggle for the curriculum in South Africa. It is my view that this controversy offers an interesting glimpse of the encounter between the institutional curriculum and a changed academic curriculum and raises important questions to think about at the current juncture.

It is October 1997 at UCT; Mahmood Mamdani, renowned African scholar from Makerere University, visiting professor at the University of Durban-Westville in 1993, winner of the Herskovitz Prize in 1997 for the best book on African Studies in English for *Citizen and Subject*, had been appointed the first A.C. Jordan Chair of African History (1996) and then director of the Centre for African Studies (CAS) in March 1997. At the time the Faculty of Humanities and Social Sciences had decided to develop a semester course on Africa. Professor Mamdani was invited by the faculty within which CAS was located to design and, presumably, lead the course. What followed has gone down in South African higher education history as the 'Mamdani Affair', an event characterised first, as a conflict of academic freedom in which university administration interfered with, and in fact blocked, the teaching of specific curriculum. The event was also characterised, much less interestingly, as a battle between personal and institutional egos. These, however, are not aspects of the controversy I deal with in this chapter. The 'Mamdani Affair' is an egregious example of the conflict between the institutional curriculum and the academic curriculum and how in the struggle between the two the academic curriculum is more often than not at a disadvantage.

The facts are relatively clear. Mamdani was requested in 1997 to develop the syllabus for a semester-long foundation course on Africa that all students entering social sciences programmes in the relevant faculty at UCT would have to take. The outcome of his efforts and the reading list for the course were to be discussed with three other academics in the faculty who constituted a working group for the implementation of the new course. The disagreement between Mamdani and his colleagues, presumably about the organisation, content and suitability of the course as foundation knowledge, took institutional proportions with the intervention of the dean, the senior deputy vice-chancellor and the vice-chancellor herself. Mamdani was first suspended from teaching the course and an alternative syllabus was developed by other academics. Although the suspension was lifted and Mamdani was invited to teach the course as part of the team, the controversy around 'Problematising Africa' and its outcome, and the eventual resignation of Mamdani have remained among the dark moments of post-apartheid UCT.

The 'Mamdani Affair' pitted UCT's professor of archaeolgy, Martin Hall, against Mahmood Mamdani. There are four papers, two per author, published by *Social Dynamics* in 1998, that present the two sides of the debate (Hall 1998a, 1998b; Mamdani 1998a, 1998b). This together with the syllabus of Mamdani's 'Problematising Africa' and that of the alternative course, which was actually taught, constitute the material publicly available to analyse the issues at stake.[12] Reading the four papers 20 years later it is possible to recast Mamdani's own characterisation of the debate as involving academic freedom, administrative decision-making in relation to academic standards and the relationship between pedagogy and content. Indeed, the debate raised these issues, and their importance then and now is undeniable. But at the core of the 'Mamdani Affair' was an epistemological problem that remained unnamed: what constituted valid knowledge of Africa; how was the subject of knowledge defined and whose knowledge of Africa should be accepted as valid. In a secondary line was the preoccupation with to whom and how this knowledge would be taught.

Besides the egos inevitably involved in academic disputation and the display of high-academic English insult in the exchanges, it is clear that what Mamdani was proposing defied UCT academics' conception of Africa and of its knowledge. Mamdani's syllabus confronted UCT with the need to examine its knowledge of Africa; where it came from; what its assumptions were; what the consequences of these assumptions were; and why it was important to examine critically the knowledge of Africa with which UCT's academics felt comfortable. With very few exceptions, too few to count, the alternative course was entirely based on knowledge of Africa developed in northern hemisphere academia. The periodisation of the course in the alternative syllabus, a particularly thorny issue in Mamdani's argument, was at best unexamined, and the conception of Africa's history implicit in it remained opaque to itself. Just as important was the unacknowledged point that knowledge itself has a history and the history of disciplines and fields of study are shaped by power relations that are themselves born in historical contexts. UCT's academics seemed unaffected by Mamdani's critique of the texts chosen in their alternative curriculum or by the fact that they did not seem to be familiar with the debates within the African academia that Mamdani was using as the organising axis in his syllabus. Finally, the vexed issue of whether and in what ways South Africa constitutes an exception to Africa's colonial history or, as Mamdani argued, very much part of the history of the African continent, was not simply a matter of interpretation, it was presented as a critique of South Africa's academic establishment both right and left. Mamdani went further and pointed out that UCT academics were offering a course that was morally and intellectually flawed. The counter argument, that the course needed to be accessible to black students who came to the university with poor schooling, did not improve UCT academics' argument, who were now accused of housing a new form of Bantu education.

Mamdani's written account of the dispute with his UCT colleagues and his reply to Hall touched on three bastions of UCT institutional curriculum: its high standards as the best university in Africa; its progressive liberal outlook; and its intellectual innocence, as a non-racist university. A close examination of the alternative curriculum found fault with all three tenets of the institutional curriculum: Mamdani found the existing expertise in African history at UCT wanting and hired a consultant from the University of the Western Cape; he regarded the alternative course as a way of teaching black students a sub-standard curriculum; and finally, he surfaced the racialised understanding of Africa presented in the periodisation and readings of the alternative curriculum.

Mamdani left UCT in 1998 to take up a position at Columbia University. There is a history to be written about what happened at UCT during this three-year period; but there is no immediately available public record showing that the 'Mamdani Affair' divided UCT or created any form of institutional examination. It is as if this was a passing moment, soon digested by the institutional curriculum, which then expelled the alien body.

Almost 20 years later UCT students under the banner of #RMF called on the university to: 'Implement a curriculum which critically centres Africa and the subaltern. By this we mean treating African' discourses as the point of departure – through addressing not only content, but languages and methodologies of education and learning – and only examining western traditions in so far as they are relevant to our own experience. (RMF 2015).

How does the Mamdani affair illuminate #RMF and more generally the call over the last three years for decolonisation of the curriculum? What are the institutional conditions that will avoid today's call for decolonisation ending up as a blip on the institutional curriculum, as Mamdani's was? What needs to be done for the institutional curriculum not to strangle opportunities for change and reflection? To answer these questions, it is necessary to compare the two moments.

Despite the publicity, the Mamdani Affair was a UCT institutional issue that died fairly quickly, while the issues raised by the #RMF movement had national proportions.

Mamdani, unlike today's UCT, Wits and Rhodes academics, did not have an institutional power base or sufficient, if any, student support.

The Mamdani Affair was kept strictly within the parameters of an academic dispute. #RMF was a political protest that took on academic matters.

In the period 2015–2017 all universities affected responded to the #RMF protest, making way to conversations on the need to decolonise the curriculum; in 1998 UCT closed ranks against Mamdani.

After #RMF some academics actually heeded the call for the decolonisation of the curriculum. At UCT in faculties as diverse as health sciences, humanities and engineering some academics are working on new courses for the undergraduate degree. The same is true at other universities.

It seems then that the main elements in avoiding the institutional curriculum 'digesting' a new academic curriculum are institutional support and the development of a critical mass of committed academics and supportive and active students. In other words, the hegemony of the institutional curriculum needs to be deauthorised from inside. Yet, I would argue that while this is a necessary condition, it is not a sufficient condition to respond more fully to the call for the decolonisation of the university. I believe that another important condition is to solve, or at least to understand, the obfuscation between identity and knowledge, and to respond to both.

CONCLUSION: TOWARDS A PEDAGOGY OF PRESENCE

In the previous sections I have tried to show how the student protest that was unleashed in 2015 must be understood especially in the context of HWUs that were experienced as fundamentally inhospitable for black students and for black academics. In section two I used Honneth's concept of recognition to explain the impact that social and epistemological misrecognition had on the capacity of black students to flourish at the university. The student protest was against both the need to assimilate into an alien culture and against the lack of recognition of their presence as black people in the university space. For this to change, I argued, the institutional and the academic curriculum need to be engaged critically. Without the acknowledgement and the impetus to effect fundamental changes in the institutional curriculum, based on the identification and acknowledgement of its characteristics, the best attempts at changing the academic curriculum, as we saw, will fail.

Across the different sections of this chapter I have argued that black students' demand for recognition as expressed during the #RMF protest cycle conflated ontological and epistemological recognition and often reduced the decolonisation of the curriculum to its Africanisation. I have explained the origins of this obfuscation through the force of an institutional curriculum that failed to see students and to see itself historically and sociologically. The historical failure of most HWUs to comprehend the implications of the presence of black students on their campuses in terms of the valorisation of blackness, especially of 'Africanness', denies students (and academics) the possibility of developing self-confidence, self-respect and self-esteem. The valorisation of African knowledge and by implication of 'African beings' implicit in the Africanisation of the curriculum is the negation of the African colonial condition as 'incomplete, mutilated, unfinished' (Mbembe 2001: 1). As important, urgent and necessary as this is ontologically, the Africanisation of the curriculum as proposed by the #RMF movement is epistemologically and politically isolating. This for me is the fundamental limit of an identitarian approach to pedagogy and curriculum.

Instead of this, I propose, following Mbembe, a pedagogy and a curriculum of presence. This represents an affirmation of the students and their blackness, of their selves, their bodies, their identities and in particular their direct and indirect (intergenerational knowledge) experiences of the world. This requires a counter movement: the acknowledgement of the identity and the position of those who teach, as well as of white students. For change in the institutional and academic curriculum to be profound and socially productive it must not only focus on black students and black academics. If the university is to play a truly transformative role in our society, a pedagogy of presence should help all of the university's inhabitants to recentre themselves away from 'white mythologies', creating the possibility of the development of new intersubjective relationships, new forms of learning and new respect for different modes of knowing. A pedagogy of presence, then, will force the entire university establishment to revise notions of student learning (Leibowitz 2017) and reconsider the manner in which students are taught. This has implications for, among other things, the language of instruction, the modalities of teaching, the notions of assessment and the understanding of the student as individual and autonomous.

At a curricular level, a pedagogy of presence makes possible two important intellectual movements: the resizing of European knowledge and its provincialisation in a global world, and the incorporation of other epistemological traditions – African, Chinese, Indian, Latin American – into the horizon of global knowledge.

Together, these two movements provide a unique opportunity for a much more radical understanding of the decolonisation of the curriculum, which focuses clearly on the social critique of the world in which we live and is, therefore, politically more hopeful.

NOTES

1   However, a small group of students was concerned about the content of the African history curriculum and about the absence of African precolonial history in the syllabi.
2   Shimla Park is the UFS rugby stadium. On 22 February 2016 the local rugby team was playing Nelson Mandela University for the final of the inter-university cup. The previous weeks had been characterised by student and contract workers protests demanding insourcing. Students

and workers decided to enter the pitch during the rugby match to bring their protest before the vice-chancellor who was present at the event. As the students interrupted the match and before police could disperse them, the public present at the match invaded the pitch and literally kicked the protesting students out of the stadium. The events at Shimla Park created a violent reaction among both black and white students, their families and white associations. In the end UFS set up a commission to investigate the events.

3   By global knowledge I mean the repository of historical and contemporary human knowledge, across all disciplines and fields of study produced by different individuals, cultures and civilisations over millennia, which becomes accessible through the Internet.

4   The Andrew W. Mellon Foundation has provided funding for a complete analysis of the #MF movement across the country. The work is being led by the Human Sciences Research Council and the principal investigator is Dr Thierry Luescher.

5   This section relies heavily on my own work on the history of policymaking in South Africa. See in particular Lange (2017).

6   I have analysed the role of the CHE and especially of the Higher Education Quality Committee in curriculum in Lange (2017).

7   A paradigmatic example of this is Jansen's (2009) analysis of a course on 'Ubuntu' at the University of Pretoria. In my own work I have shown aspects of the monolithic curriculum at the UFS.

8   The policy frames that were produced with a view to addressing these objectives were the report of the National Commission on Higher Education (NCHE 1996), White Paper 3 (DoE 1997) and the Higher Education Act (1997).

9   This figure, as the CHE report indicates, also includes foreign African students, which means that in actual fact, UCT's enrolment of South African African students was considerably lower than this figure indicates.

10   Currently UCT has approximately 40 per cent black students; 40 per cent white students and 20 per cent international students, many of whom come from other African countries.

11   C.R. Swart (1894–1982) was senior National Party politician. A Fascist sympathiser during Second World War, he was a hard-line Afrikaner nationalist and staunch republican. He was minister of justice under prime ministers Malan, Strijdom and Verwoerd. In 1961, after South Africa became a republic, he was appointed state president. The building of the Faculty of Law at UFS was named after him and in 2016 students and workers attacked his statue outside the faculty building.

12   Although the Mamdani Affair has raised its public head every so often in the last 20 years, there are to my knowledge no full accounts of what happened, how different actors reacted, what the role of the administration at faculty and university level was in dealing with the controversy and what its consequences were for the teaching of Africa at UCT.

REFERENCES

Ballim, Yunus. 2015. 'Reflections on "Epistemological Access" and the Analytical Frameworks that May Guide Institutional Responses to Student Learning in South African Higher Education'. Unpublished manuscript.

Barnett, Ronald and Kelly Coate. 2005. *Engaging the Curriculum in Higher Education*. Maidenhead: Society for Research into Higher Education & Open University Press.

Biko, Steve. [1978] 2004. *I Write What I Like: A Selection of His Writings*. Johannesburg: Picador Africa.

Bond, Patrick. 2016. 'To Win Free Education, Fossilised Neoliberalism Must Go'. In *Fees Must Fall: Student Revolt, Decolonisation and Governance in South Africa*, edited by Susan Booysen, 192–213. Johannesburg: Wits University Press.

Booysen, Susan. 2016. 'Two Weeks in October: Changing Governance in South Africa'. In *Fees Must Fall: Student Revolt, Decolonisation and Governance in South Africa*, edited by Susan Booysen, 22–52. Johannesburg: Wits University Press.

Boughey, Chrissie and Sioux Mckenna. 2016. 'Academic Literacy and the Decontextualised Learner'. *Critical Studies in Teaching and Learning* 4 (2): 1–9. doi: 10.14426/cristal.v4i2.80.

Chaturvedi, Vinayak. 2000. *Mapping Subaltern Studies and the Postcolonial*. London: Verso.

CHE (Council on Higher Education). 2004. Monitoring Directorate. 'University of Cape Town Institutional Profile'. Unpublished.

CHE (Council on Higher Education). 2008. Higher Education Quality Committee. 'Report on the Institutional Audit of the University of the Free State'. Unpublished.

CHE (Council on Higher Education). 2015. *VitalStats Public Higher Education 2015*. Pretoria: Council on Higher Education. http://www.che.ac.za/content/vitalstats-public-higher-education-2015.

Cloete, Nico, Peter Maassen, Richard Fenhel, Teboho Moja, Trish Gibbon and Helene Perold. 2006. *Transformation in Higher Education: Global Pressures and Local Realities*. Dordrecht: Springer.

Cloete, Nico, Malegapuru William Makgoba and Donald Ekong, eds. 1997. *Knowledge, Identity and Curriculum Transformation in Africa*. Cape Town: Maskew Miller Longman.

Cross, M. and B. Johnson. 2008. 'Establishing a Space of Dialogue and Possibilities: Student Experience and Meaning at the University of the Witwatersrand'. *South African Journal of Higher Education* 22 (2): 302–321. doi: 10.4314/sajhe.v22i2.25787.

Davies, Brian, Johan Muller and Ana Morais. 2004. *Reading Bernstein, Researching Bernstein*. London: RoutledgeFalmer.

DoE (Department of Education). 1997. *Education White Paper 3: A Programme for the Transformation of Higher Education*. Pretoria: Department of Education.

Ensor, Paula. 2003. 'The National Qualifications Framework and Higher Education in South Africa: Some Epistemological Issues'. *Journal of Education and Work* 16 (3): 325–346. doi: 10.1080/1363908032000099476.

Ensor, Paula. 2004. 'Contesting Discourses in Higher Education Curriculum Restructuring in South Africa'. *Higher Education: The International Journal of Higher Education and Educational Planning* 48 (3): 339–359. doi: 10.1023/B:HIGH.0000035544.96309.f1.

Fanon, Frantz. [1952] 2008. *Black Skins, White Masks*. London: Pluto Press.

Fraser, Nancy. 2009. *Scales of Justice: Reimagining Political Space in a Globalizing World*. New York: Columbia University Press.

Fraser, Nancy and Axel Honneth. 2003. *Redistribution or Recognition? A Political-Philosophical Exchange*. London: Verso.

Gee, James Paul. 2012. *Social Linguistics and Literacies: Ideology in Discourses*. London: Routledge.

Godsell, Gillian and Rekgotsofetse Chikane. 2016. 'The Roots of the Revolution'. In *Fees Must Fall: Student Revolt, Decolonisation and Governance in South Africa*, edited by Susan Booysen. Johannesburg: Wits University Press.

Gqola, Pumla Dineo. 2017. *Reflecting Rogue: Inside the Mind of a Feminist*. Johannesburg: MFBooks.

Graham, S. 2016. 'Achieving Transformation at the University of Pretoria (UP) in the Face of Diversity'. Paper submitted to the #MustFall: Understanding the Moment Colloquium, Bloemfontein, October.

Griesel, Hanlie. 2004. *Curriculum Responsiveness: Case Studies in Higher Education*. Pretoria: South African Universities Vice-Chancellors Association.

Hall, Martin. 1998a. '"Bantu Education"? A Reply to Mahmood Mamdani'. *Social Dynamics* 24 (2): 86-92. doi: 10.1080/02533959808458651.

Hall, Martin. 1998b. 'Teaching Africa at the Post-apartheid University of Cape Town: A Response'. *Social Dynamics* 24 (2): 40–62. doi: 10.1080/02533959808458648.

Hall, Martin. 2009. 'New Knowledge and the University'. *Anthropology Southern Africa* 32 (1–2): 69–76. doi: 10.1080/23323256.2009.11499980.

Higgins, John. 2007. 'Institutional Culture as a Key Word'. In *Review of Higher Education in South Africa: Selected Themes*. Pretoria: Council on Higher Education.

Higher Education Act. 1997. https://www.gov.za/sites/default/files/a101-97.pdf.

Honneth, Axel. 1995. *The Struggle for Recognition: The Moral Grammar of Social Conflicts*. Cambridge, MA: Polity Press.

Jansen, Jonathan D. 2009. *Knowledge in the Blood: Confronting Race and the Apartheid Past*. Stanford: Stanford University Press.

Jansen, Jonathan D. 2017. *As by Fire: The End of the South African University*. Cape Town: Tafelberg.

Johannesburg Salon. 2015. *Johannesburg Salon* 9. http://jwtc.org.za/resources/docs/salon-volume-9 /FINAL_FINAL_Vol9_Book.pdf.

Kerr, Philippa and Thierry M. Luescher. Forthcoming. 'What Do We Know about Students' Experiences beyond the Curriculum'. In *Pathways to the Public Good: Access, Experiences and Outcomes of South African Undergraduate Education*, edited by Paul Ashwin and Jennifer M. Case. Cape Town: African Minds.

Kessi, Shose and Josephine Cornell. 2015. 'Coming to UCT: Black Students, Transformation and Discourses of Race'. *Journal of Student Affairs in Africa* 3 (2): 1–16. doi: 10.14426/jsaa.v3i2.132.

Lange, Lis. 2014. 'Rethinking Transformation and Its Knowledge(s): The Case of South African Higher Education'. *Critical Studies in Teaching and Learning* 2 (1): 1–24. doi: 10.14426/cristal.v2i1.24.

Lange, Lis. 2017. 'Twenty Years of Higher Education Curriculum Policy in South Africa'. *Journal of Education* 68: 31–57. https://journals.ukzn.ac.za/index.php/joe/article/view/379/819.

Le Grange, Lesley. 2016. 'Decolonising the University Curriculum'. *South African Journal of Higher Education* 30 (2): 1–12. doi: 10.20853/30-2-709.

Leibowitz, Brenda. 2017. 'Cognitive Justice and the Higher Education Curriculum'. *Journal of Education* 68: 93–111. http://www.scielo.org.za/pdf/jed/n68/06.pdf.

Luckett, Kathy. 2016. 'Curriculum Contestation in a Post-colonial Context: A View from the South'. *Teaching in Higher Education* 21 (4): 1–14. doi: 10.1080/13562517.2016.1155547.

Luckett, Kathy and Veeran Naicker. 2016. 'Responding to Misrecognition from a (Post)/Colonial University'. *Critical Studies in Education*. doi: 10.1080/17508487.2016.1234495.

Maldonado-Torres, Nelson. 2007. 'On the Coloniality of Being: Contributions to the Development of a Concept'. *Cultural Studies* 21 (2–3): 240–270. doi: 10.1080/09502380601162548.

Maldonado-Torres, Nelson. 2011. 'Thinking through the Decolonial Turn: Post-continental Interventions in Theory, Philosophy, and Critique: An Introduction'. *Transmodernity: Journal of Peripheral Cultural Production of the Luso-Hispanic World* 1 (2). https://escholarship.org/uc/item/59w8j02x.

Mamdani, Mahmood. 1996. *Citizen and Subject: Contemporary Africa and the Legacy of Late Colonialism*. Princeton: Princeton University Press.

Mamdani, Mahmood. 1998a. 'Is African Studies to be Turned into a New Home for Bantu Education at UCT?' *Social Dynamics* 24 (2): 63–75. doi: 10.1080/02533959808458649.

Mamdani, Mahmood. 1998b. 'Teaching Africa at the Post-apartheid University of Cape Town: A Critical View of the "Introduction to Africa" Core Course in the Social Science and Humanities Faculty's Foundation Semester, 1998'. *Social Dynamics* 24 (2): 1–32. doi: 10.1080/02533959808458646.

Mbembe, Achille. 2001. *On the Postcolony*. Berkeley: University of California Press.

Mbembe, Achille. 2015. 'Decolonizing Knowledge and the Question of the Archive'. Presentation at the University of the Witwatersrand, Johannesburg, 22 April. https://wiser.wits.ac.za/system /files/Achille%20Mbembe%20-%20Decolonizing%20Knowledge%20and%20the%20 Question%20of%20the%20Archive.pdf.

Mbembe, Achille. 2016. 'Decolonizing the University: New Directions'. *Arts and Humanities in Higher Education: An International Journal of Theory, Research and Practice* 15 (1): 29–45. doi: 10.1177/1474022215618513.

Mbembe, Achille. 2017. *Critique of Black Reason*. Johannesburg: Wits University Press.

Moore, Rob and Johan Muller. 1999. 'The Discourse of "Voice"' and the Problem of Knowledge and Identity in the Sociology of Education'. *British Journal of Sociology of Education* 20 (2): 189–206. doi: 10.1080/01425699995407.

Ndebele, Njabulo S., ed. 2013. *A Proposal for Undergraduate Curriculum Reform in South Africa: The Case for a Flexible Curriculum Structure*. Report of the Task Team on Undergraduate Curriculum Structure. Pretoria: Council on Higher Education.

NCHE (National Commission on Higher Education). 2016. *A Framework for Transformation*. Pretoria: Human Sciences Research Council.

Nyamnjoh, Francis B. 2016. *#RhodesMustFall: Nibbling at Resilient Colonialism in South Africa*. Bamenda, Cameroon: Langaa Research & Publishing.

Pillay, Pundy. [2016]. 'Financing of Universities: Promoting Equity or Reinforcing Inequality?' In *Fees Must Fall: Student Protest, Decolonisation and Governance in South Africa*, edited by Susan Booysen, 256–268. Johannesburg: Wits University Press.

RMF (Rhodes Must Fall). 2015. 'UCT Rhodes Must Fall Mission Statement'. Facebook, 25 March. https://www.facebook.com/RhodesMustFall/posts/uct-rhodes-must-fall-mission/1559394444336048/.

Santos, Boaventura de Sousa. 2013. *Epistemologies of the South: Justice against Epistemicide*. Boulder: Paradigm Publishers.

Santos, Boaventura de Sousa and Juan Carlos Monedero. 2015. *El Milenio Huérfano: Ensayos para una Nueva Cultura Política*. Madrid: Editorial Trotta.

Scott, Ian, Nan Yeld and Jane Hendry. 2007. *A Case for Improving Teaching and Learning in South African Higher Education*. Higher Education Monitor 6. Pretoria: Council on Higher Education.

Shaughnessy, C. 2015. 'A Report on a Needs Analysis of Language at the University of the Free State'. Unpublished Research Report.

Soudien, Crain, ed. 2008. *Report of the Ministerial Committee on Transformation and Social Cohesion and Elimination of Discrimination in Public Higher Education Institutions*. Pretoria: Department of Education.

Steyn, Melissa E. and Mikki van Zyl. 2001. 'Like That Statue at Jammie Stairs: Some Student Perceptions and Experiences of Institutional Culture at the University of Cape Town in 1999'. Research Report. Cape Town: Institute for Intercultural and Diversity Studies of Southern Africa, University of Cape Town.

Tabensky, Pedro Alexis and Sally Matthews, eds. 2015. *Being at Home: Race, Institutional Culture and Transformation at South African Higher Education Institutions*. Pietermaritzburg: University of KwaZulu-Natal Press.

UCT (University of Cape Town). 2015. 'Curriculum Change Working Group'. http://www.uct.ac.za/main/teaching-and-learning/curriculum-change-working-group.

Van der Merwe, J.C. and Dionne van Reenen. 2016. *Transformation and Legitimation in Post-apartheid Universities: Reading Discourses from "Reitz"*. Bloemfontein: SUN Press.

Young, Michael F.D. 2008. *Bringing Knowledge back in: From Social Constructivism to Social Realism in the Sociology of Education*. London: Routledge.

CHAPTER 5

What Counts and Who Belongs? Current Debates in Decolonising the Curriculum

Ursula Hoadley and Jaamia Galant
University of Cape Town

When discussions around decolonising the curriculum take place, it is often diffi-cult to discern what the decolonising is referring to, and whether the discussion is about curriculum at all. Many of the major decolonisation scholars, such as Walter Mignolo, Nelson Maldonado-Torres and Ramón Grosfoguel are concerned with the 'colonial power matrix,' which continues to structure the world system, and with how to bring about 'the epistemic decolonial turn' (Grosfoguel 2007). Certain scholars who are more critical of some of these current ideas point out the complexity of changes in the forms of knowledge production. Achille Mbembe (2015) argues that rather than a sustained attack on the Western canon (that is not purely Western), decolonisation entails a radical rethinking of the purpose of knowledge produc-tion. He gives the example of a shift in orientation to 'deep time' and 'to rethinking the human not from the perspective of its mastery of the Creation as we used to, but from the perspective of its finitude and its possible extinction' (2015: 25). For Mahmood Mamdani (2017), decolonising knowledge entails 'a series of acts which sift through the historical legacy, and the contemporary reality, discarding some parts and adapting others to a new-found purpose', and, crucially, institutionalising the gains made.

Scholars such as Mbembe and Mamdani are concerned with questions of epis-temology and knowledge production, while those working in the decolonial frame often cast arguments in broad socio-political terms ('geo-politics' and 'bodypolitics') rather than in relation to questions about particular knowledge forms or disciplines and their organisation in curriculum. As both Kathy Luckett and Suellen Shay (2017) and Shannon Morreira (2017) argue, there is a gap between their 'high-level meta-epistemological debates' and questions around education systems, curriculum and pedagogy. A result of this gap is that it is difficult for those tasked with curriculum work to draw on decolonial theorising in addressing questions relevant to their work. There is no substantive decolonial theory of curriculum that can guide curriculum change, nor analyse it sufficiently. So, although we may be charged with being part of the problem, we draw on the work of a European theorist, Basil Bernstein, in order to understand the debates more clearly. Bernstein does something unique in the sociology of education. He is not only concerned with what is relayed/(re)produced through pedagogy (for example, external power relations, class, gender, ethnicity) but is also concerned with the *relay*, that which carries these messages, and is often perceived to be neutral. Bernstein describes the inner logic of pedagogic practice by means of an analytic construct consisting of three interrelated rules that are implicated in relations of power and control. It is important to signal that we are interested in the *structuring* of curriculum and pedagogic messages, and how calls for decolonisation imagine this structure.

We suggest a theorising of current debates around decolonising the curriculum, such that we may begin to discern, across different contexts and actors, what the call for decolonising the curriculum is all about. Is it about radical rupture in the forms of knowledge? Or is it about a shift in the ways that received knowledge is taught? Does it concern issues relevant to the field of production of knowledge (from which curriculum selections are made)? Or problems related to recontextualising that knowledge in curriculum, or reproducing it in classrooms and lecture theatres? One of our central concerns is around identity. Understanding curriculum as a process of identity formation, we consider the structure of knowledge and the nature of social relations in the curriculum as they pertain to questions of identity formation in a decolonial space.

WHO'LL BE THE JUDGE? A BRIEF LOOK AT LOCAL RESEARCH

Much of the current writing on decolonising the curriculum approaches the issue in relation to curriculum content on the one hand, or the teaching of that content on the other. One of the most developed accounts of different positions in the debate is Jonathan Jansen's (2017) work that identifies a typology of six different conceptions of 'decolonisation' in relation to knowledge in the university curriculum. The positions deal with (1) the location of 'Western' or 'European' knowledge in the curriculum in relation to African knowledge – a decentring (of European knowledge) approach; (2) an additive-inclusive one; (3) or a replacement approach with an Africanisation of the curriculum. Jansen's other positions are essentially complex pedagogic proposals which entail (4) 'critical engagement with settled knowledge'; (5) 'encounters with entangled knowledges' that suggest knowledge is intertwined between coloniser and colonised in the course of daily living. Finally, he suggests (6) a curriculum position that involves political conscientisation – 'Decolonisation as the repatriation of occupied knowledge (and society)'. While the descriptive account of the possible permutations of curriculum and pedagogy is interesting, the distinctions don't get to the actual entailments, and don't touch on *what will count* in the end – from what knowledge field will the rules for evaluation be derived?

Luckett and Shay's (2017) work is another prominent identification of decolonial positions, and they mark these out from the perspective of academic development in relation to Bernstein's (1990) pedagogic device. At each level of the device – the production of knowledge, its recontextualisation in curriculum, and at the level of teaching and learning – they generate the implications and a set of questions for a decolonial academic space. At the level of production, the questions are about opening up and legitimating knowledge production from sites other than the academy (Bernstein 1990: 11). At the level of pedagogy, questions concern giving teachers/lecturers/students more control over how the contents of the curriculum are taught and interpreted. But here, too, the issue of evaluation is evaded. What will count in the end? Is this about opening up access while the rules of the game and the requirements for mastery remain the same?

Morreira (2017) comes closer to considering evaluation. Although the main focus of her piece is on 'epistemic disobedience', which for the most part is greater control by lecturers over the selection of contents and texts used in the courses, she does refer to the nature of assignments and assessments in courses. But it is not clear whether the mode of critique marked out for successful performance in exams is different from that required in conventional social science or humanities course assessments; whether, in her words, the course is 'deliberately disruptive of monocentrist thinking' or whether it can 'promulgate alternative ways of being in the world' (2017: 296). Her example of 'epistemic disobedience' in the introduction of flexibility in awarding duly performed status to students, allowing for different 'personhoods' and 'cultural responsibilities' of students to be recognised, is unconvincing. But this has nothing to do with the instructional context but rather with cultural expression and bending the bureaucratic rules of the institution.

This is a small sample of the writing on decolonising the curriculum. There are others, including Saleem Badat (2017), who describes different outcomes for decolonising the curriculum when treated as 'a knowledge programme' or 'an education programme' or a 'social justice programme'. Other authors make calls in relation to curriculum for 'expansive imagination' (Sayed, Motala and Hoffman 2017); 'cognitive justice' (Leibowitz 2017); 'social dialogues' (Nyamupangedengu 2017); and 'Africanisation' (Msila and Gumbo 2016). In each case, the focus is on contents, their selection and organisation. All are silent on evaluation. These are mostly writings in the humanities, where the ability to engage in *reasoned critique* is the privileged outcome. Where will the tools that students will use to critique come from and what form will that critique take? And what will be used to judge students' entry to or membership status in the discipline? Within thin theories of curriculum, most of the writing considers curriculum in terms of the explicit voice of the ideology (the content that is formally relayed) rather than the implicit structure of the academic discourse itself. Central to this structuring is evaluation – or the determination of what counts as successful mastery of discourse.

CHANGE IN EDUCATIONAL CODE: A THEORETICAL FRAMING

Bernstein (1990, 1996) understands curriculum as an instantiation of power. Classification refers to the accretion within, or assertion of, boundaries. Boundaries can be thought of as strong where subject disciplines are bounded from one another and the contents are well defined, separate and highly *specialised*. Where classification is weak, boundaries between subject disciplines, or between the everyday world or world of work, are blurred. Power is central to the idea of classification because there are boundary maintainers who establish and defend boundaries. Mostly, they operate overtly in a strongly classified curriculum and power is explicit, while power is more masked or covert under conditions of a weakly classified curriculum.

Bernstein introduces the concept of framing which, like classification, can be strong or weak, and refers to the control that transmitters (teachers, lecturers) and acquirers (learners, students) have over different dimensions of the pedagogy. These are the selection, sequencing, pacing and evaluation of pedagogic knowledge, as well as the nature of the social relations established in the pedagogic space (more hierarchical, strongly framed, or more personalised and negotiated, weakly framed). Classification (power) operates at the level of curriculum, and control, or his term 'framing', operates at the level of pedagogy.

In Bernstein's (1975) original formation of classification and framing, he was interested in the shift from the old (elite) strongly classified and framed code in the United Kingdom to a more (progressive) weakly classified and framed code at the level of schooling. He understood this shift as a change in education knowledge codes – from the strong classification and instantiation of power of the dominant curriculum to a weakly classified code with more diffuse, implicit enactments of power. The implications of the change in code for knowledge, curriculum, pedagogy and the system as a whole, including ideas of assessment and the production of texts, were extensive. In South Africa an analogous change in code was the move from the last apartheid curriculum to Curriculum 2005, the first post-apartheid curriculum for the schooling system, which presented an interesting (though in the long term, devastating) experiment in a total shift in all aspects of the code from a strongly classified and framed modality to a radically weakly classified and framed code.

A strongly classified and framed code entails strong boundaries between formal knowledge and everyday experience or cultural expression, and a more weakly classified and framed code entails more open exchange between formal knowledge and everyday lived experience and know-how. Different codes have implications for the formation of educational identities, for the ways in which consciousness is shaped: robust subject identities in the strongly classified and framed code, and more tentatively defined academic identities in weaker forms, where there is a far greater range in the privileged ways of organising experience and making meaning than those shaped by academic knowledge alone. For Bernstein, education is the shaping of consciousness or the shaping of an academic identity.

In the 'pedagogic device' Bernstein (1996: 39) provides an account of how knowledge generated through research (or elsewhere) is transformed into the curriculum knowledge that is taught at the level of the lecture theatre, tutorial group or classroom. Research knowledge passes through different levels with sets of rules as it becomes transformed into pedagogic communication. Classification and framing describe these transformations at the different levels. At the first level, of production of knowledge, knowledge is established in disciplines. This is where boundary maintainers (or researchers, academics, processes of peer review) establish classifications between different disciplines and work at the limits of these boundaries – engaging in the 'unthinkable' (new knowledge). Curriculum is a selection from this knowledge that is produced, and involves a *recontextualising* of disciplinary knowledge for the purposes of transmission. In other words, knowledge is selected, reordered and refocused to create curriculum. Finally, in the field of reproduction (where 'evaluative rules' operate), knowledge is transmitted and acquired in the lecture hall, classroom or other setting. It is at this level that 'what counts as knowledge' is either implicit or made explicit to learners/students. At all levels, there is play of ideology: in how boundaries are established, in what is selected for curriculum and in how knowledge is taught and evaluated in the teaching of that knowledge. Power and control run through the pedagogic device, understood in terms of classification and framing.

Crucially, Bernstein contends that evaluation 'condenses the device' (1996: 50). It is at the level of pedagogy, or evaluative rules, that the work of transforming knowledge into acquisition is accomplished, deferred or terminated. He calls the evaluative rules the 'ruler of consciousness', for this is where we can measure whether mastery is attained. As above, the nature of the educational code, the strength or weakness of classification and framing, has implications for the way in which identity is constituted. It is against evaluative rules that mastery, or the accomplishment of an academic identity, is judged, in the form of right or wrong in an exam, a first or a fail in an assignment, a nod or shake of the head in a tutorial room. To be engaged in education is to be engaged in evaluation.

If classification tells us about the boundaries of knowledge and the limits of possibility for the kind of educational identity that may formed, it only tells us about the knowledge. But there are sets of social relations, practices and social arrangements that institutionalise and legitimise these limits. Paul Dowling (2009: 81) introduces the notion of institutionalisation, which functions at a lower level of abstraction than classification, and refers to 'the extent to which a practice exhibits an empirical regularity that marks it out as recognisably distinct from other practices'. Specialised academic disciplines in this conception become 'strategic spaces whereby subjects are positioned and practices distributed'. In this way, Dowling, for us, describes the social relations of the processes of induction into academic knowledge. Classification is about the knowledge relations and boundaries of possibility; institutionalisation extends this to the social relations of knowledge production and reproduction. Classification tells us what's in and what's out of a discipline. Institutionalisation tells us who belongs or has claim to that disciplinary space.

In what follows, we consider a debate on decolonising Science, which took place at the University of Cape Town (UCT) in relation to classification, framing and institutionalisation; and the ways in which the positions and arguments of the main speaker, Professor Chandra K. Raju can be read in these terms. The purpose is to understand the nature of the educational code and the nature of the challenge that is made to that code in the seminar – taken as an example of a decolonial challenge to curriculum.

THE CURIOUS CASE OF PROFESSOR RAJU

In November 2017, a controversial panel discussion was held at UCT. Professor C.K. Raju was invited by the Deputy Vice-Chancellor for Transformation, Professor Loretta Ferris and UCT's Curriculum Change Working Group to speak on 'decolonising science'. Raju's reputation preceded his presentation at the seminar and, prior to the debate, a number of articles ran in the local press concerning his standing in the scientific community (GroundUp 2017), calling him a 'crank' and a 'conspiracy theorist'. A number of members of staff within the university took offence at the invitation, and the dean of science at the time refused to participate on the panel.

What was offensive to these staff members, on the one hand, and what did those promoting the debate condone, on the other? What was Raju actually arguing in his talk? While Raju's presentation was peppered with errors,[1] several fringe ideas and the trivialising of important issues, these weaknesses should not entirely detract from what he was actually arguing for or making claims to. By attempting to understand his talk in terms of arguments around the structuring of knowledge and the structuring of social relations, we hope in this and other cases to gain a clearer curriculum perspective on the terms of the debate.

The seminar, which we take as a case study in debates on the decolonisation of the curriculum, consisted of a presentation by Raju that lasted 43 minutes. This was followed by three responses, from a mathematician (Dr Henri Laurie), a philosopher of mathematics (Professor Bernhard Weiss), and a curriculum scholar (Professor Leslie Le Grange). Questions were then taken from the floor and Professor Raju responded to the panellists and to these questions. We included both Raju's presentation and his responses as sources of data for our analysis. We also included the paper that was distributed in advance to the respondents, summarising the talk. Although the talk was ostensibly about science, much of the presentation focused on mathematics, which is the focus of this chapter as well.

In his presentation, Raju touched on a number of issues and made a number of key points. The first was the idea that science (as well as its foundations of mathematical reasoning) is based on a false history, and therefore the entire body of work or discipline of science needs to be interrogated, especially in relation to a purported basis in Christian theology and metaphysics. The second issue that Raju raised was that institutionalised mathematics is 'formal mathematics', which, he argued, differed from the 'normal' mathematics that prevailed for thousands of years prior to the institutionalising of mathematics. Formal mathematics is deductive mathematics, as opposed to empirical, inductive, 'normal' mathematics. The third issue that he raised was in relation to the ways in which science and mathematics are institutionalised, in particular in relation to peer review, publication and reputation. We take each issue in turn below, with an interest in how the issues suggest a shift in classification and framing, and what the issues around institutionalisation and identity formation are.

WHOSE MATHEMATICS IS IT ANYWAY?

Raju's first main assertion was that the history and philosophy of Western science and mathematics suggest that these sciences originated in Europe, and this idea has become entrenched in the academy and in schools. It is, he argued, 'a false history'. It is false because many of the ideas in mathematics and science originated in India centuries ago and were stolen and changed by the West. And it is false because there is scant evidence to support the idea that some of the earliest known mathematicians (for example, Euclid) were in fact European or even men. For Raju, the consequence of this 'false history' that has come to be institutionalised in the Western academy is that the contribution of earlier Indian mathematicians and scientists has been written out of the history and their voices and practices have been silenced and marginalised.

In particular, for Raju, the centrality of empirical investigations and demonstrations and numerical solutions (as opposed to abstracted, algebraic ones) that were a feature of mathematics developed in India, is now seen as antithetical to the practice of mathematics, given the strongly institutionalised formalism and use of logico-deductive methods of proof in mathematics today. In other words, he claims that because this earlier Indian history has been 'forgotten/lost', formal mathematics today is considered purely 'anti-empirical'.[2]

What are the implications of these claims? It is not evident that Raju suggests a different mathematics in relation to the past, aside from the idea that it should be first and foremost empirical (see below). Although he questions the historical origins of the ideas, he is not fundamentally proposing a shift or a rupture in mathematics as an institutionalised discipline. This was clear in his response to a question posed by one respondent, Le Grange, who asked whether there was a space for indigenous knowledge within the science curriculum; whether science could be multicultural rather than universal (he did not elaborate on this). Raju dismissed this appeal to culture outright, saying that his concern was with Western science, 'And I am suggesting that there is a whole lot of dogma there which needs to be eliminated'.

While Raju challenges *who* produced the mathematics in the first place, he does not seek a reconfiguration of the boundaries of mathematics in relation to cultural expression (multiculturalism) or other disciplines. Rather, he asks for a more accurate representation of the progenitors of the discipline and the history of mathematics. The implication, therefore, is not a change in the fundamental classification of mathematics, but a challenge to ownership and membership of mathematics as a discipline (that is, that which is dictated by the 'dogma' in mathematics).

THE DOGMA IN THE DETAIL

Raju's other historical claim is around the influence of Christian theological dogma at the time of the development of mathematics, resulting in the adoption of a particular metaphysics of infinity. He claims this metaphysic of infinity is intimately related to the Christian metaphysic of eternity that was dominant in Europe at that time. For Raju, it is the theological foundations, and what he calls church dogma in Europe at the time, that could give rise to Newton's 'Laws of Nature', influencing not only the calculus that was developed with its notions of infinity, but also the formalisation of mathematics into a logico-deductive system. All these developments, he claimed, pushed empirical observations and demonstrations and numerical solutions out of formal mathematics, and relied on a metaphysics of 'superstition' (for example, the vanishing point, infinity), and on proofs that could not be refuted by observation – similar to items of church dogma or faith. Raju argued that the consequence is that Western science and mathematics has been built on the reputability of its authors and adherence to logico-deductive reasoning and proofs, rather than refutability of its proofs through empirical observations. For him, bringing the empirical back into mathematics is key, making the refutability of proofs through numerical solutions central to the practice of mathematics.

Raju's repeated reference to the history and philosophy of science and mathematics is to make claims about the silencing of non-European histories of mathematics and science, and about how dominant thought and practices in mathematics influenced by church dogma (for example, logico-deductive methods; non-empirical demonstrations; infinity, and so on) dominated the field of production, excluding alternative thoughts and practices in mathematics (for example, empirical observations, numerical solutions). For Raju, decolonising science and mathematics is to interrogate and challenge how these dominant thoughts and practices were produced and reclaim the 'lost' histories. Again, however, the foundations of mathematics are not challenged.[3] Mathematics as a strongly classified and institutionalised discipline remains undisturbed, despite questions about its historical production.

THE (NOT SO?) NEW NORMAL

One of Raju's central concerns is the distinction he sets up between 'formal' mathematics, which is anti-empirical and deductive, and 'normal' mathematics, which is empirical and relies on inductive reasoning and numerical solutions. For him, formal mathematics is exclusionary, and normal mathematics makes mathematics 'easy'. He asserts that mathematics needs to be derived from the real world of mathematical problems, the context of application, as it was developed originally in relation to demands from agricultural problems and the challenges of navigation.[4]

Raju's concerns were clearest, perhaps, when he addressed the issue of pedagogy directly, in his response to the panellists and to questions posed in the seminar. Here his emphasis is on relevance:

> So we are doing it [teaching mathematics in the context of engineering] with very clear and pragmatic goals of improving the applicability of mathematics, improving the widest calculus without limits, because you can solve harder problems. That is the logic that engineers understand. You can solve harder problems that are not solved in normal calculus courses. … I am very clearly teaching in an engineering college, they are not interested in philosophy, they are not interested in history, they are only interested in the practical applications of mathematics for engineering.

Raju suggests a weakening of framing over selection, such that contents selected for inclusion in the pedagogy are *relevant* to the context of practice (engineering). The question, again, is how new and radical is this? Reneé Smit (2017) argues that there has been a long-standing distinction between science and engineering, whereby the former strives for predictive power through its theories and models, whereas the predictive aspect of a theory in an engineering context is only of value in relation to problem-solving or the function of an artefact in engineering. The issue of relevance was also referred to tangentially by Weiss on the panel, when he argued that there are different ways in which a cultural setting *may* influence a discipline, some of those being pernicious and some guiding the discipline to greater relevance. He specified:

> Relevance, in a distinctively cultural sense, may be more or less of an imperative for a discipline depending on how much it looks beyond itself for direction. Pure mathematics throws up particular problems for the decolonial enterprise because it aims at truth; it doesn't explicitly aim to be a form of cultural expression; *and* because it pretends not to look beyond disciplinary boundaries in determining its own direction.

The well-entrenched tradition of ethnomathematics (see D'Ambrosio 1985) does seek direction from local cultural contexts for the learning, teaching and understanding of mathematics. Common examples are Mozambican basket-weaving (Gerdes 1985) and Bengali boat-builders (Mukhopadhyay 2013). But the broader issue is around the addition of contents (also raised earlier in relation to the literature) that doesn't change the basis for evaluation. Raju is not shifting the goals for mathematics towards 'the upliftment of the soul' or 'to make man more virtuous', as he remarks. He is concerned with the practical value of mathematics, which is evaluated in terms of mathematics: students are engaged in solving practical problems, and without reliance on formalised mathematics their proofs can be refuted by empirical observations and numerical solutions.[5]

SMOKE AND MIRRORS

The panellists Laurie and Weiss both claimed that the history and philosophy of mathematics did not have direct implications for the knowledge and practice of mathematics as a discipline in the university nor its teaching in classrooms. Raju's claims suggest that going back to antique history and philosophy is key to opening up the boundary/ strongly institutionalised practices and knowledge in mathematics because it will elevate empirical and numerical approaches into the practice of mathematics and challenge the dependence on formalised mathematics and logico-deductive reasoning and proofs. What is this 'opening up'? Is it a strategy of questioning and positioning or of rupture or replacement? It would seem that Raju is seeking to pluralise epistemic positions rather than to replace one with another.

Raju's arguments about mathematics hinge on the strongly institutionalised formalisation of mathematics, not on the numerical foundations of mathematics, nor calculation procedures. Raju does not call for everything we know about mathematics to be thrown out, but rather calls for a clearer historical record of the genesis of mathematical ideas on the one hand, and on the other hand challenges the notion that what counts as 'pure mathematics' is only that which aligns with the form and practice of the formalised logico-deductive method. For Raju, mathematics and science curricula should reflect empirical situations or real-world problems that students are engaged in when 'doing mathematics'.

While initially presented as strongly and weakly classified and framed ideal-type educational codes, Bernstein's later work indicates that classification and framing values can vary independently of one another. In the Raju case, we find that classification remains strong – the challenge is to framing, in particular around selection. His concern is for relevance (in relation to engineering pedagogy). This appears similar to many academic development courses – there is less a challenge to the classification, but rather a 'complementary' or plural epistemological position – adding on to existing offerings alongside a strongly classified knowledge field (Morreira 2017). Or the focus is on framing over pacing, for example, the four-year degree programme, instituting a repair system that largely leaves the strong classification of the code intact (Luckett and Shay 2017).

WHY CAN'T I SEE MYSELF?

Raju's presentation was interspersed with references to issues around the institutionalisation of mathematics. He cited his engagement with prominent scientists, including

Karl Popper, as well as his battles with journal editors around attribution of his ideas. He talked at length about his struggles for recognition, despite an array of publications with reputable publishers. He caricatured the positions of prominent mathematicians and derided established ideas. At one point he took issue with the major cosmologist Frank Tipler:

> This is what I said to students today. Why don't you challenge Stephen Hawking? Why don't you challenge what this Tipler says, who has published six papers in *Nature*. And what does he say? He says that Judeo-Christian theology is true and can be proved on the strength of present-day physics. So this is what he said. So this is his book *Physics of Immortality* about 'modern cosmology, God and the resurrection of the dead'. And this is the table of contents: 'When will the dead be raised, why will the dead be raised?' And why don't you laugh at it the way you laughed at that lady who didn't know any science?

Here Raju equated Tipler to the statements of a second-year social science student in the infamous 'Science Must Fall' seminar at UCT, where she suggested that science be scrapped because it was based on Western modernity and failed to describe truths such as being able to use 'black magic' (witchcraft) to strike someone with lightning.

In Raju's case, we may dismiss his claim to disciplinary membership, given his cynical tactics of derision, caricature and misrepresentation and the ludicrous nature of some of his claims. But Raju is raging against the rules of membership (within mathematics; within engineering), asking why he is not recognised. Identity, we indicated earlier, entails both a knowledge relation and the formation of consciousness, and a social relation, which entails acquiring a position and claim to the discipline. Raju's torment stems from his conviction that he has grasped the evaluative rules (he has been published and he can solve engineering problems using numerical solutions in mathematics), but he still has not gained membership – he is not recognised as a mathematician.

This issue of membership appears in the end to dominate Raju's contribution to the decolonial debate: the wounding of exclusion when the perception is that the knowledge of the discipline has been grasped and membership is consequently merited or earned. We recall the case of the murder of a mathematics professor, Brian Hahn, at the University of Cape Town by a former doctoral student and assistant lecturer whose contract had not been made into a permanent academic position. The merits of the defence and prosecution in the case aside, a response years after the incident was telling. An academic, Professor Pumla Gqola, asked whether the incident was not a reflection of some other deep flaw in the nature of our relations as a community across race, gender and student and staff lines: 'A few years ago, a PhD candidate (it may have been a postdoc) repeatedly hit a white professor with an umbrella. While the media and UCT officially expressed shock, Black people who had graduated from UCT with a postgraduate degree or (had) worked at UCT expressed shock only that it had taken this long and one incident' (Crowe 2016).

Perhaps one of the difficulties around institutionalisation and rules of membership is the instability, whoever you are, of being in a discipline and in the place of the yet-to-be-thought. It is objectively unstable, it is where the unknown is to be produced and therefore those on the inside are defensive, and responsive to threats to the boundary. Those entering are anxious to know the rules and meet the criteria. Where is Raju? He is described on the Internet as 'a computer scientist, mathematician, educator, physicist and polymath researcher'. He is located in an engineering college, but seeks recognition in all these listed fields. In the course of the seminar, it appears that Raju's call for change relates more to membership than to curriculum. Essentially, his is a challenge to the ontological premise of mathematics, not its epistemology. He makes no case around a change in the evaluative rules for mathematics. They apply in the same way whether the mathematics is formal or 'normal'.

CONCLUSION

Recall that earlier we noted that Bernstein (1996) argues that evaluative rules condense the process whereby knowledge becomes pedagogic communication in classrooms, lecture theatres and tutorials. These rules refer both to control over selection, pacing, criteria and the social relation between lecturer and student (framing), *as well as* to the knowledge transacted (classification). It would seem that much of the discourse around decolonising the curriculum focuses on framing and relations of control over the selection of what is to be taught, or its pacing or the social relation between teacher and taught. Less consideration is given to the evaluative rules (which concern classification as well). These evaluative rules distil the social-formative dimension of knowledge (Muller and Hoadley 2010) and shape what counts in the end. 'What counts' goes beyond listing new topics in a curriculum. 'What counts' in this sense is not just what you know, but how you demonstrate what you know. Evaluative rules shape what questions get asked, as well as how questions are answered.

Current debates on decolonising the curriculum as read through the Raju debate and the nascent body of writing around decolonial curriculum appear to be tinkering with framing, or to be less generous, producing pedagogies that bluff their way to the end until strong evaluative rules kick in and students find failure after all. This feels not dissimilar to the most recent instalment in the Raju affair. After considerable local contestation following the seminar, including the argument by a professor in the mathematics department that what Raju was advocating in his decolonising mathematics project amounted to a 'neo-Bantu Education' (GroundUp 2017), an abridged version of the seminar was published online five months later (UCT 2018). Here the argument was made: 'Whether we agree with it or not is not really the point. The important thing is that it opens up the scope for conversation'. It appears, at this juncture, that the point of debate is not to clarify the evaluative rules but to valorise the open without the horizon of the closed. Whether this openness and instability will be a necessary step towards decolonising the curriculum or a permanent state, time will tell.

The current, dominant strongly classified and framed code in the university offers strong specialisation into existing knowledge forms and strong academic identities. The stakes in the debates around decolonising curriculum are high because the debate is around how consciousness is shaped. This is the knowledge relation. But there is also the social relation. Established classifications exclude at the same time they include, and membership rules are not always available, even to those who claim mastery over the evaluative rules. While he somewhat cynically co-opts the decolonial debate for his own ends, this is Raju's torment: I am in, but I am not recognised. The decolonial curriculum challenge is two-fold: the classification of new forms of curriculum knowledge, and their institutionalisation with new sets of membership rules.

Current debates in decolonising the curriculum appear to focus on shifts in content and its organisation, and shifts in pedagogy, especially its social relations and pacing. There is a silence, however, on the evaluative rules and how changes in these are imagined. What counts in the end remains undisturbed. The very difficult task of decolonising the curriculum, for reimagining our human purpose, and the implications for knowledge recontextualisation and reproduction is for now unrealised.

NOTES

1   George Joseph (1991, 2009) is a historian of mathematics, and provides a comprehensive history of non-European roots of mathematics that clearly refutes some of the historical claims Raju makes in the seminar.

2   While Laurie agreed that there is a lack of evidence for some of the historical claims around the origins of some of the earliest mathematicians, in his response he disputed the claim that later European mathematics 'stole' and 'changed' the mathematics from earlier Indian mathematicians. He questioned the claim that the mathematics used to develop calculus was 'imported' from India and that Indian texts were suppressed. Laurie argued that the majority of mathematics developed in Europe much later, so calculus used today came much later in Europe and does not go back directly to foundations of calculus in Indian mathematics.

3   Raju is not, for example, suggesting a new number system or new ways of counting or different rules for numerical or algebraic operations. What he challenges is 'how we do mathematics' and what counts as doing 'proper mathematics'. Raju argues that the formalisation and logico-deductive methods privileged in mathematics have come to mean that empirical observations and numerical solutions do not count as 'doing mathematics'.

4   Raju's issue with formal mathematics is also that it is possible to have computational propositions that create inconsistencies when inserted into so-called deductive mathematics. It is not actually clear that Raju would have a problem with 'logico-deductive approaches' in general. His objection is to the possibility of starting from false premises and deriving false conclusions.

5   Weiss disputed Raju's assertion that formalism in mathematics necessarily renders mathematics a metaphysics. For Weiss, formalisation in mathematics was a way of making the concepts in mathematics explicit, and he links this to the universality of mathematics; so too with the role of proofs. Laurie also challenges Raju's idea that formal mathematics is anti-empirical, exemplifying his argument by way of the development of cell phones and computers out of the calculations based on formal logic.

REFERENCES

Badat, Saleem. 2017. 'Trepidation, Longing, and Belonging: Liberating the Curriculum at Universities in South Africa'. Lecture presented in the Public Lecture Series on Curriculum Transformation Matters: The Decolonial Turn, University of Pretoria, 10 April.

Bernstein, Basil. 1975. *Class, Codes and Control.* Vol. 3, *Towards a Theory of Educational Transmissions.* London: Routledge and Kegan Paul.

Bernstein, Basil. 1990. *Class, Codes and Control.* Vol. 4, *The Structuring of Pedagogic Discourse.* London: Routledge.

Bernstein, Basil. 1996. *Pedagogy, Symbolic Control and Identity: Theory, Research, Critique.* London: Taylor & Francis.

Crowe, Tim. 2016. 'Getting Away with Murder'. *Politicsweb,* 29 June. http://www.politicsweb.co.za/opinion/getting-away-with-murder.

D'Ambrosio, Ubiratan. 1985. 'Ethnomathematics and its Place in the History and Pedagogy of Mathematics'. *For the Learning of Mathematics* 5 (1): 44–48.

Dowling, Paul. 2009. *Sociology as Method: Departures from the Forensics of Culture, Text and Knowledge.* Rotterdam: Sense Publishers.

Gerdes, Paulus. 1985. 'Conditions and Strategies for Emancipatory Mathematics Education in Undeveloped Countries'. *For the Learning of Mathematics* 5 (1): 15–20.

Grosfoguel, Ramón. 2007. 'The Epistemic Decolonial Turn: Beyond Political-Economy Paradigms'. *Cultural Studies* 21 (2–3): 211–223. doi: 10.1080/09502380601162514.

GroundUp. 2017. 'UCT Invites "Conspiracy Theorist" to Talk about Decolonisation of Science'. *GroundUp,* 28 September. https://www.groundup.org.za/article/uct-invites-conspiracy-theorist-talk-about-decolonisation-science/.

Jansen, Jonathan D. 2017. *As by Fire: The End of the South African University.* Cape Town: Tafelberg.

Joseph, George Gheverghese. 1991. *The Crest of the Peacock: Non-European Roots of Mathematics.* London: I.B. Tauris.

Joseph, George Gheverghese. 2009. *A Passage to Infinity: Medieval Indian Mathematics from Kerala and Its Impact.* Thousand Oaks, CA: SAGE Publications.

Leibowitz, Brenda. 2017. 'Cognitive Justice and the Higher Education Curriculum'. *Journal of Education* 68: 93–111. http://www.scielo.org.za/pdf/jed/n68/06.pdf.

Luckett, Kathy, and Suellen Shay. 2017. 'Reframing the Curriculum: A Transformative Approach'. *Critical Studies in Education.* doi: 10.1080/17508487.2017.1356341.

Mamdani, Mahmood. 2017. 'Decolonising the Post-colonial University'. T.B. Davie Memorial Lecture. Cape Town, 22 August.

Mbembe, Achille. 2015. 'Decolonizing Knowledge and the Question of the Archive'. Presentation at the University of the Witwatersrand, Johannesburg, 22 April. https://wiser.wits.ac.za/system/files/Achille%20Mbembe%20-%20Decolonizing%20Knowledge%20and%20the%20Question%20of%20the%20Archive.pdf.

Morreira, Shannon. 2017. 'Steps towards Decolonial Higher Education in Southern Africa? Epistemic Disobedience in the Humanities'. *Journal of Asian and African Studies* 52 (3): 287–301. doi: 10.1177/0021909615577499.

Msila, Vuyisile and Mishack Thiza Gumbo. 2016. *Africanising the Curriculum: Indigenous Perspectives and Theories*. Stellenbosch: SUN Press.

Mukhopadhyay, Swapna. 2013. 'The Mathematical Practices of Those without Power'. In *Proceedings of the Seventh International Mathematics Education and Society Conference, Cape Town, 2–7 April*, edited by Marot Berger, Karin Brodie, Vera Frith, and Kate le Roux, 94–102. Cape Town: MES 7.

Muller, Johan and Ursula Hoadley. 2010. 'Pedagogy and Moral Order'. In *Toolkits, Translation Devices, and Conceptual Accounts: Essays on Basil Bernstein's Sociology of Knowledge*, edited by Parlo Singh, Alan R. Sadovnik and Susan F. Semel, 161–176. New York: Peter Lang.

Nyamupangedengu, Eunice. 2017. 'Investigating Factors That Impact the Success of Students in a Higher Education Classroom: A Case Study'. *Journal of Education* 68: 113–130.

Sayed, Yusuf, Shireen Motala and Nimi Hoffman. 2017. 'Decolonising Initial Teacher Education in South African Universities: More Than an Event'. *Journal of Education* 68: 59–91. http://www .scielo.org.za/pdf/jed/n68/05.pdf.

Science Must Fall. 2016. 'UCT Science Faculty Meets with "Fallists"'. YouTube, 12 October. https://www. youtube.com/watch?v=C9SiRNibD14.

Smit, Reneé. 2017. 'The Nature of Engineering and Science Knowledge in Curriculum: A Case Study in Thermodynamics'. PhD thesis, University of Cape Town.

UCT (University of Cape Town). 2017. 'Decolonising Science Panel Discussion: Part 1'. YouTube, 21 September. https://www.youtube.com/watch?v=ckbzKfRIi6Q.

UCT (University of Cape Town). 2018. 'UCT Panel Discussion on Decolonising Science'. YouTube, 2 March. https://www.youtube.com/watch?v=vWdqR-z6jIc.

DOING DECOLONISATION

3

CHAPTER 6

Scaling Decolonial Consciousness? The Re-invention of 'Africa' in a Neoliberal University

Jess Auerbach, Open University of Mauritius,
Mlungisi Dlamini and Anonymous[1]

WHAT HAS BEEN AT STAKE

Imagine three moments in the same room. The first was at sunset, in January 2017 during the very early days of establishing a social science programme at a newly established institution of higher education, referred to here as Institution Q, located in Mauritius. It was evening; the programme had run for about three weeks; and we had finally secured lab space in which we planned to develop what we imagined would become one of the most serious social science degree programmes in Africa, building on an institution-wide programme of 'African Studies' that had also just been launched. Light from the setting sun poured into the room, and our expectation and trust in each other, our students and what we could build felt golden. The second moment was almost a year later: two cohorts of social science students had collectively created a mural in which they represented Africa in a way that they felt captured the nuances of the continent. This mural stood alongside a 'Wall of African Languages' where students from across the institution wrote expressions in their home languages, representing words spoken in almost 40 different countries, to add to prevalent institutional discourses in English. In the third moment, the room had been cleared and was about to be redeveloped as a corporate space.

This chapter was written at a moment when Institution Q confirmed a new strategy that shifts it away from established notions of the vision and mission of 'universities' (see Davidson 2017; Kosslyn, Nelson and Kerrey 2017) and firmly towards what its founder describes as a 'leadership institution.' Prior to this shift, Institution Q staff living and working on the Indian Ocean island of Mauritius numbered just over 100, only a small proportion of whom were Mauritian. Most had come to 'the island' out of a sense of alignment with the broad mission laid out during a TED (derived from Technology, Entertainment and Design) Global talk in 2014 and on other online platforms. The broad message of the online messaging was that by 2060 this organisation would have trained 'x million leaders' through what was then envisioned as a chain of universities spread across the African continent – the first of which was to be located in Mauritius. As might be expected of a space where so many had gathered to create transformative social change, there were multiple and competing visions of what it might take to train these 'leaders', and indeed, what the term 'leadership' even meant.

Institution Q is a private for-profit business that generates revenue through fees and investment, as well as its own financing scheme, an Income Sharing Agreement (ISA). This ISA is self-styled 'innovative tuition financing model' that claims to ensure higher education will become accessible to thousands of students across Africa. It is need-based aid, and awards funds to allow a student to attend Institution Q and, in exchange, the student pays back a percentage of their income for a set period of time. Beyond fees and investment, Institution Q does not receive any government subsidies, nor is it supported by research-generated grants. It is emphatically not a research institution. It is a 'start-up university' and was initially referred to as that, with more emphasis on the start-up than the university and eventually 'university' omitted from public discourse almost entirely. This ambiguity created a cultural tension amongst staff, many of whom had joined precisely because it *was* a university, particularly those responsible for academic delivery.

The new direction developed at Institution Q over the course of 2017 and early 2018 resolved many of these tensions, and has given Institution Q a clear identity going forward– a direction in which 'scale' and 'impact' are prioritised over and above the 'traditional' goals of higher education, particularly public critical reflection on social orders and their transformation. In so doing Institution Q's decision closes off the possibility of the goal that the three founding faculty who write this chapter collectively imagined. We envisioned and worked towards shaping an institution in which a critical and knowledge-based engagement with 'Africa' truly was front and centre, epistemologically, ontologically, socially, politically and economically. This, we hoped, would be a base from which our students might be equipped one day to 'transform the continent', rather than unquestioningly replicate economic models and practices with a record of disservice to the best aspirations of African peoples.

This chapter was written as reflection on what we had done. It was formulated and submitted while we all worked at Institution Q, and finalised after we had all resigned. We emphasise here that we hold no ill-will towards the institution, but rather want to offer a critical contribution to educators who hope to move the needle on curriculum design that places 'Africa' at the centre of student learning. The 'Africa' that we envision and have worked towards is one that is historicised, nuanced and informed by insights from many localities and different ontological traditions. This stands in contrast to more popular narratives of 'Africa' that often reflect the imagination of the Global North. This Northern imagination was often and uncritically reproduced at Institution Q, essentialising and homogenising a continent of some 1.3 billion people.

This chapter is written in three parts. We each brought different perspectives to begin with, yet shared enough common ground to find in one another a solace and intellectual camaraderie that sustained the scholarly and pedagogical project through its arc – however imperfect that arc proved to be. We were all trained, to some extent, in anthropology and the critical study of that canon. Mlungisi Dlamini is from the Kingdom of eSwatini and was responsible for the design and development of a programme called 'Africas Core', which, for the period of his stay, was offered to all Institution Q students. He discusses the discursive place of that course here. Jess Auerbach is South African and worked with two colleagues (not named in order to protect institutional identity) to develop the social science programme. In this chapter she explores broad institutional receptivity/ fear around the notion of decoloniality, which was introduced at inception but met with significant resistance – not from students, but from senior management. Nothing will be said of the third author. We present our separate narratives below, before assessing their converging theoretical approaches and findings.

THE VOICE OF ANONYMOUS: AFRICA RISING FROM WHERE, AND TO WHAT ENDS?

The narrative of 'a rising Africa', discussed in detail from corporate, investment and consultancy spaces (Gelb 2000; Roxburgh et al. 2010; Sizemore 2012; UNECA 2012; Ernst & Young 2014; Bhorat and Tarp 2016) and critiqued from a variety of perspectives (Ayers 2013; Bush 2013; Mkandawire 2014; Sylla 2014; Taylor 2016; Beresford 2016; Wengraf 2018) sits at the centre of Institution Q's institutional decision-makers' conception and construction of Africa. These mindsets and approaches were/are captured in the 'five values' declared by Institution Q, which were displayed on signboards on office walls and at times on the website (see Lyons, 2017 for an informative discussion on start-up institutional values). With these logics and values working both implicitly and explicitly, choices were made and mindsets adopted to achieve the larger vision and support the rhetoric at play.

The urgency of Africa's supposed 'challenge' from the impending population boom has been summarised in a new slogan of '6000 days', that is until 2035 when Africa is expected by some analysts to have the largest workforce in the world. This, according to the founder, creates an absolute urgency to the entrepreneurial task of 'impact'. It justifies fast-tracking scaling efforts to other countries and across sectors, and actively encourages and praises students who move 'beyond theory' into 'action' by founding initiatives that are celebrated in social media marketing campaigns and public speeches. The messaging is that the wild, unpredictable and at times dangerous nature of doing business in Africa, combined with the static and bureaucratic nature of African states, is the basis for the argument that Africa needs these self-styled 'maverick' people (staff and students) and institutions (Sizemore 2012; Swaniker 2014; Probyn 2017).

These individuals, it is hoped, can be trained to circumvent, subvert and/or actively remove barriers such as onerous and complex regulations, and even (it is implied but never explained how) corruption and clientelism. These barriers might be defined by borders, or based on localised identities inconvenient to the entrepreneurial consumer. Moreover, 'academic theory' as opposed to '21st Century Learning' (Trilling and Fadel 2012) is assumed to not produce the agility and flexibility necessary to 'do hard things', to quote a maxim often heard in the corridors of Institution Q. These barriers would otherwise make it impossible for entrepreneurial leaders to have the supposedly equal playing field and openness required for integration into regional and global systems, a prerequisite for Africa's presumed rise and progress (Ernst & Young 2014).

These barriers are to be overcome using 'modern' tools, techniques and instruments that are 'global', 'reputable', 'replicable', 'relevant' and 'productive'. There is emphasis on knowledge produced from globally recognised, reputable and/or innovative institutions (read: usually not African) as captured by staff educational backgrounds from institutions with top continental and international rankings, as displayed on Institution Q's website. The website declares that this knowledge is curated and disseminated using 'the most innovative and effective methods [of education].' Significantly, the choice of English as the lingua franca and language of instruction for close to 1000 staff and students across the Mauritian and second campus (located in mainland Africa), who collectively represent close to 50 countries, strengthens, rather than disrupts, existing hierarchical flows of capital, networks and information, to and from dominant sites of global knowledge production and control – largely, at Institution Q, plugged into Silicon Valley, California.

The seemingly transformative/innovative statements made by the Institution Q publicity machine argue that desired social change will not come from what it calls ivory-tower institutions, but through massive social change driven by entrepreneurship. In this vision, 'Africa' is almost always described as one homogenous space, reifying an understanding of Africa that continues to be informed by a Western lens and that leaves no room for the transformation of political, social or economic structures except by and congruent with the venture-capital driven 'entrepreneurialism'. These narratives enable (a) continued inequality and exclusion in the form of fragmented class structures of post-independence Africa (that is, they focus on elites and expanding the middle class with little or no consideration of those 'at the bottom'), and (b) continued focus on 'progress' in Western terms, which here are largely determined by economic balances (Bayart 2000; Taylor 2016). These take for granted that 'Africa' should one day 'catch up' with the consumption levels of the wealthiest enclaves of the world rather than asking any critical questions related to this enterprise, for Africans, humanity, or the planet.

Creating and propagating curriculum, relationships and 'culture' that focus on remaking Africa with 'entrepreneurship at the core' assumes and produces a one-dimensional 'Africa' where the multiplicity of such 'African' contexts is erased and rarely considered important. The students produced by this approach are supposed to become willing workers in like-minded institutions, 'culture carriers' who will teach the 'Institution Q-way' to those unfortunate enough to have not yet been exposed. These like-minded institutions are deliberately cultivated. In the context of Institution Q, one of the parallel ventures, here called the IQ Network (IQN), provides a space in which such institutions gather, and through which personal relationships are curated in the broad service of the entrepreneurial African vision. Building and maintaining a 'personal brand' that 'sells well' in this space is seen as an essential component of undergraduate life, and the career development unit routinely sends out emails reminding students of this fact. The effect is a flattening definition of excellence that appears to be based on an understanding of a 'rising', 'modern' and 'innovative' Africa that has open trade borders, less regulation, and ease of business facilitated by a lingua franca, personal friendships and a common set of 'values'. Any thinking outside this particular vision is rapidly shut down, especially if it occurs on social media, when students are asked to take into consideration the sensitivity of the brand that feeds them.

The question is, in this vision of Africa, who is left out? And the answer is everyone who does not subscribe – quite literally in many cases – to the platform. Or, to put it more colloquially, everyone who does not or cannot drink the Kool-Aid. This is a circle of leadership that exists because it has proclaimed itself to do so. Companies who choose to become part of the IQN and associated spin-offs find themselves with a ready group of pre-trained workers, produced by both Institution Q and the Institution Q High School (IQHS), an extremely successful elite college in Southern Africa. People who have participated as students in IQHS, Institution Q, The IQ Data Science Programme, the IQ Business Training School or the recently launched 'Short IQ courses' that will be taught at hubs throughout the continent, will have access to employers who can hire them either as interns or as full-time staff. What is proposed is expertise, contacts, influence and a network that infiltrates the geographic space of Africa and connects it to the centres of financial and social power worldwide – for better, or for worse. If this is our Africa, it is important to interrogate how it is imagined. Here it is worth turning to the one programme at Institution Q where students briefly had space to think of 'Africa' beyond these flattening tropes.

MLUNGISI'S VOICE: LEARNING TO UNLEARN: THE EXPERIENCE OF BUILDING AN AFRICAN GENERAL EDUCATION CORE

> In this new landscape, knowledge will be defined as knowledge for the market.
> – Achille Mbembe, 'The Age of Humanism Is Ending'

First: A Telltale Try

A small group of young 'Great Books'-educated Institution Q employees (largely citizens from different African countries educated at elite liberal arts colleges in the USA) managed to fight for and be awarded a budget for African Studies. In July 2016, I was hired to create and teach the course. It was 'a win', in Institution Q parlance, although far from enough, and belated. The inaugural cohort of 'future African leaders' was already completing the first year of their degrees, consisting solely of the signature job-readiness skills curriculum called 'Q Core'. Q Core comprised a 'skills-based' handful of courses largely derived from corporate consulting. They covered a much talked about but little understood 'entrepreneurship' course as well as writing, data literacy and project management. All members of the small group had designed and taught Q Core. 'It gives them strong hands,' one of them said, 'but there is nothing that trains their minds or their hearts.' My task, therefore, was to create the afterthought 'African Studies' curriculum. I felt overawed even as I believed – wrongly, it later turned out – that the team would grow to reflect the weight of the task. We named the course 'The Africas Core'. I insisted on the plural. Partly, this was to introduce dissonance to the eerily essentialist 'Africa' thrown about in everyday talk and official company speech; but primarily to signal dissociation from Cold War Era Studies. From the outset, we set out to decolonise the very teaching of 'Africa' itself.

The new faculty brief at our 'disruptive' education start-up (complete with office bean bags, shipping pallet desks, open office plans, in-office games and sometimes yoga) was the same: create something new and best-in-the-world. It was meant seriously and we took it seriously. I arrived with the new faculty, sometimes called 'facilitators', who were coming in to 'deliver' the degree programme majors alongside Institution Q's chosen accrediting partner, (here referred to as University A). All of us were new and unsure of what the University A teaching material was. The overall brief was continued: innovative and more effective learning approaches, testable and iterative, cutting-edge pedagogy, and most importantly, scalable – the latter meaning the same 'great learning experience' replicable for hundreds of thousands of our eventual 'X million leaders' in the timeframe of one generation). The brief included aiming at 'student enjoyment'. Some of us balked at this and pushed instead for 'engagement', with what we thought was a common-sense respect for the fact that learning can at times be hard and dispiriting, even though we would of course seek in all ways to prevent that where possible. But it certainly had a higher aim than pleasure, and student entertainment could hardly be the primary metric of assessing its value.

Protestations noted, the word 'enjoyment' changed to 'engagement', but still 'The Africas Core' relied on students grading each session from one to five in 'exit tickets', where one was 'unengaging' and five was 'extremely engaging' and this was the metric by which the value of the course was to be assessed institutionally. Unlike 'Q Core', Africas Core (or ASC) was not central to the founding/founder's vision. Unlike the University A majors, it wasn't a regulatory requirement to Institution Q's existence in Mauritius. ASC was unaccredited. Its future relied on responses to the above 'exit tickets', received and emailed back at the end of each session using Google Forms. Bar charts were compiled to 'build a case' for the value of this course – to show to senior management that there was 'student demand'. This was the logic of the institution to the study (serious or not) of 'the continent' for whose 'transformation' students were enrolled to be prepared. It was also by appropriating this logic – it's a thin line between this and buying into it – that the small group maneuvered to have ASC 'tested' with my hiring.

By a combination of student hunger, 'facilitator' ingenuity, and small group labour of love, the bar charts were tall, and testimonials and tracks of student feedback many and long. This was despite timetabling in which University A majors took precedence over ASC sessions, which had to be held off campus in the late afternoon and evening. The ASC content had to be narrowed down to fit around the University A majors. The first-year aim of the course we had boldly called a 'Core' – building sound grounding in key areas of general education about the global world from an African vantage point – shrank to what was meagerly possible. Yet ASC attracted and sustained student engagement without institutional sanction for student attendance or work. The hopeful seed of a decolonial African general education curriculum, taught for Africans by Africans, found itself cast on stony ground at this 'Pan African' institution.

Second: 'Africa' Must Still Out-Rise Itself

The dream of a pan-African Humanities in a pan-African university is the original predecessor to our decolonial project, its sentiments well expressed by that intellectual fountain of pan-Africanism: Edward W. Blyden in the Sierra Leone and Liberia College debates of the 1860s to 1880s (Ajayi et al. 1996: 16—27; Blyden 1882). The incarnation of that dream was snuffed out as colonial-modernity, then manifest by racist missionary Christianity (Ndlovu-Gatsheni 2015), closed off the free, or liberal, thinking of globally conscious and able Africans who saw themselves as equals in all ways to their white 'saviours' and colonisers. They have since then never been anywhere allowed to succeed at constituting themselves at this global scale in a well-funded teaching institution or at daring to think their human questions as human beings at the centre of global history in their own right and with their own right. If they 'enter history' (read: Hegel's [(1821) 1956] anti-African anthropology, to Sarkozy's [2007] Dakar Discourse, to *The Economist*'s [2011] promulgatory cover story) they are supposed to enter it, particularly the ideational site of its formulation, through the received ideas and grace of the Eurocentric tradition. Critical African intellectual work has shown that this tradition places 'Africa' at the bottom of the rung of liberal thought by a process of 'othering' the dignity of African thinking – to the point of posing as a question its suitability or, worse, possibility – thereby constituting 'the West' (its being, thought, and action) as central to globality and historicity (Eze 1997: 8—13).

The epistemic crimes against the status of the African as an actor driven by the confidence of their own knowledge of the global world, not by grace of European cartography of the world, are familiar and known to be linked in complex ways to economic, gender, political, environmental, creative and artistic restrictions (Mkandawire 2006). The personal experiences of shame and cultural alienation (P'Bitek 2013) are woven into larger tapestries of continuous anti-African discourse present in so many avenues of global orders: from international trade practices, to international law, to international media representations, to migration and violence and incarceration of the African body. It is this context that informs the varied experiences of so many multitudes of Africans, no less the young students at Institution Q. It is a speechless scandal that these experiences of 'Africa' as well as the best historical and contemporary work addressing them – continental and diasporal – can simply be muted, assumed to be absent, swept under the carpet and barred from being discussed: for their experience is the very texture of inhabiting a continent 'not yet risen'.

Institution Q pretends that African history does not exist, and that complex African experiences of structural struggle do not exist, by narrowing the discourse of what 'Africa' is to a performative 'Culture' (see Jess's discussion below); by denying space and resources to allow a nuanced and informed navigation of these issues at 'university'. Its branding invited this plane of reference and could not escape being judged by its openness to allowing this complex work to be done by its members – students and staff – who are first of all people, before they are carpenters or shopkeepers or shareholders or CEOs. Institution Q has since changed direction, a less disingenuous move. However, to remain credible, it will still need to live up to a robust conceptualisation of what leadership in Africa means – beyond starting a private or social enterprise. We must ask ourselves what ethical African leader would, in the name of such a deeply meaningful symbol and often harrowing experience, think it permissible to draw so many of the brightest and the best to come and work and learn to *think* of themselves not as global humans among so many others, but able to acquire their humanity only if they serve corporations, start enterprises or apply 'entrepreneurial thinking' to other aspects of their lives.

W.E.B. Du Bois (1903) long ago discredited Booker T. Washington's 'Atlanta compromise', an historically analogous position to that which Institution Q appears to be positioning itself on now. To educate Africans almost exclusively as labour or agents of capital in a world where for them capitalism has always and continues to also mean being bound through complex legal and political and ideational structures in relationships of inequality, complicit or not, is to undercut all the imagined benefits of 'playing the game that exists', an Institution Q Group maxim. It is a contradiction and does not achieve the aim. This debate was held before the First World War, and we find ourselves here today having to revive Du Bois's and Blyden's position. The historic dimension of, say, a Barack Obama becoming president of the United States is an expression not of the Washington vision but the Du Bois tradition – ideologically, but also in historical lineage of re-dignifying the black body through respecting and cultivating its humane mind. African transformation needs to be up to the complex task of forging new cosmopolitanisms, impossible if little room exists in one's university education to know more about the context of leadership in Africa. At Institution Q, the public framing from the founder is that African agency came into existence in the 1960s and that Africa has been poorly led until you, young hopeful entrepreneur, get our Institution Q 'special sauce' training to transform it. Africas Core sought to go beyond that.

Third: A Transient Triumph

The course that was developed for ASC is called 'An Idea of Africa'. As of my leaving, it was, ironically, the only 'scalable' course in the Institution Q system, using a combination of in-person and online sessions. It had an introductory 'un-learning' element that helps students understand where pervasive toxic knowledge about Africa comes from, historically, but also conceptually. The course sketches the role of colonial racial capitalism in the formation of the modern world system, and the continuing prevalence of Enlightenment coloniality (Eze 1997; Dabashi 2015) in conceptions of 'Africa'. It explores the origins of capital accumulation, and looks at ways of measuring development. It considers the teleologies upon which that measurement is based, and how such teleologies occlude knowledge of economic relations. We look at the varieties of African social organisation, and critically appraise normativities and erasures of gender and sexuality in parts of Africa. We even read ('scaffolded') critical science studies as it relates to colonised and gendered subjectivity (Harding 2011) to understand how neutralities of science can be instrumentalised. All this was achieved through five in-person sessions per term in the first iteration of the course, which changed to a majority online 'experience' thereafter.

The online version of the course was popular with students, who met together in person only once to discuss 'Africa and modernity' with Sabelo Gatsheni-Ndlovu's (2015) 'Genealogies' and then work online. Through their excitement and the work that they produced, I became convinced that one can indeed teach 'quality at scale' if we got the technology right and our students knew how to use it. The course ignited tremendous discussions across campus, with some students sending organisation-wide emails stating in politic terms the rage of not having been 'offered' this in their first year. 'Why, Mr. Mlungisi, why! I am so angry', one went so far as to say. 'Why aren't we being taught more of this!?'

Many have written about the need for Africans to control their own education (see, for example, Nhlapo and Garuba [2012]). Part of the allure of Institution Q was and remains that it promises to teach skills that will create the jobs Africans must make for themselves, but they will do that so much more meaningfully and strategically if their skills are framed by engagement with what we might call the 'African Humanities' (Blyden 1882; Ajayi et al. 1996). The emergence of 'An Idea of Africa' at Institution Q is testimony to the reality that even in a neoliberal institution, embracing new technologies and opportunities can potentially produce a postnationalist, pan-Africanist space of thought, desperately needed in this time of continental-scale solidarities and action across the globe. At present, however, we risk what a colleague familiar with the start-up education climate across Africa calls 'Silicon Valley Bantu Education'.

We do not say in this chapter that being a private, for-profit, institution prevents a serious investment in critical scholarship and teaching of Africa. We are not vulgar materialists. Instead, as we consistently discuss in our analysis, the combination of extractive economic structures and incentives, together with received geo-imaginations of a space colonially invoked as 'Africa', were reproduced uncritically by the institution. These reproductions made natural and acceptable pronouncements and decisions that many committed to the genuine transformation of global systems would find quite shocking. Most significant of these effects for us whilst teaching was that institutionally, to consider Africa from an African vantage point was considered completely unnecessary inside the supposedly pan-African institution.

This is a historic tragedy – continued. It is a tragedy of coloniality where, at one level, we have the cruel irony of an unblushing invocation of pan-Africanism as brand to undercut pan-Africanism as substance. It is a tragedy of coloniality where, at another level, knowledges of moral guidance and human dignity are excluded for Africans, as they long have been, but now at the moment where their African varieties should come into their own, the Africans are finally met supposedly for transformative action. At Institution Q, most of our students know that the chancellor is famous; certainly that she is close to the founder CEO. Too few, however, know the transnational context of Lusophone African liberation that lead to the chancellor's rise, or can articulate the role and significance of people like the chancellor's generation in it. If they can, it is not because of an Institution Q education, but in spite of it. That is not the leadership story for which the chancellor is invoked by Institution Q. The chancellor is rather a convenient image, a signifier, for an emergent continental brand in the making. Institution Q's use of the iconic faces of African liberation leaders, including of course Nelson Mandela's, is useful to promote a veneer pan-Africanism, complete in pictures and other advertising materials, and in no need of further thought, study or critical discussion to inspire vision and action. To do the latter, is precisely to begin threatening Institution Q's use for 'Africa' and the institution itself.

After taking 'An Idea of Africa', students posed complicated questions about meaning and global systems in historical and critical contexts. They held up a moral and strategic mirror to the personal and collective questions that matter to them today, with a critical cartographical eye to read received and wished-for maps. There are many who simply repeated unmoored slogans before the course, convinced that Africa's 'transformation' is reducible to personal traits, regardless of the structural context of action. The course came out of necessity (not enough people, not enough resources). It is skeletal but solid. But because institutional decisions are what matter, all trace of it may soon be lost. After two years of teaching at Institution Q, Africas Core was discontinued. In theory, there remains a full online course with seven optional seminars to complement and build on what had been learned online, a selection of which would launch students towards questions and (creative) action of their own interests. My hope is that in the future serious investment is made to develop and curate knowledge about the contexts of African lives and, in this way, this and other institutions truly place Africa at the core. As of late 2018, Institution Q shows no sign of this at all. Across the institution, there is no study of Africa on offer other than two University A-accredited semester courses in the social science major in Mauritius.

JESS'S VOICE: TEACHING YOUNG LIONS HOW TO SPEAK: ON THE FEAR OF DECOLONIALITY

I arrived at Institution Q in January 2017 having been told I was to build from scratch, with my colleagues, the best social science programme/department/unit/'team' in Africa. Our curriculum was to take students who had already finished the one-year Q Core towards full undergraduate degree completion and, at least initially, we were told we would have complete freedom. It was a very exciting project to begin at a new institution. I had just finished my doctorate in anthropology, based in part on the emerging university sector in Angola. I was full of ideas and energy. My colleague (unnamed for privacy concerns) had done most of the groundwork, having been at Institution Q for several months already, but neither of us had much sense of what content we would actually be teaching within the curricula of our partner institution, University A.

We were part of a group of nine people, two for each of the degree programmes offered - the remainder being in business and technical fields – plus Mlungisi teaching Africas Core, with a mid-twenties 'manager', fluent in institutional discourse but with no academic managerial experience and little administrative training, standing between us and the rest of the organisation. Over the course of the year, we collectively had to 'contextualise' the British courses we were required to teach, and much as Mlungisi described above, make them 'relevant' and 'engaging' to our students, and use them as a baseline with which to build a 'world class education' that was distinctly 'non-traditional' (pers. comm.). We were aware that we had to do this in the context of global discussions from #RhodesMustFall to #BlackLivesMatter, which many of our students were highly involved with. We also quickly realised that those students who had self-selected into our course were largely those who had felt alienated by many of the discourses of Q Core that echo the logics described by Anonymous and Mlungisi above, who were seeking alternative language with which to describe and determine their life courses.

When I began at 32, to the best of my knowledge I was the fifth-oldest person in the organization. I was one of four staff with PhDs, all on the degree programmes team, but I had yet to graduate and was green behind the ears in every way. What Institution Q referred to as 'culture' was something that was frequently discussed and endlessly instilled through a host of rituals and I found myself immediately feeling out of place. According to Melissa Daimler, writing in the *Harvard Business Review*, there are three elements to a corporate culture: behaviours, systems and practices, all guided by an overarching set of values. 'A great culture is what you get when all three of these are aligned,' she writes, 'and line up with the organisation's espoused values. When gaps start to appear, that's when you start to see problems' (Daimler 2018).

Working in a corporate space was an enormous adjustment at a personal level. Institution Q claimed (at the time) to be a university, but consciously operated as a start-up corporation. My own preconceived ideas about what a university should be, and how it should operate (at least in terms of student-facing components of the process) led me to experience significant cognitive dissonance. The values – as described by Daimler –

were easy to agree to. As Anonymous has already described, they were placed visibly on signage on the walls. These values supposedly drove the creation and iteration of a static and bounded 'culture' which we were constantly reminded was critical to institutional success. Culture was created through rituals and PowerPoint presentations that often seemed divorced from the values just described.

For example, the open-plan work space where one had to fight for a chair, move daily, and be interrupted continuously was part of the 'culture' because it brought us close together. Communicating in emojis, not words, on the institution's Slack channel (Slack is a Silicon Valley alternative to email) was part of 'culture', posting pictures of people whose clothing happened to match under the tagline 'fashion@IQ' was part of the 'culture' and, most significantly, attending weekly organisation-wide meetings on Friday afternoons and to literally be expected to cheer and 'shout out' one another's achievements (never failures) was also part of 'culture'. It was extroverted, manifestly happy, and highly social, and for many people in the organisation appeared to work very well. However, a significant portion of the academic staff struggled, because as Daimler observes, the components of culture have to accord with the organisation's purpose.

What the purpose of the organisation was, was precisely the critical question. Institution Q was growing rapidly and becoming more and more complex, and new hires arrived on a weekly basis for teams such as marketing and tech, operations, student life, and so on. Organisational structures had yet to be established at a senior level and about 100 very bright people, almost all under the age of 30, were trying to build a university from scratch without a master plan. In retrospect, it was like the analogy cited by Francis Nyamnjoh (2012) in which he draws on the parable of blind people around an elephant to explore epistemology in South Africa. The story goes that a group of blind people are gathered around an elephant and each one touches a different part of it, describing what they feel as truth. One hundred staff members, each describing what they experience and know to be valid, and everybody absolutely committed to their own reality, and working long hours for relatively low pay in order to bring it into being.

Given the context of global student politics circa 2015, we in the social sciences programme quickly concluded that ours was a decolonial elephant, and we set out to describe it with the conviction of the evangelical millennials we almost were. One of the informal mottos of Institution Q at that time – presumably in response to the general lack of structure, but also inspired by Silicon Valley norms of institutional disruption, was #askforgivenessnotpermission. We took that to heart, but with no idea of the intensity of the effects that rocking the corporate boat in this way would have on our personal experiences of Institution Q, on the student body as a whole, and on the way that the institution was read internationally.

First, we wrote a blog. Second, we established an extra-curricular reading group on decolonial theory. Third, we formulated and wrote up a series of commitments to how we would teach social science, which went viral and put the institution as a whole in a spotlight we could not have imagined and which senior management made clear they did not want. Fourth, we set up a lab space where students could gather and think, and fifth, we held a retreat. Below, I assess each of these activities: the impact they had, and the ways in which they were received at Institution Q. We also hired [name retracted], a legal anthropologist from South America with a strong record in community partnerships and human rights, to help us ensure our programme remained grounded in the very real-world issues that Institution Q had purportedly been founded to address.

In the central choice of the word 'leadership' in the advertising of an institution of higher education, a distancing took place between Institution Q and 'traditional' universities, where 'leadership' is largely read in many circles as a proxy for money-making and treated with moral and intellectual scepticism. My task, as I saw it, was to bridge the gap. I was the founding social science faculty member who *did* have a PhD and came with the very traditional pedigrees of three of the globe's most recognised higher education institutions. I wanted to enable a dialogue between two kinds of logic that I thought – and still believe – could collectively make a tremendous contribution to the emergence of different kinds of knowledge and action in the world. Shortly after we began, I therefore wrote a blog. In retrospect I blush, but only a little, for the tone was somewhat naïve but also deliberately brash: in my view, we needed to acknowledge to other scholars how strange Institution Q appeared, and then to point out that something fresh could therefore come from it.

I wrote about the complexity of establishing a social science programme in this context, in what I called a university in the making 'run by MBAs'. I asked the international community for help, because at the time, it was only [name retracted] and me, and the intellectual project was clearly very complicated. Scholars around the world responded with enthusiasm and began to engage, but Institution Q itself was not amused. 'We have students, we have classrooms, we have faculty,' I was told with genuine puzzlement by one of the organisation's most significant players. '*How* are we not a university?' Another member of senior management literally cried when he described the feeling of betrayal he experienced when reading my blog – a moment that captured the mutual bewilderment of two competing logics: the corporation, where one should work only within set structures (although ours were not yet set at all), and the 'traditional university' committed to scholarly debate. In the former, loyalty to the brand is key – *especially* when that brand is still emergent and fragile. Critique is automatically read as criticism, and most attempts at analytic argumentation were, in this case, read as exclusionary, elitist and counterproductive to the mission. Universities, of course, are very different. Institution Q has since resolved its existential tension and no longer claims to be a university at all. For most of 2017, however, this was an area of tremendous flux in the organisation as we all tried to make sense not only of the elephant, but of how to critique it if we felt, in some way, that it was about to step into a hole.

Our tasks as faculty were both aided and abetted by the partnership with University A. Mauritian law requires that a new institution be guided into being by one that is already established, and the country has several satellite campuses of global universities. The choice of University A had been made long before faculty were hired and with little understanding of the nuances of the curricula that would need to be designed. University

A is a respected institution and the people who work there are committed as both teachers and scholars. This is by no means a critique of the excellent, rigorous and careful work that they have done. Yet the curriculum is firmly rooted in the epistemologies and needs of the Global North and no amount of 'contextualisation' could change that at a fundamental level. Our students in the founding class, however, came from 16 countries, spoke 29 languages between them, and were deeply committed to learning both content and ways of thinking that were *not* of the Global North, but of Africa – the space, after all, that they were constantly being told they were learning to lead.

Both pre-empting and responding to various calls from students, we initiated what we called the 'decolonial reading group' – a space where students gathered on a fortnightly basis to read and discuss a wide range of authors who have influenced the development of what we might think of as decolonial curricula: Ngũgĩ wa Thiong'o, Frantz Fanon, Steve Biko, Angela Davis, Francis Nyamnjoh, Nelson Maldonado-Torres, and a host of others. This group gathered at 8 pm on Thursdays at the student residences, and frequently the debates continued late into the night. It equipped a group of committed students from across the institution with linguistic and conceptual tools to begin making sense of their second year of undergraduate experience, and to ask potent questions pertaining to ideology, language and the expected impact of their work. Soon, some of these students began to be openly critical of senior management during public engagements between Institution Q and the student body – exacerbated by significant institutional uncertainty at that moment in organisational unfolding. They also found the language to describe the sense of intellectual alienation that the University A curriculum at times provoked.

From the discussions in the reading group and our initial experiences of the University A curriculum, it was clear that students were feeling increasingly depressed, lost and alienated by the knowledge they were receiving. We formulated a series of commitments towards decolonial social sciences, which we started introducing into our teaching on a regular basis. These included a commitment towards open access materials, towards languages beyond English, to a student exchange ratio that would not allow inequities of affordability to shape the kinds of learning experiences that our students had. We also committed to teaching beyond text, in partnership with other organisations, and in ways that allowed students to produce knowledge actively, not only to consume it. We wanted all of this to be grounded in ethical best practices.

Under pressure from the marketing team to write about what we were doing as we established our nascent programme, I wrote a short piece for a public academic blog platform outlining these goals. The article circulated widely. Suddenly, the work in our Social Science team came to be associated, in the outside world, with the brand of Institution Q, and senior management were not happy about that at all, as was communicated very clearly in in-person meetings. Nor were University A particularly pleased, because in the piece I had chosen not to name them, unwilling to open up the complexities of North–South institutional partnerships to public scrutiny, and also keen to carve out for us a freer space in which to work. Added to this, our commitment to open access educational resources went against their own agreements with academic publishing houses.

Decoloniality is not, and has not become, a core focus area of University A either. Some individuals have articulated a very genuine desire to learn more about it, but others expressed a feeling of being challenged that was uncomfortable, very similar to the language used by senior management when they repeatedly asked us to 'tone it down'.

So what is so threatening about decoloniality, about a concept that has as its premise an undoing of received systems of thinking, in an institution that claimed to be innovating higher education? Achille Mbembe provides helpful analysis:

> Every human being becomes a market actor; every field of activity is seen as a market; every entity (whether public or private, whether person, business, state or corporation) is governed as a firm; people themselves are cast as human capital and are subjected to market metrics (ratings, rankings) and their value is determined speculatively in a futures market. (Mbembe 2015, 3)

In the logics of the firm, the 'entity' of decoloniality was unknown. It also, however vaguely, introduced a host of sensitive subjects that might sit uneasily with funders: history, violence, subjugation, the critique of Western power, and perhaps even the critique of capital. Engaging decoloniality at an institutional level would have required an organisation-wide understanding of Africa that would be costly to instil and perhaps lead to discomfort – a feeling that was distinctly antithetical to the publicly performed 'culture' described above and in part contributed to the ambivalence around Africas Core that Mlungisi has already described. It represented a potential hornet's nest that the institution could not acknowledge or handle. As another senior manager said to me directly, 'It [decoloniality] has to go. I didn't know it existed until a year ago, I don't have any interest in understanding it, and I don't want it to be associated with the brand.'

It should be made clear that at no point were we asked to close down discussions of decoloniality in the social sciences programme itself. For the most part, the organisation at least temporarily appreciated the 'fire that we had lit' and the way students were clearly thinking (senior manager, pers. comm., April 2018). Both my colleague and I presented on the topic at conferences, and staff members from across the organisation occasionally attended the reading group and expressed an appreciation of the space it provided in the very short term. As such, decoloniality as a stream of philosophical thinking could be *facilitated* at Institution Q in the context of very particular classroom discussions, but as soon as students began to ask deep questions about the emergent structures around them outside of social sciences, it was shut down, with the spaces for decolonial thinking and debate steadily silenced.

As students attempted to make sense of these experiences, again and again they came back to a text that had been written on the classroom wall. In the social sciences lab described at the beginning of this chapter was a wall of words. The wall emerged after several discussions of the place of African languages at Institution Q, inspired to a large degree by the work of Ngũgĩ wa Thiong'o, after whom the lab was named (it has since been demolished). Anyone was welcome to write on it, and in April 2018 it had text in upwards of 27 languages, amongst them Amharic, Mauritian Kréol, Yoruba, isiZulu, Berber, Lingala, Arabic, Hindi, Somali and ChiShona, inscribed in six different alphabets. Sometime in late 2017 a proverb appeared on the wall: 'Until the lion learns how to write, every story will glorify the hunter', it proclaimed, and students started to refer to this over and over again in class discussions and in their written work.

Our goal in establishing the social sciences programme had been to create a learning environment in which students were empowered from the very beginning of their education to think from a place of confidence. What we wished to do was to expose them to the kinds of knowledge that would recentre students so that they left Institution Q confident not only in their skills, but in their epistemologies, which in some cases their formal schooling had already attempted to erase. Ironically, there have been few institutions in Africa that have done what the historically black colleges in the USA have achieved, namely the creation of spaces of unapologetic black excellence that exist beyond a dialogue with sites of European or North American knowledge production and dissemination, and eloquently described by Ta-Nehesi Coates (2015) in his book *Between the World and Me*. Other African universities have of course engaged with these questions very deeply, but most have done so after a formative encounter with what we might conceive of as knowledge from the North. An example is the founding of Ashesi University in Ghana, which comes out, to a large extent, of Patrick Awuah's very personal experiences as a student at both Swarthmore and Berkeley (Gouillart 2009).

The question that many of us began with at Institution Q, and that brought so many of us to work at the institution in the first place, was what could be different if we were to start from scratch? This chapter as a whole, perhaps, stands as a tribute to our own naivety in that regard, and our failure to recognise that 'from scratch' meant deeply grounded in the structures of neoliberal market responses to global challenges and informed by the corporate consulting backgrounds of many of the founders. We wanted to teach young lions how to speak, and to a large extent we have succeeded, but what happens when their institution does not want to hear what they have to say? At the risk of sounding cheesy, what happens when a young lion roars? Does it provoke fear, or ignorance, or delight in anticipation of what is to come?

In a corporate environment where brand loyalty is absolutely crucial, how do students learn to interrogate the systems and the structures that enable the flourishing of brands in the first place? If they have studied at Institution Q, IQHS, The IQ Data Science Programme and so on, and they choose to be critical, what will be the consequences for them in time, and how should we, as faculty, therefore teach them? What we did not know at first, and refused to accept for a very long time, was that no matter how much we believed in, agreed on, and cared for the elephant that we felt with our hands (returning to the allegory of the blind people and the animal), that elephant belonged to the CEO. When he said jump, change colour, turn into a mouse or fly – the elephant was obliged to do just that. At the risk of mixing too many metaphors, right now at Institution Q the elephant has been told what it will become and been given a set of committed trainers. However, our students are not, in fact, blind old men, but young people aware of the systems at play around them. What they see, what they are told, and what they know to be true may not align, and if they do not, the students will be the first to ask searching questions. Soon to graduate, this batch of students are currently keeping their voices to a low purr, but in the near future, they will be out in the world. Our hope is they are able to speak truth to power – and if they do, that we are wise enough to listen to them.

CONCLUSION: EDUCATING FOR THE FUTURE OF AFRICA?

Working at Institution Q was an invaluable experience. All three of us gained tremendous insight into and experience of setting up an institution of higher education. We have been privileged to guide a cohort of phenomenally talented students in the founding class whom, it should be said, were all given scholarships in exchange for being guinea pigs, and most of whom had many other options but chose Institution Q for personal reasons largely to do with their reading of the vision of the founder. They have worked hard in an unpredictable environment to better both themselves and the communities they are part of. Based on our knowledge of the kinds of human beings our students are, we are confident of positive outcomes for them, and we look forward to the future that these young people will help shape. Yet as young African scholars ourselves, now reflecting on what to take from Institution Q and what to leave behind, on the steps we need to take outside of the Institution Q system as well as how to continue to work alongside it, we are left with almost as many questions as we had when we commenced, and it seems prudent to pose them here.

First, what is 'traditional education' – what Institution Q constantly pitted itself against. Whose traditions count, and what should be 'disrupted'? At Institution Q, 'traditional education' meant brick and mortar universities that conduct research, are reliant on resources that are scarce in many poorer parts of the world, including in Africa (think libraries and laboratories), and apparently put the interests of the professor above those of students. Students, the founder has publicly argued, are what Africa has in abundance – both a pragmatic truth and a way of tapping into global anxieties pertaining to Africa's 'youth bulge' that have been well articulated by scholars and policymakers alike (Sommers 2006; Lin 2012). The project of decolonial social science deliberately tried to put student learning and student production of knowledge at the forefront, but it was deemed incompatible with the institution's vision. As Mlungisi has described, Africas Core remained marginal and has currently been abandoned, despite it being the one common space for *all* students to seriously engage questions pertaining to the social and economic realities they had experienced (and sought to change) that led to many of them choosing Institution Q in the first place. In taking out 'traditional education', what are we then putting in its place?

Institution Q is of course, by no means the only institution to use new technologies in interesting ways either. San Francisco-based Minerva has done far more to develop and to think carefully through proprietary software (Kosslyn, Nelson and Kerrey 2017), and most higher education institutions now use some form of blended learning (Davidson 2017). The 'traditions' decried by Institution Q come largely from the Global North's university sector, but the knowledge being transmitted through Institution Q's Core curriculum is deeply influenced by corporate consulting, which emerged just as much 'outside' of African realities as the metonymic 'Ivy League'. Is this not, also, a tradition of knowledge production and dissemination, and should one not ask just as careful questions to explore the likely impacts of learning and doing under 'consulting culture'?

Secondly, in an age where most information is, indeed, available on the Internet (with a caveat on the variety, quality and sources of knowledge from and about Africa), what scaffolds of thinking do students need to be able parse knowledge such that they can go on to lead fulfilling lives that enable meaningful contributions to society? Embedded in that question is the need to interrogate which society/societies our students comprise and, if mobility is to happen, in what directions? *If* the goal is to become part of the global elite, then they should absolutely be exposed to extractive capital as quickly as possible, but many – even at Institution Q – question if that is really desirable. Either way, if young Africans are 'leading', who else will have to fall behind? What is a meaningful contribution, and who determines that, and how do we reward our alumni and our donors and our faculty and staff for supporting our young charges in that endeavour? How do we choose a curriculum that teaches them not what to think, but *how* to think – the goal of almost every higher education institution in the world today? Like most clichés, *how to think* remains in circulation because it is broadly true, and in this case very difficult to respond to, because it depends so much on what base of knowledge our students already have when they arrive.

Finally, what is an 'African' education? Institution Q has succeeded where the likes of Kwame Nkrumah and Aimé Césaire only dreamed. It has brought together some of the brightest from around the geographic entity of Africa, and enabled them to mix and learn from one another in ways that are likely to bear fruit only in the decades to come. Yet it has not been as deliberate in its self-construction as an African powerhouse as the University of Cape Town's formulation of 'Afropolitanism', nor evinced a political self-awareness such as that found at the Makerere Institute for Social Research (Nhlapo and Garuba 2012). Indeed, Institution Q has avoided politics almost altogether – presumably so as to not alienate shareholders, potential funders or future parents. But can an institution be both African, which after all implies pan-African, and apolitical? This chapter has argued otherwise, suggesting that the logics of neoliberalism are just as potent a politicising force as any, and that the deliberate creation of Institution Q within that framework will have serious impact on the continent to come. How this is manifest remains to be seen, and certainly, we will all be watching with interest.

NOTES

1   The third author has withheld their name but asks that their text still be included. This chapter does not reflect the authors' current institutions.

REFERENCES

Ajayi, J.F. Ade, L.K.H. Goma, G. Ampah Johnson and Wanjiku Mwotia. 1996. *The African Experience with Higher Education*. Accra: Association of African Universities.

Ayers, Alison. 2013. 'Beyond Myths, Lies and Stereotypes: The Political Economy of a "New Scramble for Africa"'. *New Political Economy* 18 (2): 227–257. doi: 10.1080/13563467.2012.678821.

Bayart, Jean-Francois. 2000. 'Africa n the World: A History of Extraversion'. *African Affairs* 99 (395): 217–267.

Beresford, Alexander. 2016. 'Africa Rising?' *Review of African Political Economy* 43 (147): 1–7. doi:10.1 080/03056244.2016.1149369.

Bhorat, Haroon and Finn Tarp. 2016. *Africa's Lions: Growth Traps and Opportunities for Six Leading African Economies* Washington, D.C: Brookings Institution Press.

Blyden, Edward Wilmot. 1882. *The Aims and Methods of Liberal Education for Africans*. Cambridge: J. Wilson and Son.

Bush, Raymond. 2013. 'Making the Twenty-First Century Its Own: Janus-Faced African (Under) Development'. *Afrika Focus* 26 (1): 51–66. doi: https://doi.org/10.21825/af.v26i1.4924.

Coates, Ta-Nehisi. 2015. *Between the World and Me*. New York: Spiegel & Grau.

Dabashi, Hamid. 2015. *Can Non-Europeans Think?* London: Zed Books.

Daimler, Melissa. 2018. 'Why Great Employees Leave "Great Cultures"'. *Harvard Business Review*, 11 May 2018. https://hbr.org/2018/05/why-great-employees-leave-great-cultures.

Davidson, Cathy N. 2017. *The New Education: How to Revolutionize the University to Prepare Students for a World in Flux*. New York: Basic Books.

Du Bois, W. E.B. 1903. *The Souls of Black Folk: Essays and Sketches*. Chicago: A.C. McClurg.

Economist. 2011. 'Africa Rising: The Hopeful Continent'. 3 December 2011. https://www.economist.com/leaders/2011/12/03/africa-rising.

Ernst & Young. 2014. 'Africa 2030: Realizing the Possibilities'. Ernst & Young. https://www.ey.com/Publication/vwLUAssets/EY-Africa-2030-realizing-the-possibilities/%24FILE/EY-Africa-2030-realizing-the-possibilities.pdf.

Eze, Emmanuel Chukwudi. 1997. *Postcolonial African Philosophy: A Critical Reader*. Cambride, Mass: Blackwell.

Gelb, Alan H., ed. 2000. *Can Africa Claim the 21st Century?* Washington, D.C.: World Bank. http://siteresources.worldbank.org/INTAFRICA/Resources/complete.pdf.

Gouillart, Emily. 2009. 'An Interview with Patrick Awuah'. *Journal of International Affairs* 62 (2): 187–192.

Harding, Sandra. 2011. *The Postcolonial Science and Technology Studies Reader*. Durham, NC: Duke Univeristy Press.

Hegel, Georg W.F. [1821] 1956. *The Philosophy of History*. Translated by J.H. Clarke. New York: Dover.

Kosslyn, Stephen Michael, Ben Nelson, and Robert Kerrey. 2017. *Building the Intentional University: Minerva and the Future of Higher Education*. Cambridge, MA: The MIT Press.

Lin, Justin Yifu. 2012. 'Youth Bulge: A Demographic Dividend or a Demographic Bomb in Developing Countries?' *Let's Talk Development* (blog), 5 January. http://blogs.worldbank.org/developmenttalk/youth-bulge-a-demographic-dividend-or-a-demographic-bomb-in-developing-countries.

Lyons, Dan. 2017. *Disrupted: My Misadventures in the Start Up Bubble*. New York: Hachette Books; Reprint edition.

Mamdani, Mahmood. 1998. 'Is African Studies to Be Turned into a New Home for Bantu Education at UCT?'. *Social Dynamics* 24 (2): 63–75. doi: 10.1080/02533959808458649.

Mbembe, Achille. 2015. 'Decolonizing Knowledge and the Question of the Archive'. Presentation at the University of the Witwatersrand, Johannesburg, 22 April. https://wiser.wits.ac.za/system" / files/Achille%20Mbembe%20-%20Decolonizing%20Knowledge%20and%20the%20Question%20of%20the%20Archive.pdf.

Mbembe, Achille. 2016. 'The Age of Humanism is Ending'. *Mail & Guardian*, 22 December. https://mg.co.za/article/2016-12-22-00-the-age-of-humanism-is-ending/.

Mkandawire, Thandika. 2006. *African Intellectuals: Rethinking Politics, Language, Gender and Development*. London: Zed Books.

Mkandawire, Thandika. 2014. 'Can Africa Turn from Recovery to Development?' *Current History* 113 (763): 171–177.

Ndlovu-Gatsheni, Sabelo J. 2015. 'Genealogies of Coloniality and Implications for Africa's Development'. *Africa Development* 40 (3): 13–40.

Nhlapo, Ronald Thandabantu and Harry Garuba. 2012. *African Studies in the Post-colonial University*. Cape Town: University of Cape Town.

Nyamnjoh, Francis. 2012. 'Blinded by Sight: Divining the Future of Anthropology in Africa'. *Afrika Spectrum* 47 (2-3): 63–92.

P'Bitek, Okot 2013. *Song of Lawino & Song of Ocol*. London: Waveland Press.

Probyn, Justin. 2017. 'Four Barriers Hindering Innovation in Africa'. *How We Made It in Africa*, 19 October. https://www.howwemadeitinafrica.com/four-barriers-slowing-innovation-africa/59929/.

Roxburgh, Charles, Norbert Dörr, Acha Leke, Amine Tazi-Riffi, Arend Van Wamelen, Susan Lund, Mutsa Chironga, Tarik Alatovik, Charles Atkins, Nadia Terfous and Till Zeino-Mahmalat. 2010. *Lions on the Move: The Progress and Potential of African Economies*. New York: McKinsey & Company. https://www.mckinsey.com/featured-insights/middle-east-and-africa/lions-on-the-move.

Sarkozy, Nicolas. 2007. 'Le Discours de Dakar de Nicolas Sarkozy de 2007'. *Le Monde Afrique*, 9 November. https://www.lemonde.fr/afrique/article/2007/11/09/le-discours-de-dakar-de-nicolas-sarkozy_1774758_3212.html.

Sizemore, Charles. 2012. 'Africa: The Last Investment Frontier'. *Forbes*, 8 August. https://www.forbes.com/sites/moneybuilder/2012/08/08/africa-the-last-investment-frontier/#151cba584f91.

Sommers, Marc. 2006. 'Fearing Africa's Young Men: The Case of Rwanda'. Social Development Papers. Conflict Prevention & Reconstruction Paper No. 32, The World Bank, Washington, DC, January. http://documents.worldbank.org/curated/en/303071468105531710/Fearing-Africas-young-men-the-case-of-Rwanda.

Sylla, Ndongo. 2014. 'From a Marginalised to an Emerging Africa? A Critical Analysis'. *Review of African Political Economy* 41 (S1): S7–S25. doi: 10.1080/03056244.2014.996323.

Taylor, Ian. 2016. 'Dependency Redux: Why Africa Is Not Rising'. *Review of African Political Economy* 43 (147): 8–25.

Trilling, Bernie, and Charles Fadel. 2012. *21st Century Skills: Learning for Life in Our Times*. San Francisco: Jossey-Bass.

UNECA (United Nations Economic Commission for Africa). 2012. *Unleashing Africa's Potential as a Pole of Global Growth: Issues Paper*. Addis Ababa: United Nations Economic Commission for Africa. http://repository.uneca.org/handle/10855/21119.

Wengraf, Lee. 2018. *Extracting Profit: Imperialism, Neoliberalism and the New Scramble for Africa*. Chicago: Haymarket Books.

CHAPTER 7

Testing Transgressive Thinking: The 'Learning Through Enlargement' Initiative at UNISA

Crain Soudien
Human Sciences Research Council

What should be in the South African higher education curriculum has been a subject of continuous debate for almost 50 years. The debate has resonances with and has been informed by the discussion in the United States about what the average graduate should be taught and should know. Leading the charge in the USA is Eric D. Hirsch (2001), the spokesperson for a group of academics calling themselves the 'core knowledge' movement:

> At the Core Knowledge Foundation, we have argued in favour of teaching topics that have the greatest potential for developing general competence and narrowing the test-score gap among student populations. We inventoried the knowledge that is characteristically shared by those at the top of the socio-economic ladder in the United States. ... People who have called this approach a collection of mere facts or labelled it Eurocentric and elitist have not bothered to find out just what is in the Core Knowledge sequence. ... It is the result of a long process of research and consensus building. (Hirsch 2001: 24)

Hirsch's critics (Coles 2014) have described his curriculum as 'a hegemonic vision produced for and by the white middle class to help maintain the social and economic status quo. It deliberately fails to consider the values and beliefs of any other particular race, class or gender.'

Similar contestations have characterised the South African discussion. At several points over the last 80 years radical scholars and activists inside and outside the university have raised the question of 'dominant knowledge' and its role in the production of inequality and particularly racial oppression. Two texts produced in the 1950s by Ben Kies (1953), *The Contribution of the Non-European Peoples to World Civilisation*, and Isaac Tabata (1959), *Education for Barbarism*, powerfully raised the question about the need for approaches to education that were culturally inclusive. During the 1970s and 1980s the campaign for what was called 'People's Education', drawing on Freierean and popular understandings of education posed the challenge sharply to the legitimacy of ruling class approaches to knowledge (see Motala and Vally 2002). From these provocations and from prolonged debate and argument inside the academy, interestingly, has emerged almost 40 years of innovative strategies and initiatives. Amongst these have been the introduction of academic development programmes in many universities and the establishment of alternative institutions such as the humanities and social science Khanya College, which was based on an explicitly Africa-centred approach to the curriculum (Soudien 2015). The debate itself, however, has until recently been relatively sedate. The rise of the #RhodesMustFall movement at the University of Cape Town (UCT), which saw the removal of one of colonialism's most dramatic symbols – the statue of Cecil John Rhodes – from the campus has changed its emotional and intellectual temperature completely. The demand for what has been called 'decolonisation' has been placed forthrightly on the table (see inter alia, Ndlovu-Gatsheni 2013; Garuba 2015; Mbembe 2015; Nyathi 2016; Essop 2016; Hendricks and Liebowitz 2016; Kamanzi 2016; Pityana 2016; Rudin 2017; Prah 2017; Jansen 2017; Paterson 2018). Interestingly, in this current phase of the discussion have appeared all the elements of contention – philosophic disagreement, polemic posturing and high rhetoric – that accompanied the debate in the United States.[1]

Interesting as all these elements are, significant for the purposes of this discussion is the question of the role of the university in processes of social development. Higher education scholar Nico Cloete, in a recent talk, bemoaned the fact that the decolonisation debate was failing to address broader issues of development (Paterson 2018). In articulating this concern, he was confirming an issue raised by key scholars in the global decoloniality movement (see, for example, Santos 2007). The issue was the high levels of inequality that have accompanied and indeed marked the kinds of development that have taken shape around the world. Speaking to this concern, Arturo Escobar says, '[What] moved me to write about the "invention of development" … in the late 1980s is still very much there: the fact that, as I see it, development continues to participate in strategies of cultural and social domination, even if academics might have a more nuanced view today of how these strategies operate' (Escobar 2011: 1). Cloete and Escobar, it is important to make clear, approach the idea of development from very different perspectives. The central challenge they pose, however, that of the place of the university in development, remains central.

To contribute to the discussion about the role, place and significance of the South African university in the country's political economy in the context of the discussion about decolonisation, I undertake a critical assessment of an important initiative begun at the University of South Africa (UNISA): the South African Research Chairs Initiative (SARChI) in Development Education (DE).[2] SARChI Chairs are a flagship programme of the Department of Science and Technology and the National Research Foundation. Their purpose is to promote high-level research. Acknowledging my biases, as I was a founding participant of this project, I foreground the significance of the initiative while also identifying the challenges both within it and around it. The analysis is stimulated by the concern of Escobar and by the need to show how South Africans are contributing to the larger global discussion on the role of the modern university in processes of social development.[3]

RECENT CURRICULUM AND EPISTEMOLOGICAL INNOVATIONS IN THE SOUTH AFRICAN UNIVERSITY

Current popular and even academic analyses of the state of curriculum development in South African higher education would have it that the coming of democracy 'has brought little or no change in their institutions and the society at large' (Fomunyam 2017, 6797). Views such as these flatten out, homogenise and essentialise the complexity of the story of curriculum and its evolution in the almost 190-year history of the South African university and particularly the history of the last 30 or 40 years (Soudien 2015). In that history, and even dominating it, was the insidious coalescence of global imperial epistemologies with local white supremacist pedagogical and ideological interventions. These took their crudest expression with the proclamation of the Extension of University Education Act, Number 45 of 1959. Out of this came the apartheid university, a deeply racialised space upon which was imposed, often but not always, academics who did not always have the interests of their students at heart. It was a place that stood in direct antithesis to the open university Cardinal John Newman had in mind, a place for 'students from every quarter for every kind of knowledge' (Newman [1852] 1907).

But, and this is neither an apology nor a defence, in every single institution there were individuals and even groups of individuals who were able to teach not just in resistance to whatever the hegemonic word was but in complete confidence about the pedagogical and moral obligation of making their students critical thinkers. They could not, of course, always do this openly. The security police were present in their classrooms as registered students. The point, however, is that in the midst of the most intense forms of oppression experienced in South Africa's history, a history not yet fully written, there were scholars who were able to generate and produce powerful learning environments, equal to the most progressive anywhere in the world. It is for this reason that a 'nothing has changed' judgement of the nature of the South African university and what is happening in its classrooms is both ahistorical and unhelpful. What would be helpful is close and unapologetically critical study – in full awareness of the blind-spots and contradictions that were there – of particular situations inside departments and faculties,[4] which help us understand how disciplines either opened up or closed down opportunities for critical thinking.[5]

In registering this appeal for historical complexity, it is important also to acknowledge the range of important initiatives around the curriculum that have taken form in recent times. These initiatives came, and continue to come, with the support, often at the instigation of, leading figures inside the university, deans, deputy vice-chancellors, vice-chancellors and university councils. Their contribution is, and this must be acknowledged, complex and, often, contradictory. They regularly provide support. They are present visibly and practically in the very genesis of many initiatives and may even have been their originators. But in having to manage extremely complex demands on their political and fiscal obligations, these very critical interlocutors of the complex change landscape of higher education in South Africa often, also, prevaricate, falter and even back-track. Small in number and even contradictory as these interventions have been, it is necessary to acknowledge that they have in important ways opened the discussion of what the university is for. The interventions essentially fall into two groups, those with an explicit ontological focus and others that seek to address questions of knowledge. They are both motivated by the urge to address the question of what the South African university could be.[6] In the first category is a group of extraordinary, again little-celebrated, initiatives, including:

- The Intercultural and Diversity Studies Unit of Southern Africa at UCT was established in 2001 and relocated to the University of the Witwatersrand (Wits) as the centre for Diversity Studies in 2011. The aim of the project is to 'build capacity to meet the challenges of diverse societies through research and education' and it 'aims to further social justice and deepen democracy' (https://www.wits.ac.za/wicds/). This unit was started to bring together 'academic theorisation and practical approaches around questions of inclusivity and diversity'. Its point of departure was the social constructedness of 'race'.
- The Centre for Critical Research on Race and Identity at the University of KwaZulu-Natal. The project seeks to study 'race thinking and changing identities', for the purpose of understanding and discussing 'the epistemological, moral, cultural and other bases for perceptions of human diversity and difference' (https://ccrri.ukzn.ac.za).
- The Apartheid Archive Project at Wits which has as its main objective 'examin[ing] the nature of the experiences of racism of [particularly "ordinary"] South Africans under apartheid and their continuing effects ... in contemporary South Africa' (http://www.historicalpapers.wits.ac.za /?inventory/U/collections&c=AG3275/R/9023).
- The Centre for the Advancement of Non-Racialism and Democracy at the Nelson Mandela Metropolitan University, now the Nelson Mandela University. It was established in 2010 as an explicit project of the University's vice-chancellor and has as its focus the building of a non-racial orientation to knowledge production and the ideal of advancing transformation through fostering difficult dialogues.

- The Reitz Institute at the University of the Free State (UFS), an International Institute for Studies in Race, Reconciliation and Social Justice on the site of its Reitz Residence where four young white men abused five black custodial members of staff (https://www.ufs.ac.za/institute/the-institute-for-reconciliation-and-social-justice-home/general/history-of-the-institute).[7]

Significantly, all of these projects share a direct interest in 'race' and racism and a concern with processes of racial formation. All of them work with the country's racial legacy and the role of the universities in the production and reproduction of 'race' and racism. They are important sites of sociological and political reflection on how the social dynamic of 'race' works, how it reinstantiates itself and how racism can be resisted.

The second category involves projects with a stronger epistemological focus. Amongst these are initiatives supported by the Department of Science and Technology's focus on indigenous inowledge systems (IKS). A critical example is a collaborative initiative between the universities of the North West, Venda and Limpopo (see http://nepadsanbio.org/about-sanbio/iks-node).

Another important initiative is the Grounding Programme at the University of Fort Hare (UFH), aimed at first-year students. The objectives of the Grounding Programme are:

- To provide UFH undergraduates with a critical and decolonising framework in which to see and understand the world, the continent and themselves.
- To provide a progressively rigorous, responsible and compassionate basis for gaining and applying their knowledge and energies to the world.
- To provide students with a deep understanding of the principles of Ubuntu, democracy, liberation and decolonising knowledge (University of Fort Hare 2007).

Yet another important example, one that has unfortunately been discontinued, was the Project for the Enhancement of Research Capacity at UCT. The significance of this project was its deliberate attempt to surface and work with the politics of different knowledge orientations. The project spawned a number of research initiatives underpinned by the ambition of producing 'new knowledge, which is transformative in that it is appropriate to our position in SA, on the continent and in the world' (https://www.news.uct.ac.za/article/-2009-05-25-new-programme-to-perc-up-research). These research initiatives came together in a series of seminars that put the question of epistemological hospitality squarely on the table.

SARCHI DEVELOPMENT EDUCATION

In the context of the broader decolonisation discussion, the DE initiative at UNISA constituted an important practical attempt to develop and model a new way of working with knowledge in the university. The DE chair was awarded to Professor Catherine Odora Hoppers at UNISA in 2008. Her purpose with the establishment of the chair, with the full support of the university, was to begin to develop and institutionalise alternative approaches to the production of knowledge for social development, hence its – name Development Education. Writing in the 2009 SARChI Annual Report Progress Plan, the university's Executive Director for Research, Professor Tinyiko Maluleke, spelled out the terms of institutional support:

The University of South Africa has set aside substantial funds and other resources of its own in order, among other things, to achieve the following goals, namely to:

- Transform the Chair into an observatory with a view to possibly continue beyond the NRF [National Research Foundation] term for support to the chair beyond the [support provided by the] NRF
- Situate the Chair firmly within UNISA's own moral and pedagogic mandate
- Give prominence to the Chair within UNISA, nationally and internationally
- Provision of further expert support for students attached to the Chair
- Provision of the relevant technological support for the Chair to have impact in an ODL (Open and Distance Learning) institutional context
- Attract top rank scholars from all over the world to periodically come and assist in the pursuit of the goals of the Chair
- Provide further logistical and administrative support to the Chair as its work-load increases and matures. (SARChI Chair Papers 2009b: 23)

The title of the Chair was significant – *Development Education*. It was not, as is the case in many other institutions, 'Development and Education' or 'Education and Development', or even 'Developmental Education'. Through it, Odora Hoppers sought to signal a shift in the ways in which the human task of learning and making sense of the world was managed and mediated. Education, the point she sought to make, was not *for* development. In a *for* development rendering, education was, in the Hirschean way of seeing the world, what *some* people thought, whatever their motives, was good for others. Her approach was implicitly that education *was* development. In its full sense, and this is elaborated below, it opened itself up to Newman's idea of 'knowledge from every quarter'.

Briefly, to put the DE initiative into perspective, Odora Hoppers established it through a set of articulated interventions which were, even in global terms, innovative. Three moves are important to highlight. The first was to assemble a group of postgraduate Master's and doctoral students from a range of disciplines and countries who were interested in exploring, in their disciplines, the question of development. Within a year of the programme's establishment, she had attracted 19 students, 10 of them doing PhDs, working in fields as diverse as bioengineering and physics, on the one end of the science spectrum, to law and politics, on the other. The second was to build a circle of 'elders and distinguished fellows … from various fields, including quantum physics, law, peace studies and business ethics' who had made the questions of human development their focus (SARChI Chair Papers 2009a). The last, and in some ways her most significant intervention, was to convene a group of indigenous knowledge intellectuals and practitioners, mostly from South Africa, but also from North America, Scandinavia, Australia and New Zealand, who were interested in the question of inclusive development. The articulation principle, discussed below, was to explore ways in which these historically located and historically determined groups could model a new articulated conversation in the classic space of the modern university about the great challenge of human development, without the cultural, social and economic presumptions of superiority and inferiority.

The DE initiative reached the end of its NRF support, after ten years, in 2017. Odora Hoppers is in the process of continuing the work she began in the DE initiative in a new independent institute called the Global Institute of Applied Governance of Science, Knowledge Systems and Innovations. In its ten-year span of life, the DE initiative produced, it is important to emphasise for the record, dozens of Master's and PhD graduates, convened annual meetings of all the critical knowledge partners and saw Odora Hoppers engage in both small and large ways with hundreds of partners inside UNISA and beyond in the wider global knowledge community around the question of DE.

Aside from retreats for the students, an annual week-long meeting took place almost each year between 2008 and 2016. To these meetings came the distinguished fellows, the indigenous knowledge specialists and the students. Amongst the distinguished fellows were some of the world's leading cultural theorists, Shiv Visvanathan from India, Dani Nabudere from Uganda, John Ralston Saul from Canada and Howard Richards from Chile and the United States. Amongst the IKS theorists were Wally Serote, Mme Grace Masuku and Oom Jan van der Westhuizen, leading South African intellectual activists. The theme for the second retreat in 2010 was 'Human Development and the Transformation of the Academy'; for the fourth in 2011 it was 'Transformation by Enlargement: From Africa to Humanity'; for the fifth in 2012 it was 'Cognitive Justice and the African and Global Commons'; for the sixth in 2013 it was 'Establishing the Discourse and Protocols for Innovations from Below as Restorative Action to Communities'; for the seventh in 2014 it was 'Healing and Restorative Citizenship Education as the First Principles in the Philosophy of Higher Education'; for the eighth in 2015 it was 'Building Excellence in Indigenous Knowledge Systems as a Science'. The retreats ended in 2016 with the ninth retreat/interface held at the University of Venda. Odora Hoppers described it as follows: 'The Retreat was combined with an Interface engagement for the first time. It was entitled "Towards Science and Technology for Humility in South Africa". ... Minister Naledi Pandor thought the Retreats should be taken nationwide. She attended for two days and gave two keynotes' (note from Odora Hoppers, 5 May 2018).

DEVELOPMENT EDUCATION'S PERSPECTIVE: ENGAGING THE 'DEFAULT DRIVE'

It is important to describe what the ideas and principles upon which the DE was constructed were. The key idea from which the initiative set off was the critical analysis that the modern university was constituted on an exclusionary 'default drive'. It is necessary to quote Odora Hoppers at length to understand the critique. She provided the critique in response to a question from an interviewer about the nature of the modern university:

Yes as modern, but like all the academies throughout the continent, they've had problems with their constitutive rules that govern knowledge production, that govern the work of the academy. The way all disciplines are structured, still retain core pin codes of the European thinking, the cultural drives are European. To that extent it's not unique to Unisa, in fact there's no big difference between Unisa and Wits or Unisa and Cape Town, only the liberal universities are much smarter in concealing themselves, they conceal and they disguise in a much more sophisticated way. But the ethnic nature of all universities, being ethnically European, tribally European for example, it is a problem where Africa's development is concerned. Core pin codes drive the thinking for example in higher education, research, teaching, learning, content, and curriculum and so on and so forth. And in the South African situation it is even more pungent because of the history of apartheid of course. But I take it that the challenge is the thinking behind the race and the unwritten, the unspoken part about the super-iority of the west [sic] which is the problem. It is not really race, it is something deeper than that because an African can get trained inside a university and behave exactly the same. So I'm not tackling the problem which I call mine. I'm not functioning at the level of first level indigenisation. First-level indigenisation is a replacement of colour and that is not my mandate. Many people can deal with that, there are legislations, there all manners of equity things. For me the problem is in the default drive itself, the cultural drive of the systems, the intolerance other ways of seeing, the closure within that, the hierarchicisation of IKS, the absolutely exclusivist way in which the produc-tion is framed, that is what I am taking on. The mandate that I carry is probably the most challenging of all mandates because to be actually looking at the systems with the intention of making propositions for the dismantling of the knots, this is some-thing that is unprecedented. So I mean what looks cosy, coming in as an expert, is not because ... [I am] dealing exactly with the past where the spooks are, where the academy hides their skeletons, I am going straight into those skeletons, not just at the barefoot level ... but the thought processes, the thought systems that determine and make exclusion okay. ... Mine is not some sort of post-colonial theorisation. It is very strategic and very tactical type of research, research leading to very strategic actions. (SARChI Chair Papers 2009c)

In this explanation were several foundational analytics and innovative propositions. Central amongst the analytics was the critique of the constitutive rules of the modern uni-versity. The point that Odora Hoppers sought to make was that the founding approaches of the institutions were essentially, as she put it, ethnic and tribal. These founding notions, predicated on a particular kind of objective European superiority, had built into them condescension, exclusion and erasure. Their deep ontic, that is their view of living entities inside the larger ecology within which they existed, was, as Odora Hoppers put it, more than simply that of 'race'. It was cultural. This cultural hubris sought to teach the world that it was in European thought that its weal was to be found. The task of the modern university, therefore, was to take this thought – European knowledge – into the world. This identity of the modern university, Odora Hoppers argued, was profoundly destructive, 'because the distance between the universities and society in Africa is untenable and the condescension that is crafted into that relationship is no longer acceptable' (SARChI Chair Papers 2009c). The effect of this condescension, she argued, was 'the hidden script at universities. It is never said aloud but it is there. The script is: Africa has nothing to offer because history has already been determined and history belongs to Europe. All Africa has to do is to imbibe it. That's why universities are so comfortable using the Western default drive' (SARChI Chair Papers 2009a).

In presenting the DE initiative's response to this culture of condescension, Odora Hoppers offered important propositions for a way forward. A critical innovation, and this is a key element of her approach to the decolonial discussion, 'is not so much to rewrite the Western script that African universities are using but to enlarge it so that Africa too has a voice' (SARChI Chair Papers 2009a). The proposition she sought to make was founded, as she said, on the inadequacy of the 'Western package': 'It is inadequate to the task of bringing up children who have other frames of reference. The system as we have it is too limited for the drama that confronts a growing African child'. In this, her line of argument was that the elite European map for world development was problematic in two ways. First of all, it presumed that it had all the answers to the past, present and future problems of the world. In response she said: 'No one has complete answers'. The problem with Eurocentric knowledge was that 'it bites a little piece of what is possible; it spits out and ignores the rest'. It was, in this logic, exclusionary and managed on a basis of contempt for others not-European. Its second problem, and this, it must be acknowledged here, is my own reading of her hermeneutic, is that the Western knowledge package was also responsible for many of the problems the world was experiencing. The 'development' it offered was responsible for the destruction of the environment and for the conceit of human mastery over all of life.

Central, in giving response to this logic, for the DE initiative was the idea of *enlargement:* 'This chair seeks to assist the system to rewire its knowledge framework so that it can take in more knowledge and expand its repertoire' (SARChI Chair Papers 2009a). Towards this – and this is where the practice Odora Hoppers sought to introduce in the initiative distinguished itself from others – she sought to bring together the knowledge affordances available to humanity and to explore their connected potential for addressing the problems of the world: 'No one has complete answers. It's about how your one-tenth of the solution can link with that one-tenth and that two-fifths and so on'. This required, distinctively, a hospitality to all knowledge forms, critically, the traditional knowledge forms of so-called high Western modernity, quantum physics, and those of 'the rural child, barefoot and in tattered clothes who has a botanical garden coming right to her doorstep. She is naturally evolving inside a system that is integrated with nature, with a grounding in plant, weather and soil systems. Western science needs to build on the knowledge the African child already has by linking up with the child's lived world'. It required, in addition to bringing into the knowledge universe IKS, but all the disciplines in the spirit of transdisciplinarity, another legacy of the Western system: 'The deeper you specialise in a specific discipline, the deeper you dig yourself into the silo. … Unless you dig sideways, you lose the capability to converse with other disciplines'.

The Odora Hoppers leitmotif, as is evident, was the idea of 'enlargement'. An explanation of this was captured in the proposal the initiative developed for its second strategic retreat in 2010:

> The Chair applies a methodology of *transformation by enlargement* in all its work. This means that all key concepts and ideas driving or anchoring policy and the academy are revisited with a view to expanding their understanding to include ways of seeing that had been previously excluded. These include the two central themes that underpin policies in higher education, science, research and innovation from the perspective of human development, and especially the marginalised. These are the *information society/knowledge economy*, AND *innovation*. These concepts are reframed from an inclusive paradigm by integrating the perspective of rural communities. The result is that *new theoretical and conceptual advances are introduced* which in turn help to provide *more nuanced conceptions and interpretations of hitherto poorly understood dimensions of livelihood in the African context*. These include expanding the understanding of innovation from only scientific laboratories and the related economic parameters, to notions such as 'social innovations', 'cultural capital', innovative practices in relation to livelihoods', 'innovations from below', the 'social good' and the 'commons'. It calls for revolutions not only in technology, *but also in the way we THINK about issues*. It furthermore enables the introduction of dynamic conceptual reversals that give dignity to rural people. (SARChI Chair Papers 2010)

In this expanded understanding of knowledge and its real and existing potential, DE sought to introduce into the university the provocation of moving beyond its narrow cultural horizons and to venture into a trans-territorial mode of thinking about itself and how it worked. The transgressive requirement for the world was to cross the bounded lines of time and space with all their exclusionary inclinations into a new enlarged human commons. Critical, moreover, to this transgressive commitment, was, as Odora Hoppers argued, an openness 'to understand the weaknesses [of the knowledge affordances available to humankind] and to [see] where enlargement can happen' (SARChI Chair Papers 2009a). She argued in this same document:

I zoom in on where I think humanity is losing out and I do not do duels. … Once people have torn up a new idea, everyone is happy. No, I only want serious thinkers who can go beyond thinking in terms of critique and make a collective contribution in creating a safe space for code determination. I am not interested in polemic at this stage; I don't have time to waste.

I return to the significance of 'enlargement' in the conclusion, where I attempt to make an argument for the distinctive contribution 'enlargement' makes to the larger discussion about decolonisation.

DEVELOPMENT EDUCATION'S PRACTICE: 'RETHINKING COMMUNITY ENGAGEMENT'

Each of the retreats was constituted as an 'interface' experience. Each was structured around conventional input papers from the fellows. Distinctive, however, was the space given to the IKS holders to talk about their work and understanding of the problems of the world. These sessions were relatively formal but allowed the IKS holders the room to speak as they chose. In this, over the period 2008 to 2015, the retreat came to constitute a critical forum, distinctive in the world and of deep significance for South Africa, for modelling how a transgressive conversation around knowledge and its limits could be engaged.[8] It was a self-conscious attempt at moving towards the centre of the university a model for managing a dialogue around knowing in critical kinds of ways. Over the period, it developed, in both organic and deliberate ways, a style of engagement that put the question of 'facing each other' at its centre.

The 2008 retreat pivoted on Odora Hoppers's explanation of the approach she wished to institute for the Chair. Her appeal was for the construction of a university experience for young people which went beyond the neoliberal market. This contribution, which is discussed in the ideas of the DE initiative below, was captured in the point that 'we need to develop young people who can traverse boundaries without fear. This University seeks to place itself at the disposal of the service of humanity – not at the service of the market – this will help us to be clear about where the university should not go. Our challenge is humanity. The minute you frame it like that, you have a problem with education. At its very best education is at the service of the market – get jobs for people, not livelihoods' (author's notes from meeting, February 2010). This provocation stimulated a discussion that lasted for several hours, involving all the participants in the retreat. The discussion allowed a glimpse of what a respectful engagement of people from different points of departure could be like.

Subsequent retreats built on this model. The fourth retreat in 2012, opened by the Minister of Higher Education, Naledi Pandor, with the theme of 'Transformation by Enlargement', was simultaneously academic and practical. It was opened with the Indian theorist Shiv Visvanathan sharing his experiences of the Indian National movement and how this movement, through the idea of cognitive justice 'tried to understand the conditions of oppression for both the oppressor and oppressed' (SARChI Chair Papers 2012: 12). His contribution introduced into the wider discussion ways of approaching the question of livelihoods that Odora Hoppers had introduced in the early moments of the DE's history. He argued that

> cognitive justice is the right of different societies to pursue the kind of knowledge on which their ways of life depend. It is not interested in the idea of voice and participation but wants cognitive representation, which should not be perceived as a kind of hostility but a 'playful dance'. Information without knowledge brings about the death of democracy, which cognitive justice is all about. It is a way of democratising democracy. (SARChI Chair Papers 2012: 12)

This focus on cognitive justice provided the opportunity for the retreat to work with the question of the constitutive rules of the university. Powerfully, from this point onwards IKS theorists began to speak about their approaches to questions of evidence and validity. The discussion had moved from a concern about their legitimacy. Critically, not without challenge, they were in the discussion about how knowledge was made and reproduced. An example of this was provided by Gogo Lizzie Nkosi, a traditional health practitioner who made the point that 'Western scientists ... test their medicines for efficacy and toxicity within laboratories and on guinea pigs – not humans. Traditional healers, on the other hand, test medicines on *themselves*' (SARChI Chair Papers 2012: 18).

The point about the approach modelled in the retreats was their deliberate attempt to examine the norms, practices and ideas of the academy in relation to the reality of people's everyday lives. Pivotal was the challenge of addressing the conditions for the integration of knowledge systems in the academy. In this, the contribution of Professor Babuuzibwa Luutu, the Vice Chancellor of the Marcus Garvey Pan Afrikan University in Uganda, was crucial during the entire life of the DE.[9] A regular participant at the retreats, he generated a critical view on how to manage the task of cognitive justice for the DE. He shared a powerful story about the dilemma a community in Uganda faced about what to do with three pythons that had entered a community. In this dilemma were religious views (mainly Muslim), traditional perspectives and official bureaucratic Western views. The position he developed helped the DE to understand how knowledge systems worked and what was required of a cognitive justice approach:

> The community gathered and some bowed in honour of nature. When they appear in two, that's something. Community turned up in supplication, giving them eggs. But they're not united. Another part of the community, Muslims, turned up and said this was satanic. There was a dilemma about what to do. They took the pythons to the police

station. The police said what must we do, this is not our work. A man then took the pythons to his home. He was then asked where he got permission to keep the pythons at his home. Then began a three-hour battle to collect the pythons. This reflects on the dangers and evils and destructiveness of disciplinarity. A discipline called biology classifies animals into wildlife and domestic life, IKS doesn't make that distinction. The state was typically paralysed in the form of the police. Islam sees nothing but ignorance and wallowing in Satanism. Now, disciplinarity, therefore, was all about taking things apart, taking things out of context, decontextualising, away from their lived relationships. All of the things didn't make sense. The African is not just wounded in that he is separated from nature, he is also set up from his fellow human beings and history. All the things which didn't make sense are presented as evidence of primitiveness. Therefore, healers who are close to nature had their science criminalised. Out of this school system, up to university, the modern African is cognitively wounded, unable to come to terms with himself. This is the African we are inviting ourselves to heal. (Author's notes from meeting, 22–24 November 2014)

The critical issue that Luutu brought to the meeting was the question of *how* to model the practice of the integration of knowledge. The story he told ended with the killing of the pythons. Dominant knowledge represented by the formal authority won the day. An opportunity had been lost, Luutu argued, to manage, respectfully, the ways of seeing of all the stakeholders in the situation. This became a focus in 2015. At this retreat the emphasis was placed on understanding the modalities of social orders for embedding and creating knowledge. The critique of the hegemonic university was returned to. The DE, through Luutu's exploration, acknowledged that it had to deal with the question of managing, in all forms of knowledge creation, the distinction between that which was known and that which was unknown. This, he urged, was the critical dynamic that needed to be worked with, to understand how to mitigate the procedures of classification and ranking instituted by hierarchical social orders. The report of the 2015 retreat articulated this challenge well: 'This distinction between known and unknown is built into the social order of hierarchy implying that questions, observations, analysis and thought are distributed in harmony with a structure of power in the academy' (SARChI Chair Papers 2015: 15).

CONCLUSION: LESSONS FOR THE CURRICULUM DEBATE

That the DE ended in 2017 is a question of some concern. The university had made a commitment at some point to look at ways of institutionalising it. It is the politics around this, I argue, that are important for the wider curriculum renewal discussion, including the discussion in its decolonisation form, to track and to deconstruct. Why was it so difficult for the university to sustain the initiative? Acknowledging the need for this deconstructive analysis should not, however, detract from the actual contribution of the DE to the curriculum renewal discussion.[10] What is this contribution? The contribution is essentially to model a way into the discussion about knowledge making and the curriculum in the university. This way is captured in Odora Hoppers's idea of 'enlargement'.

'Enlargement' in relation to the wider decolonisation repertory is distinctive in two respects. The first is in terms of its conceptual underpinnings and the second with respect to its approach to the procedures or modalities for knowledge production and engagement.

The idea of 'enlargement' as a concept emanates, of course, directly out of the critique of the knowledge ecology of the modern university. Important in this critique is the way the discursive universe of the modern university is constituted and reproduced and its fundamental modes of privileging the methodologies and content of Western epistemologies. The critique is focused on the claim of dominant Western knowledge, through its 'scientific method', of having discovered scientifically objective pathways to 'truth'. This, its central gift to civilisation, is deeply problematic. It is deeply problematic in its narrativisation of itself as a discovery of Europeans alone. The European 'Enlightenment' came on the back of successive transfers of knowledge from ancient Egyptian times and, most critically, the Islamic presence on the southern European peninsula for a few centuries. It is also problematic to the extent that it accords to itself the status of the 'only truth'. This critique is not new. The DE initiative's analysis of the politics of the university is entirely consonant and in keeping with standard criticisms, including decolonial ones, of the problems of dominant Western knowledge systems. What is new, I suggest, is the shift towards the axiological in the DE's ways of beginning to reason. In the transactions and dynamics of the DE, this shift is under-articulated. This under-articulation, as a critical observation of its self-awareness and its self-understanding, is an important area the DE would need to, in its future iterations, pay attention to. Important about it, however, is that it arises and presents itself as a challenge of and a consequence of the process of *thinking* in the DE. Thinking, understanding, is in and of itself an ethical experience. This understanding of the ethical arises through Howard Richards's (2010) arguments about the logics of the colonialist mentality and the ethical incontrovertibles – things one cannot argue against – produced by this mentality. An example provided by Richards (2011: 3) is the global economy's need and justification for protecting its stability: 'There are certain … features of western modernity, now expanded to become the global economy, that make it immune to certain kinds of change. … Modernity is like a homeostatic system that responds to certain kinds of change with built in mechanisms that restore certain aspects of the status quo. … It allows for some hotter or cooler temperatures for a while, but after a time regresses automatically to where it was set'. In this, he argues, one sees the law providing and legitimating the processes for the reproduction and the stability of the economy when it is 'out of equilibrium', such as, for example, when profits fall. To restore profits an economy has to reduce government spending. This produces what Richards describes as 'economic stability with injustice' – austerity measures, wage cuts, lay-offs and a critical reduction in social welfare.

The point that Richards emphasises is that apart from the social and economic ways of looking at the world, which the 'economic stability with injustice' logic brought to modernity, it also constituted the world in ethical terms. He argues that this is not what transformation by enlargement is all about: 'It is not about excluding options. It is about becoming more rational by considering a greater number and variety of options before making a decision. [It is about] making us less dependent on a single logic, a single dynamic, a single metaphysic' (Richards 2011: 8). There are values towards which the world should be reaching that should not depend on the homeostasis of neoliberalism. Here is education *as* development.

The second contribution of 'enlargement' is its deliberate attempt at managing the integration of knowledge. The dialogues created the conditions for a multiplicity of views, beyond the binaries of science versus tradition or 'hard science' versus indigenous knowledge, to be brought to bear on a discussion. In this debate were raised the challenges of 'hard science': validity, proof and warrant. The IKS specialists, interestingly, came into these engagements fully aware of the challenge raised for them by 'hard science'. The strength of the dialogues was their willingness to hear the IKS holders explain themselves. Supporting this was the powerful position of cognitive justice introduced by Visvanathan. Supplementing this, the discussions also engaged directly with the commensurability of different knowledge forms. This attempt at speaking directly to the politics of knowledge was an important distinguishing feature of the initiative. It introduced into the curriculum discussion a question that was not evident either in the Hirschean discussion in the United States or in the decolonisation discussion, the practical question of procedure. How did one take forward practically the discussion about the multiple knowledge affordances in the modern university? In the initiative this was, following the ethical inflection of the discussion, a moment of civilisational hospitality.

In bringing this discussion to a close, it can be argued that the contribution the DE initiative made, in its ethical and procedural innovations, amounts to a strategic pragmatism. How to move forward knowing what we do, about our opportunities and challenges, was well understood within the Initiative. UNISA's Vice Chancellor, Professor Mandla Makanya, reiterated these objectives:

> What kind of transformative actions must be brought to bear to create restorative action? How can areas of knowledge production be reconstituted to create a just and human centred-development?
>   What are terms of integration into public arena?
> Given the ambivalent distance between universities and societies what kind of realignment is needed to make universities feel part of the commons? These are questions that occupy us every day. (SARChI Chair Papers 2012)

The response of Odora Hoppers and Richards was for the university to enlarge its vision and understanding of the world. Richards argues that it is a mistake to make the argument that the 'university should cease teaching social sciences derived from and embedded in the dominant paradigm' (Richards 2011: 7). At the heart of this positioning is essentially a set of strategic practical questions. Pragmatism is its essential approach.

But, and this is the final point, the question of how one manages the task of holding different logics in one place remains a challenge. Beyond giving people an opportunity to voice their epistemic commitments and positions, how one manages knowledge integration, how one brings one knowledge tradition to the point of finding entry ways into another, of inviting possibilities of commensurability – as opposed to setting up impermeable boundaries – is as yet not clearly spelt out. But in its commitment to dialogue the DE was conscious of how the power of position was constituted and how the terms of dialogue in any context created the conditions of possibility. It recognised the sociology of the academy, its structured biases and inequalities, and how this inequality cried for change. It recognised too that, if a dialogue of respect was to be constructed between the space and world of tradition against the deliberately constructed modalities for thinking and debate of the university, a set of basic orders of engagement was necessary. Central to this was the mutual awareness on the part of the participants in the dialogue of their points of departure being rooted in logics with histories. The project, each time it met, it needs to be emphasised, attempted to model these values. This notwithstanding, the point needs to be made, questions remain. And they are large. The project had, however, within itself, suggestions of ways forward. One provided by another of its interlocutors, Dr Gavin Andersson, is that the problem was not now simply one of dialogue but also of how knowledge communities were organised. The problem, he argued, drawing on activity theory, was in proposing common engagement around real problems and the placing at the disposal of the problems the real expertise that the various parties can draw on (SARChI Chair Papers 2010). In this, Richards argues, is the work of 'humanising modernity', of making 'the university a celebration of what humans are and have been, and will be. Bring modernity's other into the curriculum, not to assimilate modernity's other into the categories the disciplines already have, but to transform the curriculum, transform research, transform community engagement' (SARChI Chair Papers 2010: 2).

NOTES

1   Amongst these has been, dramatically, as there has been in the United States, a preoccupation with the *tincture* of knowledge. The abstract for a seminar by Leigh-Ann Naidoo at the School of Education, University of Cape Town, is described in the following way: 'One of my key arguments is that black intellectuals have something very important to say about the relationship between knowledge and its context, and that "blackening the curriculum and the classroom" is a project of decolonisation: the restructuring of the relationship between the university and society, between knowledge and being' (Invitation sent by email by Azwihangwisi Muthivhi, 23 March 2018).

2   The SARChI initiative was introduced into the South African higher education system in 2006 by the Department of Science and Technology, based on a Canadian model, to attract and retain excellence in research in the local university system.

3   It is important to indicate my own role in this initiative. I was one of the original Distinguished Fellows gathered together by the Chair holder, Professor Catherine Odora Hoppers. This contribution is based on my subjective, not uncritical I hope, engagement with the DE. Through this I was able to document much of the DE's external activity, including being able to put together field notes of events, speeches and discussions during the work of the DE. Professor Odora Hoppers also, thankfully, provided me with all the official reports made by the DE to the funders of the Chair, the National Research Foundation. These documents are referenced in this contribution as the 'SARChI Chair Papers'.

4   The Mamdani case at UCT is one celebrated example but there are examples that go back to the most contentious of fields, anthropology, at the University of Cape Town in the 1920s (Phillips 1993: 23).

5   This contribution seeks to situate itself in that spirit. It is not, however, a full deconstruction of the DE initiative.

6   It is necessary to make the point that many other initiatives and projects in the South African higher education community have been established, which less directly have the same objectives as the ones that are listed here. These include the Wits Institute for Social and Economic Research (WISER) at Wits and the Institute for the Humanities in Africa (HUMA) at UCT. They were, however, not established explicitly as *knowledge* or *social inclusion* projects.

7   That there were other initiatives, beyond these profiled here, is without question. It is our job to bring these into the broader discussion. It is critical that the discussion has a critical working knowledge of all of these initiatives to understand, much more empirically and in much more grounded ways, what the politics of knowledge making, through the curriculum, are in the South African university.

8   A similar experience arose at a gathering on 'race' and racism organised by scholars at the University of South Australia in the middle of the first decade of the new century. It was one of the few occasions when academics and unapologetic IKS holders spoke to their points of departure for how they explained life in its complexity.

9   Interesting here is understanding Luutu's Marcus Garvey Pan Afrikan University with its commitment 'to epistemological rediscovery, relocation, promotion, management and development of African indigenous knowledge and wisdom so they can become part and parcel of the global knowledge systems and recognized as such' (Marcus Garvey Pan Afrikan University n.d.).

10   Already in 2009 Odora Hoppers would say to her interviewer Andersson, in response to his implied criticism about not seeing the impact of what she was trying to do, that the modern university was constituted over a 400-year period and that remaking it could not happen in a day (SARChI Chair Papers 2009c).

REFERENCES

Coles, Tait. 2014. 'Critical Pedagogy: Schools Must Equip Students to Challenge the Status Quo'. *The Guardian*, 25 February. http://www.theguardian.com/teacher-network/teacher-blog/2014/feb/25/critical-pedagogy-schools-students-challenge.

Escobar, Arturo. 2011. *Encountering Development: The Making and Unmaking of the Third World*. Princeton: Princeton University Press.

Essop, Ahmed. 2016. 'Decolonisation Debate Is a Chance to Rethink the Role of Universities'. *The Conversation*, 16 August. https://theconversation.com/decolonisation-debate-is-a-chance-to-rethink-the-role-of-universities-63840.

Fomunyam, Kehdinga G. 2017. 'Decolonising the Engineering Curriculum in a South African University of Technology'. *International Journal of Applied Engineering Research* 12 (17): 6797–6805.

Garuba, Harry. 2015. 'What Is an African Curriculum?'. *Mail & Guardian Online*, 17 April. https://mg.co.za/article/2015-04-17-what-is-an-african-curriculum/.

Hendricks, Cheryl and Brenda Leibowitz. 2016. 'Decolonising Universities Isn't an Easy Process – But It Has to Happen'. *The Conversation*, 23 May. https://theconversation.com/decolonising-universities-isnt-an-easy-process-but-it-has-to-happen-59604.

Hirsch, E. D. 2001. 'Seeking Breadth and Depth in the Curriculum'. *Educational Leadership* 59 (2): 22–25.

Jansen, Jonathan D. 2017. *As by Fire: The End of the South African University*. Cape Town: Tafelberg.

Kamanzi, Brian. 2016. 'Decolonising the Curriculum: The Silent War for Tomorrow'. *Daily Maverick*, 28 April. https://www.dailymaverick.co.za/opinionista/2016-04-28-decolonising-the-curriculum-the-silent-war-for-tomorrow/#.W0jsIi2ZPq0.

Kies, Ben. 1953. *The Contribution of the Non-European Peoples to World Civilisation*. Cape Town: The Teachers' League of South Africa.

Marcus Garvey Pan-Afrikan University. n.d. 'Marcus Garvey Pan-Afrikan University Profile'. http://www.friends-partners.org/utsumi/Global_University/Global%20University%20System/List%20Distributions/2011/MTI2220_20110120/MPAU-PROFILE-MODIFIED%20copy.pdf.

Mbembe, Achille. 2015. 'Decolonizing Knowledge and the Question of the Archive'. Presentation at the University of the Witwatersrand, Johannesburg, 22 April. https://wiser.wits.ac.za/system/files/Achille%20Mbembe%20-%20Decolonizing%20Knowledge%20and%20the%20Question%20of%20the%20Archive.pdf.

Motala, Shireen and Salim Vally. 2002. 'People's Education: From People's Power to Tirisano'. In *The History of Education under Apartheid*, edited by Peter Kallaway, 174–191. Cape Town: Maskew Miller Longman.

Ndlovu-Gatsheni, Sabelo. 2013. *Coloniality of Power in Postcolonial Africa: Myths of Decolonisation*. Dakar: CODESRIA. http://www.codesria.org/spip.php?article1791.

Newman, John Henry. [1852] 1907. *The Idea of a University*. London: Longmans. http://www.newmanreader.org/works/idea/.

Nyathi, Nceku. 2016. 'Decolonising the Curriculum: The Only Way through the Process Is Together'. *Moneyweb*, 27 December. https://www.moneyweb.co.za/news/south-africa/decolonising-the-curriculum-the-only-way-through-the-process-is-together/.

Odora Hoppers, Catherine A. and Howard Richards. 2012. *Rethinking Thinking: Modernity's "Other" and the Transformation of the University*. Pretoria: UNISA Press.

Paterson, Mark. 2018. 'Bringing "Development" into the Decolonisation Debate'. *University World News*, no. 499 (30 March). http://www.universityworldnews.com/article.php?story=20180330165321638.

Phillips, Howard. 1993. *The University of Cape Town, 1918–1948: The Formative Years*. Cape Town: University of Cape Town.

Pityana, Barney. 2016. 'The 2015 Student Revolts in South Africa: A Call for Dialogue'. Unpublished paper.

Prah, Kwesi Kwaa. 2017. 'Has Rhodes Fallen? Decolonizing the Humanities in Africa and Constructing Intellectual Sovereignty'. The Academy of Science of South Africa (ASSAF) Inaugural Humanities Lecture. Pretoria, 9 March. https://www.assaf.org.za/files/ASSAf%20news/Has%20Rhodes%20Fallen.docx%20ASSAF%20Address%2015.2.2017.pdf.

Richards, Howard. 2010. 'Human Development and the Transformation of the Academy'. Lecture delivered at the University of South Africa, 20 July.

Richards, Howard. 2011. 'Human Development and the Transformation of the Academy'. *Journal of Developing Societies* 27 (2): 201–216. DOI: 10.1177/0169796X1102700205.

RMF (Rhodes Must Fall). 2015. 'Rhodes Must Fall Statements'. *Johannesburg Salon* 9: 6-19. http://jwtc.org.za/resources/docs/salon-volume-9/FINAL_FINAL_Vol9_Book.pdf.

Rudin, Jeff. 2017. 'Deconstructing Decolonisation: Can Racial Assertiveness Cure Imagined Inferiority?' *Daily Maverick*, 22 January. https://www.dailymaverick.co.za/opinionista/2017 -01-22-deconstructing-decolonisation-can-racial-assertiveness-cure-imagined-inferiority/#. W0jwLS2ZPq0.

Santos, Boaventura de Sousa. 2007. 'Beyond Abyssal Thinking: From Global Lines to an Ecology of Knowledge'. *Revista Critica de Ciencias Sociais* 78: 3–46. https://www.eurozine.com /beyond-abyssal-thinking/.

SARChI Chair Papers. 2009a. 'About the SARChI Chair in Development Education'. Unpublished.

SARChI Chair Papers. 2009b. 'SARChI Annual Progress Report 2009'. Pretoria: UNISA.

SARChI Chair Papers. 2009c. 'The Most Challenging of All Mandates: NRF Educational Development Chair, Catherine Odora-Hoppers'. Transcript of interview with African Literature PhD student 'Andersson'. Unpublished.

SARChI Chair Papers. 2010. 'Human Development and the Transformation of the Academy: An Intellectual, Strategic and Pragmatic Response from Development Education'. Pretoria: UNISA.

SARChI Chair Papers. 2012. 'Report of the 4th Retreat: Development Education and Systems Transformation. Transformation by Enlargement: From Africa to Humanity!'. Pretoria: UNISA.

SARChI Chair Papers. 2015. 'Final Report: Building Excellence in Indigenous Knowledge Systems as a Science'. Pretoria: UNISA.

Soudien, Crain. 2015. 'Looking Backwards: How to Be a South African University'. *Educational Research for Social Change (ERSC)* 4 (2): 8–21.

Tabata, Isaac Bangani. [1959]1980. *Education for Barbarism: Bantu (Apartheid) Education in South Africa*. London and Lusaka: Unity Movement of South Africa.

University of Fort Hare. 2007. 'Grounding Programme Proposal'. Document submitted to the University of Fort Hare Senate, August 2007. Unpublished.

CHAPTER 8

Between Higher and Basic Education in South Africa: What Does Decolonisation Mean for Teacher Education?

Yusuf Sayed and Tarryn de Kock, University of Sussex,
Shireen Motala, University of Johannesburg

In the context of the student-led #RhodesMustFall and #FeesMustFall protests, there has been a renewed call for the decolonisation of the higher education curriculum.[1] This has been underpinned by an often-unexamined assumption that the curriculum is largely an artefact of colonial and/or apartheid education. A range of views emerged: from one arguing that a decolonised curriculum must place at its epistemic centre writers and views from Africa, to those demanding that such a curriculum must expunge all vestiges of 'Western' thought. There has been a constant refrain that indigenous knowledge be placed at the core of the curriculum. This chapter examines what these ideas imply for curriculum and pedagogy in higher education, specifically as it relates to initial teacher education (ITE). It assesses multiple and contested scholarly understandings of decolonisation as they relate to the curriculum (Hountondji 1990; Garuba 2015; Mama 2015; Mamdani 2016).

We focus on ITE, which connects the school to the university. The focus in decolonisation debates on disciplines such as philosophy, literature and the sciences in decolonisation of the higher education curriculum ignores the importance of the decolonising agenda to the preparation of teachers, and fails to see the interconnection between higher education in general, teacher education in particular and the education system as a whole (Mamdani 2007). We build upon a meta-analysis of teacher education curricula at five selected universities.[2] The meta-analysis provided a snapshot of the curricula for final-year ITE students in the year following the rise of the South African student movements and the call for the decolonisation of university curricula. We explored the written literature and topics that lecturers formally cover in their modules. In addition, we conducted semi-structured interviews with teacher education lecturers (one black female, two black males, one white female and one white male).

This chapter reveals what a more comprehensive decolonisation of higher education might mean, particularly as it relates to the transformation of an education system marked by historic racial, class and spatial inequalities (Bray et al. 2010; Soudien 2012; Sayed, Motala and Hoffmann 2017). It seeks to shed light on a contemporary education policy debate regarding what a transformed higher education curriculum might entail. In particular, it focuses on initial teacher preparation in higher education, challenging analyses that see school and higher education as disconnected elements.

SITUATING THE DEBATE ON CURRICULUM DECOLONISATION IN SOUTH AFRICA IN THE CONTEXT OF AFRICA

In many respects, recent calls for decolonisation in South African higher education are not unique in the regional context. It can be argued that the colonial project was simultaneously a political, economic, epistemic and cultural project engendering particular ways of being, knowing and doing. On the one hand, it subjugated economies and resources were mobilised towards metropolitan economies and networks rather than being directed towards local dynamics, needs and processes. This is evident in the export of natural resources and division of labour that relegated former colonial states to the margins of the global economy (Hountondji 1990). On the other hand, colonisation created forms of knowledge production and dissemination, and the sites through which knowledge is transmitted, organised and authorised (Hountondji 1990; Nyamnjoh 2016) in ways that marginalised local knowledge and traditions. It privileged particular identities that embodied Western, European, capitalist, Christian and heteronormative identities as the global norm, while casting other identities as local, particular, parochial and often inferior (Nyamnjoh 2016). Colonisation was a process of epistemological conquest (Ngũgĩ 1986); a cultural hegemony that destroyed the sense of identity and undermined indigenous knowledge. Thus decolonisation is as much economic and political as it is a cultural process; a process Ngũgĩ (1986) has claimed has no end point but acts as a reference for continual struggle.

In epistemic terms, decolonisation is the affirmation of the colonised. Yet the question is: What exactly should the outcomes of decolonisation be? In curriculum terms, this is most evident in the debates between Ali Mazrui and Walter Rodney in the 1960s on the function of the university in Africa – and analysed at length by Mahmood Mamdani in Chapter 1 of this volume. Their exchanges highlight a fundamental tension inherent in any debate on the role of universities, namely the line between excellence and relevance and the power dynamics inherent in who and what defines them. Such tension is also evident in the debate around the ideas of Ngũgĩ wa Thiong'o, concerning African literature in English. Ngũgĩ's point of departure was the assertion, particularly within nationalist movements, that colonial languages such as French and English served as rallying points around which struggles could be organised, particularly in contexts where a multiplicity of local languages had served colonial 'divide and rule' strategies (Mamdani 1998; Ngũgĩ 2005). Ngũgĩ and his colleagues proposed the abolition of the English Department at the University of Makerere and its replacement with a Department of African Literature and Languages. He wrote: 'The aim, in short, should be to orientate ourselves towards placing Kenya, East Africa, and then Africa in the centre. All other things are to be considered in their relevance to our situation, and their contribution towards understanding ourselves' (Ngũgĩ 2005: 439).

These debates reflect two key positions within debates on decolonising the curriculum, which can be characterised as 'nativist' or 'Afroradicalist' (Mbembe 2012). The former deployed a metaphysics of difference that emphasised Africa's uniqueness; subverting negative stereotypes about African societies (such as their primitivism and communitarianism) by transposing them into a positive interpretation of a glorious African humanity. Where nativism fails is precisely in its reduction of 'Africanness' to essentialisms that reinscribe racial logic and do not challenge racist thinking. Afroradicalism draws on the Marxist tradition and African nationalism to conflate class struggle with struggle against white domination. While this may not seem inherently problematic, in practice Afroradicalism's emphasis on political authority plays into a demonisation of critique and dissent as representative of 'inauthentic' Africans, racialising political orientation in a manner that mirrors the colonial politicisation of race and ethnicity (Mamdani 1998; Mbembe 2012). Fundamentally, both forms of Africanisation failed to problematise the notion of race and its use as a category of belonging, and as such reproduced the very categorisations that decolonising movements sought to overcome (Nyamnjoh 2016).

In this context, scholars (Mama 2015; Pillay 2015) have reminded us that South Africa's intellectual community is only now beginning a conversation that others long had in post-independence universities such as Cheikh Anta Diop (Bathily, Diouf and Mbodj 1995), Ahmadu Bello (Mustapha 1995), Ibadan (Ake 1982), Dar es Salaam (Shivji 1996) and Makerere (Mamdani 1990). The decolonisation debate in South Africa is not unique or new, though often assumed to be so. Such exceptionalism is evident in how students framed the debate at some universities, failing to make decolonisation visible as a historical process on the continent and seemingly unaware that the struggle is both continuous and reshaped over time, albeit conjuncturally different.

CENTRING STUDENT UNDERSTANDING OF DECOLONISATION: A TALE OF A BIFURCATED HIGHER EDUCATION SYSTEM

Popular debates on decolonisation in South Africa grew rapidly in 2015 following the now widely known incident when student Chumani Maxwele threw faeces at the statue of

Cecil John Rhodes at the centre of the University of Cape Town's (UCT) Upper Campus. Maxwele's actions galvanised growing dissent around lack of transformation, inadequate access and curriculum reform, as well as the alienation of black students at this historically white university (Nyamnjoh 2016). These issues became broadly identified with 'decolonisation', which then branched into different strands, for example #FeesMustFall, focusing on more specific issues. Initial arguments about decolonisation broadened into calls for insourcing campus workers, and subsequently the demand for free tertiary education and an end to a 'rape' culture at the country's institutions (Naicker 2016).

Students in South Africa have re-energised the debate about what decolonisation means through collective political action across the country. This movement is, as Saleem Badat (2015: 98) noted, multiple in form, variegated in its understanding and transitory, without a single source of organisation and leadership. He has argued that the 'transitory status of students means that institutional memory and organisational continuity and sustainability are major challenges'. This is both its strength and a source of frustration to administrators and academics seeking to address the collective actions of students as they often do not have a clear leadership, are not generally nationally organised, and formed around a single issue (Naicker 2016).

The decolonisation movement in its different forms and guises spoke to the largely unchanged nature of many of South Africa's historically white elite universities. It also demonstrated the divide between the country's tertiary institutions. Protests around fees, access and curriculum had taken place at poorer historically black working-class institutions regularly since 1994, but were largely cast within a discourse of violence and academic poverty, with the result that Maxwele's actions were seen as the 'start' of the movements for decolonisation and free education, although in reality they were not (Ndelu 2017; Vilakazi 2017). This divide reflects the highly unequal nature of higher education institutions (HEIs) in South Africa, a division based on class as much as race. The view is premised on an assumption that historically black working-class institutions were somehow limited to material concerns such as fees and access (Langa 2017), while historically white elite institutions were concerned with questions of epistemology. There is a tendency to see student movements at institutions such as Rhodes and UCT as something new and important, ignoring the legacy of protest that had taken place at different stages at HEIs following the end of apartheid, and more generally, in higher education elsewhere in Africa (Nyamnjoh 2016; Vilakazi 2017).

The dating by many to 2015 of the student protests around decolonisation mirrored the way in which academic work is constituted around the higher education divide. Following the changes and mergers of HEIs (CHE 2010), South Africa has a higher education landscape where racial, economic and intellectual conditions have created a two-tier system, with historically white universities (HWUs) deracialising, as schools have done, by attracting middle-class black students. In contrast, historically black universities (HBUs) are home to mostly black working-class students from schools in the lower quintiles. In this context, Mamdani (2016) notes that the division between HEIs in South Africa indicates the ongoing divide between excellence and relevance, where historically white institutions appeal to excellence to retain not only their privileges and networks, but their academic autonomy. For historically black institutions, which had not enjoyed the same level of autonomy due to their direct subordination to apartheid administration, 'any struggle of significance … took on an immediate political significance' (Mamdani 2016: 77). This generated the image of black academics as public intellectuals, as opposed to the 'scholars' in the bounded intellectual spaces of the traditional elite universities, but furthermore of a division between 'one who produces theory [the scholar] and one who applies it [the public intellectual]' (Mamdani 2016: 81). This locates the current hierarchy of tertiary institutions where HWUs (such as UCT, University of the Witwatersrand [Wits], Rhodes University, Stellenbosch University and the University of Pretoria [UP]) are bastions of academic excellence and producers of the research and innovation upon which HBUs and universities of technology rely. A participant in Sandile Ndelu's (2017) research into protests at the Cape Peninsula University of Technology (CPUT) argued that 'UCT students predominantly go in the upper end of the market place. CPUT [students] predominantly go into what they call the white-collar employment – banks, industries. They have knowledge. But their knowledge is applied knowledge and not theoretical' (Ndelu 2017, 17). There is certainly scholarly work from black institutions. This bifurcation does suggest, however, how knowledge production and scholarly work as currently constituted perpetuate divisions and inequities justified by standards of language and 'excellence'.

DECOLONISATION AS POLITICAL AND EPISTEMIC

As noted above, the student movement articulated multiple demands for decolonisation. Of significance was the view that decolonising the curriculum cannot be disassociated from a wider political call for decolonising higher education specifically and society in general. This idea is illustrated in the quotations below.

> We are an independent collective of students, workers and staff who have come together to end institutionalised racism and patriarchy at UCT. … We want to be clear that this movement is not just concerned with the removal of a statue. … The statue was therefore the natural starting point of this movement. Its removal will not mark the end but the beginning of the long overdue process of decolonising this university. (RMF 2015b)
>
> We have realised that the systems of exploitation which confront oppressed people at this institution cannot be tackled internally, precisely because they are rooted in the world at large. … The decolonisation of this institution is thus fundamentally linked to the decolonisation of our entire society. (Matandela 2015)

The student movement programme of decolonisation differentiated itself from government and its student organisations. … [It] called instead for deeper structural change of the university as an institution, issuing from concerns with staff demographics,

Eurocentric curricula, institutional racism and other forms of oppression such as patriarchy and homophobia. (Naidoo 2016)

The decolonising debate clearly does not exist in a temporal vacuum from the colonial and postcolonial experience. It encapsulates political, economic and epistemological
concerns about the impact of colonial domination (Mamdani 2016) and the reconstruction of a society founded on belief in the humanity of the colonised (Mbembe 2012;
RMF 2015a). The curriculum concerns of decolonisation thus include political and economic concerns relating to equity, access and social justice. In this sense, the debate about
decolonisation speaks to the 'unfinished business' of higher education transformation:
HEIs still reflect the colonial and apartheid legacy with inequities in relation to funding,
research productivity, student experiences and graduate employability, to name but a few.
Intersectional politics foregrounded the end for a decolonial approach:

> In our belief, the experiences seeking to be addressed by this movement are not unique
> to an elite institution such as UCT, but rather reflect broader dynamics of a racist and
> patriarchal society that has remained unchanged since the end of formal apartheid …
> An intersectional approach to our blackness takes into account that we are not only
> defined by our blackness, but that some of us are also defined by our gender, our
> sexuality, our able-bodiedness, our mental health and our class, among other things.
> (RMF 2015a)

Intersectionalism foregrounded both the symbolic and material reconstruction of the
institution, as well as society at large. While limited on programmatic detail, it affords space
for discussion and transformation of a racist, sexist, classist, chauvinistic, Afrophobic
and exclusionary institutional culture (RMF 2015a; Nyamnjoh 2016). It privileged the
experiences of students politically and epistemically, introducing new configurations of
race/ethnicity, class and gender in public spaces where images of white, able-bodied, cis-
heterosexual, middle-class and often Christian men had generally been considered as
normative (RMF 2015a; Wekker et al. 2016).

FROM REJECTING CURRICULA FORMS TO RECENTRING THE CURRICULUM

The student movement argued strongly for a decolonised curriculum that did not
emphasise Western knowledge and pedagogies (RMF 2015a; Nyamnjoh 2016). This
was an attempt to end 'the domination of Western epistemological traditions, histories
and figures' (Molefe 2016: 32), wherein 'it is surely part of the distinctiveness of South
Africa, that its politically majority "black" African population can change the "language"
and break the bonds of pain and suffering through renouncing self-imposed marginality and embracing better conditions of inclusion to create new forms of life' (Nyamnjoh
2016: viii). Western traditions and knowledge are understood as the element to be

questioned, for 'to be a radical African intellectual, is to challenge, on fundamentally personal, institutional and societal levels, this form of alienation that colonial education encourages' (Gamedze and Gamedze 2015: 1). As Archie Mafeje (2000: 66) has argued, 'to evolve lasting meanings … we must be "rooted" in something'. That 'something' is specifically African conditions, discourses and experiences.

What is most apparent in the perspectives of the student movement is what decolonisation must reject. In curricular terms, this is a view that a decolonised curriculum is one that removes canons of Western knowledge and forms of modernity tied to colonisation. In the words of a leader of the student movement:

> The current curriculum dehumanises black students. We study all these dead white men who presided over our oppression, and we are made to use their thinking as a standard and as a point of departure. Our own thinking as Africans has been undermined …
>
> We cannot be decolonised by white people who colonised us. … For decolonised education to be introduced, the existing system must be overthrown and the people it is supposed to serve must define it for themselves. (UCT student Athabile Nonxuba quoted in Evans [2016])

In a similar vein, it has been argued that in science there is a need to reject and replace Western canons of thought:

> How do we even start to decolonise science, because science is true, because it is science. Science as a whole is a product of Western hegemony, and the whole thing should be scratched off. If you want a practical solution as to how to decolonise science, we have to restart science from an African perspective, from our perspective of how we have experienced science. Western modernity is the direct antagonistic factor to decolonisation because Western knowledge is totalising … So, Western modernity is the problem that decolonisation directly deals with, to say that we are going to decolonise by having knowledge that is produced by us, that speaks to us and that is able to accommodate knowledge from our perspective. Decolonising the science, doing away with it entirely and starting all over again to deal with how we respond to the environment and we understand it. (Science Must Fall 2016)

These students conceive of a decolonised curriculum as a tangible artefact that simultaneously consists of new forms which that in the present curriculum and those that hark back to a pristine and pure past, which has been subjugated by colonisation and requires epistemological excavation. It is a binary approach posited on a knowledge canon ascribed to geographical spaces and figures. Knowledge forms and ways of knowing and reasoning are reduced to the ephemeral surface elements of content.

Underpinning this geography of knowledge, however, is the more important point of the language used to create, transmit and develop the curriculum. The marginalisation of African languages is argued to be a key gap in current curricula, reflecting colonisation, according to these students, as the following quotation indicates:

> White lecturers teach students African music and the base of music studies is classical European music. The curriculum does not accommodate creativity and expression in African languages. For example, drama students feel they are marked lower if they produce work in an African language. (UCT student Athabile Nonxuba quoted in Evans [2016]).

A key strand in the student understanding of a decolonised curriculum is the need to make it more relevant and for it to accommodate what has been marginalised and subjugated. This requires a curriculum which embeds African ideas, writers, philosophies and knowledge. For some, this means near-wholesale rejection of knowledge seen as originating elsewhere, particularly from the West; for others, Western canons of knowledge are complemented and added to by indigenous knowledge. The following quote succinctly expresses this idea:

> The current anti-black curriculum is designed to reproduce systems of oppression. This anti-black education is driven by the exclusion of the majority. FMF [Fees Must Fall] believes that the purpose of education is to allow for the transmission of knowledge and wisdom of society from one generation to another. This will prepare young people to actively participate in the development of South Africa. This type of education system will conserve the integrity of the community, perpetuating the agreed norms and values of society. (Fees Must Fall Western Cape 2016)

The binary curricular forms noted above stand in stark contrast to the idea of decentring curricula in favour of an African-focused, recentred curriculum. Achille Mbembe (2015) argues for a decolonisation project of recentring what is at the root of Africa's consciousness, placing African agency at the centre (Mungwini 2016). In curricular terms decentring and recentring are simultaneous processes that seek to create knowledge forms in which the positionality and geography of what is taught is decentred from the Western canon so that it has not just its roots but its location in the African imaginary and context. In this sense, the recentred curriculum, which is African, is both an expression of political struggle for agency as well as an assertion and validation of African identity. It is a curriculum that 'critically centres Africa and the subaltern … treating African discourses as the point of departure – through addressing not only content, but languages and methodologies of education and learning – and only examining Western traditions in so far as they are relevant to our own experience' (Mungwini 2016: 525). In this sense, it transcends versions of curricular decolonisation that seek to either replace or add to existing canonical forms.

This idea of a recentred curriculum, shorn of the more uncompromising aspects of rejectionist or additive models, is captured in this view of philosophy in higher education:

> There are at least three forms the decolonisation of the philosophy curriculum could take. First, some people conceptualise the decolonising of the philosophy curriculum as entailing the retention of the themes currently engaged with by the current curriculum but including African thinking in those conversations. The problem with this approach is that it proceeds by suggesting that we force African thinking into moulds pre-determined by Western philosophy. ... A second conceptualisation of decolonisation demands that we boot every text of philosophy from the West, or more generally from outside the African continent, from the current philosophy curriculum, and teach only African philosophical texts. I think that this approach depends on a serious misunderstanding of what decolonisation is. Decolonisation, as I understand it, demands a centring of African knowing and being. To centre a thing metaphysically implies the existence of other surrounding objects. ... This leads us into the third possible conceptualisation of what a decolonised philosophy curriculum should look like. Philosophy on the continent should have African thought at its centre ... But we cannot lock other voices out of that debate. ... The basic starting point, nonetheless, needs to be and remains the African life experience and African thinking about that life experience. ... This third form is the form I think a decolonised philosophy curriculum should take. (Nwogbo 2017)

Conceptualisations of a decolonised curriculum like these reflect two different ideas of what it means to validate other types of knowledge and what are conceived of as colonial knowledge systems. On the one hand, similarly to 'Nativist' approaches (Mbembe 2012), the decolonial imperative in curricular transformation is conceived of as that which valorises African indigenous knowledge and harks back to a past marked by essentialised renditions of being African as a reaction to colonisation. Narrow interpretations of this kind run the risk, similar to the post-independence moment in other African states, where calls for indigenisation of the academic staff (RMF 2015a) often take the form of Afrophobia, where scholars from other countries on the continent are seen as scapegoats put in place in institutions to avoid filling posts with local scholars (Nyamnjoh 2016).

On the other hand, in attempting to respond to the colonial imperative in curricular transformation, and to develop knowledge forms while recovering subjugated knowledge, it should be recognised how remembrance and reclamation may ossify, crystallise and reify difference as essence (Ndlovu-Gatsheni 2013; Garuba 2015; Nyamnjoh 2016). This attempt at recentring seeks to straddle both continuity and change and challenge forms of indigenisation of curricula that inscribe racist and primordial interpretations of the African experience and that relegate Africa to the 'particular' interpolated within the universal (assumed as Western) human experience (Hountondji 1990). As such, it seeks to avoid the double bind of selective memorialisation of a glorified precolonial past, and the reliance on languages and codes that reinscribe colonial stereotypes of difference according to race, ethnicity, class, gender, faith, language and other signifiers, in the process of trying to imagine a radically different future.

A recentred decolonised curriculum needs to engage specifically and critically with what decentring and recentring mean and what subjugated knowledges are to be centred. In particular, what does it mean to incorporate indigenous ways of knowing into the curriculum and who decides? In this respect, it is instructive to note Linda Tuhiwai Smith's (2012) argument that there is no single source of indigenous ways of knowing. They are as diverse as communities, languages, cultures and beliefs. In positioning the idea of indigeneity, this transcends the widespread but simplistic idea that the curriculum must reflect the various ways of knowing, and must be a balance between local and global cultural identity at a time of globalisation (Semali and Stambach 1997). A decolonised curriculum is more than a celebration of benign forms of diversity and multiculturalism, reinscribing colonial logic (Santos 2014).

The idea of multiple and competing ways of knowing is inherent in the pluralisation of the term 'indigenisation' as it relates to decolonisation. The idea that the epistemic is a site of struggle and contestation is then inimical to the idea of decoloniality. Boaventura de Sousa Santos (2014: 14) has stated that epistemologies of the South are 'ways of knowing developed by social groups as part of their resistance against the systemic injustices and oppressions caused by capitalism, colonialism, and patriarchy', as a decolonised curriculum is a continuous epistemic struggle and a curriculum always in the process of becoming and not being.

As a site of epistemic struggle, a decolonised curriculum privileges the agency of the student in processes of learning and in how the curriculum is defined and produced in higher education. Intellectual interventions were made in both oral and written exchanges between students from different elements in the student movement, challenging assumptions about the inability of black students to think and reason critically about their experiences of alienation and marginality (Nyamnjoh 2016). Students issued a challenge to higher education, and society at large, while themselves grappling with the complexity of their own post-apartheid experiences and the fractured nature of identities that had been contested, reconfigured and reimagined after 1994. The movement created the conditions for agency by opening up public space to enable dialogue about what a decolonised curriculum might look like. Many workshops, seminars and sessions, led by students, were dedicated to thinking through this question. Debates also revealed a 'darker' side of student movements, which included the dominance of males, sexism and gender violence, and the co-option of the movement by party political interests and members (Langa 2017). However, the space opened revealed the agency that is necessary to give expression to the idea of a decolonial turn in the curriculum as one of contestation and critical interrogation. In so doing, the movement enabled the prising open of a public space to engender a dialogue about a new imaginary. As Camalita Naicker (2016) explains:

> For the moment, student movements and others have been more concerned about calling for decolonisation and experimenting with different ways of thinking and

organising, than about prescribing the particular shape that decolonised curricula should take. In this regard, Naidoo (2016) characterises the student movements as '… clarifying the untenable status quo of the present by forcing an awareness of a time when things are not this way. They have seen things many have yet to see. They have been experimenting with hallucinating a new time'. In this sense the call to decolonise the curriculum can be understood as a challenge to give expression to an imaginary beyond existing thought and institutions that have become normalised as unchanging and unchangeable.

The recentred, decolonised curriculum is therefore one that affords space for dangerous conversations about race, to challenge the actions complicit in the continuation of tragic realities (Yancy 2017). This transformation represents and opens up the possibility of moving from 'knowledge as regulation' to 'knowledge as emancipation' (Santos 2007: li). A recentred, decolonised curriculum is then more than additive, or a replacement of forms of knowledge with others. It is about disrupting established canons of knowledge, engaging in pedagogies of discomfort, engendering radically critical conversations and seeing the epistemic at the heart of the struggle for decolonisation that confronts space and time, geography, body and positionality.

Fundamental to the idea of the decolonised and recentred is what Francis Nyamnjoh (2016) considered to be fundamentally a 'critical universalism' or alternative universalism (Connell 2016). Here, the Other is not absent but always present and binaries are transcended. Such an approach takes as its point of departure questioning the comfort of our taken-for-granted belonging to racial categories, gender groups, and so on. This requires, as the student movement shows, a reimagining of the terms we use to relate to and name the Other in our imaginations. Scholars such as the late Neville Alexander (2013) also held this position, arguing that the continued resort to race as a signifier of difference in post-apartheid South Africa would not serve the purpose of creating a raceless future; that race continued to lock individuals into particular experiences and interpretations of reality and that only through doing the difficult work of interrogating and experimenting with what a world without race could look like, and not before, would South Africa be able to create it. Raewyn Connell (2016) similarly pointed to the dialectic of the past and present, the dominated and dominant, the modern and primitive, as not in opposition but relational, in which the presence of the one implies the existence of the Other. Cast in this way the problem of the knowledge form of the marginalised is not about absence but 'its subordination within the mainstream economy of knowledge' (Connell 2016: 3).

SILENCES, GAPS AND OMISSIONS

Laudable as calls for decolonisation may be, there is a failure to undertake a relational analysis of the curricula at several levels. There is a remarkable silence about pedagogy and the practice of teaching. What are to be the relationships between students and academics in pedagogy and in determining which knowledge is to be valued? Decolonising the curricula is about much more than notions of its content, but encompasses the whole ideology of what it represents, for whom, and based on whose knowledge. Additionally, it is about more than simply decolonising the curricula in a limited sense, but involves considering the whole system, the project of the university, teaching practices and academics' attitudes (Heleta 2016). Mbembe (2015) notes the relational nature of a decolonised curriculum by distinguishing four stages of decolonisation required in the process of freeing university systems and enabling transformation to occur. They are (1) decolonisation of buildings, (2) decolonisation of classrooms – deconstructing what counts as valid teaching practices, (3) decolonisation of management – engaging in possible alternative ways of doing things, and (4) decolonisation of knowledge – validating indigenous knowledge and epistemic traditions supressed as different from the Eurocentric canon. Similarly, the Council on Higher Education (CHE) (2016) highlights some ways of thinking about a decolonised curriculum, including (1) changing the content: ensuring curricula are relevant to students' real-world experiences and match the needs of the local society, (2) changing how it is taught: curriculum as 'co-constructed', involving student voices and teaching practices, (3) changing the understanding of knowledge and interrogating whose knowledge it is, and (4) changing whose knowledge and who is teaching/researching. These frameworks point to the idea of a decolonial turn in curricula as multi-layered and relational.

Perhaps the biggest critique of the decolonisation movement as it relates to higher education is the failure to see higher education change as part of a broader transformation of the education system (Santos 2014). The student protests were characterised by limited and sporadic engagement with basic education that struggles to overcome historic racial, class and spatial inequalities (Soudien 2012; Sayed, Motala and Hoffmann 2017). The focus on disciplines such as philosophy, literature and the sciences excluded any focus on teacher education and the importance of transferring the decolonising agenda to the preparation of teachers, with a view of generating long-term gains across the whole education system (Mamdani 2007). There has been limited analysis of whether and how the schooling system and the curriculum are (de)colonised and how they shape student experiences. There is thus a need to excavate the roots of this system and examine the way in which colonial schooling systems have fed into the colonial intellectual project, creating subjects who are willing participants in its expansion and maintenance. The gatekeeping of universities begins much earlier – in the constitution of the schooling system and the way in which it sorts and accords value to particular modes of being and knowing, of knowledge acquisition and the place of higher knowledge as an indicator of class status (Ngũgĩ 2005; RMF 2015a). Decoloniality is also a project of decolonising schooling and teacher education.

DECOLONISING INITIAL TEACHER EDUCATION

The critical role of ITE programmes at universities in contributing to the process of decolonisation in tertiary institutions and schools is often underestimated. As Mamdani (2007: 213) argues: 'Higher education is where teachers are trained and curricula developed.

Without research in higher education to develop curricula for the entire system of education, all curricula will be as an off-the-shelf imported facility.… If our object is to transform general education, we need to begin with higher education.' The implication is that teacher education matters because teachers' agency is critical to decolonising our schools.

As African states became independent, processes of Africanisation and decolonisation took root. The role of teachers became part of the political project of nationalisation, and, at the same time, issues of culture and relevance became apparent. N'Dri Assie-Lumumba (2012) highlights the significant role of teachers in the process of Africanisation of states and the postcolonial emphasis on teacher education, describing teachers as 'catalysts' for rebuilding African nations. Due to educational expansion, most nations experienced teacher shortages, mainly in secondary schools, and the use of many unqualified teachers (Chivore 1986). Therefore, teacher education focused on solving the issue of demand. The emphasis of teacher education was that 'these secondary teachers should be in a position to pass on the country's goals, values and commitments that must in the end become part of the character of the youth of the new state' (Chivore 1986: 226).

Returning to the South African context, perhaps counterintuitively, the majority of teachers are not educated at HWUs. In 2012, 29 per cent of teachers graduated from the University of South Africa (UNISA) and 19 per cent from the University of the North West. Only 1 per cent of teachers graduated from UCT (DHET 2013). From this perspective, historically disadvantaged institutions that produce the majority of teachers in South Africa are crucial to what generations of children in South Africa learn. Thus, while black students and staff at HWUs have dominated the public debate about decolonisation, it is in fact the epistemic agency of their counterparts at black working-class universities that is critical to transforming our education system. The scholarly community and the public should pay much greater attention to intellectual work in these institutions. Scholars and students at historically white institutions should seriously consider measures such as research collaboration, co-development of curricula, student exchanges and stronger cooperation with their counterparts at black working-class universities, particularly in relation to teacher education.

The decolonisation of teacher education requires the dismantling of the system of education that produced 'generations of teachers, of all races, with distorted and deficient understanding of themselves, of each other, and of what was expected of them in a divided society' (DBE and DHET 2011: 19). In its teacher education policy, the post-apartheid government has taken into account the need to equip teachers to fulfil a number of roles and functions in the construction of a democratic and inclusive society. This culminated in the *Norms and Standards for Educators* (DoE 2000) and the *Minimum Requirements for Teacher Education Qualifications* (DHET 2011, 2015), providing clearer direction to providers for structuring teacher education. These policies set out the minimum norms, standards and criteria that should inform the construction of teacher education programmes, with issues of inclusivity, diversity and equity at their core (Sayed, Motala and Hoffmann 2017). For a number of reasons they do not, however, redress the coloniality of teacher education.

LECTURERS' VOICES

A meta-analysis of teacher education curricula at five selected universities in the Eastern and Western Cape provinces, was complemented by semi-structured interviews with teacher education lecturers, exploring their understandings of various factors that inform their curriculum decisions, such as personal intellectual backgrounds, institutional contexts and national policy requirements.[3]

Following on the work of Linda Chisholm, M. Friedman and Q.A. Sindoh (2017), a notion of colonialism is used that identifies continuities in power relations and representations between past and present; we also follow Leon Tikly (1999), who highlights the centrality of African agency in approaches that challenge Eurocentrism. Our findings below highlight epistemological concerns about who writes, from which perspective, and whether localisation of content is sufficient to signal decolonisation – issues that resonate with student views in the institutions surveyed.

While black authors were a minority across programme curricula, there were important differences across institutional types. At HBUs black female authors and white male authors contributed equally to the reading materials (33 per cent each), followed by white female authors (25 per cent) and black male authors (8 per cent). At HWUs, white male authors made the largest contribution (49 per cent), followed by white female authors (24 per cent) and black male authors (16 per cent), with black female authors contributing a negligible 3 per cent. At the merged university, the majority of authors were white females (53 per cent), followed by white males (29 per cent). Black female and male authors each contributed only 5 per cent.

The bibliographic data also reflect a specific geographic pattern. There was a strong emphasis on authors based at South African institutions. At HBUs, over 90 per cent of the authors were based in South Africa, while at HWUs and at the merged university, nearly 60 per cent of the authors were based in South Africa. There were few authors from other African countries in the curricula of HWUs, while they contributed only 9 per cent at HBUs and just over 3 per cent at the merged institution. Authors from South America and Asia were almost wholly absent from the five universities' curricula. In contrast, authors based in Western countries contributed just over 40 per cent of the written material at historically white and merged universities but were completely absent from the HBUs.

The presence or absence of authors in the curricula suggests that students are mostly isolated from intellectual debates in African scholarship and across the global South more generally, despite countries in these regions typically sharing certain experiences of colonisation and education.

While the content analysis suggests that considerable attention is paid to the history of apartheid, there seems to be limited coverage of the colonial and missionary roots of the education system or of other kinds of education systems such as initiation schools (Matobo, Makatsa and Obioha 2009), Islamic schools (Chohan 1988) and schools started by the descendants of slaves (Williams 2016). Nevertheless, at one of the universities surveyed, a week is set aside for oral discussion of indigenous knowledge systems, and at another a week for discussions of the relationship between the philosophy of Ubuntu and that of existentialism. This suggests a (very) slowly expanding imagination of what counts as important intellectual work. Several institutions emphasise dialogues and conversations, in order to develop a shared understanding of what decolonisation is and is not (Crowe 2017). A focus on local authors to the exclusion of authors from the rest of Africa and the Global South may, however, reinforce a kind of parochialism that reinscribes narratives of South African exceptionality, suggesting that Africans' intellectual capacities are dependent on the colonial encounter. This could, as Mamdani (1998) suggests, create the impression that colonialism is the pivot upon which history turns.

Arguably lecturers' curriculum decisions are shaped in part by their own intellectual biographies. Much of this is a product of their own higher education, which plays a strong role in moulding their intellectual outlooks and the bodies of knowledge with which they are most familiar. However, the influence of one's intellectual community is not always direct or obvious. As one interviewee pointed out, when he moved to South Africa to pursue his doctoral studies, he was exposed to a university that is a centre of Western knowledge in an African context:

> There's nothing really speaking about the African heritage, unless you go to a small unit in the library on African academic material, where people who really write from an African perspective – many of them … are white people who have steeped themselves in African thought, they have studied African philosophies, African knowledge forms, and they have something to say about it. … [That got me thinking] why don't we have more of that kind of ethos in our faculty of education? (Lecturer C2 2016)

The notion of intellectual identity was a recurring theme in lecturers' understanding of what it means to decolonise the curriculum – echoing a frequent theme of the student movement. While there seemed to be no consensus on the details of what decolonisation entails – some emphasised the use of African languages as a medium of instruction, and others a more South African-focused set of references – there was common acknowledgement among all interviewees that decolonisation involves a transformation of one's intellectual worldview and ways of understanding. As one interviewee argued, unless South Africa and other countries of the Global South uses a different lens, 'which says we are different from other parts of the world, this is what we have to offer the world, this is what is unique about us, and these are the unique contributions that our cultural development … can contribute to the rest of the world', it is not possible to 'seriously talk about decolonising anything (Lecturer C2 2016)'.

Similarly, another interviewee argued that decolonisation involved growing self-knowledge, with people beginning to grasp their own identities as teachers: 'You are beginning to learn a new way of operating in the world, and it's not just about you and the classroom, it's about you and the world (Lecturer B2 2016).'

A focus on language is a recurring theme, yet its implementation appears to be diffi-cult. Ngũgĩ (2017), speaking at Wits, said that the mother tongue was a powerful tool for the decolonisation of knowledge: 'Knowledge of mother tongue is empowerment, lack of this knowledge is enslavement.' Language policy continues to be one of the most contested areas, featuring extensively in the protests in 2015 and 2016. Examining language and its purpose is just one of the ways in which decolonisation of knowledge is taking place in South African universities. Students call for a recentred curriculum; echoing the calls for a shift from the benign approach to diversity and language. Pessimism about the dominance of Western curricula and ways of knowing emerged powerfully from the interviews. As one lecturer put it, the existing curriculum came largely from the West: 'The more globalised the world becomes, the more privileged Western thought becomes, Western ways of knowing become. So that is what we teach, we can't run away from that (Lecturer C2 2016).'

Interviewees expressed a strong awareness of the hegemony of Western knowledge. One remarked that 'whether you like it or not, it's a dominant, overarching hegemony of ideas' and described decolonising the curriculum as the attempt to accommodate local understandings within a dominant Western canon: 'Are there ways in which we can respond ... that derive from our own understandings of the world?' This interviewee was one who understood decolonisation as a process of struggle not only with the self but with one's broader historical context: 'We need to recognise our historical constraints ... [but] work with ourselves in the recognition of how that hinder hinders us simultan-eously' (Lecturer B2 2016).

None of the interviewees reported engaging deeply in their courses with the stu-dent movement on decolonising the curriculum. They made little mention of formal discussions about these issues within their faculties, despite the striking resonance with their own concerns. Several interviewees argued that the reason for this was that stu-dent teachers were reluctant to engage in student politics due to financial pressure. Interviewees also claimed that the student movements themselves were unclear about the nature of their demands regarding decolonisation. Academics had asked what decolonising the curriculum might mean, in concrete terms; but 'people are very unclear about all of that ... The parameters have never been awfully clear, and I doubt whether they ever will be. The minute you put a parameter on it then it's "why this boundary, why not that boundary?" You know how that goes. Whether that's obfuscating, or ducking and weaving, or genuine intellectual concern, it's a mixture of all of those things' (Lecturer B2 2016).

While echoing these sentiments, another interviewee pointed out that academics' own relative lack of engagement with the student movements may contribute to students' lack of understanding about the movement's goals. This lack of engagement, coupled with a sense that the movement's goals were shifting and changing over time, perhaps helps explain why not one interviewee planned to change her or his curriculum in direct response to student activism. It is perhaps also for these reasons that the interviewees struggled to articulate what they understood by decolonisation and related concepts such as indigenous knowledge. Although all of them highlighted the role of self-knowledge and contextual relevance as being part of these concepts, they had difficulty describing how they might change the curriculum to manifest this more concretely. Instead, what emerged from the narrative was an understanding of decolonisation as a process of multiple struggles, both within the university and the self.

What is evident is that teacher education and diversity in all their interrelated aspects have not been adequately investigated. Diversity must be viewed as part of decoloniality, and as Lungi Sosibo (2013) notes, diversity of culture and knowledge must be incorporated into teacher education. She further noted that teachers play an important role in socialising learners in the real world, and need to be equipped with the knowledge and skills to demonstrate and impart to their learners what cultural diversity is. Yusuf Sayed, Shireen Motala and Nimi Hoffman (2017: 84) suggest that trainee teachers need to empower themselves with epistemic agency so that they can instil in the learners they will teach the ability to be creative, accepting all forms of knowledge. One of the institutions that served as a case study in Sayed, Motala and Hoffmann's (2017) research on ITE programmes took up these concerns, implementing a faculty-wide 'humanising pedagogy', rooted in the work of scholars such as Paulo Freire and Antonio Gramsci and feminist and critical race theories. The implementation of this pedagogy coincided with the decolonisation moment in South Africa, with the result that the faculty took these concerns into consideration in shaping its programmes. Staff and management took the view that teaching was a 'moral, ethical and existential practice' (Sayed, Motala and Hoffmann 2017: 72) that required their responsibility to realise the worth and dignity of the learner, as part of the mutual and reciprocal recognition of their humanity by teacher and learner in the educational encounter.

INSTITUTIONAL AND SYSTEMIC ISSUES: FURTHER OBSERVATIONS ON FUNDING AND COORDINATION MECHANISMS IN INITIAL TEACHER EDUCATION

Two other important observations emerged related to lecturers' abilities to rethink curricula. First, there is declining public investment in higher education and second, a lack of mechanisms for lecturers and students to reflect and deliberate together about the curriculum. This resonates powerfully with the student postulation that their struggle was inextricably tied to broader issues.

Since 1994, HEIs have sought to increase access to higher education. They have followed a global trend towards massification of universities, but have also sought to redress historical inequalities by increasing the number of African students enrolled. Since 1994, the number of students enrolled at HEIs has more than doubled (MacGregor 2014). However, massification has not been adequately supported through government funding. Government funding as a proportion of university revenue decreased from 49 per cent in 2000 to 40 per cent in 2014. The shortfall was largely made up by student fees, which increased by 42 per cent from 2010 to 2014. To maintain a competitive edge in a rapidly transforming knowledge economy and achieve quality education at all tertiary levels, South Africa needs to invest more. Historically, South Africa has not invested enough in higher education; in 2015 higher education funding was only 0.67 per cent of gross domestic product (GDP). South Africa has failed to reach its own target of 1 per cent of GDP for research and development – a figure well below most international spending levels. From 2010 to 2014, the growth in permanent academic staff was 20 per cent, while the staff to student ratio grew to an alarming 1:55 from an earlier 1:40. These financial pressures on universities have negative effects on the quality of what is taught and how it is taught.

Lecturers often seem to be simply trying to survive amidst these financial pressures, which have increased under the impact of student demands. One lecturer explained that meeting student demands for insourcing workers meant that:

> The original money that was saved by outsourcing, which funded student bursaries, then got lost, and that then meant – and that's where I think things started to get very complex and emotional – is that what in effect it meant is that all academics have had to take a salary cut this year. We've lost two professorial posts, and likely to lose more posts … So now those who were championing the students' rights are not so happy as they were a year ago. … I think by the end we were all so completely exhausted that the thought of recurriculating the whole thing, and trying to understand what the heck we were doing, just became too much; let's just survive this year and we'll see how we go from there. (Lecturer B2 2016)

Within this institutional context of mounting pressures and multiple struggles, a number of interviewees spoke of the need to find space to think through curriculum decisions. Such collective reflection and deliberation between students and staff requires a coordinating mechanism, of which there was little evidence. Universities see student fees as a central form of revenue to sustain their operations. As a result, more and more students are admitted while universities face staffing cuts. Teaching and learning are directly affected: fewer tutorials, larger classes, the employment of cheaper and underqualified staff and staff attrition because of untenable working conditions. Lecturers described these conditions as having the greatest single impact on the already limited scope for consolidating knowledge and understanding, particularly in terms of conceptual development (Rusznyak et al. 2017: 23). This limits epistemic access.

The consequence seems to be that while the student movements have substantially influenced public discourse, they have had a very limited ability to provide a unified coordinating mechanism for rethinking our universities in general and teacher education curricula in particular.

Asked whether their university had collaborated with other institutions in thinking through their teacher training curricula, all interviewees indicated that there were no such communities of practice, even for the theoretical components of their programmes, where they might have been particularly valuable. One interviewee, who had been deeply involved in redesigning the curriculum in response to *Minimum Requirements for Teacher Education Qualifications* (DHET 2015), first introduced in 2011, stated flatly that they had worked in isolation: 'Our recurriculation was done solely by us within the faculty. I don't even remember us bringing in any experts from outside, from the other universities in the country. So it was purely done internally here' (Lecturer C2 2016). Another lecturer reflected that there had been some attempts at coordination across universities in the Western Cape in the late 1980s and early 1990s, but with the restructuring of the system through mergers the 'impetus just fell away completely, if there had been an impetus at all' (Lecturer B2 2016).

In addition, the interviewees noted that in their experience none of the teacher unions has been involved in facilitating discussions around curricula, nor the professional body of teachers, the South African Council for Educators (SACE). In one interviewee's experience, teacher unions and SACE had been 'non-existent in higher education … there's no real working together' (Lecturer E5 2016).

In this situation, government policy on teacher education curricula might have provided the space for collective reflection. However, one interviewee saw policies such as *Minimum Requirements for Teacher Education Qualifications* as specifying desirable graduate attributes, but failing to embed these 'in a regular basis in your teaching and learning' (Lecturer E5 2016). For this respondent, *Minimum Requirements for Teacher Education Qualifications* was not a framework enabling collective reflection on curricula, but an additional bureaucratic burden on overworked and resource-constrained staff.

Lack of opportunities for discussion seems inherent in current teacher education policies. *Minimum Requirements for Teacher Education Qualifications* emphasises the development of a mix of knowledge and skills appropriate for student teachers but is remarkably silent on curriculum content (Sayed and Novelli 2016). This may be understandable in an approach that seeks to protect academic freedom and autonomy, but it leaves open the issue of coordination, which even the Teacher Education Programme Accreditation and Qualifications Committee – a technical committee of the DBE, SACE, CHE and the Sector Education and Training Authorities – does not fill, though it seeks to align teacher education programmes with policy requirements for teacher education qualifications (Sayed and Novelli 2016). Consequently, specification of content is left to the discretion of teacher education providers, who may or may not collaborate with other universities, let alone the students. Nevertheless, the recent Teaching and Learning Development Capacity Improvement Project seems to have picked up the challenge of forming communities of practice (in Foundation Phase literacy and numeracy) in order to deliberate upon and reach voluntary consensus on what should constitute key subject and pedagogical content knowledge in their respective domains (DHET 2016). If encouraged by policy and supported by institutions, such communities of practice could respond to the call to decolonise the curriculum by creating similar spaces for discussion and consensus building, which in turn could make possible the collective development of

ITE curricula that would provide student teachers with common learning and knowledge experiences whilst recognising differing academic traditions and institutional histories.

Overall, the picture that emerges is an absence of robust coordinating mechanisms for collective deliberation between staff, students and practising teachers on what decolonising the curriculum might mean and how to go about it. This is compounded by the financial pressures on, and dwindling resources of, universities, which hinder attempts actively to tackle the creation of decolonised academic curricula in initial teacher education.

CONCLUSION

Decolonising the curriculum in higher education, specifically in relation to teacher education, reveals four key features. First, there are multiple and contested understandings, infused with diverse meaning, about what decolonisation currently is and should look like. These encompass perspectives that on the one hand suggest that decolonisation implies a curriculum that expunges what is perceived as an undifferentiated Western/Northern knowledge in favour of knowledges that colonialism and apartheid have subjugated. On the other hand, it implies a curriculum centred on African epistemologies that shifts the focus from hegemonic Western forms of knowing without repudiating them.

Second, material and institutional constraints reflect the political and economic legacy of colonisation and apartheid. These constraints have been deepened by the chronic underfunding of higher education, which has left academic staff and students with limited time and resources to engage in debates about the curriculum. Such constraints have most deeply affected universities that cater to black working-class students. Decolonisation of the curriculum is both an epistemic and material project. As such, both the material conditions that influence students being in university and conditions of labour for academics shape the limits and possibilities for a decolonised curriculum. To decolonise the curriculum is more than a project of what is taught and how, and any effort at decolonisation must call for targeted and sustained economic investment, particularly in black working-class universities. This should enable scholars to devote time and energy to explore these issues in a systematic and coherent way.

Third, lecturers and the student movements often seem unable to articulate in concrete terms what a curriculum might look like outside hegemonic forms of understanding and knowing. This dialectic between hegemonic forms of knowing and challenges speaks to the incompleteness, fragility and contested nature of knowledge creation as a collective enterprise. This is particularly relevant to decolonisation debates that require an expanded imaginative grasp, but where such grasp can be limited by this very incompleteness and fragility.

Fourth, it is unclear who should bear the responsibility of seeing the process through (Crowe 2017). Emmanuel Mgqwashu (2016) points out that decolonisation is not the responsibility of just one racial group, nor is it a project that degrades any particular race, while acknowledging that whites still retain a large percentage of wealth and knowledge production (Landsberg and Hlophe 2001: 25). It is also important to note that transformation is not the same as decolonisation but transformation could be viewed as a catalyst for the decolonisation of knowledge in South African universities.

What, then, are the possibilities for decolonised higher education as it relates to initial teacher education? There are no easy answers but it is evident that decolonisation of the curriculum in higher education in general and teacher education in particular must transcend binary forms of thought. It must be more than simply white versus black or Western versus African writers. It should be premised on an approach where what knowledge is and how it is constituted are critically interrogated, engaging with the position of the knower in local, regional and global contexts. Difference as a foundational element of knowing cannot be taken for granted and must be subjected to scrutiny. In this we need to challenge how the traditional and the indigenous are constituted while we also engage with how Western thought is constituted as a hegemonic form of knowing. For this to occur, we need a notion of a decolonised teacher education curriculum founded on a radical and critical universality that recognises epistemology as complex and in which disruptive conversations about knowledge take place. Where they do so, the binaries of colonial/decolonial and indigenous/Western are subject to critical scrutiny, and can be seen in their totality and engaged with as such. A decolonised teacher education curriculum should be one in which there are multiple possibilities, points of rupture, and encounters, always uneasy, with the power dynamics inherent in interactions between the self and Other, between curriculum and society, between what is and what could be and between the indigenous and the Western.

In teacher education, a decolonised curriculum should seriously engage with issues of language. Additionally, decolonising teacher education cannot take place in isolation from systemic shifts in how teachers are positioned as professionals in relation to the school curriculum, and the diverse schooling contexts in which graduates from university ITE programmes will find themselves. As such, decolonising teacher education is about addressing the education system more systemically, including in relation to teachers' working conditions, how they teach and how they are positioned in relation to education policy. Thus, the agency of student teachers and their critical positioning must be foregrounded within teacher education programmes to realise the laudable aims of decolonising the curriculum in higher education.

Even while every tertiary institution in South Africa has demonstrated a commitment towards the decolonisation of knowledge, whether through conversation, establishing new units, promoting dialogue, renaming spaces, creating manuals for curriculum change or through curriculum reform, more needs to be done. As Mbembe (2012) notes, there is a need for significant reform of institutional processes and for changes in institutional cultures and ethos. The task is multi-layered and complex and, as Mamdani (2016: 79) argues, epistemological decolonisation is different from political and economic decolonisation. It follows that decolonisation of the curriculum is not an easily achievable event but is rather a process of continuous negotiation and struggle with the self, with institutions and with others.

Finally, we suggest that the decolonisation of the curriculum should also be addressed as a political and economic project. The application of social justice to a diversity framework is hardly visible in the discussion. Some of the key proposals for decolonisation in our current context could include a diversity-rich curriculum, transformation of what is being taught and how it is being taught; universities' critical role in reproducing the modern/colonial division of knowledge; epistemic violence and the reproduction of the hegemony of dominant knowledge; universities' role in addressing global and social environmental justice through actively engaging with epistemic justice; a decolonial and intersectional approach that illustrates that diversity-poor practices are monocultural, and understanding that diversity and access are not only about inclusion but also about what knowledge is reproduced at the university through research, teaching, and so on. Most importantly, these ideas must be addressed at all levels. In this way, we can reinvigorate a radical conception of decolonisation as anti-capitalist and anti-neoliberal, which does not result in the maintenance of the status quo or the superficial papering-over of deep clefts in society (Nyamnjoh 2016). Decolonisation of higher education in general and teacher education in particular creates the possibility of realising substantive equity and quality in the process of learning in changing times and in a changing global context. For this we owe much to the student movements' call for decolonised curricula, and for the decolonisation project that is always in a state of becoming rather than being.

Decolonising teacher education requires an eco-systems approach to education transformation, spotlighting the complex interconnection between school and higher education. Preparing teachers in higher education institutions for teaching, then, is a necessary though not sufficient condition for transforming the legacy of colonisation and racism that marks South African society. However, decolonisation as part of the strategy of transformation raises complex questions about who decides what should be taught, how, and why. This chapter seeks to provides answers to these challenging questions as a way of opening up the space for informed and deliberative dialogue about the trajectory of South African education, more than 20 years after the formal abolition of apartheid.

NOTES

1   This chapter is part of a broader project at the Centre for International Teacher Education at the Cape Peninsula University of Technology, which aims to develop a systematic understanding of teacher education in South Africa in terms of the potential for teachers to contribute towards a more just and equitable education system. An earlier version was prepared for a special edition of *Journal of Education* (Sayed, Motala and Hoffmann 2017) and we acknowledge the contribution of Nimi Hoffman to that article. This chapter is a substantially reworked and extended version.

2   The universities included were two historically black universities, two historically white universities, and one university that merged to combine these two institutional types. Of these, two are in the Eastern Cape and three in the Western Cape.

3   This section draws heavily on Sayed, Motala and Hoffmann (2017).

REFERENCES

Ake, Claude. 1982. *Social Science as Imperialism: The Theory of Political Development*. Ibadan: Ibadan University Press.

Alexander, Neville. 2013. *Education and the Struggle for National Liberation in South Africa*. Cape Town: The Estate of Neville Edward Alexander. https://www.marxists.org/archive/alexander/education-and-the-struggle.pdf.

Assie-Lumumba, N'Dri T. 2012. 'Cultural Foundations of the Idea and Practice of the Teaching Profession in Africa: Indigenous Roots, Colonial Intrusion, and Post-colonial Reality'. *Educational Philosophy and Theory* 44 (S2): 21–36. doi: 10.1111/j.1469-5812.2011.00793.x.

Badat, Saleem. 2015. 'Deciphering the Meanings and Explaning the South African Higher Education Students Protests of 2015–16'. *Pax Academica: African Journal of Academic Freedom* 1–2: 71–106. http://paxacademica.codesria.org/IMG/pdf/Pax_Academica_12_2015_Guest_Editor_Nyamnjoh.pdf

Bathily, Abdoulaye, Mamadou Diouf and M. Mbodj. 1995. 'The Senegalese Student Movement from Its Inception to 1989'. In *African Studies in Social Movements and Democracy*, edited by Mahmood Mamdani and Ernest Wamba-dia-Wamba, 368–408. Dakar: CODESRIA.

Development Community (SADC)'. *Scientometrics* 84 (2): 481–503. doi: 10.1007/s11192-009-0120-0.

Bray, Rachel, Imke Gooskens, Sue Moses, Lauren Kahn and Jeremy Seekings. 2010. *Growing up in the New South Africa: Childhood and Adolescence in Post-apartheid Cape Town*. Pretoria: HSRC Press.

CHE (Council on Higher Education). 2010. *Teaching and Learning beyond Formal Access: Assessment through the Looking Glass*. HE Monitor 10. Pretoria: Council on Higher Education. http://www.che.ac.za/sites/default/files/publications/Higher_Education_Monitor_10.pdf.

CHE (Council on Higher Education). 2016. *South African Higher Education Reviewed: Two Decades of Democracy*. Pretoria: Council on Higher Education.

Chisholm, Linda, M. Friedman and Q.A. Sindoh. 2017. 'Decolonising History of Education in South African Teacher Education'. Paper prepared for the National Institute for the Humanities and Social Sciences. Johannesburg: University of Johannesburg and the University of the Witwatersrand Centre for Edcuation Rights and Transformation.

Chivore, B.R.S. 1986. 'Teacher Education in Post-independent Zimbabwe: Problems and Possible Solutions'. *Journal of Education for Teaching* 12 (3): 205–231. doi: 10.1080/0260747860120301.

Chohan, Ahmed. 1988. 'Muslim Education in South Africa: Its Present Position'. *Muslim Education Quarterly* 5 (2): 67–75.

Connell, Raewyn. 2016. 'Decolonising Knowledge, Democratising Curriculum'. Paper for the University of Johannesburg discussions on Decolonisation of Knowledge. https://www.uj.ac.za/faculties/humanities/sociology/PublishingImages/Pages/Seminars/Raewyn%20Connell's%20Paper%20on%20Decolonisation%20of%20Knowledge.pdf .

Crowe, Timothy. 2017. '"Decolonisation" at the University of Cape Town: What Is It? How Should It be Achieved? *UCT News*, 26 September. https://www.news.uct.ac.za/article/-2017-09-26-decolonisation-at-the-university-of-cape-town-what-is-ita-how-should-it-be-achieveda.

DBE (Department of Basic Education) and DHET (Department of Higher Education and Training). 2011. *Integrated Strategic Planning Framework for Teacher Education and Development in South Africa, 2011–2025: National Diagnostic Report on Learner Performance*. Pretoria: Department of Basic Education and Department of Higher Education and Training. http://www.dhet.gov.za/Teacher%20Education/Intergrated%20Strategic%20Planning%20Framework%20for%20Teacher%20Education%20and%20Development%20In%20South%20Africa,%2012%20April%202011.pdf.

DHET (Department of Higher Education and Training). 2011. *Minimum Requirements for Teacher Education Qualifications*. Pretoria: Department of Higher Education and Training. http://www

.dhet.gov.za/Teacher%20Education/Policy%20on%20Minimum%20Requirements%20for%20 Teacher%20Education%20Qualifications%20(2011),2022%20July%202011.pdf.

DHET (Department of Higher Education and Training). 2013. *Statistics on Post-school Education and Training in South Africa*. Pretoria: Department of Higher Education and Training.

DHET (Department of Higher Education and Training). 2015. *Revised Policy on the Minimum Requirements for Teacher Education Qualifications*. Pretoria: Department of Higher Education and Training. http://www.dhet.gov.za/Teacher%20Education/National%20Qualifications%20 Framework%20Act%2067_2008%20Revised%20Policy%20for%20Teacher%20Education%20 Quilifications.pdf.

DHET (Department of Higher Education and Training). 2016. *Teaching and Learning Development Capacity Improvement Project: Primary Teacher Education (PrimTEd) Project*. Pretoria: Department of Higher Education and Training.

DoE (Department of Education). 2000. *Norms and Standards for Educators*. Pretoria: Department of Education.

Evans, Jenni. 2016. 'What Is Decolonised Education?' *News24*, 25 September. https://www.news24.com/ SouthAfrica/News/what-is-decolonised-education-20160925.

Fees Must Fall Western Cape. 2016. 'Statement'. Facebook, 25 October. https://www.facebook.com/ FeesMustFallWC/posts/547974228740044.

Gamedze, Thuli, and Asher Gamedze. 2015. 'Salon for What?'. *Johannesburg Salon* 9: 1–2. http://jwtc. org.za/resources/docs/salon-volume-9/FINAL_FINAL_Vol9_Book.pdf.

Garuba, Harry. 2015. 'What Is an African Curriculum?' *Mail & Guardian Online*, 17 April. https:// mg.co.za/article/2015-04-17-what-is-an-african-curriculum/.

Heleta, Savo. 2016. 'Decolonisation: Academics Must Change What They Teach, and How'. *The Conversation*, 20 November. https://theconversation.com/decolonisation-academics-must -change-what-they-teach-and-how-68080.

Hountondji, Paulin. 1990. 'Scientific Dependence in Africa Today'. *Research in African Literatures* 21 (3): 5–15.

Landsberg, Chris and Dumisani Hlophe. 2001. 'The Triple Black Burden: Race, Knowledge Production and South Africa's International Affairs'. *South African Journal of International Affairs* 8 (1): 23–39.

Langa, Malose. 2017. *#Hashtag: An Analysis of the #FeesMustFall Movement at South African Universities*. Johannesburg: Centre for the Study of Violence and Reconciliation. http://www.csvr.org.za/pdf/ An-analysis-of-the-FeesMustFall-Movement-at-South-African-universities.pdf.

Lecturer B2 [pseud]. 2016. 'Interview about Curriculum Decisions in the ITE Programme', edited by Nimi Hoffmann, 17 August.

Lecturer C2 [pseud.]. 2016. 'Interview about Curriculum Decisions in the ITE Programme', edited by Nimi Hoffmann, 16 August.

Lecturer E5 [pseud.]. 2016. 'Interview about Curriculum Decisions in the ITE Programme', edited by Nimi Hoffmann, 18 August.

MacGregor, Karen. 2014. 'Major Survey of International Students in South Africa'. *University World News* 333 (6 September). http://www.universityworldnews.com/article.php?story=20140905134914811.

Mafeje, Archie. 2000. 'Africanity: A Combative Ontology'. *CODESRIA Bulletin* 2 (1–2): 66–71.

Mama, Amina. 2015. 'Decolonizing Knowledges 101: In the Master's House'. YouTube, 7 May. https:// www.youtube.com/watch?v=pXoisspygxU&feature=share.

Mamdani, Mahmood. 1990. *The Intelligentsia, the State and Social Movements: Some Reflections on Experiences in Africa*. Dakar: CODESRIA.

Mamdani, Mahmood. 1998. *Teaching Africa: The Curriculum Debate at UCT*. Cape Town: University of Cape Town, Centre for African Studies.

Mamdani, Mahmood. 2007. *Scholars in the Marketplace: The Dilemmas of Neo-Liberal Reform at Makerere University, 1989–2005*. Dakar: CODESRIA.

Mamdani, Mahmood. 2016. 'Between the Public Intellectual and the Scholar: Decolonization and Some Post-independence Initiatives in African Higher Education'. *Inter-Asia Cultural Studies* 17 (1): 68–83. doi: 10.1080/14649373.2016.1140260.

Matandela, Mbali. 2015. 'Rhodes Must Fall: How Black Women Claimed Their Place'. *Mail & Guardian Online*, 30 March. https://mg.co.za/article/2015-03-30-rhodes-must-fall-how-black-women-claimed -their-place/.

Matobo, T., M. Makatsa and E. Obioha. 2009. 'Continuity in the Traditional Initiation Practice of Boys and Girls in Contemporary Southern African Society'. *Studies of Tribes and Tribals* 7 (2): 105–113. doi: 10.1080/0972639X.2009.11886600.

Mbembe, Achille. 2012. 'At the Centre of the Knot'. *Social Dynamics* 38 (1): 8–14. doi: 10.1080 /02533952.2012.699243.

Mbembe, Achille. 2015. 'RMF in Conversation with Achille Mbembe: Part 1'. YouTube, 1 May. https:// www.youtube.com/watch?v=g-lU4BCsL8w&feature=youtube_gdata_player

Mgqwashu, Emmanuel. 2016. 'Universities Can't Decolonise the Curriculum without Defining It First'. *The Conversation*, 22 August. https://theconversation.com/universities-cant-decolonise -the-curriculum-without-defining-it-first-63948.

Molefe, T.O. 2016. 'Oppression Must Fall: South Africa's Revolution in Theory'. *World Policy Journal* 33 (1): 30–37.

Mungwini, Pascah. 2016. 'The Question of Recentring Africa: Thoughts and Issues from The Global South'. *South African Journal of Philosophy* 35 (4): 523–536. doi: 10.1080/02580136.2016. 1245554.

Mustapha, A. 1995. 'Society and the Social Sciences in Northern Nigeria, 1962–1994: A Case Study of Ahmadu Bello University'. *CODESRIA Bulletin* 2 (1): 12–16.

Naicker, Camalita. 2016. 'Camalita Naicker: Academy and Activism Panel'. Decolonizing the Academy Conference. YouTube, 22 April. https://www.youtube.com/watch?v=laDIAAwZ6-A.

Naidoo, Leigh-Ann. 2016. 'Hallucinations'. The 15th Annual Ruth First Memorial Lecture, University of the Witwatersrand, Johannesburg, 17 August. http://witsvuvuzela.com/wp-content/uploads /2016/08/Hallucinations_RUTHFIRST_August2016_FINAL.pdf.

Ndelu, Sandile. 2017. '"A Rebellion of the Poor": Fallism at the Cape Peninsula University of Technology'. In *#Hashtag: An Analysis of the #FeesMustFall Movement at South African Universities*, edited by Malose Langa, 13–32. Cape Town: Centre for the Study of Violence and Reconciliation. http://www.csvr.org.za/pdf/An-analysis-of-the-FeesMustFall-Movement-at-South-African -universities.pdf.

Ndlovu-Gatsheni, Sabelo. 2013. *Coloniality of Power in Postcolonial Africa: Myths of Decolonisation*. Dakar: CODESRIA. http://www.codesria.org/spip.php?article1791.

Ngũgĩ wa Thiong'o. 1986. *Decolonising the Mind: The Politics of Language in African Literature*. London: James Currey.

Ngũgĩ wa Thiong'o. 2005. 'Europhone or African Memory: The Challenge of the Pan-Africanist Intellectual in the Era of Globalization'. In *African Intellectuals: Rethinking Politics, Language, Gender, and Development*, edited by P. Thandika Mkandawire, 150–170. Dakar: CODESRIA.

Ngũgĩ wa Thiong'o. 2017. 'Language at the Centre of Decolonisation'. Lecture delivered at the University of the Witwatersrand, Johannesburg, 2 March. https://www.wits.ac.za/news/latest-news/general -news/2017/2017-03/language-at-the-centre-of-decolonisation-html.

Nwogbo, Johnbosco. 2017. 'Decolonising African Philosophy: What the Curriculum Should Look Like'. *The Journalist*. http://www.thejournalist.org.za/spotlight/decolonising-african-philosophy -what-the-curriculum-should-look-like.

Nyamnjoh, Francis B. 2016. *#RhodesMustFall: Nibbling at Resilient Colonialism in South Africa*. Bamenda, Cameroon: Langaa Research & Publishing.

Pillay, Suren. 2015. 'Decolonizing the University'. *Africa Is a Country*, June. https://africasacountry
.com/2015/06/decolonizing-the-university.

RMF (Rhodes Must Fall). 2015a. 'Rhodes Must Fall Statements'. *Johannesburg Salon* 9: 6–19. http://jwtc
.org.za/resources/docs/salon-volume-9/FINAL_FINAL_Vol9_Book.pdf.

RMF (Rhodes Must Fall). 2015b. 'UCT Rhodes Must Fall Mission Statement'. *Johannesburg Salon* 9: 6–8.
http://jwtc.org.za/resources/docs/salon-volume-9/FINAL_FINAL_Vol9_Book.pdf.

Rusznyak, L., L. Dison, M. Moosa and M. Poo. 2017. 'Supporting the Academic Success of First-year
Students in South Africa: A Study of the Epistemological Access They Acquired through a Lecture
and Text'. *South African Journal of Higher Education* 31 (1): 207–226.

Santos, Boaventura de Sousa. 2007. *Another Knowledge Is Possible: Beyond Northern Epistemologies.*
London: Verso.

Santos, Boaventura de Sousa. 2014. *Epistemologies of The South: Justice against Epistemicide.* Boulder:
Paradigm Publishers.

Sayed, Yusuf and Mario Novelli. 2016. 'The Role of Teachers in Peacebuilding and Social Cohesion:
A Synthesis Report of South Africa, Uganda, Pakistan and Myanmar Case Studies'. Brighton:
Research Consortium on Education and Peacebuilding, University of Sussex.

Sayed, Yusuf, Shireen Motala and Nimi Hoffman. 2017. 'Decolonising Initial Teacher Education in
South African Universities: More Than an Event'. *Journal of Education* 68: 59–91. http://www
.scielo.org.za/pdf/jed/n68/05.pdf.

Science Must Fall. 2016. 'UCT Science Faculty Meets with "Fallists"'. YouTube, 12 October. https://www.
youtube.com/watch?v=C9SiRNibD14.

Semali, Ladislaus and Amy Stambach. 1997. 'Cultural Identity in an African Context: Indigenous
Education and Curriculum in East Africa'. *Folklore Forum* 28 (1): 3–28.

Shivji, Issa G. 1996. *Intellectuals at the Hill: Essays and Talks, 1969–1993.* Dar es Salaam: Dar es Salaam
University Press.

Smith, Linda Tuhiwai. 2012. *Decolonizing Methodologies: Research and Indigenous Peoples.* 2nd ed.
London: Zed Books.

Sosibo, Lungi. 2013. 'Accountability in Teacher Education: Positioning Pre-service Teachers
as Evaluators of Their Performance'. *Africa Education Review* 10 (S1): 159–182. doi:
10.1080/18146627.2013.855441.

Soudien, Crain. 2012. *Realising the Dream: Unlearning the Logic of Race in the South African School.*
Cape Town: HSRC Press.

Tikly, Leon. 1999. 'Postcolonialism and Comparative Education'. *International Review of Education* 45
(5–6): 603–621.

Vilakazi, Marcia. 2017. 'Tshwane University of Technology: Soshanguve Campus Protests Cannot be
Reduced to #FeesMustFall'. In *#Hashtag: An Analysis of the #FeesMustFall Movement at South
African Universities*, edited by Malose Langa, 49–57. Cape Town: Centre for the Study of Violence
and Reconciliation. http://www.csvr.org.za/pdf/An-analysis-of-the-FeesMustFall-Movement-at
-South-African-universities.pdf.

Wekker, Gloria, Marieke Slootman, Rosalba Icaza, Hans Jansen and Rolando Vázquez. 2016. 'Let's Do
Diversity. Report of the University of Amsterdam Diversity Commission'. Amsterdam: University
of   Amsterdam.   https://www.researchgate.net/publication/310649646_Let%27s_do_diversity
_Report_of_the_University_of_Amsterdam_Diversity_Commission.

Williams, Karen. 2016. 'Martha Solomons: The Slave's Daughter and Countess of Stamford Who
Made My Life Possible'. *Media Diversified*, 31 August. https://mediadiversified.org/2016/08/31
/martha-solomons-the-slaves-daughter-and-countess-of-stamford-who-made-my-life-possible/.

Yancy, George. 2017. *On Race: 34 Conversations in a Time of Crisis.* Oxford: Oxford University Press.

REIMAGING COLONIAL INHERITANCES

4

CHAPTER 9

Public Art and/as Curricula: Seeking a New Role for Monuments Associated with Oppression

Brenda Schmahmann
University of Johannesburg

In a lecture delivered in 1927, the Austrian writer Robert Musil (2006: 42) suggested that 'there is nothing in this world so invisible as a monument'. Characterising monuments as 'conspicuously inconspicuous', he ventured that this paradox is true even of larger-than-life figurative statues:

> Every day you have to walk around them, or use their pedestal as a haven of rest, you employ them as a compass or a distance marker, when you happen upon the well-known square, you sense them as you would a tree, as part of the street scenery, and you would be momentarily stunned were they to be missing one morning. But you never look at them, and do not generally have the slightest notion of whom they are supposed to represent, except that maybe you know if it's a man or a woman. (Musil 2006: 42)

Although Marion Walgate's larger-than-life portrait of mining magnate and politician Cecil John Rhodes, formerly at the University of Cape Town (UCT), was one of the most prominently located commemorative sculptures in South Africa, Musil's insights seem to have tallied with the sentiments of many regularly passing the sculpture. Since the early 1960s, this work commemorating the benefactor of lands on which the primary

Fig. 9.1: Marion Walgate's *Cecil John Rhodes* (1934), bronze, on the upper campus of the University of Cape Town prior to its removal in 2015.

Source: Photograph by Paul Mills

campus was built had been poised above the rugby field and at the base of stairs leading to Jameson Hall,[1] where Rhodes sat with hand on chin, his acquisitive gaze surveying Cape Town and beyond (Figure 9.1).[2]

But despite its loaded iconography and the sculpture's being positioned in such a way that it was necessarily a point of focus for anybody standing lower down on the campus and looking upwards towards Jameson Hall, routine exposure to it by those in its surrounds appears to have rendered it somehow unremarkable to many. While concern was voiced now and then about the appropriateness of a commemorative statue of a figure such as Rhodes on a post-apartheid campus, these articulations – at least those recorded in the media – appear to have been occasional rather than frequent.[3]

This scenario changed decisively in March 2015, however. On the ninth of that month, about a dozen protesters gathered around the sculpture, where they called for its removal as well as an end to the racism they considered operative at the university, and one participant – Chumani Maxwele – then tossed a bucket of human excrement at the sculpture. The event, rather than simply being reported and then disappearing from memory, ignited a large-scale protest. On 11 March, the university's

Student Representative Council (SRC) issued a formal statement that the display of such a work was symptomatic of the lack of transformative actions being taken by the institution. In contrast to Musil's contention that monuments tend to go unnoticed, the SRC argued that the portrait of Rhodes served as 'a constant reminder for many black students of the position in society that black people have occupied due to hundreds of years of apartheid, racism, oppression and colonialism'.[4]

The immediate upshot of the protest against the sculpture is well known. While Max Price, then vice-chancellor of the university, had hoped initially for a relocation of the work, events took a different turn. Following escalating student protest which, included occupying the offices of the university administration in its Bremner Building, on 8 April the university council ratified a decision on the part of its senate to remove the sculpture, and it was taken to an off-campus storage site a day later. Meanwhile the so-called Rhodes Must Fall movement had developed in such a way that resistance did not limit itself to this work, other commemorative sculptures of Rhodes or indeed statuary of other individuals associated with oppression. Rather, removal was mooted as the first step towards addressing a lack of transformation on campuses more generally. In the words of Advocate Rod Solomons (2015), chair of the UCT Association of Black Alumni: 'It is our view that the challenge around the so-called Rhodes statue is code for something else that is bubbling under at UCT and at many of our universities and colleges.'

The removal of Walgate's sculpture, it should be noted, involved deviating from the general approach recommended by the post-apartheid government, where the policy has been to foster reconciliation by sustaining and maintaining inherited monuments and simply adding new ones to them.[5] But regulations to respect works from apartheid and colonial eras notwithstanding, a question arises as to whether the decision to remove the offending sculpture from UCT ought to mark the start of a fundamentally new approach to managing visual culture in the public domain and at universities in particular. Are monuments from colonial and apartheid eras irrelevancies that, if they are observed at all, do nothing but cause offence? Is there any sense in retaining prominently placed and larger-than-life sculptures at other universities, ones that – like Walgate's sculpture of Rhodes – are of individuals whose values and approaches are now generally questioned and critiqued?

I propose that, while seeming to symbolise a commitment towards enabling the transformation of campuses into spaces where prejudicial values and attitudes that held sway during colonial and apartheid eras are no longer tolerated, a removal of sculptures and monuments does not in fact ultimately work productively towards enabling such change. In much in the same way that reading a novel such as Joseph Conrad's *Heart of Darkness* in 2019 in light of postcolonial theories will yield insights and understandings that are distinct from what a reader might have gleaned in 1899, when it was originally published, so too might current bodies of thought affect the way in which contemporary viewers interpret historical monuments. If engaging with *Heart of Darkness* is more likely to enable a critical understanding of stereotypes about Africa and their damaging implications than a banning of the novel from public libraries might achieve, so too – surely – is the act of making available monuments associated with prejudicial histories rather than rendering them inaccessible. Proposing that monuments might contribute towards the acquisition of enhanced critical insight into the imperatives and biases at play within the colonial and apartheid eras, I suggest that they might be helpfully viewed as valuable for a contemporary student body rather than as tired remnants from the past that remain in place only because one is not allowed to remove them. Supporting this position by outlining creative strategies that have been deployed to negotiate objects and sites with loaded histories and connotations, I suggest how such interventions enable commemorative monuments and sculptures to constitute a type of 'curriculum' with the capacity to elicit enriched knowledge and understanding on the part of viewers. My overall purpose is to suggest that creative interventions with respect to monuments may assume an educative role, whether these are undertaken by invited artists or by students themselves.

After briefly outlining some problematical implications of removal, as well as referring to alternative forms of critical engagement that have been undertaken internationally, I turn my attention to three creative interventions in response to monuments on South African campuses. These are valuable to consider together because, while undertaken at different periods (one half a decade after the first democratic election, another nine months prior to the commencement of the Rhodes Must Fall movement and a third during the last phase of student protests), they all respond critically to monuments associated with the influence of Afrikaner nationalist ideas.

RETHINKING THE ROLE OF MONUMENTS

Cities are dynamic entities with structures that necessarily change rather than being frozen in time. Consequently, monuments and sculptures have historically been adapted or moved in response to changed circumstances, and, like other structures, they are also susceptible to the effects of the elements. While we tend to think of monuments as permanent, this is mostly the result of the connotative impact of materials they may include, such as marble and bronze, or their stylistic allusions to 'timeless' works from ancient Greece or Rome. But viewing monuments as structures that are amenable to modification and relocation, rather than being sacrosanct, does not mean advocating the automatic destruction or placement in storage of those associated with unpalatable histories.

A perception that systematically purging public spaces of artworks commemorating regimes, groups and individuals whose actions were associated with colonial or apartheid values is necessary for those spaces to be suitably 'decolonised' tends to involve understandings that works of art have definitive and fixed meanings. In the case of the Walgate sculpture, it overlooked 'how changed understandings of Cecil Rhodes and the influence of highly critical views about British imperialism will necessarily affect the degree of authority the sculpture might exert in the twenty-first century' (Schmahmann 2016: 100). I have indicated that a principle of evaluating people represented in art as either 'good' or

'bad' has a flattening effect on how one reads history, encouraging one to overlook the complex imperatives that underpin choices they make. Such perspectives tend also to reduce
the value of works of art to who they represent, neglecting how such objects may also speak
in valuable ways of aesthetic and representational traditions. A sad irony in the case of the
Walgate work is that UCT ended up removing from view one of the comparatively few early
twentieth-century public sculptures made by a woman artist. 'While claiming that this was
a necessary first step for transforming the campus, and even now and then mentioning
gender in their calls for equity,' I have remarked elsewhere, 'those arguing for the removal
of the sculpture displayed a total blind-spot about how such an act would in fact perpetuate
a marginalisation of women artists in the public sphere' (Schmahmann 2016: 101).

Perhaps most importantly, as I have also observed, removal is often the modus oper-
andi of choice for those leaning more toward the right than the left of the political spectrum. Commemorative objects are in some sense material evidence of past allegiances
that may be potentially embarrassing or compromising for those seeking to obfuscate
or deny such links, while those intractably rooted in right-wing movements may find
removal a useful assurance that their heritage treasures will not be vulnerable to dese-
cration by people unsympathetic to their viewpoints. An example of removal being used
to halt rather than foster transformative actions occurred at Rhodes University in the
immediate post-apartheid period. In 1994, the institution's senate received a proposal for
a name change – one that was defeated through a disingenuous argument that the name
was simply a 'brand' and involved people making no connection to Cecil Rhodes as an
historical figure. As a consequence, however, the university found itself obliged to remove
from view the various portraits of the mining magnate and politician that were in key
positions on its two campuses. Taken away first was a large framed photograph that was
then at the official entrance to the university's East London campus and subsequently two
sculpted busts by Henry Pegram – one of Cecil Rhodes and the other of Alfred Beit – that
the university had been bequeathed in the early twentieth century and that had been
displayed ceremoniously at the official entrance to the university buildings on the primary Grahamstown (Makhanda) campus since the 1960s. In other words, by removing
these portraits, the university was certainly not aiming to facilitate left-wing interests.
On the contrary, it was resisting calls for transformative actions and instead taking the
line of simply denying that it had been founded with seed money from the Rhodes Trust
and had in fact spent its history constructing Cecil Rhodes as what a reporter described
in 1909 as 'the parent' of the institution (*Grahamstown Journal* 1909: 2).[6] In so doing, it
was also of course removing imagery that might allow a current student at that university
a critical engagement with the institution's own problematic history and how this might
have a bearing on its present.

But if the monuments in question are not to be, at best, invisible and, at worst,
interpreted as ratifications and support for the actions and attitudes of those whom they
commemorate, they call for active intervention. In other words, if they are to become
dynamic prompts for engaging with South African histories, cues of one kind or another
are needed. Such interventions or cues need not assume literal apologies or statements

of disassociation: plaques with wording in which institutions distance themselves from the actions of the individuals or groups commemorative objects represent, besides being unsophisticated, are most likely to close off discussion. If monuments are to serve as a rich form of 'curriculum', one might instead look for engagements that prompt the workings of memory (and postmemory)as well as discursive engagement.[7]

Amongst the numerous successful examples of such interventions that have taken place internationally are superimpositions over monuments from the past. When regulations on the part of English Heritage prevented adaptations to murals by Jan Juta and J.H. Pierneef in South Africa House in London, a scheme was devised to overlay the murals with glass that would enable discursive and critical engagements with their content. Thus, for example, Sue Williamson engaged with a painting by Juta depicting Simon van der Stel at the Castle involved in an exchange of copper by proposing to overlay the mural in question with a transcription of a ledger revealing Van der Stel's various slave transactions – information left out of sanitised accounts of Dutch settlement at the Cape (see Coombes 2004: 293–295). Relatedly, in 2011 Arnold Holzknecht and Michele Bernardi undertook a creative intervention to a monumental frieze in a civic building in the small town of Bolzano in northern Italy that represents fascist leader Benito Mussolini on horseback and includes the slogan *Credere, Obbedire, Combattere* (Believe, Obey, Combat). Leaving the original discernible, they superimposed over the frieze, in LED illumination, a quote by Hannah Arendt that reads 'Nobody has the right to obey' in Italian, German and Ladin, a local Romance language (see Invernizzi-Accetti 2017).

Some interventions around monuments are intended to be temporary. These have included image projections – most famously perhaps those of the Polish-born USA-based artist, Krzysztof Wodiczko. Amongst his initiatives was one involving South Africa House, which he undertook in 1981 in response to the Thatcher government's refusal to impose sanctions on South Africa. While working on another commission in Trafalgar Square, Wodiczko surreptitiously projected a swastika on to the emblem of the Cape of Good Hope on the pediment of the embassy, an installation that remained up for only a couple of hours. While one might argue that such a juxtaposition may have flattened out differences between apartheid South Africa and Nazi Germany, the monument was nevertheless highly effective in terms of what Ewa Lajer-Burcharth (1987: 148) describes as its 'strategic disruption of the architectural language of Trafalgar Square': Herbert Baker had 'used a deliberately anachronistic style' in this twentieth-century building so that it might 'give the embassy the cultural authority evoked by other public agencies located there', but Wodiczko denies it 'this comfortable architectural fit'. Works intended to be of short duration also include performance-based works. For example, in a 1982 incarnation of her *Body Configurations* series, the Austrian performance artist, VALIE EXPORT, adopted exaggeratedly deferential postures at ideologically loaded sites in Vienna, such as its *Heldenplatz* (Heroes, Square) where Hitler gave his victory speech following his march into Austria in 1938 (see Widrich 2014: 78–79).

Interventions may also take the form of alternative monuments placed alongside or in the vicinity of ones associated with ideologies that are considered problematic. A work of this type is regarded as dialogical in the sense that, as Quentin Stevens and Karen Franck (2016: 68) explain, it 'draws critically from an existing memorial's formal vocabulary and values, and in doing so, enriches that language by redeploying or inverting the meanings of existing forms and adding new inflections'. A South African example of this type can be found at the site of the so-called Battle of Blood River near Dundee in KwaZulu-Natal, where a 1970s, monument by Cobus Esterhuizen comprised of 64 bronzed cast-iron wagons was joined by a 1999 Wall of Remembrance invoking the horn-like battle formation used by Dingane's army (see Marschall 2010: 311). Dialogical monuments are sometimes also counter-monuments – a term James Young (1992) first used to designate works that challenge the traditionalist form of the monument. For example, as Stevens and Franck point out, Maya Lin's Vietnam Veterans Memorial in Washington, DC has a dialogical relationship with two traditionalist monuments – the Washington Monument and Lincoln Memorial – in the sense that its shape 'frames sightlines' to them. But it nonetheless 'contrasts thematically and experientially with these works. Its black polished surface reflects them. Its dark form sinks into the landscape rather than rising up. It encourages intimate, introspective experience rather than distant viewing' (Stevens and Franck 2016: 72). Particularly when it assumes the form of a counter-monument, a new monument placed in proximity to an old one, and which is designed to have a dialogical relationship to it, can thus serve to challenge its messages and meanings in important ways.

MNEMONIC MONUMENTS ON SOUTH AFRICAN CAMPUSES

Some of these various strategies have informed and underpinned interventions to monuments on campuses. While I am not aware of instances where universities have sought physically to adapt monuments on a permanent basis, a number of performance-based or temporary adjustments to monuments have come to my attention. New works have also been designed and placed in such a way as to enable dialogical relationships with older ones, and, working in light of discourse about the counter-monument, some of these new monuments have self-consciously avoided traditionalism.

When it became the University of Johannesburg, in 2005, the newly merged institution inherited the former Rand Afrikaans University (RAU) campus – and with it, two monuments that have a dialogical relationship to one another.

The earlier of the two (Figure 9.2), unveiled on 12 August 1975, and in the same year as the new RAU campus in Auckland Park was itself opened, is located within the grounds surrounded by the circular main building. Jan van Wijk, architect of the Taalmonument (Language Monument) in Paarl, was also on the team of architects that had recently completed the RAU buildings. Approached by the university for his ideas about something enduring for campus to coincide with the centenary of the founding of Die Genootskap van Regte Afrikaners, an organisation promoting Afrikaans, he suggested transporting rocks from the site of the Taalmonument to the campus.[8]

Figure 9.2: Monument with three stones conceptualised by Jan van Wijk for the former Rand Afrikaans University (1975) on the Kingsway Auckland Park campus of the University of Johannesburg.

Source: Photograph by Paul Mills

The second, begun in 1999 and completed in 2000, is by the well-regarded South African artist Willem Boshoff, whose work often includes a focus on the complexity of Afrikaans identities and histories, and is between and surrounding the primary entrance to the main building of the campus and the library. Entitled *Kring van Kennis* ('Circle of Knowledge'), it reiterates the monument installed in 1975 in the sense that it is comprised of boulders – but in this instance 11 of them – and engages with language. Made from black granite, each boulder (Figure 9.3) includes on its planed top a spiral of script in which definitions for obscure English words are offered in one of South Africa's 11 official languages.

The rock or boulder in the 1975 monument draws on a motif with allusions to the Great Trek. While in fact a having terrible impact on the lives of various groups within the interior, intrinsic to Afrikaner nationalism was the idea, as Jennifer Beningfield (2006, 35) expresses it, that this new nation of Voortrekkers 'had been able to discover itself in the isolated and empty interior' that 'was depicted as being without history, ripe for inscription'. Along with reinforcing a misconstruction of white Afrikaners as pioneers taking occupation of virgin territory, the focus on rocks that were seemingly constituted either by nature or by long-departed prehistoric cultures as part of their spiritual rites

Figure 9.3: The granite boulder with sand-blasted text that includes English definitions of English words in Wilhelm Boshoff's *Kring van Kennis* (Circle of Knowledge) (2000).

Source: Photograph by Paul Mills

enables the language monument to create the impression of having predated the development of the campus and Johannesburg by hundreds of years – almost as if Afrikaner nationalist ideas were authenticated prehistorically.

But Boshoff's later monument critically inverts and upsets Afrikaner nationalist ideas rather than reinforcing them. *Kring van Kennis* reiterates the circular structure of the RAU buildings. Whereas the architecture of RAU may be read as a concrete bastion resistant to outside forces through its laager-like form and thus of intractability and an impetus to intellectually and ideologically separate the group from others, Boshoff's circle invokes reference to seating used for an *imbizo* (gathering/meeting) and thus to a context that offers opportunities for the democratic exchange of different perspectives. And, while sharing with the 1975 language monument on campus allusions to prehistoric structures such as Stonehenge, this similarity serves to emphasise their differences. Whereas the 1975 monument was, as Boshoff explains, 'regarded as fighting for the supremacy of Afrikaans at the expense of all the other languages spoken in South Africa' (interview with the author, 4 February 2010), *Kring van Kennis* gives equal status to all those tongues. And whereas the 1975 language monument is an imposing structure that does not invite physical inter-action, the Boshoff work lends itself to being climbed on and sat upon – that is, it avoids all the deferential awe that traditionalist commemorative objects are designed to elicit.

The words included in Boshoff's work are all 'ologies' or 'isms', thus invoking reference to the kinds of topics studied at universities. But as I have remarked in another publi-cation, these 'ologies' and 'isms' are somewhat remote from usual themes. Some allude to fields too esoteric to be probable in a contemporary context while others describe actions that, while sounding erudite, are in fact far removed from the highbrow. But while many amuse, others discomfort the viewer by 'invoking reference to prejudice or guilt, and thus to "ologies" and "isms" which we perhaps ought to study rather more than we do' (Schmahmann 2013: 4). 'Ethnophaulism', for example, refers to 'insulting speech in a racial sense' and 'Hamartology' designates 'the doctrine that deals with sin'. These allusions to conflict on the basis of difference are reinforced through the iconog-raphy of the rock which, while having connotations to do with occupying virgin territory in Afrikaner nationalist uses, as indicated, is also more generally associated with stone-throwing. Crucial here, however, is the fact that Boshoff's boulders are in fact far too weighty to throw and thus point to the conversation, the *imbizo*, as a far preferable way of resolving difference.[9]

Completed six years after the first democratic election, Boshoff's monument was made in a context in which RAU's founding vision of itself as an academic home for white Afrikaners was clearly untenable. The university had consequently begun seeking to increase enrolments of black students by providing tuition in both English and Afrikaans, and by the turn of the new millennium, more than half its students preferred English as their medium of instruction (Voort 2002: 8). Five years after the unveiling of Boshoff's sculpture, however, a decisive change meant that this would not continue to be a uni-versity where Afrikaans enjoyed any special privilege: RAU was merged with the former Wits Technikon and components of Vista University to form a completely new entity, the University of Johannesburg. A language policy approved by the new university's senate on 25 October 2006 indicated on the university's website that it 'promotes multilingualism and designates Sesotho sa Leboa, English, isiZulu and Afrikaans as its primary languages for academic, administrative, communication and marketing purposes'. These ambitious plans would be somewhat modified in time, however. In its most recent language policy, approved by its council on 3 April 2014, the university indicated on the university's web-site that all its modules and programmes 'are offered in English, and wherever possible and reasonably practicable, will also be offered in the other three designated languages', but English was designated specifically as 'the primary language of internal governance, administration, marketing, and internal and external communication'.

Although the 1975 monument has not itself been physically altered since its original installation, it is *conceptually* altered through the presence of *Kring van Kennis* on campus. When considered alongside the Boshoff work, which sets up a dialogue with it, the earlier monument lends itself to being used for a discursive engagement with the history of the campus, with how educational institutions were enmeshed and involved in promoting Afrikaner nationalist interests, and how such interests may have had an impact on the visual domain. While it is yet to be deployed in this way, it has the potential to become an exciting and vital prompt for critical consideration of questions about language and identity on South African campuses, as well as historical engagements with the impact of Afrikaner nationalism on institutions and their visual culture.

While *Kring van Kennis* operates as a dialogical counter-monument, there have also been various temporary interventions to works on South African campuses. Particularly notable in this regard is an intervention that responded to two prominently placed commemorative sculptures on the University of the Free State campus (Figure 9.4).

Figure 9.4: Anton van Wouw, *Marthinus Theunis Steyn* (1929), bronze, on the left and Johann Moolman, *C.R. Swart* (1991), bronze, on the right.

Source: Photographs by Paul Mills

The earlier of the two works under scrutiny was of Marthinus Theunis Steyn, the sixth and final president of the Orange Free State. Unveiled on 29 September 1929, this twice-life-size work in bronze was made by the prominent sculptor of Afrikaner statesmen and heroes, Anton van Wouw, and was paid for by the Afrikaanse Studentebond (Afrikaner Student Union), an organisation with an Afrikaner nationalist orientation. Also included in the intervention was a stylised and larger-than-life bronze portrayal of C.R. Swart, the first state president of the Republic of South Africa and the chancellor of the university between 1950 and 1976. Made by Johann Moolman, it was acquired considerably later – in 1991.

Figure 9.5: The preparation of works for Cigdem Aydemir's *Plastic Histories* (2014): Left: Van Wouw's *Marthinus Theunis Steyn* shrink-wrapped in plastic and prior to being spray-painted pink; top right: Cigdem Ayemir (front) organising the shrink-wrapping of Van Wouw's *Marthinus Theunis Steyn*; bottom right, Moolman's *C.R. Swart* in the process of being spray-painted pink.

Source: Photographs by Paul Mills

In 2014 and as part of the Vryvees, an annual arts festival in Bloemfontein, an Australian artist, Cigdem Aydemir, shrink-wrapped and sprayed pink these representations of Steyn and Swart (Figure 9.5) as part of a work called *Plastic Histories*.

While she hoped to also cover with pink shrink-wrapping four commemorative sculptures of Afrikaner nationalist figureheads and heroes in the city,[10] she was unable to secure permission to do so. Hence, working with a colleague, Warren Armstrong, she devised an application that viewers could access on their cell phones or tablets that would instead create the impression that these various sculptures had received this treatment. Simultaneous with the exhibition was a show at the Johann Stegmann Gallery on campus that included digital prints and videos of these interventions as well as some portrait busts from the university collection that had been covered with the same shrink-wrapping and which, displayed on their sides, seemed as if they had been toppled. Also simultaneous were walking tours that enabled the artist to discuss the sculptures on-campus as well as off-campus.

Seeking to reveal how memory may be 'plastic in the sense that it is constantly shaped and moulded by our new knowledge of the past',[11] Aydemir's intervention also suggests plastic as a metaphor for how the sculptures can themselves transform thinking. As André Keet observes in his essay on her intervention: 'Our historical statues, celebrating a history of "racism", "sexism" and all other kind of violence, require such transformative observations: importing them into the present because of their innate plasticity; and thus, as teachers of "justice"' (Keet 2014: 24). Pink was particularly provocative in this regard. Jonathan Jansen indicates in his commentary on *Plastic Histories* that 'pink suggests softness, even gayety, with all the kinds of homophobic reaction the colour evokes' (Jansen 2014:12). The colour pink, one might argue, enables a 'queering' of the monuments – that is, a rendering of them as at odds with heteronormativity and in alliance with all those who refuse to be bound by conservative moralities and conventions. In so doing, the strategy of 'queering' draws attention to the ways in which monuments are usually exclusivist and narrow in terms of who they celebrate and commemorate. For Aydemir, using pink offered 'an opportunity to empower and commemorate the unacknowledged and equally deserving rather than those simply in power'.[12]

Aydemir undertook her intervention about nine months prior to the commencement of the Rhodes Must Fall movement. Had it been undertaken a couple of years later, she would not have had available to her Moolman's portrayal of Swart. On 22 February 2016, a riot broke out in the wake of a racialised conflict at a rugby match on campus. Some of the protestors then set fire to the work and used hammers and rocks to dislodge the figure, which ended up in a pond. Following its restoration, it was arranged that the sculpture be relocated to the heritage site of the Voortrekker Sarel Cilliers on Doornkloof farm in the Kroonstad district of the Free State province (see Schmahmann 2017: 48–49). On 15 March 2018, an internal notice to staff and students at the university conveyed a message that the Steyn sculpture's placement on campus was also under consideration. An 'Informational Transformation Plan' had included the setting up of a team to work on statues and artwork, but students were apparently unhappy with the pace of transformation of the campus. Francis Petersen, the new rector and vice-chancellor, decided to escalate the speed of decisions made in regard to the statue of Steyn by setting up another task team to propose 'clear time frames on key deliverables, cognisant of what is legislatively required in terms of heritage authorities'.[13] After completing its deliberations in compliance with the heritage permit, the task team's recommendation that the statue be relocated off campus was approved by the university council in November 2018.[14]

Figure 9.6: View of *Intersection* by Ledelle Moe, Isabelle Mertz, et al. (photographed in 2017) in relation to Steynberg's *J.H. Marais* (1950), stone, on the Rooiplein of Stellenbosch University.

Source: Photograph by Paul Mills

In contrast to the University of the Free State, which embarked on a process of removing an offending large-scale artwork, Stellenbosch University has begun enabling discursive engagement with a sculpture of parallel impact. The monument concerned is Coert Steynberg's marble sculpture of J.H. Marais on the Rooiplein (Red Square) at the institution (Figure 9.6).

Completed in 1950, the one-and-a-half-times life-size work celebrates Johannes Henock Marais (born 1850), better known as Jannie Marais, whose bequest of £100 000 had enabled the transformation of Victoria College into the University of Stellenbosch in 1918. Marais' intention had been to establish a fully-fledged and independent university where Afrikaans (Dutch) was foregrounded. Undertaken in counteraction to Cecil Rhodes' plan to establish a university in Cape Town, his bequest was underpinned by a conception that Stellenbosch had been 'closely bound up for many years with the spiritual, moral and national life of the Dutch-speaking part of the nation' and 'is the place where the Afrikaner people have been best able to realise their ideals and from which they have been able to exert the strongest influence on South Africa' (memorandum by D.F. Malan, Professor Morrees of the Theological Seminary and Mr J.G. van der Horst, quoted in Brink 2006: 41).

Organised in collaboration with Isabelle Mertz, a Master's candidate working with her in 2016, Ledelle Moe, a Visual Art Department staff member, devised a work called *Intersection,* which provided a forum for second-year Visual Arts students to respond to the history of the campus and environment in general while also establishing a dialogical engagement with Steynberg's sculpture. A concrete object that might be read as either a Greek cross or an 'X', *Intersection* has on top of it small postcard-sized bronze panels or objects, each designed by a different person. When I examined the work in February 2017, there were 21 panels on the object, but the work had space for further additions which were being conceptualised for 2018, when it would once again serve as part of the second-year curriculum.

While its title – *Intersection* – indicates on one level 'these white lines kind of intersect the Rooiplein and the X', Moe explains that it also refers to 'the intersecting of different voices, different conversations'.[15] Moe indicates that she sought to position the sculpture in relation to that of Marais: 'I chose this spot in particular because it is right in front of him. There's a sight line towards him that's of a particular nature, so that you could sit here and look at him, and look away'.[16] I have noted in a detailed exploration of the history of the sculpture and recent interventions to it that, when viewed as a Greek cross, the shape might be understood to refer to the architecture of Dutch Reform churches, including the Moederkerk (Mother church) in Stellenbosch, and thus to focus critical attention on an entity that played a primary role in shaping values and attitudes that held sway at the institution. When read as an 'X', however, a different set of associations are brought into play. Alluding to the mark used in voting or the idea that 'X' marks the spot, it was apparently also used historically by the British army, who designated someone they were about to execute by positioning a piece of paper with a black X close on his heart.[17] As I note in my discussion of the intervention: 'Interpreted in light of this latter association, it could be understood as a displaced and symbolic "execution" of the sculpture of Jannie Marais, to which it has a critical relationship'.[18]

The bronze forms on top of it were each researched and produced by a different person. Involving each participant in learning bronze casting as a technique, the production of the form simultaneously demanded independent research about the Stellenbosch campus and environment. In one of the bronzes, called *Message from Stellenbosch,* for example, Charles Palm explores the contradictions surrounding attitudes to education amongst the Dutch in the Cape. A keyhole motif is cast from the front door of the Ou Hoofgebou (Old Main Building), the oldest building in the Stellenbosch University complex, that was constructed, Palm observes, 'as a monument to education and progress in Stellenbosch'. Home to the Law faculty, he notes, it is still used as an important ceremonial space for important university events'.[19] However, as I have noted, 'this reference to a building associated with education, law and progress is juxtaposed with the allusion to a letter emanating from Stellenbosch that, in antithesis, speaks of a Dutch ruling order whose actions were characterised by suspicion of education, lack of justice and retrogressive thinking'.[20] The message, written in 1760, was from Upas, an enslaved man in Stellenbosch, to September van Bugis, who was enslaved in Cape Town and known as a healer. While Upas was asking only for assistance with a health complaint, his letter – found by a commando amongst September's few possessions – was treated as evidence of the latter's complicity in murder committed by a group of men in the course of endeavouring to escape their enslavement. The lack of learning, disregard for justice as well as inhumanity on the part of the Dutch resulted ultimately in September being sentenced to death by being broken at the rack.[21]

Information about the bronzes, which Moe has made available on the site, indicates that, in addition to enabling enhanced knowledge about the campus as well as research capacities on the part of those involved in the project, the initiative clearly has potential to educate other students as well. Important to note in this regard is that, while Moe initially experienced some difficulty in getting permission for this project to take place, her way has been smoothed by recent reconsiderations of ways of managing visual culture on campus. A 'visual redress' committee has been established under the ambit of the vice-rector for social impact and the Transformation Office. Working in light of projects and research on student responses to art on campus under her ambit since 2014, Elmarie Costandius, an associate professor in the Visual Arts Department, drew up its 'First Draft Visual Redress Plan' (26 September 2017) in which it is indicated that, while the 'erection of new statues of relevant and popularly agreed-upon figures will assist in diversifying the University's visual landscape and would aid in fostering inclusivity', it would potentially be more beneficial for the institution to create a scenario in which the Rooiplein might serve as a forum for the staging of weekly exhibitions, performances or other events that would enable critical engagement with visual culture.[22] In the context of such an approach, initiatives such as Moe's project can now find a ready home on campus.

CONCLUSION

In *As by Fire: The End of the South African University*, Jansen (2017: 161) identifies six broad directions that calls to 'decolonise' the curriculum have taken. One of these, he indicates,

> is less concerned with either repositioning or replacing the existing curriculum than with empowering students to engage that knowledge by asking critical questions such as: Where did this knowledge come from? In whose interests does this knowledge

persist? What does it include and leave out? What are its authoritative claims? What are the underlying assumptions and silences that govern such knowledge.

He observes further that this approach has implications for debate about what to do with commemorative monuments in the sense that simply removing them from access prevents their enabling these kinds of critical questions.

Jansen's observation tallies with what I have been proposing in this chapter. Believing that existent monuments can become a means for reflecting critically on how unequal relations of power have shaped commemorative practices themselves, I have suggested that they have the potential to become *part of* a new and vital curriculum, rather than seeming to be remnants from the past that *hamper* transformation. But ensuring that monuments should be accessible does not mean they should also be regarded as sacrosanct. On the contrary, their capacity to serve as vehicles for critique and historical engagement is best enabled through creative interventions. Whether through dialogical monuments introduced in their vicinity, such as Boshoff's *Kring van Kennis* at the University of Johannesburg, temporary adaptations to sculptures such as those undertaken by Cigdem Aydemir at the University of the Free State, or by being incorporated into class projects, as in the case of the *Intersection* initiative organised by Ledelle Moe at Stellenbosch University, inherited commemorative objects can readily become dynamic and vital prompts for enhancing and enriching the education of students at South African universities.

ACKNOWLEDGEMENTS

My sincere thanks to Jonathan Jansen for inviting me to be part of this exciting publication and to Paul Mills for taking photographs for me. My research towards this chapter was made possible through generous financial support from the National Research Foundation (NRF) of South Africa. Please note, however, that any opinions, findings, conclusions or recommendations expressed here are my own, and the NRF accepts no liability in this regard.

NOTES

1   The sculpture was acquired in 1934, six years after building had been completed on lands donated to the institution from Rhodes' estate. It was initially placed just above De Waal Drive, where the figure looked towards a rose garden. The widening of De Waal Drive necessitated it being moved, and it was then relocated to a more elevated position. I outline these circumstances in full in *Picturing Change: Curating Visual Culture at Post-apartheid Universities* (2013: 53–58).

2   His imperialist inclinations were further conveyed through a poem by Rudyard Kipling engraved on the sculpture's pedestal:
I DREAM MY DREAM
OF ROCK AND HEATH AND PINE

OF EMPIRE TO THE NORTHWARD

AY, ONE LAND

FROM LION'S HEAD TO LINE.

3   Anthony Holiday, a staff member at the University of the Western Cape, argued in a letter published in the *Cape Times* in 2005 that all images of Rhodes ought to be taken down and that Njabulo Ndebele, vice-chancellor at the time, might encourage this by removing the sculpture from the University of Cape Town (see Holiday 2005). There is also the report by Melissa Steyn and Mikki van Zyl (2001) suggestively titled 'Like That Statue at Jammie Stairs: Some Student Perceptions and Experiences of Institutional Culture at the University of Cape Town in 1999'. Additionally, a group of anonymous activists, the Tokolos Stencil Collective, articulated opposition to the sculpture both through leaving their trademark stencilled graffiti on its pedestal in May 2014, and via their webpage. While there was doubtless additional discourse of this type within UCT, these are the only public arguments for the sculpture to be removed that I have found from the period between the first democratic election and March 2015.

4   Ramabina Mahapa, 'Press Release on UCT Student Protest,' 11 March 2015. http://www.scribd.com/doc/258502122/UCT-SRC-Press-Release-on-UCT-Student-Protest.

5   Indeed, the National Resources Heritage Act of 1999 indicates that public monuments and memorials would require 'the special consent of the local authority … for any alteration or development affecting' them and that, should such an alteration or development be undertaken 'without the consent of the local authority, the local authority may require the owner to stop such work instantly and restore the site to its previous condition within a specified period'. National Heritage Resources Act, no. 25 of 1999, Chapter II, section, 30, pp. 23–24. See Chapter II, section 37, p. 30, where it is indicated that 'public monuments and memorials must, without the need to publish a notice this effect, be protected in the same manner as places which are entered in a heritage register referred to in section 30'.

6   More details can be found in Schmahmann (2013: 42–53).

7   I am using the term as it was coined by Marianne Hirsch (2008): 'Postmemory describes the relationship of the second generation to powerful, often traumatic, experiences that preceded their births but that were nevertheless transmitted to them so deeply as to seem to constitute memories in their own right.'

8   Initially five boulders were brought to campus. But, unloaded from the bulldozer, the third rock fell in place on the first two in a way that seemed perfect to those involved. It was then decided to exclude two of the boulders. These circumstances are outlined in an unpublished email from Ritszema de la Bat, the former vice-rector (Operations), dated 11 November 2005, in the archives at Paarl.

9   The fact that the rocks may allude to stone-throwing but are too heavy to throw was observed by the artist in an interview with the author on 4 February 2010.

10   President Johannes Hendrikus Brand (fourth president of the Orange Free State) by J.W. Best in 1893; General De Wet (celebrated for his leadership in the Afrikaner struggles against British rule) by Coert Steynberg in 1954; James Barry Hertzog (prime minister when the National Party won the election in 1924) by Danie de Jager in 1967; and Francis William Reitz (fifth state president of the Orange Free State) by Laura Rautenbach in 1986.

11   Video commentary by Cigdem Aydemir on 17 June 2014 posted on 'Situate: Art in Festivals' website. http://www.situate.org.au/artwork/plastic-histories-by-cigdem-aydemir/.

12   Video commentary by Aydemir, 17 June 2014.

13   Lacea Loader, 'Task Team Focusing on President Steyn Statue', 15 March 2018. Internal letter to staff and students.

14   The special task team made a submission to the Free State Provincial Heritage Resources Authority for a permit to cover up the sculpture during the review process. But the terms of the permit

were rather that the sculpture needed to be kept accessible. Working in light of this, the university devised a temporary installation around the sculpture that included a reflective triangular column that featured questions about the sculpture in three languages spoken locally (English, Afrikaans and Sesotho) and that in fact blocked the sculpture if it was viewed from the east by a person heading down the pathway towards the main building. The installation also included a suggestion box in which comments could be deposited as well as various concrete benches where individuals might themselves reflect on the work, its history and its significance within the present. The idea was that submissions (which could be made online, in hard copy or orally) would be examined by a heritage expert who would in turn enable the institution to come up with a decision in regard to the work. (My thanks to J.C. van der Merwe, acting director of the Institute for Reconciliation and Social Justice at the University of the Free State, for outlining the process that was followed during a visit I made to campus on 21 August 2018.)

15   Interview by the author with Ledelle Moe at Stellenbosch University, 21 February 2017.
16   Interview with Moe at Stellenbosch University, 21 February 2017.
17   http://www.theidioms.com/x-marks-the-spot/.
18   Brenda Schmahmann, 'Knocking Jannie off His Pedestal: Two Creative Interventions to the Sculpture of J.H. Marais at the University of Stellenbosch'. Chapter in volume titled *Troubled Images: Visual Culture and the Politics of Afrikaner Nationalism*. In progress.
19   Pdf file with explanations of the various works that are made available at the site.
20   Brenda Schmahmann, 'Knocking Jannie off His Pedestal: Two Creative Interventions to the Sculpture of J.H. Marais at the University of Stellenbosch'. Chapter in volume titled *Troubled Images: Visual Culture and the Politics of Afrikaner Nationalism*.
21   See Koolhof and Ross (2005) for a discussion of the sequence of events and the misreading of Upas's letter.
22   Document that Elmarie Costandius supplied to the author.

REFERENCES

Beningfield, Jennifer. 2006. *The Frightened Land: Landscapes and Politics in South Africa in the Twentieth Century*. New York: Routledge.
Brink, Chris. 2006. *No Lesser Place: The Taaldebat at Stellenbosch*. Stellenbosch: Sun Press.
Coombes, Annie. 2004. *History after Apartheid: Visual Culture and Public Memory in a Democratic South Africa*. Johannesburg: Wits University Press. First published by Duke University Press in 2003.
Grahamstown Journal. 1909. 'Rhodes University College: Unveiling of Beit Bust'. 18 February 1909.
Hirsch, Marianne. 2008. 'The Generation of Postmemory'. *Poetics Today* 29 (1): 103–128.
Holiday, Anthony. 2005. 'Rhodes Statue Insults the New Order'. *Cape Times*, 14 March.
Invernizzi-Accetti, Carlo. 2017. 'A Small Italian Town Can Teach the World How to Defuse Controversial Monuments'. *The Guardian*, 17 December. https://www.theguardian.com/commentisfree/2017/dec/06/bolzano-italian-town-defuse-controversial-monuments.
Jansen, Jonathan D. 2014. 'Waiting to Exhale'. In *Plastic Histories: Public Art Project by Cigdem Aydemir*, 12–13. https://issuu.com/joh_designs/docs/plastic_histories_catalogue2014.
Jansen, Jonathan D. 2017. *As by Fire: The End of the South African University*. Cape Town: Tafelberg.
Keet, André. 2014. 'Plastic Knowledge, Memory and History'. In *Plastic Histories: Public Art Project by Cigdem Aydemir*, 24–25. https://issuu.com/joh_designs/docs/plastic_histories_catalogue2014.
Koolhof, Sirtjo and Robert Ross. 2005. 'Upas, September and the Bugis at the Cape of Good Hope: The Context of a Slave's Letter'. *Archipel* 70: 281–308.
Lajer-Burcharth, Ewa. 1987. 'Urban Disturbances'. *Art in America* 75 (11): 146–153, 197.

Marschall, Sabine. 2010. *Landscape of Memory: Commemorative Monuments, Memorials and Public Statuary in Post-apartheid South Africa*. Leiden: Brill.

Musil, Robert. 2006. *Posthumous Papers of a Living Author,* translated by Peter Wortman. Brooklyn, NY: Archipelago Books.

Schmahmann, Brenda. 2013. *Picturing Change: Curating Visual Culture at Post-apartheid Universities.* Johannesburg: Wits University Press.

Schmahmann, Brenda. 2016. 'The Fall of Rhodes: The Removal of a Sculpture from the University of Cape Town'. *Public Art Dialogue* 6 (1): 90–115.

Schmahmann, Brenda. 2017. 'A Thinking Stone and Some Pink Presidents: Negotiating Afrikaner Nationalist Monuments at the University of the Free State'. In *Public Art in South Africa: Bronze Warriors and Plastic Presidents*, edited by Kim Miller and Brenda Schmahmann, 29-52. Bloomington: Indiana University Press.

Solomons, Rod 2015. 'UCT Association of Black Alumni (UCTABA) View on Rhodes Statue'. University of Cape Town News, 29 March. https://www.news.uct.ac.za/article/-2015-03-29-uct-association -of-black-alumni-uctaba-view-on-rhodes-statue.

Stevens, Quentin and Karen Franck. 2016. *Memorials as Spaces of Engagement*. New York: Routledge.

Steyn and Mikki van Zyl. 2001. 'Like That Statue at Jammie Stairs: Some Student Perceptions and Experiences of Institutional Culture at the University of Cape Town in 1999'. Research Report. Cape Town: Institute for Intercultural and Diversity Studies of Southern Africa UCT.

Voort, Thea. 2002. 'Purchasing Governance and Control for the Rand Afrikaans University'. DCom thesis. Rand Afrikaans University.

Widrich, Mechtild. 2014. *Performative Monuments: The Rematerialisation of Public Art*. Manchester: Manchester University Press.

Young, James. 1992. 'The German Counter-Monument'. *Critical Inquiry* 18 (2): 267–296.

CHAPTER 10

The Plastic University: Knowledge, Disciplines and the Decolonial Turn

André Keet
Nelson Mandela University

The idea of the 'the plastic university' suggests a straightforward proposal: the university's essence is transformability.[1] In the context of present debates on knowledge and curriculum within South African universities, this idea signifies a decolonial undertaking, an excavation of sorts. Such shovelling is an uneasy and awkward task given the present over-proximity of the decolonial discourse (Keet 2017) in South African higher education. While draping and masking much of the necessary contestations that need to emerge, the immediacy of the decolonial academic 'chatter' and 'clutter' since the #MustFall movements, which took shape from 2015 onwards, is performing itself as a collective existential crisis within the academy.

Thus, to retrieve itself, the academy in South Africa had to produce the 'decolonial' as the reigning epithet, as in decolonial pedagogies, and decolonial this or that. The upshot of these decolonial adventures is the systematic evasion of engagement with the nature and politics of disciplined knowledge, and how it constitutes the university and its practices. A classic case in point of shallowing the debates is the message in Jenna Etheridge's (2018) newspaper article 'Decolonising Education: How One SA University Is Getting It Done', which focusses on Stellenbosch University. That is, the academy seldom reflects on the transformative resources embedded within the disciplines and the concomitant knowledges with which they work. For this reason, the academy, for the most part, simply grasps transformation work as a series of interventionist strategies. By superimposing these approaches on the plastic transformability of knowledge and teaching and learning, transformation strategies run the risk of being counter-productive.

This chapter argues for an interpretive orientation that can sense the 'origin' of the university, from which it has detached itself, as plastic; that is, flexible, malleable, with an inscribed transformative ability rooted in the 'nature' of the knowledge and the disciplines with which it works. To wit, the university's essence is transformability. As our ways of disciplining the university have concealed this essence, the decolonial turn, in my reading, is a call to excavate and recover the innate plasticity of the university, which speaks to a kind of unburdening of epistemic freedom as a key notion in any definition of the decolonisation of knowledge. I build, self-referentially, on my previous attempts to style Catherine Malabou's (2005, 2008, 2010a, 2010b, 2011, 2012, 2016) notion of plasticity into a useful tool for university transformation praxes in South Africa (Keet 2012, 2014a, 2014b, 2014c, 2014d, 2017). On this basis, I suggest an interpretive schema that can grasp and re-animate, in decolonial terms, the university's originary position as plastic. Not as an exercise in fruitless thinking, but to disclose, to itself, to ourselves, the university's intuitive aptitude for deep transformation. In this vein, I put forward the plastic university to be imagined as a self-transforming machine, with infinite possibilities for doing just, and doing right.

KNOWLEDGE, DISCIPLINES AND THE ACADEMY

I joined the university sector, formally, in the late 2000s, after spending 14 years in the fields of human rights and human rights education (HRE). In 'Does Human Rights Education Exist?' (Keet 2017), I tracked my shifts in praxes over these years with an interest in the renewal of social practices, traditions and institutions as I came to experience and appraise HRE as inherently conservative and uncritical in relation to 'human rights universals'. The critique of HRE, accompanied by a search for productive reformulations of its praxis, started with my doctoral studies in 2004, and was later formulated as 'Discourse, Betrayal, Critique: The Renewal of Human Rights Education' (Keet 2012) ('Betrayal') and 'Plasticity, Critical Hope and the Regeneration of Human Rights Education' (Keet 2014c) ('Critical Hope'). Relating these ideas to the university transformation space, I have subsequently engaged with knowledge transformations and the notion of plasticity in 'Epistemic "Othering" and the Decolonisation of Knowledge' (Keet 2014a) ('Epistemic Othering'), 'Plastic Knowledges: Transformation and Stagnations in the Humanities' (Keet 2014b) ('Plastic Knowledges') and 'Refractions: Social Theory, Human Rights and Philosophy' (Keet 2014d) ('Refractions').

In 'Epistemic Othering', I track the history of disciplining knowledge, and the rapid expansion of disciplines in the twentieth century, in relation to the history of the university. From a transformation perspective, this tracking was necessary because the disciplines, more so than any other social, intellectual or administrative arrangement, permeate and rule the life of the university (Keet 2014a: 29):

> Academics and students are streamed; professional, academic and student identities are constructed; scientific authorities are established and maintained; social statuses are affirmed; social spaces are mapped out; recognitions, rewards and sanctions are distributed; and epistemic injustices are legitimated. A series of classes, textbooks, study guides, tutorials, practicals, conversations, seminars, journals, conferences and assessment regimes, each charted according to the status of the disciplines within the university space, animate the university. Ritual behaviours, symbolic expressions, ceremonial practices, triumphal architectures and artefacts add to this picture of the university as an institution steeped in the self-referential logics produced within the disciplines.

Accepting that disciplines are regarded as the architectures for producing and organising knowledge, we are, socially and conceptually, disciplined by our disciplines; they help produce our world (Messer-Davidow, Shumway and Sylvan 1993: vii). The argument posed by Ellen Messer-Davidow, David Shumway and David Sylvan (1993) is that disciplines significantly influence the 'ruling relations' within institutions,[2] that is, what Dorothy Smith (2005: 11) describes as the 'extraordinary yet ordinary complex of relations that are textually mediated, that connect us across space and time and organise our everyday lives – the corporations, government bureaucracies, academic and professional discourses, mass media, and the complex of relations that interconnect them'. With due regard for the disciplinary power of the disciplines, Messer-Davidow, Shumway and Sylvan (1993) reiterate that their influence includes the distribution of scientific authority according to positions that have been historically acquired and reproduced. These scholars put forward an understanding of the disciplines as operating on four planes: they specify the objects we can study, the relations that obtain among them, and the criteria for such study; they produce practitioners; they produce economies of value; and, finally, the disciplines produce the idea of progress.[3] Academic practices that are tagged to disciplines are all part of a system of strategies that produce and maintain the rules of scientific recognition.

Representations of science, however, correspond to positions already occupied on the scientific field; moreover, 'these representations are *ideological strategies and epistemological positions*' (Bourdieu 1975: 40). Agents, generally, aim to justify their own positions and the strategies employed to maintain them (Bourdieu 1975: 40). This is at the heart of the transformative challenges of the academy – and it explains, in part, why the decolonisation of knowledge has emerged as a key demand over the past few years. The decolonisation of knowledge is meant to disrupt the disciplines in order to dislodge the rules that generate the existent patterns of rewards and sanctions within the academy.

The present 'chatter' and 'clutter' of decolonising talk within the academy – decolonising this, decolonising that – is intended to turn decolonisation into a metaphor and, thus, an ideological strategy to maintain epistemological orientations and justify existing positions. This development towards the manicurist and veneerist application of the decolonial as an abstract, or an aesthetic, troubled Eve Tuck and Wayne K. Yang (2012: 2) some time ago: 'One trend we have noticed, with growing apprehension, is the ease with which the language of decolonisation has been superficially adopted into education and other social sciences, supplanting prior ways of talking about social justice, critical methodologies, or approaches which decenter settler perspectives'.

The present South African higher education scene resembles the images embedded in this quotation. The reproductive schema at work should not be underestimated; such a game plan, more than anything else, aims to preserve disciplinary practices and their prevailing conditions of privilege and disadvantage. I argue that the social structure of the academy, though embedded, is disclosed in equity patterns, promotions, privileges and sanctions; the way in which scientific authority is distributed and transferred; and the constitution of university committees, such as disciplinary, ethics and research committees, and so on, as well as the regulatory, material and discursive power and authority assigned to them. That is, I came to view the social structure of the academy and the institutional culture of universities as co-constituting each other. I have pursued this argument in 'Epistemic Othering', through the critique of post-structural, postcolonial and African studies, and their colonising complicities, by considering the work of Paul Tiyambe Zeleza (2007, 2009), Simon Gikandi (2001) and Sabelo J. Ndlovu-Gatsheni (2013). My aim was not to dismiss these intellectual trends and scholarly contributions, but to demonstrate how these knowledge formations can, if we are not careful, inscribe that which they critique. In essence, 'Epistemic Othering' attempts to show, via the nature of the disciplines and Michel Foucault's (2013: 204) idea that ideology is registered at the very point at which science is articulated upon knowledge, how difficult the project of decolonising knowledge is:

> The hold of ideology over scientific discourse and the ideological functioning of the sciences are not articulated at the level of their ideal structure (even if they can be expressed in it in a more or less visible way), nor at the level of their technical use in a society (although that society may obtain results from it), nor at the level of the consciousness of the subjects that built it up; they are articulated where science is articulated upon knowledge.

Thus, the task of decolonising knowledge may not be able to escape the hold of ideology over science; as such, it runs the risk of re-inscribing existing epistemic injustices and inventing new ones. Zeleza's critique of Eurocentrism within postcolonial, post-structural and African studies points precisely to these risks: 'The African response, too, even in its militant Afrocentric forms, has largely consisted of investing Africa with the imagined positive attributes of Europe, rather than dismantling the very foundations of this colonising epistemological order. Can African studies escape – even transcend – the

Eurocentric coding, the seductions and sanctions of writing Africa by analogy?' (Zeleza 2009: 103).

Thus, we need to reject and work against the present metaphorisation of decolonisation, its easy appropriation in anything and everything we say and do, in the South African university's academic landscape. The patience and deep reflexive work required for the decolonisation of knowledge would be a better, more productive option, whilst we continue to toil towards social inclusion and more socially just arrangements within higher education; this is the hard work of excavation, the task of shovelling, required of a decolonial undertaking. On this basis, I argue for an interpretive orientation that can grasp and re-animate the university's originary position as plastic.

While in 'Epistemic Othering' I argue that decolonising knowledge would be a demanding task, in 'Plastic Knowledges' I suggest that knowledge itself holds transformative reserves that should find institutional expression within universities. The point I argue in 'Plastic Knowledges' is that the disciplines already produce the principles of their own production, so determined historically. Hence, I maintain that knowledge transformations would be challenging. Further, I make the point that although we generally think of ourselves as 'free agents', the regularities of social practices do not support our agency claims. The question thus arises: 'How can behaviour be regulated without being the product of obedience to rules?' (Bourdieu 1990: 65). Enter the notion of *habitus*: 'systems of durable, transposable *dispositions*, structured structures predisposed to function as structuring structures, that is, as principles of the generation and structuring of practices and representations which can be objectively "regulated" and "regular"' (Bourdieu 1981: 94).

The habitus has a reproductive impulse, and agents are not necessarily conscious of the structuring of their practices, which are ordered independently of themselves based on a 'durably installed principle of regulated improvisations ... [that produce] practices which tend to reproduce the regularities immanent in the objective conditions of the production of their generative principle' (Bourdieu 1977: 78). Both the semi-permanency of institutional cultures within universities and the practices that produce them can be accounted for within this interpretive scheme; so too is it possible to explain the slow shift in the demographics of the academy. Even so, if, in the South African context, equity imperatives may sluggishly change the demographics of the academy, new entrants, who are meant to renew the academy, are quickly institutionalised via habitus.

Habitus, in the academic context, has frequently been doused with 'intellectual hair spray' (Hey 2003) without doing real praxis work. Thus, even as the challenges of higher education transformation demonstrate the reproductive impulse of the system via habitus, it has been widely criticised for undercutting human agency. Nevertheless, without marshalling habitus as an interpretive scheme, how do we account for the predispositions that social agents within the academy have towards reproductive ways of behaving (Reay 2004)? For Pierre Bourdieu (1990: 77), 'the habitus, as a system of dispositions to a certain practice, is an objective basis for regular modes of behaviour, and thus for the regularity of modes of practice, and if practices can be predicted ... this is because the effect of the habitus is that agents who are equipped with it will behave in a certain way in certain circumstances'.

There is sufficient empirical evidence to suggest the regularity and predictability of reproductive social practices within universities, even as we claim otherwise. The challenge, as it relates to the social structure of the academy, is its weak categories of self-understanding. The academy has become too accustomed to modes of life and thought 'which remain opaque to him [*sic*] because they are too familiar' (Bourdieu 1988: xi). Transforming the social structure of the academy, however, is dependent on whether academics are capable of studying the 'historical conditions of [their] own production, rather than by some form or other of transcendental reflection'; in doing so, they can gain 'theoretical control of [their] own structures and inclinations as well as over the determinants whose products they are'. The project is further hamstrung by the fact that academics are seldom responsive to empirical research about the academy itself; science is not 'credited when it encroaches on the world of the scholar' (Bourdieu 1988: xiv). In this regard, the academic's apathetic responses to reports on institutional racism and transformation are cases in point. This suggests a link between the will to know and the will to power, which in the end disallows analyses of the individual and collective defence mechanisms of the academy itself. For instance, one would probably encounter significant bureaucratic and political institutional obstacles in attempting to obtain ethical clearance to study the historical production of the professoriate linked to the political construction of the disciplines at any university in South Africa: *we do not want to know*. In short, we, in the academy, first, lack a critical ontology of ourselves (Foucault, as read by Malabou 2010a: 14); that is, our incapacity for 'objectivication' is laid bare (Bourdieu 1990). Second, we lack the methodological and intellectual dispositions and tools to study the hidden determinants that constitute our own habitus.

Part of the conditions for the arduous, yet necessary and rewarding work demanded by the task of decolonising and de/re-disciplining knowledge is delineated in 'Epistemic Othering'. 'Plastic Knowledges' builds on this by setting out the limited agency available to us within the context of the habitus of the academy. That is, it is more productive to acknowledge agency's detention by habitus and to systematically work against it, than it is to claim an unburdened agency that can at best lead to self-indulgent reflexive studies that serve as moral hideouts. Nevertheless, the history of knowledge implies that its very nature has been expelled from itself within the academy, together with the project of organising knowledge and the academic practices associated with it. The resources that are available to work against the reproductive impulses of the academy reside in the very nature of the knowledge with which it works, as captured in the concept of 'plasticity'. With this in mind, the interplay between habitus and plasticity emerged for me as a possible way for grounding the transformation of the academy. That is, we have to think of ways to mobilise the very nature of the knowledge with which we work, to challenge our habitus. Because, we are, in essence, disciplined by our disciplines, and habitus is, in part, a function of this process of disciplining.

AGENCY AND PLASTICITY

'The Future Is Plastic' is the interesting title of Alexander Hope's (2014) refiguring of Malabou's notion of plasticity. The 'future of the humanities is the future of plasticity', and the sciences have plastic limits, Malabou (2010a) argues. In essence, the originary position of knowledge is plastic; so is that of the disciplines, and the university.

A shovelling, excavation, delayering is required to 'look' for plasticity and generate interpretive schemes that would reveal the university's innate capacity for transformation. But, we first have to restate the interesting proposition that is taking shape. If we are disciplined by our disciplines, then we are organised and ordered by the organisation of knowledge; we are literally our disciplines, we title ourselves according to our disciplines, and we authorise ourselves via our disciplines. Accepting this as a plausible proposition, it is evident that disciplines, in part, generate the systems that constitute the habitus of the academy. Further, it is possible to suggest that 'undisciplined knowledge' (DeSouza and Purpura 2013) and the de/re-disciplining of knowledge as well as the fracturing of the discipline (Klein 1993) represent, in one or another form, the 'plasticity' of knowledge, of which Malabou speaks.

I had this logic in mind when developing the argument for 'Plastic Knowledges' and followed it up with example-driven arguments in 'Refractions'. Influenced by the pragmatic possibilities of knowledge transformation as key to deep change within universities, I had to engage with the constraints imposed on us by habitus. In modest terms, habitus simply suggests that if we are to proceed in scientific enterprise, we require a non-narcissistic reflexivity because 'we are implicated in the world [and thus] there is implicit content in what we think and say about it' (Bourdieu 2000: 9). Following Bourdieu, I came to have little faith in 'reflection' that turns thought onto itself and makes us 'believe that the most radical doubt is capable of suspending the presuppositions, linked to our various affiliations, memberships, implications, that we engage in our thoughts'. That is, the unconscious, collective history that produces our categories of thought is not so easily dislodged. Thus, according to Bourdieu, we require scientific reflexivity (Wacquant 1990: 681), a sort of double objectification (Bourdieu 2000: 10), as opposed to naïve, self-indulgent reflexivity. For Bourdieu (2000: 10), 'the most effective reflection is the one that consists in objectifying the subject of objectification. I mean by that the one that dispossesses the knowing subject of the privilege it normally grants itself and that deploys all the available instruments of objectification (statistical surveys, ethnographic observation, historical research, etc.) in order to bring to light the presuppositions it owes to its inclusion in the object of knowledge'.

The overproduction of reflection-related inquiries in South African universities is of the naïve type: an innocence-making project that releases us from the responsibility to constantly reconstitute ourselves. Upon noticing the outbreak of reflection studies and 'fair lady' methodologies of this type, post-1994, in South African universities, I took my leave from an action research that has lost its connection with the emancipatory intellectual project of the 1980s, which has since been conscripted into the desire for guiltlessness.

To put forward the demanding task of working against and on oneself as individual actions that should feed into the transformation of the social structure of the academy, I, in a sense, had to put forward at least two arguments to foreground a burdened agency within the academy: one that is closer to social reality and another that requires the hard work of reconstitution. That is, there is little value in trying to elude one's own captivity.

The first argument relates to the knowledge and the history of the disciplines within which the social agent within the university is located. For Foucault (1998: 95–96), the subject is

> neither a radically free or self-originating agent nor the passive interpellate of some overdetermining structure, but is always in some sense an active participant in the interplay of power relations which produce her as a subject. Consequently, resistance is always possible – the exercise of power is always vulnerable to reversals, disruptions, refusals – but resistances never originate from a position of exteriority to power, rather a plurality of points or strategies of resistance exist within the web formed by power relations, as its immanent and irreducible opposite. (Foucault: Agency, Subjectivity, Power 2014)

The second argument is associated with the specificity of the academic field and its habitus, as put forward by Bourdieu. Elsewhere, I refer to the Bordieuan idea of reflection as 'reflection-on-the-verge', the kind that dispossesses us from the privileges we grant ourselves (Keet 2017). Such demanding reflection is rare within the South African academy, which has hamstrung its transformation. However, even as a determinism is tracing Bourdieu's logic, reflexivity as part of academic struggles will 'increase the autonomy of the scientific field and thereby the political responsibilities of its participants' (Wacquant 1990: 681). Loïc Wacquant wants 'a rupture with the doxic acceptance of the existing academic world that may help open up new spaces for intellectual freedom and action'.

For the academy, limited agency, as argued in 'Plastic Knowledges', is a function that relates to how 'scientific authorities, are established and maintained, and how social statuses are affirmed, by the reproductive power of habitus within the university setting.' Thus, the possibility of knowledge transformation is slim, especially in a higher education climate in which academics seem not to study their own social structures in order to disclose the categories of their self-understanding and the social derivation of thought that they employ. To counter this trend, 'Bourdieu calls for scientific reflexivity as opposed to naïve self-analysis to construct an 'equally rigorous and uncompromising political economy of the ... [academy] ... in order to uncover its invisible structure, to locate the specific forms of capital that are efficient in it, and to raise our collective awareness of the hidden determinisms that regulate our practices as symbolic producers' (Keet 2014b).

The taxed agency that allows for resistance and renewal intuitively corresponds with my experiences in social institutions and, I suspect, has a stronger foothold in social reality. Further, in the concept of 'plasticity', I found a formulation of renewal and regeneration that is intimated but not formulated in Foucault's subject and Bourdieu's agent. The venture into these interpretive schemes also affirmed for me the centrality of knowledge renewals in the higher education transformation project across the different types of universities in South Africa. The disciplining of knowledge that inscribes ideology into science also alerted me to the possible risks that could shadow the decolonisation and the renewal of knowledge projects. In an effort to address these concerns, in 'Epistemic Othering' (Keet 2014a), I shift away from arguments that see knowledge disruptions mainly as content, organisation or packaging matters. I also reject simplified arguments on knowledge inclusivity and epistemological pluralism, because they do not have an associated political 'ethics'. Moreover, while I avoid the invalidation of Western epistemologies, I remain sceptical of assimilatory arguments for an African voice into a Western epistemological network. In 'Epistemic Othering' (Keet 2014a), I 'propose that the "decolonisation of knowledge" is viewed as the collective processes by which disciplinary practices are successful in working against the inscribed epistemic injustices of all knowledge formations'. At the core of my proposal is a speculative conviction that by adopting this view we will be able to avoid the pitfalls of the trends referred to above and, at the same time, offer productive 'real-existing' options for 'decolonising knowledge'; options with rational political form.

The interpretive and pragmatic possibilities around transformability and transformation have been given new impetus in Malabou's formulations of plasticity since the publication of her first book *The Future of Hegel: Plasticity,* Temporality *and Dialectic* (2005). These possibilities have since been taken through and advanced in *Plasticity at the Dusk of Writing: Dialectic, Destruction, Deconstruction* (2010), *The Heidegger Change: On the Fantastic in Philosophy* (2011), *The New Wounded: From Neurosis to Brain Damage* (2012) and *Before Tomorrow: Epigenesis and Rationality* (2016). In 'Critical Hope' (2014c), I trace Malabou's (2005: 9) re-introduction of Hegel's concept of plasticity to mean 'the capacity to receive form and the capacity to produce form'. Malabou initially attempted to show that Hegel's conception of subjectivity can essentially be described as 'plastic' in character; in this connection, plasticity describes the constitutive character of something that lies between the extremes of rigidity and sheer flexibility.[4] Plasticity thus occupies an intermediate position insofar as whatever is truly plastic must always be capable at once of receiving form and bestowing it. Plasticity also refers to a philosophical attitude that Hegel describes as a 'sense of receptivity and understanding on the part of the listener' (Malabou 2005: 10). Malabou interprets Hegel's dialectic as a process of plasticity, 'a movement where formation and dissolution, novelty and anticipation, are in continual inter play' (Malabou 2000: 191). Hegel's dialectic does not lead, as generally interpreted, to a closure, but to a future that is open (Malabou 2000: 192). The dialectic is regenerated as a forward movement because of its plasticity (Crockett 2010: xii) and therefore 'plasticity' might 'power social, economic, political and personal transformation' (Shread 2010: xxx).

Steering away from 'transcendentalist' readings of Hegel, Malabou (2011: 65) insists that plasticity is 'not an empty, transcendental instance'. Rather, plastic reading is a 'new, transformed type of structural approach' that 'moves beyond what might appear to be the decisive limitations' of the deconstructive readings inaugurated by her teacher, Jacques Derrida (James 2012: 84). In essence, plasticity is the 'shape or form of that which remains or survives in the wake of deconstruction', it is a 'movement or passage between the formation and dissolution of form'. In *Plasticity at the Dusk of Writing*, Malabou (2010: 1) declares the book a portrait of the concept of plasticity, generally viewed as her signature concept, which refers to 'mutability, change, exchange, morphing, metamorphosis, transformation' (Galloway 2012). Plasticity is a well-known concept in the scientific disciplines (Moser 2007); for instance, the scholarship of Mark Solms (Solms and Turnbull 2002), a South African psychoanalyst and neuropsychologist, features prominently in Malabou's work. In addition, via the neurosciences and the plasticity of the brain and its regenerative possibilities, Malabou develops 'plasticity' as a basis for social and political analysis.[5] She 'reads recent scientific research to suggest ... that the organisational structures and functioning of the brain offer us, above all, a model of freedom' (Shread 2010: 129) but also a model of destruction, 'that is, to blow up or bomb using plastic explosives' (Shread 2010: 129–130). Malabou's work also provides analytical resources in various spheres of study: the 'natural sciences', law, education, the humanities, the social sciences, and so on, with her work gaining traction outside the parameters of philosophy conventionally understood. In accord with this understanding of Malabou's work, Brenna Bhandar and Johnathan Goldberg-Hiller (2015: 2) introduce their recent anthology by making explicit the fact that the volume is dedicated to how they 'grasp Malabou's central concept of plasticity to facilitate political praxis. In the making of [the] volume, [they] asked the authors to liberally but critically explore the economic, psychoanalytic, and sociocultural dynamics that Malabou has also identified as her political field'.

Earlier, Malabou (2010a) already brought her plastic analysis to bear on the disciplines in general, and the humanities in particular. I presented these arguments in 'Plastic Knowledges' in which I emphasised that she suggests that the 'future of the humanities as a future of plasticity ... is already woven into the humanities – and into disciplinarity as such – from the start' (Williams 2013: 8). As discussed in this chapter, Malabou (2010a: 10) suggests three limits: 'the limits of knowledge, the limits of political power, [and] the limits of ethics'. To be at the limits and to think at the frontiers, presumes an outside; a space partly delineated by the natural sciences. The challenge, according to Malabou, is that we constitute the 'frontier' in a way that 'always already rigidifies the meaning of the outside, and consequently of the inside as well'. She intimates that plasticity is undermined right from the start 'by the fixity and determination of the spaces it is supposed to limit in a supple and malleable way'.

In 'Refractions' I pursue plasticity as a form of renewal within philosophy, social theory and human rights. Plastic is a medium for refraction; plasticity is its condition, so I argued. Adrian Johnston (Johnston and Malabou 2013: xii), in his collaboration with Malabou, suggests that the refractions offered by Malabou's sustained philosophical and political projects, in her engagement with biology, neurosciences and psychoanalyses, point to the necessity of rethinking 'philosophical concepts and the categories of contingency, continuity, event, selfhood and subjectivity'. In this respect, the entirety of the philosophical institution and the intellectual discourse of philosophy need to be refracted.

'Change', dependent on plasticity, is crucial to Malabou's refractions within discourses, because she believes that 'now that capitalism, political liberalism, and techno-science have become the chief modes of thought' (Skafish 2011: xix), a new humanities and social sciences can only engage with these dominant modes if it crosses the borders of its own metaphysics, its own frontiers. Irrespective of the radicality of the changes that human beings are undergoing (cultural hybridisations, biotechnologies, and so on), they are lined into conformity with techno-capitalist regimes and forms of value; beings are now tradable equivalents. Working against seemingly inevitable forms imposed upon us by capitalism, Malabou argues for opposing the 'ontologico-capitalist form of transform-ation with a counterform', that is, being-as-change (Skafish 2011: xix). Thus, 'not only will the humanities have to stand down from their dominant, effectively ontological pos-ition', the humanities, social and natural sciences need to recover their plastic reserves to be able to engage with these developments. The ensuing dialogue has to be steered by new categories, new philosophies. A new philosophy of plasticity, for instance, is a real possibility.

CONCLUSION: THE PLASTIC UNIVERSITY

If the disciplines preside over the university, and the university represents the uncondi-tional freedom to question and to assert (Derrida 2001: 24), then the university ought to be plastic; but it has been undercut by its own discipline, in every sense of the word. The question is not whether 'plasticity' provides for a new way of being a university. Rather, it implies modes of epistemological, ontological and political reorientations that would allow it to return to its origin via the transformative ability rooted in the nature of the knowledge and the disciplines with which it works.

If we accept this, and there is good reason why we should, decolonising knowledge will not emerge as a battle of additions, assimilations or displacements, but as prefigured within knowledge itself. Knowledge plasticity intimates an epistemic freedom of sorts; a kind of epistemic justice etched in itself in its transformations, and the disciples of the disciplines who have organised it. It is plasticity that may affirm, for now, the definitional parameters of the decolonisation of knowledge that I have formulated in 'Epistemic Othering': 'the collective processes by which disciplinary practices are successful in working against the inscribed epistemic injustices of all knowledge formations' (Keet 2014a: 35). Such academic practices will already have a socially just orientation to the 'human figure that is by definition plastic' (Mbembe 2017: 133).

'Plasticity' presents itself as one of the productive tools within the broad body of crit-ical thought for my own processes of deciphering and self-clarification, as well as for how to think and do transformation work in order to advance social solidarity through and within universities. In its emergence, the 'plastic university' has been imaged in multiple ways and has been expressed as the plastic interface between self and structure. Derived from this is the premise that the transformation of the university in socially just directions is intrinsically tied to knowledge and pedagogy, and the constant plastic reconfigurations of ourselves and our social practices and its expression in real, programmatic work.

To this end, in my work I explore how one can reimagine a whole cluster of the present humanities and social sciences disciplines under a new plastic arrangement of 'Social Praxes', as well as reformulations for the study of human rights and law. Moreover, my colleagues at a variety of universities thoughtfully work on the Africanisation of their disciplines, in the natural and social sciences. They wield intellectual shovels – excavating, lifting, scooping out the plasticity of knowledge to reveal the university's innate capacity for transformation: unearthing, digging up the epistemic injustices resident in knowledge, and reforming it … in true plastic fashion. The work of these colleagues is premised on plasticity and the transformation of the knowledge project as key to change in higher education.

There are more and more practices that present avenues of disciplinary resistance and possibilities for new paths to open up; which supports the argument that undisciplined knowledge together with the fracturing and re-/de-disciplining of knowledge are becoming standard concepts and actions in our daily practices as academics.[6] These practices show that 'every situation can be cracked open from the inside' (Rancière 2011: 49), even if institutions are so obviously powerful. In this context, the responsibility of the academic is to give better expression to the fact that we are plastic human beings, engaged with plastic knowledges, building a plastic, self-transforming university and higher education sector.

NOTES

1   This chapter is adapted from André Keet's speech on his inauguration as Professor in Higher Education Studies at the Nelson Mandela University, delivered in Port Elizabeth on 23 July 2018. The inaugural address is titled *The Plastic University: Knowledge, Disciplines and Decolonial 'Circulations'*.

2   Smith's notion of 'ruling relations' is integrated into her method of inquiry, institutional ethnography (2005: 11), which is 'designed to create an alternative to the objectified subject of knowledge of established social scientific discourse'. In this respect, Smith (in Widerberg 2004) explores 'the institutional order and the relations from the point of view of people who are in various ways implicated in and participating in it'.

3   For a more detailed rendering of these concerns, and their relationality, see the preface to *Knowledges: Historical and Critical Studies in Disciplinarity*, by Messer-Davidow, Shumway and Sylvan (1993: vii–viii).

4   For something that is incapable of taking on form because it rigidly sticks or elastically returns to its original form, cannot be described as plastic (Malabou 2005: 8; 2008: 15). On the other hand, something that does not preserve any particular form, but assumes the most various forms either at the same time (polymorphy) or one after another (flexibility), cannot be described as plastic either (Malabou 2008: 12). Plasticity thus lies between mere malleability and rigid intractability, between polymorphy and restriction to one specific form.

5   A search for scientific journals and books with 'plasticity' in their title revealed titles devoted to plasticity in evolutionary biology and ecology, where species are known to develop in response to their current environment, or in materials science and physics, where 'plasticity' refers to the property of materials to undergo irreversible changes of shape in response to applied forces. Further, in neuroscience, 'plasticity' is an umbrella term that covers a wide diversity of processes and mechanisms involved in small-scale or large-scale remodelling of the nervous system.

6   See, for instance, De Souza and Purpura (2013).

REFERENCES

Bhandar, Brenna and Jonathan Goldberg-Hiller, eds. 2015. *Plastic Materialities: Politics, Legality, and Metamorphosis in the Work of Catherine Malabou.* Durham, NC: Duke University Press.

Bourdieu, Pierre. 1975. 'The Specificity of the Scientific Field and the Social Conditions of the Progress of Reason'. *Sociology of Science* 14 (6): 19–47. doi: 10.1177/053901847501400602.

Bourdieu, Pierre. 1977. *Outline of a Theory of Practice.* Cambridge: Cambridge University Press.

Bourdieu, Pierre. 1981. 'Structures, Strategies and the Habitus'. In *French Sociology: Rupture and Renewal Since 1968*, edited by Charles C. Lemert. New York: Columbia University Press.

Bourdieu, Pierre. 1988. *Homo Academicus.* Stanford: Stanford University Press.

Bourdieu, Pierre. 1990. *In Other Words: Essays towards a Reflexive Sociology.* Stanford: Stanford University Press.

Bourdieu, Pierre. 2000. *Pascalian Meditations.* Stanford: Stanford University Press.

Crockett, Clayton. 2010. 'Foreword'. In *Plasticity at the Dusk of Writing: Dialectic, Destruction, Deconstruction*, by Catherine Malabou, xi–xxvi. New York: Columbia University Press.

Derrida, Jacques. 2001. 'The Future of the Profession or the University without Condition (Thanks to the "Humanities", What Could Take Place Tomorrow)'. In *Jacques Derrida and the Humanities: A Critical Reader*, edited by Tom Cohen. Cambridge: Cambridge University Press.

DeSouza, Allan and Allyson Purpura. 2013. 'Undisciplined Knowledge'. In *African Art, Interviews, Narratives: Bodies of Knowledge at Work*, edited by Joanna Grabski and Carol L. Magee. Bloomington: Indiana University Press.

Etheridge, Jenna. 2018. 'Decolonising Education: How One SA University Is Getting It Done'. *News24*, 7 May. https://www.news24.com/Analysis/decolonising-education-how-one-sa-university-is -getting-it-done-20180507.

Foucault, Michel. 1998. *The History of Sexuality.* Vol. 1, *The Will to Knowledge.* Harmondsworth: Penguin.

Foucault, Michel. 2013. *Archaeology of Knowledge.* London: Taylor & Francis.

Foucault: Agency, Subjectivity, Power. 2014. *Automatic Writing* (blog). https://automaticwriting1 .wordpress.com/2014/10/09/foucault-agency-subjectivity-power/.

Galloway, Alexander R. 2012. 'Plastic Reading'. *Novel* 45 (1): 10–12. doi: 10.1215/00295132-1541297.

Gikandi, Simon. 2001. 'Globalization and the Claims of Postcoloniality'. *South Atlantic Quarterly* 100 (3): 627–658. doi: 10.1215/00382876-100-3-627.

Hey, Valerie. 2003. 'Identification and Mortification in Late Modernity: New Labour; Alpha Femininities and Their Dis/Contents'. Keynote address presented at the International Conference on Gender and Education, University of Sheffield.

Hope, Alexander. 2014. 'The Future Is Plastic: Refiguring Malabou's Plasticity'. *Journal for Cultural Research* 18 (4): 329–349. doi: 10.1080/14797585.2014.959308.

James, Ian. 2012. *The New French Philosophy.* Cambridge: Polity Press.

Johnston, Adrian and Catherine Malabou. 2013. *Self and Emotional Life: Philosophy, Psychoanalysis, and Neuroscience.* New York: Columbia University Press.

Keet, André. 2012. 'Discourse, Betrayal, Critique: The Renewal of Human Rights Education'. In *Safe Spaces: Human Rights Education in Diverse Contexts*, edited by Cornelia Roux, 7–27. Rotterdam: SensePublishers.

Keet, André. 2014a. 'Epistemic "Othering" and the Decolonisation of Knowledge'. *Africa Insight* 44 (1): 23–37.

Keet, André. 2014b. 'Plastic Knowledges: Transformations and Stagnations in the Humanities'. *Alternation* 21 (2): 99–121.

Keet, André. 2014c. 'Plasticity, Critical Hope and the Regeneration of Human Rights Education'. In *Discerning Critical Hope in Educational Practices*, edited by Vivienne Bozalek, Brenda Leibowitz, Ronelle Carolissen and Megan Boler, 69–81. London: Routledge.

Keet, André. 2014d. 'Refractions: Social Theory, Human Rights and Philosophy'. *Acta Academica* 46 (4): 132–158.

Keet, André. 2017. 'Does Human Rights Education Exist?' *International Journal of Human Rights Education* 1 (1): art. 6. https://repository.usfca.edu/cgi/viewcontent.cgi?article=1006&context=ijhre.

Klein, Julie Thompson. 1993. 'Blurring, Cracking, and Crossing: Permeation and the Fracturing of Discipline'. In *Knowledges: Historical and Critical Studies in Disciplinarity*, edited by Ellen Messer-Davidow, David R. Shumway and David Sylvan. Charlottesville: University Press of Virginia.

Malabou, Catherine. 2000. 'The Future of Hegel: Plasticity, Temporality, Dialectic'. *Hypatia* 15 (4): 196-220. doi: 10.1111/j.1527-2001.2000.tb00362.x.

Malabou, Catherine. 2005. *The Future of Hegel: Plasticity, Temporality, and Dialectic*. New York: Routledge.

Malabou, Catherine. 2008. *What Should We Do with Our Brain?* New York: Fordham University Press.

Malabou, Catherine. 2010a. 'The Future of the Humanities'. *Theory@Buffalo* 14: 8–16.

Malabou, Catherine. 2010b. *Plasticity at the Dusk of Writing: Dialectic, Destruction, Deconstruction*. New York: Columbia University Press.

Malabou, Catherine. 2011. *The Heidegger Change: On the Fantastic in Philosophy*. Albany: State University of New York Press.

Malabou, Catherine. 2012. *The New Wounded: From Neurosis to Brain Damage*. New York: Fordham University Press.

Malabou, Catherine. 2016. *Before Tomorrow: Epigenesis and Rationality*. Cambridge: Polity.

Mbembe, Achille. 2017. *Critique of Black Reason*. Johannesburg: Wits University Press.

Messer-Davidow, Ellen, David R. Shumway and David Sylvan, eds. 1993. *Knowledges: Historical and Critical Studies in Disciplinarity*. Charlottesville: University Press of Virginia.

Moser, Edvard I. 2007. 'Integrative Comments: Plasticity: More than Memory'. In *Science of Memory: Concepts*, edited by Henry L. Roediger, Yadin Dudai and Susan M. Fitzpatrick, 93–100. New York: Oxford University Press.

Ndlovu-Gatsheni, Sabelo. 2013. *Coloniality of Power in Postcolonial Africa: Myths of Decolonisation*. Dakar: CODESRIA. http://www.codesria.org/spip.php?article1791.

Rancière, Jacques. 2011. *The Emancipated Spectator*. London: Verso.

Reay, Diane. 2004. '"It's All Becoming a Habitus": Beyond the Habitual Use of Habitus in Educational Research'. *British Journal of Sociology of Education* 25 (4): 431–444. doi: 10.1080/0142569042000236934.

Shread, Carolyn. 2010. 'Translator's Note'. In *Plasticity at the Dusk of Writing: Dialectic, Destruction, Deconstruction*, by Catherine Malabou, xxvii–xxx. New York: Columbia University Press.

Skafish, Peter. 2011. 'Translator's Foreword'. In *The Heidegger Change: On the Fantastic in Philosophy*, by Catherine Marabou, xxiv. Albany: State University of New York Press.

Smith, Dorothy E. 2005. *Institutional Ethnography: A Sociology for People*. Walnut Creek, CA: AltaMira Press.

Solms, Mark and Oliver Turnbull. 2002. *The Brain and the Inner World: An Introduction to the Neuroscience of Subjective Experience*. New York: Other Press.

Tuck, Eve and K. Wayne Yang. 2012. 'Decolonization Is Not a Metaphor'. *Decolonization: Indigeneity, Education & Society* 1 (1): 1–40. https://decolonization.org/index.php/des/article/view/18630 /15554.

Wacquant, Loïc. 1990. 'Sociology as Socioanalysis: Tales of Homo Academicus'. *Sociological Forum* 5 (4): 677–689. doi: 10.1007/BF01115399.

Widerberg, Karin. 2004. 'Institutional Ethnography – Towards a Productive Sociology: An Interview with Dorothy E. Smith'. *Sosiologisk Tidskrif* 12(2). https://www.idunn.no/st/2004/02/kommentar _institutional_ethnography_-_towards_a_productive_sociology_-_an_i .

Williams, Tyler. 2013. 'Plasticity, in Retrospect: Changing the Future of the Humanities'. *Diacritics* 41 (1): 6–25.

Zeleza, Paul Tiyambe. 2007. *Global and Transnational Engagements.* Vol. 2 of *The Study of Africa,* edited by Paul Tiyambe Zeleza. Dakar: CODESRIA.

Zeleza, Paul Tiyambe. 2009. 'African Studies and Universities since Independence'. *Transition* 101: 110–135. doi: 10.2979/TRS.2009.-.101.110.

CHAPTER 11

Decolonising Knowledge: Can Ubuntu Ethics Save Us from Coloniality? (Ex Africa Semper Aliquid Novi?)

Piet Naudé
Stellenbosch University

THE QUEST FOR 'DECOLONISED' KNOWLEDGE

One of the core demands of the #FeesMustFall student protest movement in South Africa over the last four years (2015–2018) has been for 'decolonised' education.[1] This concern is not unique to (South) Africa and expresses a global concern about 'colonial' knowledge. For example, the Centre of Study and Investigation for Decolonial Dialogue in Barcelona, Spain, explains its decolonising effort as follows: 'A basic assumption of the project takes knowledge-making, since the European Renaissance, as a fundamental aspect of coloniality – the process of domination and exploitation of the Capitalist/Patriarchal/Imperial Western Metropolis over the rest of the world'. This coloniality 'denies the epistemic diversity of the world and pretends to be mono-epistemic'. The Western tradition of thought 'is the hegemonic perspective within the world system with the epistemic privilege to define for the rest of the world, as part of an imperial universal design, concepts such as democracy, human rights, economy, feminism, politics, history, etc. Non-Western traditions of thought are concomitantly inferiorized and subalternized.[2] … There is no modernity without coloniality'. (CSIDD n.d.)

The same sentiments are expressed by Achille Mbembe (2015). He asks what a Eurocentric canon is and responds: 'A Eurocentric canon is a canon that attributes truth only to the Western way of knowledge production. It is a canon that disregards other knowledge traditions' (2015: 9). He proceeds: 'The problem – because there is a problem indeed – with this tradition is that has become hegemonic' (2015: 10). Mbembe concludes that the decolonising project has two sides: a critique of the dominant Western models of knowledge and the development of alternative models. 'This is where a lot remains to be done' (2015: 18).

Indeed, a lot remains to be done. One could summarise the concerns of knowledge decolonisation as follows: Western knowledge traditions have become the norm for all knowledge; the methodologies underlying these traditions are seen as the only forms of true knowledge, which has led to a reduction in epistemic diversity; because of the institutional and epistemic power that Western traditions hold, they constitute the centre of knowledge so that other forms of knowledge are suppressed and are seen as inferior – a situation described as 'coloniality'. Decolonisation has specific relevance to Africa, as this continent finds itself in a postcolonial era, but its knowledge and university curricula still reflect the dominance of Western knowledge forms.

This chapter speaks to some of the salient issues raised in the decolonisation of knowledge debate via the case study of an African (business) ethic. It uses key aspects of attempts to construct an African ethics as an illustration of the cultural and epistemological claims underlying coloniality. The concern of centre-periphery power asymmetry so eloquently expressed by decolonisation academics will be confirmed. As Mbembe intimates, this is the easy part. The constructive effort to build an alternative is the difficult task. This chapter discusses different ways in which one can talk about 'African' ethics, taking the Ubuntu debates as illustrative of the potential and constraints of such an 'African' ethic. The chapter ends with a short evaluation of whether Ubuntu ethics holds potential to rescue African intellectuals from coloniality.

It is important to raise the concern that to talk about 'African' ethics rests on the questionable assumption that it is indeed possible to speak about '*an* African' approach abstracted from the complex histories, cultures and geographies of Africa.[3] This is a familiar paradox where one attempts to build a model based on generalisations while knowing that such generalisations are distortions of the particularities from which they are abstracted. Where these generalisations are mostly filtered through the lenses of colonial and postcolonial views, the task for abstracting an 'indigenous' or 'traditional' African view becomes even more complex.

It would therefore technically be more appropriate to speak of African knowledges or ethics or value traditions in the plural form. This is, however, rarely done, as we have grown accustomed to explaining particular complexities with a singular and a universal approach. Models gain their explanatory value exactly from such generalisations and this chapter therefore refers to 'African ethics' in the singular, though concerns about the empirical validity of the very general value claims made in the name of 'sub-Saharan African people' are raised below.

Advocates for decolonisation are right that by adding the adjective 'African' (or Chinese, or Japanese) to ethics, the marginal intellectual and geo-ethical position of Africa may be reinforced. In the 'centre' there is (an assumed) 'universal' ethics derived from the dominance of Western philosophy, which is taken as the norm and point of reference, but rarely described as 'Western'.[4] And on the margins are the adjectival ethics with curiosity value and an overt contextuality.[5]

The reality facing a scholar from Africa (or other marginal sites) is that there is no way to escape the already well-developed traditions in ethics with the accompanying technical terms and canonical/classical texts. This is in fact the very way in which African-based scholars are introduced to 'ethics'. There is no *tabula rasa* or Archimedean starting point 'in Africa' from which one can subsequently approach the established canons of ethics built over a 2, 400-year reflective, written tradition in the West.

The intellectual journey to Africa always starts in Europe: an African scholar travels an arduous intellectual journey to first understand the rich and complex traditions of 'ethics'. We learn the names of the great thinkers such as Plato, Aristotle, Kant, Schopenhauer, Marx and Nietzsche. We hear about the established models of ethics explained in terms such as virtue, deontology and utility. Once this tradition is understood, our hermeneutical lenses have already been shaped. So when we 'return' our gaze to Africa to reflect upon 'traditional values' or 'indigenous knowledge systems', the only categories and intellectual apparatus at our disposal are the Western ones. Whatever we seek and might find locally will have to be explained in English and in terms of the established academic tradition, otherwise it simply does not 'make sense' to outsiders. The local voice, if heard at all, will only be taken seriously if judged and legitimised in terms of the accepted standards already established. The homogenising power of academic globalisation renders 'local' ethics as an interesting variation on the normative tradition, with which it is always compared.

MODELS OF 'AFRICAN' BUSINESS ETHICS

Let us – for argument's sake – accept this centre-periphery configuration as the reality of doing ethics, but take on the challenge to develop (business) ethics from an 'African' perspective. Three broad options for an 'African' business ethics, in ascending order of localisation, are discussed below: a direct transfer of Western ethics to Africa; different attempts to translate Western ethics into the context of Africa; and the development of a uniquely African position via the so-called Ubuntu principle, this latter explored in more depth.

The Transfer Model
In this model, Western ethics is taken as the norm and held up as the ideal approach to ethics. This dominant tradition is then read and simply transferred to the context of Africa. There is very little 'translation', no contextual adaptation, and rarely any critical

reception. This can happen with any standard Western textbook. When, for example, James Rachels's (1989) fine collection, *The Right Thing to Do*, with its readings in moral philosophy drawn inter alia from Thomas Aquinas, Immanuel Kant, John Stuart Mill and Thomas Hobbes, is used in an African classroom, those names are simply held up by lecturers as 'basic readings' that everyone interested in moral philosophy should know.

The consequence is that the adjective 'Africa' in this case, if used at all, describes nothing more than a geographical reading location. Whether one reads Aristotle and Kant in Lagos, Cairo, Nairobi or Berlin, it makes no difference. This is the way in which most African students (like myself) are taught ethics and philosophy. We neither realise that we are introduced to a 'Western' tradition, nor that there are 'Africans' (such as Augustine and the Alexandrian School) who made significant contributions to this tradition. The question of an 'African' approach to ethics always comes later, if at all – and then it is impossible to jump over our own European shadows.

The Translation Model

There are at least three possible forms of translation that one may discern from a reading of business ethics literature. In each case, the normative position of Western ethics is accepted, but there is an interaction with the African context that goes further than a mere transfer of knowledge.

First, there is an elucidation of Western ethics from an African perspective. In this case, there is an (uneven) reciprocal relation between Western ethics and African contexts: Western insights are taken as basis from which to interpret local contexts with the consequence that these contexts themselves are made sense of, or are critically appraised, in terms of the accepted Western perspective with an illuminating effect on the Western idea itself.

Second, a popular way to make a contextual, African contribution to ethics is the translation of local case studies into the frameworks of Western theories or ideas. One of the tasks to indigenise business school curricula is exactly by providing local case studies instead of dominant examples from the North.[6] Typical questions could be the following: What does the Walmart takeover or SAB Miller merger teach us about *stakeholder theory*? How can a *utilitarian approach* be used to argue for/against implementation of a minimum wage in South Africa? In what way does Islamic finance in Africa illustrate the potential of a *deontological* ethics?

A third form of translation occurs when context-specific African ethical problems are addressed with recourse to insights from the Western tradition. In this case, African ethics focuses on moral dilemmas that are particular to our context and seeks resolution of these questions by making use of Western theories. For example: Can corrupt business practices in Africa be explained by recourse to Lawrence Kohlberg's *stages of moral formation* (Kohlberg 1981–1984)? How can extensive management-labour conflicts be resolved by using the *creating shared value notion* developed by Michael Porter and Mark Kramer (2011)?

It is clear that the translation model does achieve a significant gain over a mere transfer, but as an example of decolonising knowledge, its contribution is minimal, as it relies on the Western insights and theories for its construction. In other words: There are local languages with some interesting variations, but the language from which and into which the translation takes place is predominantly 'English' (as a metaphor for the Western traditions).

The Substantive Model: Ubuntu Ethics

In this model, Western ethics is taken as a valuable tradition, but there is an endeavour to develop a distinct ethics that could be called 'African'. The claim is that Ubuntu ethics constitutes an additional, competing and alternative theoretical framework to those received via the Western tradition. Hence I call this model 'substantive'.

There has been a considerable growth in literature to design an 'Ubuntu ethics' deriving from the African continent. Here I engage with some of the most important representatives in furthering the argument about the possibility of an African ethic. The most advanced analytical work in this field has over recent years been done by Thaddeus Metz, who, in a seminal essay 'Toward an African Moral Theory' (Metz 2007b), outlines at least six senses in which Ubuntu is used. He comes to the conclusion that there is indeed an indigenous African ethics that expresses the communitarian approach of Africans in distinction to the individualism of Europe. This qualifies his work as a substantive approach to African ethics. According to him, this Ubuntu ethic may be summarised in the following principle of right action: 'An action is right just insofar as it promotes shared identity among people grounded on good-will; an act is wrong to the extent that it fails to do so and tends to encourage the opposites of division and ill-will' (Metz 2007b: 338; see also Metz 2012).

To advance this important debate, my contribution – framed in the quest for decolonised knowledge – argues that the Ubuntu project is based on a number of questionable claims.

First, the claim is that Ubuntu derives from a universal respect for being-through-the-other, but it will be shown that its origin and social setting are tribal kinship relations.

Second, the claim is that Ubuntu is a uniquely African phenomenon, but it will be argued that the values associated with Ubuntu are based on generalisations that are not empirically proven and, even if accepted, are prevalent in most pre-modern and small-scale communities.

Third, the claim is that Ubuntu expresses African communitarian views in contrast to Western individualism and rationalism. It will be argued that personhood and autonomy are inherent in all societies, including those in Africa, and sociality or being-through-the-other is indeed integral to Western philosophy as well.

The classical academic discussion of what became known as the Ubuntu idea derives from John Mbiti (1969) in his book *African Religions and Philosophy*.[7] I will use this work as primary reference point to develop a critical assessment of *ubuntu*.

According to Mbiti (1969: 108–109), 'whatever happens to the individual happens to the whole group, and whatever happens to the whole group happens to the individual. The individual can only say: "I am, because we are; and since we are, therefore I am". This is a cardinal point in the understanding of the African view of man.'

First Argument

One should carefully note that the quotation above is set in Mbiti's discussion of ethnic groups, kinship, (extended) family life and the individual. Mbiti wishes to avoid the negative connotation of the word 'tribe' and prefers to speak of 'people' or 'peoples'. He emphasises that African peoples are to be differentiated by a number of factors: language, geographical boundaries (however fluid), a common culture expressed via a history with particular national figures and common ancestors, as well as common customs. He adds that 'each people has its own distinct social and political organisation' with tribal chiefs, extended families and persons with special status. Each people also has its own religious system: 'Traditional religions are not universal: they are tribal or national' (Mbiti 1969: 4). It therefore warrants speaking of African religions in the plural (Mbiti 1969: 1), while 'a person cannot be converted from one tribal religion to another', just as it is impossible to change tribal membership that is based on birth (Mbiti 1969: 103–104).

When proceeding to discuss kinship, Mbiti points out that the 'deep sense of kinship, with all it implies, has been one of the strongest forces in traditional African life'. He immediately explains: '*Kinship is reckoned through blood and betrothal* (engagement and marriage).[8] It is kinship which controls social relations between people *in a given community*: it governs marital customs and regulations, it determines the behaviour of one individual toward another' (Mbiti 1969: 104; emphasis added). This kinship is extended to the living dead (ancestors) and even covers animals and non-living objects through the totemic system. For Mbiti 'almost all the concepts connected with human relationship can be understood and interpreted through the kinship system. This is what largely governs the behaviour, thinking and whole life of the individual *in the society of which he* [*sic*] *is a member*' (Mbiti 1969: 104; emphasis added).

Although Mbiti points out that cultural exchange occurs among African peoples and that ideas found in one people may be found in a different form in another people (Mbiti 1969: 103), his discussion of the 'Ubuntu' idea is fundamentally situated within the social boundaries of a particular people.

One can obviously abstract the idea of Ubuntu from its social embeddedness in a particular people, and then develop a kind of universal goodwill idea with some moral force. This is what African (and other) ethicists do. But to claim that traditional Africans in general upheld a universal notion of Ubuntu that includes 'all others' is simply not supported by Mbiti's discussion or by empirical research. If it is said that 'I am, because we are', the 'we' that shapes the 'I' has a particular ethnic and kinship character, and not a universal ('I am through all others') connotation.[9] Translated into current contexts, Ubuntu could consequently mean that I use my power in society to benefit those who are 'of my own'. I am a person through the ones close to me and they benefit from my patronage to the exclusion of others who are not from my nation, tribe, family or political party. This bounded notion of Ubuntu lies at the heart of factionalism in Africa.

Second Argument

It is claimed that Ubuntu is a uniquely African phenomenon, but it will be argued that the values associated with it are not proven empirically and are prevalent in most pre-modern and small-scale communities.

Mbiti points out that he is discussing African philosophy in its 'traditional' sense: traditional religions, traditional beliefs, traditional attitudes and traditional philosophies. He is aware of 'modern' influences such as education, urbanisation and industrialisation 'by which individuals become detached from their traditional environments'. He is also keenly aware of the global power of modernity: 'The man [*sic*] of Africa must get up and dance, for better and for worse, on the arena of world drama. His image of himself and of the universe is disrupted and must make room for the changing "universal" and not simply "tribal" man' (Mbiti 1969: 216). Some Africans are less affected by the changes (rural and illiterate people), but even where outward change to a 'modern' life takes place, many still hold on to some traditional beliefs.

The first problem is that the list of values associated with 'traditional' African society and therefore seen as expressions of Ubuntu is as varied as there are authors on the topic: empathy, care for others, dignity, harmony, inclusivity, respect, reciprocity, forgiveness, community orientation, and so forth. The consequence is 'that Ubuntu comes to mean no more than what is good or virtuous' in a very vague sense (West 2014: 49), without enough particularity to be of ethical use.[10]

The second problem is that the claims made in academic literature about these purported 'African' values have thus far not been supported by credible and reliable empirical research. Almost all Ubuntu writers make the general claim that Africans (at least traditional ones) are 'communal' (with the kind of value list as above) while Westerners are 'individualistic'. Two prominent authors serve as example of this.

Mogobe Ramose (1999, 2003a, 2003b, 2003c, 2007) bases his argument of Ubuntu as 'the root of African philosophy' on a fine etymological analysis of Ubuntu. This linguistic base for Ubuntu is prevalent among what Ramose calls 'the Bantu-speaking people' of Africa (Ramose 2003c, 230), and it is on this analysis that he builds the philosophy and ethics of Ubuntu. But nowhere does Ramose empirically verify the transition from a linguistic feature to a moral world. He takes his cue for this linguistic analysis from Martin Heidegger, but Heidegger does not make general claims about purported moral convictions held by 'German-speaking people' as derived from his existentialist philosophy or language ontology. In other words, Ubuntu and its associated values – insofar as they are derived from a linguistic feature – are not entirely convincing.

Metz is at pains to state that his effort to build a theory of right action on the basis of Ubuntu 'is a constructive project not an empirical one' (Metz 2007a: 333). This is a fair admission. But he then proceeds on the same page to say that he attempts to build a theory that is different from Western ones. The 'evidence' (his word) that he gathered for this 'African' claim is from reading books on moral beliefs of Africans, engaging in conferences on the theme, listening to his students from Africa, and speaking to colleagues

(Metz 2007a: 333, footnotes 3 and 4). He then proceeds: 'So far as I can tell, *it is a fact* that there are several judgments and practices that are spatio-temporally extensive in Africa, but not in the West' (Metz 2007a: 333; emphasis added).[11]

As Andrew West rightly points out, empirical claims (such as claiming as a fact that sub-Saharan Africans hold distinctive communal values) that are only based on personal experience, anecdotes and impressions are not 'evidence' in the academic sense of the word. Empirical claims must flow from valid questionnaires, administered to an acceptable proportion of participants via random sampling followed by credible statistical inferences. West discusses a number of empirical cross-cultural studies on the collectivism-individualism divide by various authors (West 2014: 50–54) and he convincingly demonstrates their inconclusive results:

> The mixed results and methodological limitations of all these studies preclude any simple generalisations regarding the values of sub-Saharan Africans being justified. It is premature to conclude, on the basis of existing evidence, that sub-Saharan Africans … do or do not maintain the values of Ubuntu. At present, we can only conclude, that such generalisations are unjustified. (West 2014: 53)

What happened in the Ubuntu literature is that claims of 'Ubuntu values' (as proliferated as they are) as 'typical of sub-Saharan Africans' (as diverse as they are) became part of the canon, and were then transmitted via academic cross-references from author to author, creating the impression of an undeniable 'fact'.

What is 'African' about a set of Ubuntu values is that it is an abstraction developed mostly by Africa-based or African-associated scholars. In this sense it is an etic, elite reinterpretation of residues of what used to be 'traditional African', devoid of the social practices and everyday realities of Africans subject to political, social and economic brutalities in sub-Saharan Africa. In this guise, it may function in two ways: as a utopian vision of society, it may inspire and give (false?) hope, like a kind of empty clarion call. And as a 'narrative of return' (West 2014: 55) it may provide Africans, subject to rapid modernisation and identity renegotiation,[12] some sense of anchorage in an idealised precolonial past (West 2014: 54–55).

But it fails as a project of decolonisation, because it 'essentialises' Africans (exactly what a colonial mind does) and as an elite abstraction it mirrors colonial power structures that exactly inhibit the move to release Africans from their oppression under coloniality.

The third problem relates specifically to the 'uniqueness' claim of Ubuntu.[13] I concur with the few Ubuntu authors who point out that Ubuntu is not unique,[14] and actually expresses a universal sense of humanity.[15]

If we, for the moment, accept the value description of Mbiti's 'traditional' African societies, the question arises as to whether what is termed 'Ubuntu' is not in fact a description of most premodern, 'traditional' or 'small-scale' societies, irrespective of their geographical location. This question can be answered in the affirmative when one reads studies on personhood in ancient Egypt (Assmann 2002: 15); concepts of autonomy in early rabbinical societies (Fishbane 2002: 125–126), the effect of monetisation on interpersonal relations in sixth-century BCE Greece (Hölscher 2014), the shifting concept of trust from 'traditional' to contemporary Chinese communities (Lu 2010: 117–127), as well as descriptions of early faith communities in the New Testament with the values embedded in, for example, the body metaphor.[16]

It is clear that in most 'traditional' societies a person is established as person when he/she is embedded in social relations, and that there is an ontological reciprocity between individual and society. This applies to Europe as well, where, for example, Ferdinand Tönnies ([1881] 1922) makes a distinction between *Gemeinschaft* (community) based on affectual loyalty so typical of premodern relations (Ubuntu-type communities) and *Gesellschaft* (society), which is marked by impersonal, functional relations, for example the rational agreements contained in commercial contracts prevalent in modern, industrial contexts.

The idea that 'I am a person through other persons' in a close-knit community of reciprocity is therefore not a uniquely African phenomenon. The only 'uniquely African' part is the depiction thereof via the concept of *umuntu ngumuntu ngabantu*.

Third Argument

Ubuntu expresses African communitarian views in contrast to Western individualism and rationalism. It will be argued that personhood and autonomy are inherent in all societies, including Africa, and sociality or being-through-the-other is indeed integral to Western philosophy as well.

THE 'INDIVIDUALIST' DIMENSION OF AFRICAN PERSONHOOD

Let us turn to the complex notion of 'making a person' and the relation between an individual and the community in which he/she lives.

On the one hand, Mbiti argues what one would call a 'communitarian' perspective: 'In traditional life, the individual does not and cannot exist alone except corporately. He owes his existence to other people. … He is simply part of the whole. *The community must therefore make, create or produce the individual*; for the individual depends on the corporate group' (Mbiti 1969: 108; emphasis added).

On the other hand, Mbiti holds on to what one could call an 'individualist' perspective: 'Just as God made the first man, as God's man, so now *man himself makes the individual who becomes a corporate or social man*' (Mbiti 1969: 108; emphasis added). An example of this is polygamy, which must, according to Mbiti, ultimately be viewed in the context of enhancing immortality: the greater the number of offspring, the greater the opportunity to be reborn in the multitude of descendants and to be remembered by and through them. A man who enters into a polygamous marriage is 'making' both himself and the community. 'Such a man has the attitude that "the more *we are*, the bigger *I am*"' (Mbiti 1969: 142).

Mbiti also qualifies his references to corporate descriptions to ensure that the element of individuation is not lost: 'Therefore, when we say in this book that such and such a society "believes" or "narrates" or "performs" such and such, we do not by any means imply that everybody in that society subscribes to that belief or performs that ritual ... *Individuals hold differences of opinion on various subjects*' (Mbiti 1969: 3; emphasis added) – a further testimony to the active presence of individuals and individuality in a given social context (though constrained by patriarchy and other social allocations of power).

This important dimension of 'self-making' or *autopoiesis* is lost in the crude contrast that African ethicists set up between 'Western individualism' and relational 'African communalism' (Comaroff and Comaroff 2002). In no society, neither Western nor African, can an individual create him- or herself *ex nihilo* or outside of social relations (Keller 2002: 200–201) because the idea that a person can exist as an unmediated sociological reality is simply that – an abstraction, an idea (Comaroff and Comaroff 2002: 67).

Based on their careful anthropological studies in Africa, John Comaroff and Jean Comaroff' make a number of important observations. There is no generic view of *the* African conception of personhood. 'There is no such thing' (Comaroff and Comaroff 2002: 68). Personhood is indeed a social construction and 'the person' is a dynamic negotiated entity, a constant work-in-progress that plays itself out in a social context that is at once highly communal and individuated (Comaroff and Comaroff 2002: 69, 72) and subject to the resistance of countervailing forces (Comaroff and Comaroff 2002: 76). The 'foundational notion of being-as-becoming, of the sentient self as active agent in the world, was so taken for granted that it went largely unsaid' (Comaroff and Comaroff 2002: 73).

The Conclusion is clear :

> Nowhere in Africa were ideas of individuality ever absent. Individual*ism*, another creature entirely, might not have been at home here before the postcolonial age. ... But, each in its own way, African societies *did*, in times past, have a place for individuality, personal agency, property, privacy, biography, signature, and authored action upon the world. ... All of which ought to underscore, yet again, why crude contrasts between European and African selfhood make little sense. (Comaroff and Comaroff 2002: 78)

This notion of personhood is confirmed by African scholar Kwama Gyekye. According to him, the first postcolonial leaders in Africa (such as Senghor and Kenyatta) overemphasised the communitarian or communalist nature of traditional African societies to provide a basis for experiments in African socialism (Gyekye 2003: 298–299). This communitarian conception, reinforced by African philosophers such as Ifeanyi Menkiti (1984), upholds the ontological primacy and independence of the community over against the individual with the implication that 'the person is *wholly* constituted by social relationships' (Gyekye 2003: 298). On the basis of moral agency (individuals are held responsible for their actions) and autonomy 'that enables one to determine at least some of one's own goals and to pursue them' (Gyekye 2003: 306), Gyekye rejects as 'misguided' the simple contrast between African and Western notions of the person (2003: 303). Geyeke holds a restricted or moderate communitarian view (2003: 306), because 'it cannot be persuasively argued that personhood is *fully* defined by the communal structure or social relationships' (Gyekye 2003: 305).

The dynamic nature of African humanness (not humanism) implies for Ramose, among others, that one's humanity is confirmed by recognising the humanity of others. This in turn implies that human subjectivity is an essential part of Ubuntu. 'If this were not so, it would be senseless to base the affirmation of one's humanness on the recognition of the same in other' (Ramose 2003a: 644). The group is neither primary to nor does it supersede the individual. 'The crucial point here is that *motho* is a never finished entity in the sense that the relational context reveals and conceals the potentialities of the individual'.

This 'individualist' dimension of African personhood implied by Ubuntu is mostly ignored by African ethicists. Although there is no interest in the individual solely as an ontological construct but always in a normative relation to others, it does not deny a focus in Africa on personal signature and relative autonomy.

Let us now turn our gaze in the other direction: Is it correct to assume that the Western tradition operates with a rational, autonomous and individualist notion of personhood and that it is therefore different from Africa, which purportedly upholds a 'relational' orientation?

AN EXPANDED VIEW ON WESTERN NOTIONS OF PERSONHOOD

One could start by pointing to the deep paradox in the very notion of an 'autonomous individual', because 'a non-contextual autonomy – autonomy in and of the self, rather than in relation to another – does not exist'. The reason is that 'autonomy always arises within a context, relative to those from which it claims its independence' (Keller 2002: 194). There is always only, paradoxically speaking, a *relational* autonomy.

Acknowledging the context dependence of any claim to 'autonomy', Catherine Keller suggests that we need a social ontology wherein we recognise 'the self always and only emergent from its matrix of relations – and therefore never strictly speaking autonomous, however free the agency of that emergence' (Keller 2002: 199). This would hold true for the 'thinking I' suggested by René Descartes as well as the enlightened person who is an autonomous rational being according to Kant. We indeed find in Descartes and Kant powerful expressions of 'the turn to the subject', but to suggest that this subject is to be equated with a purely decontextualised self-referential individualism is to overlook the fundamental ambiguity of relational autonomy in principle.

René Descartes

It has become the custom of some African ethicists to build a contrast between *cogito ergo sum* (Western thinking) and the African notion *umuntu ngumuntu ngabantu* (Mbigi 2005: 69–70). This interpretation is a misreading of Descartes, as it assumes that his view of the human person is fully expressed in the *cogito ergo sum* dictum. The confusion arises because Descartes's epistemology is isolated from and simply conflated with this anthropology. African ethicists therefore make a category mistake by comparing Cartesian apples (How do I know?) with African pears (How do I relate to others?).

As is well known, Descartes's aim was to establish an irrefutable basis for knowledge. Via a process of methodical doubt he came to the conclusion that the only certainty is in fact doubting all existing knowledge. But to doubt means that I, the doubting individual, must exist. He wrote in his Meditations II: 'So that after having reflected well and carefully examined all things, we must come to the definite conclusion that this proposition: I am, I exist, is necessarily true each time that I pronounce it, or that I mentally conceive it' (Descartes [1641] 1952: 78). Descartes's further conclusion, after positing that thought is a vital attribute belonging to him, is that he is a real thing and really exists. 'But what thing? I have answered: a thing which thinks' (Descartes [1641] 1952: 79).

This summary of himself as 'a thinking thing' early in the Meditations reflects his search for an irrefutable basis for true knowledge, but does not exhaust his view of himself as a human person. As Descartes addressed the difficult question of sense perceptions such as feeling pain and hunger and thirst, he asserted that nature taught him that

> I am not only lodged in my body as a pilot in a vessel, but that I am very closely united to it, and so to speak so intermingled with it that I seem to compose with it one whole. … For all these sensations of hunger, thirst, pain, etc. are in truth none other than certain confused modes of thought which are produced by the union and apparent intermingling of mind and body. (Descartes [1641] 1952: 99)

In his last published work, *Passions de l'Ame* (Passions of the Soul) (published in 1649), Descartes (as the title suggests) turned his attention to discuss the feelings and experiences that arise from the interaction between body and spirit (Perler 2002). The six basic passions are wonder, love, hatred, desire, joy and sadness, which are seen as physiological phenomena to be studied from a natural scientific perspective to ensure that they are beneficial to humans because they are understood and controlled. The freedom of the human person lies in the ability to reflect on and steer the reciprocal interaction between mind and body, constituting the person as a 'master of his experiences' (Perler 2002: 161).

While Descartes maintained his dualism as well as the primacy of the thinking soul, it would be inappropriate to reduce his richly developed view of the human person to a mere 'thinking I' and then build upon this reductionist basis a perception of 'the Western tradition'.

Immanuel Kant

It is, further, a misreading of Kant to claim that he was only promoting a self-confident, rational being who has the courage to seek knowledge with his own mind,[17] without recourse to assistance from other people. Kant, in his essay 'Was ist Aufklärung?', indeed famously described the enlightened person in these terms, and said that it is very difficult to escape from immaturity and to use our own mind, because the immature state (relying for knowledge and truth on the insights of tradition or others in authority) has become a natural part of who we are. But this essay and the epistemology contained in *Critique of Pure Reason* (Kant [1781] 1998) should always be read in conjunction with his ethics in the *Groundwork of the Metaphysic of Morals* (Kant [1785] 1964).

In this latter work Kant explains that the free will that practises the categorical imperative is not merely subject to the law, but is so subject that it must be considered as also making the law for itself. This co-construction of the law with its sensitivity to all human beings as ends in themselves comes to pass because it is 'in no way based on feelings, impulses, and inclinations, but *only on the relation of rational beings to one another*' (Kant [1785] 1964, 102; emphasis added; see Keller 2002, 197).

Via his ethics, Kant demonstrated the importance of relationality: Not only does the imperative of treating people as ends and not merely as means point towards a striving precisely beyond 'individualism', but its very formulation depends on the relation of rational beings to one another in the kingdom of ends.

Karl Marx

It is, further, a selective reading and distortion to portray 'the Western tradition' as not being open to the purported Ubuntu idea of being a person through others.[18] In his famous theses on Feuerbach, Marx ([1888] 1969) states unambiguously in the sixth thesis that Feuerbach dissolves the religious essence into the human essence. The problem is that Feuerbach presupposes 'an abstract – isolated – human being' whereas 'the human essence is no abstraction inherent in each single individual. In its reality *it is the ensemble of the social relations*' (Marx [1888] 1969; emphasis added). This must be understood from Marx's theory of social classes, steering him sociologically speaking towards an explanation of individuals from their embeddedness in material, historical social relations, exactly against strands of individualism that view the single, autonomous person as a unit of social analysis.

The intention for constructing relational personhood by the philosophers referred to above is not to merely make an abstract ontological point about the human person, but to infuse a moral dimension into their philosophy. This is apparent from Descartes's notion of moral perfection, Kant's communal law-making and Marx's class struggle toward a more just society.

In their efforts to create an African ethic, most Ubuntu scholars work with false generalisations of both Africa and the West, as well as with assumed dichotomies between them. This is a well-known rhetorical strategy: one creates space for one's own view by building an exaggerated contrast position of the other. In terms of a decolonising project, it would, however, be a deep irony and a sign of a colonised hermeneutic if African ethicists call on a decontextualised and selective interpretation of Western philosophy to argue for their own uniqueness and contextuality.

DOES UBUNTU ETHICS PROVIDE AN ESCAPE FROM COLONIALITY?

The background to this chapter is the debate about whether one could steer between the 'immovable rock' of Afrocentric and 'the bad place' of Eurocentric knowledges (Cooper and Morell 2014: 2). On the assumption of an agreement that the current situation requires acts of 'decolonisation', a possible option is to enter into a process of decentring the West and replacing it with Africa. In other words, Eurocentrism is replaced by Afrocentrism. Mbembe (with reference to Ngũgĩ) explains decolonisation exactly as such a process of decentring. 'It is about rejecting the assumption that the modern West is the central root of Africa's consciousness and cultural heritage. It is about rejecting the notion that Africa is merely an extension of the West' (Mbembe 2015: 16). A new centre should be created: '*With Africa at the centre of things,* not existing as an appendix or a satellite of other countries and literatures, things must be seen from the African perspective' (Mbembe 2015: 17; emphasis added).

Apart from the question of how this should happen in practice, it seems unethical in the end to mimic the coloniality from which we try to escape in creating a new power asymmetry where Africans exercise power over others.[19]

A variation of this idea and a 'softer' version of Afrocentrism is the proposal for 'Africa-centred knowledges'. This implies that 'knowledge can become Africa-centred regardless of where they originate. But they do so only when they get entangled in African realities, lexicons and matrices and are shaped by these contexts' (Cooper and Morrell 2014: 4–5). Africa is then not so much a new centre, but a legitimate context which is taken seriously in the pursuit of multiple knowledges in an intermediate space between the West and Africa.[20]

It is fairly straightforward to see that the transfer model of business ethics does not qualify to fit into either an African- or Africa-centred paradigm, and in fact prolongs a colonial mindset. Insofar as the three forms of the translation model are each in their own way a contextualising of Western knowledge in Africa, they do weaken the dominant Eurocentric or Western view and indeed provide a minimal level of recourse from coloniality. But because the assumption of Western theories remain, this effort at decolonisation only functions at the level of de- and recontextualisation with minimal, if any, *epistemological* challenge to prevailing Western moral philosophies.

The question then remains: Do the efforts to build a substantive, alternative Ubuntu ethics transcend decolonisation-as-contextualisation towards a genuine escape from epistemological coloniality? The critical exposition above indicated just how difficult it is to escape from coloniality.

The dominant languages expressing Ubuntu ideas are colonial English and French, and the means of knowledge production and distribution are via mainline universities, conferences, journals and publishers. Even Ubuntu requires the very infrastructure and means seen as oppressive colonial power structures. The reason is simple: Ubuntu scholars also wish to be taken seriously. And they know that 'acceptance' and 'validation' of Ubuntu scholarship are still subject to the hegemony of the North. The rule is clear: so-called indigenous knowledge is only 'knowledge' once endorsed by the centre.

For Ubuntu to be taken seriously as alternative rival ethical theory (see Metz 2007b), it must be contrasted with dominant and standard Western traditions.[21] Its own particularity is premised upon that which it tries to undermine, escape or complement.[22] The postcolonial thinker is forever bound to the colony and the thought patterns underlying Western paradigms. The methods and interpretative categories are borrowed from the West. Ramose premises his linguistic analysis of Ubuntu on Heraclitus's view of motion (Ramose 2003a: 645) and Heidegger's etymological discussion of *aletheia* (Ramose 2007: 354). And in his development of an African philosophy he uses standard Western categories such as epistemology, ontology, ethics and metaphysics. He, and others, cannot jump over the shadow of the European tradition.

WHY IS AN ESCAPE FROM EPISTEMIC COLONIALITY SO DIFFICULT?

To understand why the task of epistemological liberation from Western models is so difficult and not particular to (business) ethics, two explanatory factors need to be taken into account:

First, efforts at constructing an African ethic like Ubuntu is a theoretical task. It therefore represents second-order knowledge. This is to be distinguished from first-order or tacit knowledge.

Tacit knowledges – including moral knowledge – are assumed by people in their everyday lives and are expressed in many forms: stories, anecdotes, beliefs, customs, songs, feasts. All social contexts, not only 'indigenous' or 'African' ones, are rich with a multiplicity of moral knowledges. These moral knowledges imply cosmologies and sustain worldviews taken for granted, and their validity is not usually called into question. Life simply goes on.

But the moment it is asked, 'What is *scientific* or (in this chapter) *ethical* knowledge?', a different epistemic realm with much stricter rules of validity comes into play. Not everything counts as 'evidence' and not just anyone is a valid 'source'. The modern Western tradition has, for now, definitively shaped the nature of what we call scientific, academic knowledge – including ethics and moral philosophy – and therefore dominates the content and paradigms of our theorising efforts.

The challenge, as was demonstrated in the ethics discussion above, is that the moment indigenous moral knowledge of 'sub-Saharan bantu-speaking peoples' is made into an object of study beyond its lived reality, the shadow of the Western canon with its particular thought forms loom large. Look, for example, at this quotation from Catherine Odora Hoppers and Howard Richards (2012: 10) who argue strongly for the epistemic deconstruction of Western science:

> Whenever we look deeply at African society, or indeed most indigenous societies, the empirical fact that stares back at us is a reality of life lived differently, lives constituted around different metaphysics of economic, of law, of science, of healing. ... The problem before us is that the academy has not adopted to its natural context, or has resisted epistemologically, cosmologically and culturally – with immense ensuing cognitive injustice to boot!'.

However, the construction of an 'empirical fact' and the description of indigenous cultures in etic, theoretical categories like 'cosmology', 'metaphysics', 'epistemology' and so forth (including 'ethics'!) are clearly inferred from the Western academic tradition and constitute acts of colonisation and epistemic injustice – the exact opposite of what the authors intended.

The second factor that complicates an escape from paradigmatic or theoretical coloniality, has to do with the global nature of 'Western' science.

What is described as 'modern scientific thinking' is indeed a fairly recent phenomenon in human history. If we take David Wootton's magisterial history of the scientific revolution as reference point (Wootton 2015), this 'new science' only finds its foothold in the period between 1492 and 1750. It introduced a new understanding of knowledge with a new language in which terms such as 'discovery', 'hypotheses', 'experiments', 'theories' and 'laws' of nature assumed a new meaning. Decolonisers are therefore right that this kind of knowledge is relative to the longer preceding history of knowledges; it is further relative to current indigenous knowledges as well as to the specific geography in which it first emerged, namely Western Europe. This particular scientific way of thinking therefore in principle qualifies for the description of a 'local' knowledge.

However, this 'locality' has in the meantime been 'universalised' in at least two ways.

First, the successful translation of Western scientific knowledge into all sorts of technologies has and will continue to shape the global world. Science constitutes the inescapable basis of our everyday lives, no matter our location. If some decolonisers call for the suspension of well-established knowledges that underlie the many positive fruits of these valid knowledges (such as flying in an aeroplane, using antiretroviral medicine, halting the spread of cholera and malaria, and talking on our mobile phones) they will not be taken seriously. Each of these technologies is the product of stable modern knowledges that are, for now, accepted as valid. Translated into technology, their trusted and stable validity, as measured in scientific terms, is indeed useful to all people. We, inescapably, live in and benefit from a 'scientific' world, shaped by modernity and the Enlightenment.

Second, the idea that 'science' is a 'local' form of 'Western' knowledge has been superseded by both academic and economic globalisation. If one takes into account the spread of scientific knowledge in its 'Western' form across the globe via the international university system, and if one, for example, looks at manufactured products with a global supply chain, it has almost become superfluous to speak of 'Western' knowledge. At this point in human history, the matrix of knowledge as scientific knowledge knows no geographic boundaries and is being advanced by scientists and being bought in consumer goods all over the globe, including Africa.[23]

The same globality holds for the development and advancement of ethical theories. Although ethics in the Western tradition predates the Enlightenment, all theoretical models from Ancient Greek to late-twentieth-century moral philosophers are now embedded in this global knowledge system, which forms the inescapable matrix against which all ethical knowledge that claims to be valid, theoretical knowledge, is both framed and measured. That is why the good efforts at a substantive Ubuntu ethics not only expresses itself via Western terminology, but also as second-order knowledge conforms to the validity standards of Western science – citing reliable and authoritative sources, making non-contradictory statements, building rational arguments, and so forth – against which decolonisation in its epistemic form exactly rebels.

IS THERE – IN PRINCIPLE – A WAY OUT?

Have we therefore reached a cul de sac in our efforts to overcome coloniality beyond contextualisation? I wish to argue to the contrary, on condition that a blind-spot in the search for epistemic diversity in the decolonisation project is avoided.

If decolonisation critique is against scientism or positivistic knowledge, where empirical observation and repeatable experiments are seen as the only form of valid knowledge, decolonisers are in fact in good company. Philosophically this critique is well established in various forms of post-positivist thinking from Karl Popper's (1959) falsification and Thomas Kuhn's (1962) paradigm theories to different strands of social constructivism. This is not a new idea.

The blind-spot of some proponents of decolonisation in seeking greater room for other forms of knowledge than 'scientific' knowledge is that they focus chiefly on the natural sciences. They consequently miss the point that 'knowledge' in any modern university includes a rich variety of perspectives that do not conform to a narrow definition of experimental validity or the requirement of quantitative exactitude that works so well in mathematics, physics or engineering.

Western science itself has developed a rich diversity of epistemologies in fields of inquiry such as economics, history, philosophy, literature, psychology, theology, art, or what one could bundle together as the humanities and social sciences. Ethics and moral philosophy form an integral part of these knowledge forms and they challenge the narrow empiricist scientific tradition. The key consequence is that this epistemic diversity beyond empiricism opens these disciplines up to embrace what has become known as 'indigenous' knowledges: historians recognise that oral histories are crucial for access to an oral past; local music and song are important sources of anthropological understanding; archaeological artefacts open doors on the lifestyle of past communities; traditional healers already assist in a richer definition of health, and – in the context of this chapter – forms of tacit moral knowledge about personhood-in-community, expressed via Ubuntu, have the potential to eventually disrupt and enhance our existing ethical theories and move from mere (de)-contextualisation to a transcendence of epistemic coloniality.

This disruptive and complementary potential is enhanced by the fact that the very nature of post-positivist knowledge invites falsification and paradigm revolutions. As African intellectuals we should exploit this inherent trait of Western knowledge and actively create space for dissenting views, especially those from the so-called margins. This will undermine current privileges and weaken current academic power nestled in conferences, universities and journals. This will expose and deconstruct the social and epistemic violence accompanying the modern Western scientific tradition. Such dissent and critique are 'rational' things to do, as they increase the likelihood of growth in scientific knowledge so eloquently described by Popper (1959) and Kuhn (1962). As Mbembe said (with reference to Enrique Dussel), for knowledge to be universal, it must also be pluriversal. We must therefore transform the university into a pluriversity (Mbembe 2015: 19) by continuing to pursue decolonisation via 'local' knowledge forms,[24] and by being more radical in our search for genuine alternative thought forms.

CONCLUSION

The conclusion of this chapter is that the substantive effort to construct an alternative moral theory via Ubuntu represents the strongest form of de- and recontextualisation of Western knowledge if compared with transfer and translation models of business ethics, and hence qualifies as a decolonised form of Africa-centred knowledge. In this limited sense, then, Ubuntu does provide a decentring of Eurocentric views and consequently a tempering of coloniality.

But on the stronger claim of actual epistemic decolonisation, it is apparent that the Ubuntu project – like all forms of theoretical-scientific knowledge – is invariably steeped in Western knowledge forms and rules of validation. From this perspective, and judged by the more fundamental epistemic demands of decolonisation, Ubuntu is in fact a perpetuation and further reinforcement of a colonial mindset.

Because post-positivist, 'Western' scientific knowledge is by definition and in principle open to falsification, efforts at decolonisation of moral philosophy may yet yield ethical theories with superior problem-solving and alternative expressive abilities, leading to new knowledge paradigms. In light of the current state of African business ethics scholarship, and the fact that relief cannot readily be expected from 'Western' ethicists, the prospect of success does not look good – unless and until we radically reconceptualise what are counted as moral 'problems', moral 'solutions' and – ultimately – moral 'theory'.

NOTES

1   This essay is a reworked version of the author's inaugural address in April 2017 at the University of Stellenbosch and was published online in December 2017 by the *Journal of Business Ethics*. Its inclusion in this anthology is with the kind permission of the author and the journal publisher.

2   Those who resist domination by Western knowledge often refer to other knowledges as 'non-Western', revealing the deep bias they are trying to overcome.

3   In the same way it is an abstraction to speak about '*a* Western' or '*a* European' approach.

4   Books with the title of 'business ethics' very rarely, if ever, explain themselves as *Western* business ethics, nor does one find an *American* business ethics journal in the same vein as the *African Journal of Business Ethics*.

5   That we in Africa are inevitably drawn toward the centre is, for example, evident from the very successful and good book, *Business Ethics*, edited by colleagues Deon Rossouw and Leon van Vuuren (2018). This book started in 1994 as *Business Ethics: A Southern African Perspective*. It became *Business Ethics in Africa* in 2002, and as from the third edition (2004) onwards, the title has just been *Business Ethics*. For an appreciative discussion of this development up to 2010, read Naudé (2011).

6   See, for example, the more than 500 cases listed by the African Association of Business Schools (www.aabschools.com) and the sources provided by the South African Business School Association (www.sabsa.co.za). See the interesting case studies listed in Chapter 23 of Rossouw and Van Vuuren (2018).

7   It must be noted that Mbiti himself did not use the actual word 'Ubuntu' in this study to describe an African philosophy, but, as is evident from the quotations in the text, and looking at subsequent discussions of Ubuntu, he does express the idea quite distinctly.

8   See Ramose's (2003c: 230) emphasis on the family (in its extended form) as social basis for an African philosophy. 'No doubt there will be variations within this broad philosophical "family atmosphere". But the blood circulating through the "family" members is the same in its basics'.

9   See Naudé (2013: 246) for a critique of the misuse of Ubuntu: 'When the supposedly universal boundaries of Ubuntu (humaneness) are drawn along ethnic or party-political lines, they become a vicious philosophy of exclusion and dehumanisation. When life-enhancing social exchange is turned into corrupt buying of favour, public resources are wasted. When the social ideal of community enhancement is replaced by enrichment for powerful individuals or elite groups, poverty and social marginalisation increase. When a communitarian sense of happiness turns into an ideology of communitarianism where dissenting voices and contrasting opinions are seen as treacherous in principle, consultation (open debate), so famous in traditional African *imbizos*, dies.'

10 This is a problem that Metz (2007b) admirably attempts to address in his Ubuntu theory of right action.

11 See Metz's list of these judgements and practices in Metz (2007b: 324–327).

12 The threat to a purported Ubuntu lifestyle has its roots in the combined effect of Africans being swept off their feet by an 'accelerated modernity' (Smit 2007: 83) and the impact of cultural globalisation (Naudé 2005) together with the interiorisation of the colonial master's image of Africans. The former implies an attitude of cultural diffidence ('global is always better than local'); the latter a deep sense of inferiority: 'If I do not look, act and talk like my former master [now the centre of the global village], then I have not "made" it yet'.

13 Metz (2007c: 375) speaks of 'distinctiveness': 'A moral theory counts as "distinctive" insofar as it differs from what is dominant in contemporary Anglo-American and Continental philosophy'. My

view is that his theory of right action indeed shows potential of being distinctive; although its claim to be 'African' on the basis of particular 'beliefs that are common among peoples of sub-Saharan Africa' is not convincing. The only sense in which Metz's work is 'African' is that is done from a geographical location in Africa and in dialogue with a body of literature developed predominantly by African and African-based scholars.

14   See Broodryk (1996: 35–36) who, after comparing Ubuntu with a variety of thought constellations (communism, capitalism, Marxism, and so on), concludes: 'If unique means unusual, incomparable, extra-ordinary, Ubuntuism then seems not to be unique. Ubuntu does not exist only in one culture; people of all cultures and races can have this magic gift or sadly lack it. In each of us some of these qualities exist.'

15   See Nussbaum (2009) on a 'common humanity' and Lutz (2009: 319) who, inter alia, forges links between Ubuntu and Confucianism.

16   See the narratives of these small-scale communities in the book of Acts and the normative vision of reciprocity, care, benevolence, service and assistance (Ubuntu values?) contained in the letters to the Corinthians, chapters 12–14; Romans, chapter 15; Ephesians, chapter 4; and Philippians, chapter 2.

17   I retain the sexist spirit of Kant's language.

18   In her recent doctoral dissertation with the interesting title *Einander Nötig Sein*, Sarah Bianchi (2016) demonstrates that intersubjective, existential recognition ('intersubjektive existentielle Anerkennung') is a recurring theme in Fichte, Hegel and, the focus of her dissertation, Friedrich Nietzsche. Literally translated, she explores the notion that 'we need one another' from a philosophical perspective.

19   The 'centre' of knowledge is not geographically fixed: There were times that Africa – via the Egyptian empire for example – was at the epicentre of architecture, mathematics and art. It is the process of globalisation in modern times that currently gives Western science its universal hold.

20   This is no easy task: 'Given the imbalance of world power, as reflected in its knowledge assumptions, those who choose to occupy this creative, suggestive third space, struggle to enlarge its archives, its case histories, and its theoretical concepts' (Cooper and Morrell 2014: 7).

21   See Metz (2007b: 321, 341), who clearly aims at designing 'a competitive African moral theory', which may be 'compared to dominant Western theories such as Hobbesian egoism or Kantian respect for persons'.

22   See Augustine Shutte's (2001) attempt to develop a complementary model synthesised from 'African' and 'Western' thinking.

23   The first successful heart transplant was done in Cape Town. No one considers medical transplant techniques as either 'African' or 'Western'. They are simply transplant techniques. The new galaxies found by the Square Kilometre Array radio telescope (SKA) in the Northern Cape (South Africa) or a new human species found in the Cradle of Humanity in Gauteng (South Africa) are not 'Western' discoveries. They are simply discoveries by scientists who happen to work in Africa.

24   In this vein, it would, for example, be advisable to include a discussion of Ubuntu, to make explicit the work of Africans in an ethics curriculum, and to use Ubuntu as the prism through which dominant Western theories are viewed. This is an act of decentring that could have a significant decolonising effect.

REFERENCES

Assmann, Jan. 2002. 'Der eine Lebt, Wenn der Andere Ihn Geleitet: Altägyptische Konzepte vom Konnektiven Leben'. In *Die Autonome Person: eine Europäische Erfindung?*, edited by Klaus-Peter Köpping, Michael Welker and Reiner Wiehl, 15–28. Munich: Wilhelm Fink.

Bianchi, Sarah. 2016. *Einander Nötig Sein: Existentielle Anerkennung by Nietzsche*. Munich: Wilhelm Fink.

Broodryk, Johann. 1996. 'Is Ubuntuism Unique?' In *Decolonizing the Mind: Proceedings of the 2nd Colloquium on African Philosophy*, edited by J. Malherbe, 30–37. Pretoria: UNISA Press.

Comaroff, John L. and Jean Comaroff. 2002. 'On Personhood: An Anthropological Perspective from Africa'. In *Die Autonome Person: eine Europäische Erfindung?*, edited by Klaus-Peter Köpping, Michael Welker and Reiner Wiehl, 67–82. Munich: Wilhelm Fink.

Cooper, Brenda and Rob Morell. 2014. *Africa-Centred Knowledges: Crossing Fields & Worlds*. Woodbridge, Suffolk: James Currey.

CSIDD (Centre of Study and Investigation for Decolonial Dialogues). n.d. 'Decolonizing Knowledge and Power: Postcolonial Studies, Decolonial Horizons'. A summer school in Barcelona, Spain, 8–12 July 2019. Course description. http://www.dialogoglobal.com/barcelona/description.php.

Descartes, René. [1641] 1952. 'Meditations on First Philosophy'. In *Great Books of the Western World*, vol. 31: 69–103. London: Encyclopaedia Britannica.

Fishbane, Michael. 2002. 'Covenantal Theonomy and the Question of Autonomous Selfhood: Three Spiritual Types'. In *Die Autonome Person: eine Europäische Erfindung?*, edited by Klaus-Peter Köpping, Michael Welker and Reiner Wiehl, 113–130. Munich: Wilhelm Fink.

Gyekye, Kwama. 2003. 'Person and Community in African Thought'. In *The African Philosophy Reader*, edited by P. H. Coetzee and A.P.J. Roux, 297–314. New York: Routledge.

Hölscher, T. 2014. 'Money and Image: The Presence of the State on the Routes of Economy'. In *Money as God? The Monetization of the Market and Its Impact on Religion, Politics, Law, and Ethics*, edited by Jurgen Von Hagen and Michael Welker, 111–136. Cambridge: Cambridge University Press.

Kant, Immanuel. (1781) 1998. *Critique of Pure Reason*. Cambridge: Cambridge University Press.

Kant, Immanuel. [1785] 1964. *Groundwork of the Metaphysic of Morals*. New York: Harper and Row.

Keller, Catherine. 2002. 'The Subject of Complexity: Autonomy and Autopoiesis'. In *Die Autonome Person: eine Europäische Erfindung?*, edited by Klaus-Peter Köpping, Michael Welker and Reiner Wiehl, 193–202. Munich: Wilhelm Fink.

Kohlberg, Lawrence. 1981–1984. *Essays on Moral Development*. San Francisco: Harper and Row.

Kuhn, Thomas S. 1962. *The Structure of Scientific Revolutions*. Chicago: University of Chicago Press.

Lu, Xiaohe. 2010. *Business Ethics: A Chinese Approach*. Shanghai: Shanghai Academy of Social Sciences.

Lutz, David. 2009. 'African Ubuntu Philosophy and Global Management'. *Journal of Business Ethics* 84 (S3): 313–328. doi: 10.1007/s10551-009-0204-z.

Marx, Karl. [1888] 1969. 'Theses on Feuerbach'. Moscow: Progress Publishers. https://www.marxists.org/archive/marx/works/1845/theses/theses.htm.

Mbembe, Achille. 2015. 'Decolonizing Knowledge and the Question of the Archive'. Presentation at the University of the Witwatersrand, Johannesburg, 22 April. https://wiser.wits.ac.za/system/files/Achille%20Mbembe%20-%20Decolonizing%20Knowledge%20and%20the%20Question%20of%20the%20Archive.pdf.

Mbigi, Lovemore. 2005. *The Spirit of African Leadership*. Randburg: Knowres Publishing.

Mbiti, John Samuel. 1969. *African Religions and Philosophy*. London: Heinemann.

Menkiti, Ifeanyi A. 1984. 'Person and Community in Traditional African Thought'. In *African Philosophy: An Introduction*. 3rd ed., edited by Richard A. Wright, 171–181. Lanham MD: University Press of America. http://www2.southeastern.edu/Academics/Faculty/mrossano/gradseminar/evo%20of%20ritual/african%20traditional%20thought.pdf.

Metz, Thaddeus. 2007a. 'The Motivation for "Toward an African Moral Theory"'. *South African Journal of Philosophy* 26 (4): 275–335.

Metz, Thaddeus. 2007b. 'Toward an African Moral Theory'. *Journal of Political Philosophy* 15 (3): 321–341. doi: 10.1111/j.1467-9760.2007.00280.x.

Metz, Thaddeus. 2007c. 'Ubuntu as a Moral Theory: Reply to Four Critics'. *South African Journal of Philosophy* 26 (4): 369–387. doi: 10.4314/sajpem.v26i4.31495.

Metz, Thaddeus. 2012. 'An African Theory of Moral Status: A Relational Alternative to Individualism and Holism'. *Ethical Theory and Moral Practice* 15 (3): 387–402. doi: 10.1007/s10677-011-9302-y.

Naudé, Piet. 2005. 'In Defence of Partisan Justice: What Can African Business Ethics Learn from John Rawls?' *African Journal of Business Ethics* 2 (1): 40–44.

Naudé, Piet. 2011. '*Business Ethics* (2010): A Review Essay'. *African Journal of Business Ethics* 5 (2): 103–105.

Naudé, Piet. 2013. '"Am I My Brother's Keeper?" An African Reflection on Humanisation'. *Nederduits Gereformeerde Teologiese Tydskrif* 54 (3-4): 241-253. doi: http://ngtt.journals.ac.za/pub/article/view/360.

Nussbaum, B. 2009. 'Ubuntu: Reflections of a South African on Our Common Humanity'. In *African Ethics: An Anthology of Comparative and Applied Ethics*, edited by Munyaradzi Felix Murove, 100–110. Pietermaritzburg: University of KwaZulu-Natal Press.

Odora Hoppers, Catherine A. and Howard Richards. 2012. *Rethinking Thinking: Modernity's "Other" and the Transformation of the University*. Pretoria: UNISA Press.

Perler, D. 2002. 'Descartes' Transformation des Personenbegriffs'. In *Die Autonome Person: eine Europäische Erfindung?*, edited by Klaus-Peter Köpping, Michael Welker and Reiner Wiehl, 141–162. Munich: Wilhelm Fink.

Popper, Karl. 1959. *Logic of Scientific Discovery*. London. Hutchinson.

Porter, Michael E. and Mark R. Kramer. 2011. 'Creating Shared Value: How to Reinvent Capitalism – and Unleash a Wave of Innovation and Growth'. *Harvard Business Review* 89 1–2: 62–77.

Rachels, James. 1989. *The Right Thing to Do: Basic Readings in Moral Philosophy*. New York: Random House.

Ramose, Mogobe B. 1999. *African Philosophy through Ubuntu*. Harare: Mond Books.

Ramose, Mogobe B. 2003a. 'Globalisation and Ubuntu'. In *The African Philosophy Reader: A Text with Readings*, edited by P.H. Coetzee and A.P.J. Roux, 626–650. New York: Routledge.

Ramose, Mogobe B. 2003b. 'The Ethics of Ubuntu'. In *The African Philosophy Reader: A Text with Readings*, edited by P.H. Coetzee and A.P.J. Roux, 324–330. New York: Routledge.

Ramose, Mogobe B. 2003c. 'The Philosophy of Ubuntu, and Ubuntu as a Philosophy'. In *The African Philosophy Reader: A Text with Readings*, edited by P.H. Coetzee and A.P.J. Roux, 230–238. New York: Routledge.

Ramose, Mogobe B. 2007. 'But Hans Kelsen Was Not Born in Africa: A Reply to Thaddeus Metz'. *South African Journal of Philosophy* 26 (4): 347–355.

Rossouw, Deon and Leon van Vuuren. 2018. *Business Ethics*. 6th ed. Cape Town: Oxford University Press.

Shutte, Augustine. 2001. *Ubuntu: An Ethic for a New South Africa*. Pietermaritzburg: Cluster Publications.

Smit, Dirkie. 2007. *Essays in Public Theology: Collected Essays 1*. Stellenbosch: Sun Press.

Tönnies, Ferdinand. [1881] 1922. *Gemeinschaft und Gesellschaft: Grundbegriffe der Reinen Soziologie*. Berlin: Curtius.

West, Andrew. 2014. 'Ubuntu and Business Ethics: Problems, Perspectives and Prospects'. *Journal of Business Ethics* 121 (1): 47–61. doi: 10.1007/s10551-013-1669-3.

Wootton, David. 2015. *The Invention of Science: A New History of the Scientific Revolution*. London: Allen Lane.

CHAPTER 12

Future Knowledges and Their Implications for the Decolonisation Project

Achille Mbembe
University of the Witwatersrand

The experience of student protests in South Africa has generated difficult but necessary debates about whiteness and the damage resulting from institutionalised racial hierarchies and violence. It has forced upon us new questions about what counts as knowledge and why. It has also obliged society at large to reflect on whether academic institutions can be turned into spaces of radical hospitality and if so, how, for whom and under what conditions; or whether they are simply sites that replay power relations already existing within society. Moreover, it has brought back to the centre perennial 'postcolonial dilemmas' such as: What should we do with institutions inherited from a cruel past? Are such institutions 'reformable' or should they simply be 'decommissioned' or, for that matter, literally burnt down in the hope that from the ashes, something new will eventually emerge (Ndebele 2016)?

At the core of these events is the hope, especially among the youth, for something new, which would not simply be a repetition of what we thought we had got rid of (Mbembe 2017). It is this hope that explains the renewed *injunction to decolonise* institutions, or for that matter, knowledge itself.

Calls to 'decolonise' are not new. In the 1960s, 1970s and 1980s they were issued under different names, the most recognisable of which were 'Africanisation', 'indigenisation', 'endogenisation' and so on. So far – and as far as Africa is concerned – the decolonising injunction has mostly consisted of a critique of the *colonial knowledge chain* (what is taught, produced and disseminated) and a denunciation of its deleterious effects on the African society, culture and psyche. To be sure, a lot of resources have been invested in the study of 'indigenous knowledge' or 'technological systems' (Mavhunga 2014; Hountondji 1997). Most of these studies could in fact be assembled under the rubric of *ethno-knowledges*, so tight are their connections with the politics of identity and ethnicity (for a critique, see Comaroff and Comaroff [2009]).

But we still do not have a precise idea of what a 'truly decolonised knowledge' might look like. Nor do we have a *theory of knowledge* as such that might compellingly underpin the African injunction to decolonise. Because of the absence of both a theory of knowledge and a *theory of institutions*, the injunction to decolonise may be, at least for the time being, better understood as a *compensatory act* whose function is to heal what amounts to racial shame (Du Bois 1903).

THE INJUNCTION TO DECOLONISE

Take for instance Ngũgĩ wa Thiong'o (1986) and his now canonical *Decolonising the Mind*. Of all the practical implications Ngũgĩ draws from his programmatic statements, the most important is arguably the necessity for curriculum reform. Crucial in this regard is, for him, the need to teach African languages. A decolonised university in Africa, he believes, should put African languages at the centre of its teaching and learning project. Ngũgĩ probably assumes that language inevitably shapes knowledge or what it is possible to know; he probably believes that language inevitably grounds knowledge in a particular culture and influences what we know and how we know it. But language alone cannot stand or compensate for the lack of a theory of knowledge as such.

Another example is Paulin Hountondji, for whom decolonising knowledge amounts to making sure that our scientific activity is not externally oriented; is 'not intended to meet the theoretical needs of our Western counterparts and answer the questions they pose' (Hountondji 2008).

For him, to decolonise knowledge is to replace such vertical relations with what he calls 'horizontalism' – which he understands as 'an autonomous, self-reliant process of knowledge production and capitalisation that enables us to answer our own questions and meet both the intellectual and the material needs of African societies'.

Hountondji makes a distinction between discourses *on*, or *about* Africa, which are coming *from*, or are produced or developed *by Africans within Africa* – the study of Africa by Africans in Africa (I do not know where this leaves the diasporas) – and any other discourse on the same subject, but which might originate *from somewhere else*.

The willingness to debunk whiteness, the over-reliance on US-made theories (black feminism, queer theory, Afropessimism, theories of intersectionality) and the idea of the university as a public good notwithstanding, the lack of a theory of knowledge – a potentially fatal weakness of the decolonising project – is also at the heart of South African late injunctions to decolonise.

To put it succinctly, 'decolonisation' in the African context has meant, pell-mell: (1) changing the curriculum, or syllabus or content (this mostly applies to the humanities); (2) changing the criteria for defining what texts are included in, or excluded from the canon; (3) changing student demographics while recruiting more black staff and transforming the academic and administrative bodies; and (4) recalibrating the activities of teaching and learning in such a way as to institute a different teacher-learner power relation.

In the process, an instrumentalist view of knowledge has generally been privileged, which reduces knowledge to a matter of power (which by the way it is – the famous Foucauldian knowledge/power nexus – but only partly). Curriculum reform is spoken about in terms of the rehabilitation of marginalised or defeated narratives but hardly in response to current shifts in knowledge landscapes (of which more later). There is hardly any critique of so-called indigenous epistemologies and in more than one instance, the latter is simply conflated with traditional cosmogonies, vernacular *arts de faire*, including crafts, narratives and proverbs.

In some instances, decolonisation is easily reduced to a matter of origins and identity, race and location. What confers authority is where one comes from, the putative community one belongs to, not the truth validity of the claims being made.

Furthermore, the concept of Africa invoked in most discourses on 'decolonisation' is deployed as if there was unanimity within Africa itself about what is 'African' and what is not. Most of the time, the 'African' is equated with the 'indigenous'/'ethnic'/'native', as if there were no other grounds for an African identity than the 'indigenous' and the 'ethnic' (see Letsekha 2013).

These observations do not constitute sufficient ground for an outright repudiation of the decolonising project. After all, an uncompromising critique of the dominant Eurocentric academic model – the fight against what Latin Americans in particular call 'epistemic coloniality' – that is, the endless production of theories that are based on European traditions, is still necessary. So is the critique of particular anthropological knowledges (knowing about Others) that never fully acknowledge these Others as thinking and knowledge-producing subjects in their own terms (see Feierman 1990).

Indeed, there is a recognition of the exhaustion of the present academic model with its origins in the universalism of the Enlightenment. Boaventura de Sousa Santos (2007, 2013) or Enrique Dussel, for instance, make it clear that *knowledge can only be thought of as universal if it is by definition pluriversal*. They have made it clear, too, that at the end of the decolonising process, we will no longer have a university. We will only have what they call a 'pluriversity' (Santos 2010). For them, a pluriversity is not merely 'the extension throughout the world of a Eurocentric model presumed to be universal and now being reproduced almost everywhere thanks to commercial internationalism'. By pluriversity, they understand a process of knowledge production that is open to 'epistemic diversity'.

The end goal is not to abandon the notion of universal knowledge for humanity, but to embrace such a notion via a '*horizontal strategy of openness to dialogue among different epistemic traditions*'. Within such a perspective, to decolonise the university is therefore to reform it with the aim of 'creating a less provincial and more open critical cosmopolitan pluriversalism' – a task that involves the radical *re-founding* of our ways of thinking and a 'transcendence of our disciplinary divisions'.

Properly understood (and in spite of its obvious limitations), the 'decolonial' 'decolonisation' project (just like postcolonial theory and feminist theory) has aimed at expanding our conceptual, methodological and theoretical imaginary. In most instances, it has resisted unified accounts of the human. Downplaying regimes of knowledge that have constituted the human or even the world as one, or have framed humanity as an undifferentiated whole, it has instead sought to map and interrogate the social, cultural and historical differences and uneven power relations that divide the Anthropos.

In this sense, the 'decolonial' 'decolonisation' project is an epistemological project premised on the idea that social worlds are multiple, fractured and contested. Thus the necessity to embrace multivocality and translation as a way not to perpetuate the knowledge/power asymmetries that currently fracture global humanity. In this model, knowledge of the empirical world is thought to be gained through the embrace of multiplicity, of a plurality of narratives from many voices and places.

Unfortunately, in the 'decolonial' 'decolonisation' project (just as in some strands of feminist and postcolonial theories), multiplicity has been theorised as 'difference'. Difference itself has been understood as that which separates and cuts off one cultural or historical entity from another. A decolonial act, in this perspective, is taken to be an act of disconnection and separation (a gesture by which one is cut, or one cuts oneself from the rest). The challenge has therefore been to understand difference as a particular fold or twist in the undulating fabric of the universe – or in a set of continuous, entangled folds of the whole.

BIFURCATIONS

Whatever the case, attempts at 'transcending our disciplinary divisions' have in fact been happening partly in response to a set of challenges universities worldwide have been facing, and ongoing contestations affecting the disciplines that constitute the foundations of modern knowledge.

Some of these challenges are of a *political* nature. In the South African case, they have to do with profound and still unresolved questions of racial justice. They have to do with the conditions under which the university can be recognised as a truly common, *public good*, and as such a microcosm of a society in which each voice counts, which is built on the idea of radical hospitality, co-belonging and openness as opposed to separation and closure. Of late, such disputes have dramatically crystallised around, amongst others, the problem of student debt and the decommodification of higher education.

Other such contestations are of a *generational* nature. Indeed massive cultural shifts are underway as we increasingly live our lives in reconfigured environments of intense informational stimuli and as digital technologies become tightly woven into the fabric of our everyday life. As suggested by N. Katherine Hayles and others, we can suspect that a 'technologically enhanced rewiring of the brain' is underway especially among the younger generations (see Pötzsch and Hayles 2014). If indeed, as we are led to believe, dealing with digital and computational media on an everyday basis entails significant neurological changes, then the assumptions we used to entertain about humans and their relations to the world may no longer be entirely valid in relation to the kind of self that is emerging among the younger generations.

Other challenges are of an *institutional* nature. Not so long ago, institutionalised knowledge was all that counted. It was an object to be taught in clearly circumscribed institutions and disciplines. Knowledge produced by the university was bounded and restricted by organisational apparatuses. As a matter of fact, there is no boundary for any knowledge today. Extra-institutional knowledge is unbounded, uncontainable and easily searchable. It is no longer so easily restricted by organisational apparatuses. To know nowadays requires the development of a range of new literacies required, for instance, by changes in writing, in reading, in forms of public presentation, in the capacity to inter-pret images, or to work on a screen. Old knowledge platforms now appear dated or in any case, are falling into obsolescence at a higher rate and pace (Svensson and Goldberg 2015).

Other contestations are of *a pedagogical nature*, triggered as they are by new learning methods, devices and publics. Traditional ways of teaching have been chan-ging thanks to a range of new practices and methods enabled by digital environ-ments. The sense, nowadays, is that everything can be searched and found. This is what Google is for – an efficient way to deliver knowledge to the public. Meanwhile, various open learning platforms are increasingly created by the learners themselves. Such platforms do challenge the very notion of disciplinarity – how to think properly, the questions that are the right ones to ask, the right method to deploy in addressing those questions.

Techno-facilitation of knowledge, with flipped classrooms, innovative project works and collaborative writing is increasingly becoming the norm. The epoch is characterised by a massive acceleration, which contrasts with the humanistic predisposition to slow down. The role of the teacher in its old form might not exist for much longer. Massive open online courses are no longer a rarity. The old vertical teacher-student relationship is increasingly replaced by the idea of a *learning community*, one in which the teacher gives away control and learning encompasses the total social experience of the students. Furthermore, it happens inside and outside the classroom, and it takes seriously the knowledge the students already have.

Yet others challenges are of *an epistemological nature*. It remains to be seen whether the perennial question of what we can know and how we came to know things will ever be resolved. If anything, old disputes are far from having been settled as standard realist, rationalist and objectivist understandings of truth and knowledge are undercut by the proliferation of new, *hybrid thought styles* and new *thought collectives*.

NEW COGNITIVE ASSEMBLAGES

As a result of technological innovations and the pressures evoked above, epistemic reconfigurations, or shifts, are under way in various disciplines and sub-disciplines. They are harnessing new kinds of data and reshaping what constitutes units of analysis. New bodies of thought are involved in rethinking the nature of knowledge itself, the nature of being, of matter, how degrees of agency are distributed across human and non-human agents. Contrary to various discourses on the crisis of the humanities, the age is characterised by heightened curiosity and accompanying experimentation.

Some of these shifts are paving the way for *the emergence of entirely new cognitive assemblages*, if not new knowledge formations. I would now like to briefly comment on those transformations that have to do with the changing epistemological landscape.

FRAGMENTATION OF THE DISCIPLINES

Not so long ago, the sciences – theoretical and applied – could still be systematically ordered and classified. For instance, life sciences, physics, the organic and the inorganic 'could be demarcated and located along methodological axes, along a set of pedagogical practices'. Now, within every discipline and every field, the ramifications are so manifold that 'they subvert any consistent totality'. Each specialisation ends up turning into further segmentations, which in turn branch out from their classical roots, in a process of incessant production of sub-specialisations within sub-specialisations (Steiner and Vilar 2008: xxii–xxiv).

Against this argument, it can be observed that fragmentation has always been part of the life of the disciplines. In fact, disciplines and fields of study have never been entirely fixed, either in form or in organisation. They have always been continuously forming and transforming, sometimes merging but never really progressing toward any general unity or truth.

But we are clearly witnessing is an acceleration of this process today. It has reached a level where many are now wondering whether disciplines as such have become obsolete. Indeed, established disciplines do no longer correspond to, or encompass the variety of 'fields of inquiry'. There is a profound disjuncture between the disciplinary taxonomies and classifications inherited from the nineteenth and twentieth centuries and the proliferation of thematic imagination, the rhythm of the constitution of diverse sub-fields.

THE VELOCITY OF SO-CALLED TURNS

A corollary of fragmentation is the velocity of so-called turns. The 1980s were marked by the linguistic turn. Nowadays, many 'turns' are happening simultaneously – the affect turn, the new materialism turn, the ontological turn, the neuro-turn, the Anthropocene turn.

To be sure, some of the turns do not last. Others are not 'real' turns since they do not affect deeper questions of epistemology or of method. They are part of a vast recycling and rebranding of disciplines that goes hand in hand with the creeping commodification of education. Yet, all these 'turns' must be taken as 'alerts', a search for different *images of thought* (St. Pierre, Jackson and Mazzei 2016).

A crucial factor behind the proliferation of fields and sub-fields of inquiry, our sense of *who is the subject of cognition and what should count as an object of knowledge* is fast changing. Of particular significance, too, is the fact that *entrenched and historic antagonisms between the sciences and humanities disciplines are breaking down*. They are breaking down as a result of a number of developments I would like to briefly single out.

First is the gradual recognition that we humans are not as special as we once thought. Nor are we as disentangled from other species as we once thought. Actually, the terrestrial sphere is not only mostly populated by beetles and bacteria in terms of biomass (Bar-On, Phillips and Milo 2018) but the future of our species will thoroughly depend on what we do to other species (principle of entanglement and mutuality).

Second is the fact that the humanities have traditionally relied on a distinction between society and nature, or culture and nature. This is reflected in the division of labour between social sciences and natural sciences. The social, in this instance, usually referred to those aspects of human life, human activity and human understanding that required some form or another of symbolisation. If nature was understood to encompass both subjects and objects, society and nature nevertheless denoted two realms that could be kept analytically distinct – the distinction between the symbolic and the pre-symbolic.

There are those who still argue for the uniqueness of human nature, or for the idea 'that humans occupy a unique position in the scheme of things' (Hayles 2005). They still believe that humans alone are capable of rational thought; they alone have a capacity to feel emotions such as empathy.

The ontological turn (which has given rise to new subfields such as post-humanist ethnography, environmental philosophy and history, Earth System science and other strands of social science research) has put such beliefs under severe stress. Common to these sub-fields is the idea of distributed agency and, to some extent, the rejection of the Cartesian dichotomies between subject and object, society and nature, human and nonhuman, living and non-living entities. The drive nowadays is to perceive the various non-human entities with which we interact as sources of agency.

Third, *a renewed dialogue is in the making between the social sciences, studies of science and technology, life and biological sciences and philosophy*. It is not without tensions and contradictions. Issues that have primarily been the subject and object of the biological sciences are, in different ways, increasingly becoming the subject of theories and methods within the humanities and vice versa. Emergent fields or sub-fields across the life and biological sciences and the humanities are engaged in the search for new terminologies and theoretical apparatuses at points of contact and interface, across disciplinary boundaries and traditions (Fitzgerald and Callard 2015). Humanities-inflected inquiries are being reshaped in ways that make them more open to biological sciences, just at the time when biological sciences are becoming more receptive to the social sciences (Meloni 2014).

Of late, this *incipient convergence* has triggered the development of new research agendas. Such agendas overtly privilege ideas of co-constitution, co-evolution and co-implication. They 'emphasize the complex, processual, indeterminate, contingent, non-linear and relational nature of phenomena constantly open to effects from contiguous processes' (Blackman 2016a: 263). In other words, they start from the assumption that there are no biological or vital processes that are not 'simultaneously technical, cultural, symbolic, material, economic and immaterial' (Blackman 2016b: 4). As for the human, not only is its emergence processual: the human is fundamentally an indeterminate entity.

At the heart of this incipient convergence is therefore a deliberate attempt not only at breaking down all kinds of distinctions 'between human and other life forms, between binary genders, between the social and the natural, the human and the technical, biology and identity, the mind and the body, self and other, material and immaterial, and many other dichotomous forms of thought and practice' (Blackman 2016b: 8), but also at *relocating the apparent newness of the present conjuncture to longer, deeper histories*. Thus, the return of deep history as the best way to elucidate the conditions under which the new emerges.

THE NEURO-TURN

Of late, the two most important turns have been the ontological turn and the neuro-turn. Both put into question a number of foundational categories the humanities have relied on for the last centuries – the category of *the human* and the category of *the social*; that of *nature* and that of *culture*. Some of the key categories of the human-istic inquiry – intention, agency, consciousness, mind, brain and language, autonomy, personhood, beliefs and feelings such as empathy, sympathy, compassion, suspicion, fear or love have also been subjected to renewed inquiry, especially by the biological sciences.

In fact, 'the webs of human social and cultural life that we had come to understand as our particular object of knowledge seem more and more open to being figured neuro-scientifically and experimentally' (Fitzgerald and Callard 2015: 4). According to Des Fitzgerald and Felicity Callard, many facets of human life that were, for much of the twentieth century, primarily understood through the abstraction of 'culture' or 'society' 'are increasingly understood as functions of the cerebral architecture of individuals or of groups of individuals' (Fitzgerald and Callard 2015: 7).

Neuroscientists are now seeking to establish the neural mechanisms that underpin almost every single human activity or emotion. For Nikolas Rose (2016), although brains are constitutively embodied, saturated by and dependent upon their constant transactions with inputs from without, mental events can now be read in the tissues of the brain.

FORMS OF KNOWING AND SUBJECTS OF COGNITION

The changes sketched above are not only affecting the nature of matter and the place of embodied humans within a material world, or how human beings are understood in the present. They are also affecting the very forms of knowing and the subject of knowledge.

Not long ago, conscious thought was seen as the defining characteristic of humans. Cognition (knowing) involved an awareness of self and others and it was associated with consciousness, symbolic reasoning, abstract thought, verbal language, mathematics and so on. The act of knowing also included perception and judgement. Today, thanks to progress in disciplines such as cognitive biology, we have a better and more complex understanding of *human cognitive ecology*.

First of all, as Hayles (2016: 789) suggests, cognition is no longer 'limited to humans or organisms with consciousness; it extends to all life forms, including those lacking central nervous systems such as plants and micro-organisms'. Being, as it is, the engagement of all life forms with their environment, cognition is a much broader capacity that 'extends far beyond consciousness into other neurological brain processes' (Hayles 2016: 783). In other words, there are non-conscious forms of cognition.

Second, she argues, cognition is not limited to humans and life forms. It is also pervasive in complex technical systems. In other words, humans and living organisms are not the only important or relevant cognisers on the planet. Technical systems are also endowed with cognitive capabilities.

Third, knowledge does not only reside in the brain. It is also acquired through interactions with the environment. It is partly about processing information, discerning patterns, drawing inferences. We live in an epoch when the informational streams we rely upon to produce knowledge are so massive, so multifaceted and complex that they can never be processed exclusively by human brains.

Cognitive abilities once resident only in biological organisms have therefore now been exteriorised into the world. 'Biological and technical cognitions are now so deeply entwined that it is more accurate to say they interpenetrate one another' (Hayles 2016).

All of this is happening amidst a return to 'big questions', the most important of which are what constitutes human life; how are we to communicate between disciplines, between cultures, between human and non-human entities; and whether there is anything we hold dear in our ways of living that we might want to preserve nurture, and foster, while overcoming the existential paradigm that has set us on a fast track to ecological collapse (Citton 2016).

KNOWLEDGE IN A COMPUTATIONAL AGE

It is not only the entire knowledge ecology that is fast changing. It is also what actually counts as knowledge. Computers have changed the way even basic concepts in science are understood. The conflation of the mind/brain with the computer is the biggest intellectual event of our times. It is at the basis of current reconfigurations of what counts as knowledge.

Knowledge has always been tied to the requisite of 'empirical validation'. Knowledge is that which has to be validated empirically; that which has undergone a methodical, systematic process of empirical validation. No knowledge is free from these constraints. Whatever is free from it represents at best wisdom, but not knowledge as such.

The epoch is in search of deterministic models of human behaviour and decision-making. Knowledge is reduced to an understanding of what lies behind people's decision-making, their responses to marketing: the figures of the citizen, the consumer, publics and their behaviour.

It is a conception of knowledge that claims to possess laws that can be discovered through the use of mathematics.

Imitating natural sciences and mimicking physics has been a crucial trend/feature in the human/social sciences since the nineteenth century – the idea that we will gain privileged insight into humanity generally if we follow or apply the laws of physics to human phenomena.

Whether we have transcended that physics envy (hierarchies of knowledge) remains to be seen. In some instances, it is back with vengeance. Take, for instance, economic theory, where this movement mostly gained steam after the Second World War. If we are to believe historians of science, this was the moment when techniques such as linear pro-gramming, statistical optimisation, matrix methods, formal logic, information theory, game theory 'and a whole raft of techniques were imported into economics'.

In the 1960s and 1970s, early developments of both electronic computers and program-ming were consolidated and an entirely new intellectual epoch was rendered possible by the computer, which 'jumpstarted' what today is known as 'econometric empiri-cism', which ranges from 'cybernetics as a theory of certain kinds of human/automaton metaphors, to the incorporation of stochastic models in decision theory, to econometrics and simulation'.

With the advent of algorithmic thinking and various forms of automated reasoning, new debates are unfolding concerning the faculties of knowing, desiring and judging as well as the meaning of truth. The same goes for intuition, understanding and imagination (Stiegler and Ross 2017).

THE PLANETARY

Each of the 'turns' evoked above has paved the way for the rise of new objects of know-ledge and new questions about the ways in which the human world could be re-imagined in terms of its relation with the Earth. With the end of the human condition as marked by agency, the times are propitious for the return to 'big questions' and 'deep history' – 'big questions' concerning the relation of human life to planetary life, in a context of geo-logical recasting of historical time.

The emerging paradigm is that 'human societies and the Earth have now forged a tenuous unity' (Delanty and Mota 2017: 10). 'Planetarity' is the consciousness of that unity and of the entanglement of nature and society.

AFRO-COMPUTATION

In this last section, I will try to draw the implications of the developments I have just sketched for the study of Africa. Africa is going through a silent techno-computational revolution. Electronic and digital footprints are everywhere – ticket sales, online searches are common.

People write blog posts. Many resort to credit card transactions. The visual and auditory landscape is fast changing. In music, we are witnessing an endless recombination and remix and mash-up of sounds and rhythms, the sampling and recombining of old and new material.

Cut-up and collage practices extend well beyond music as such, as old and new creative practices keep generating innovative, useful content in almost every single domain of everyday life – in visual art, film, video, literature, culinary arts, fashion and of course Internet applications.

So, here like everywhere else in the world, life behind screens is fast becoming a fact of daily existence. People are exposed to, are producing and are absorbing more images than they ever have before.

They are increasingly surrounded by all kinds of devices, dream machines and ubiquitous technologies – cell phones, the Web, videos and films. Connection to the Internet is not simply a preoccupation for the middle class. It is increasingly in the interest of the urban poor to be connected too. Even before food, shelter and access to electricity have been secured, the first thing the African urban poor strive for is a mobile phone, then television and especially cable TV. And of course the Internet.

It follows that as the boundaries of perception are being outstretched, more and more Africans are projected from one temporal regime to another. Time now unfolds in multiple versions. Its shapes are more protean than they have ever been. The struggles to capture these protean shapes of time have hardly been documented and yet, they are paving the way for an Afropolitan aesthetic sensibility we still need to map and properly study.

A prime example of the ongoing Afro-techno-revolution is the mobile phone. The introduction of the mobile phone on the continent has been a technological event of considerable singularity. Three comments in this regard are necessary.

First, the mobile phone is not simply an object of use. It has become a portable storage (*grenier*) of all kinds of knowledges and a crucial device that has changed the way people speak, act, write, communicate, remember and imagine who they are and how they relate to themselves, to others and to the world at large.

Second, along with the advent of other computational media, the introduction of the mobile phone has also been a major *aesthetic and affect-laden event*. In Africa, this device is not only a medium of communication. It is also a medium of *self-stylisation and self-singularisation*. People spend a lot of time with it. It is as if they wear it. It has become an extension of one's being, a container of lives it in turn shapes. The way people treat their phones and the way they take care of these objects is itself an indication of how they would like to be taken care of and, eventually, of the way they would like to be treated.

Third, from a philosophical point of view, the biggest impact of the mobile phone – and of digital technologies more broadly – has been at the level of *the imaginary*. The interaction between humans and screens has intensified, and with it, the experience of life and the world as cinema – the cinematic nature of life.

The argument I want to make, which is slightly different from a classical Afrofuturist argument, is that *the plasticity of digital forms speaks powerfully to the plasticity of African precolonial cultures and to ancient ways of working with representation and mediation, of folding reality.*

African precolonial cultures were obsessed with the interrogation concerning the boundaries of life. As evidenced by their myths, oral literatures and cosmogonies, among the most important human queries were those concerning the world beyond human perceptibility, visibility and consciousness. The time of objects was not unlike the time of humans. Objects were not seen as static entities. Rather, they were like flexible living beings endowed with original and at times occult, magical and even therapeutic properties.

Things and objects, the animal and organic worlds were also repositories of energy, vitality and virtuality and, as such, they constantly invited wonder and enchantment. Tools, technical objects and artefacts facilitated the capacity for human cognition and language. They belonged to the world of interfaces and as such, served as the linchpin to transgress existing boundaries so as to access the Universe's infinite horizons. With human beings and other living entities, they entertained a relationship of reciprocal causation. This is what early anthropologists mistook for 'animism'.

Turning now to knowledge as such, it must be said that precolonial African ways of knowing have been particularly difficult to fit into Western analytical vocabularies. According to Jane Guyer and Samuel Eno Belinga (1995), in their study of Equatorial knowledge, such ways of knowing were not 'specialist, in the sense of a closed esoteric system with its classifications, propositions'. Nor were they 'controlled and monopolised by a small cadre of experts or a secret society hierarchy' (1995: 93).

Collectively, they tells us, 'knowledge was conceptualised as an open repertoire and unbounded vista. Then, within collectivities the vista was divided up and quite widely distributed on the basis of personal capacity' (Guyer and Eno Belinga 1995: 93). 'Adepts were many and varied,' they say, 'each pushing up against the outside limits of their own frontier of the known world, inventing new ways of configuring, storing and using' what must have been an ever shifting spectrum of possibility. Citing Jan Vansina (1990) and James Fernandez (1982) in particular, Guyer and Eno Belinga argue that these were societies that knew much more about their local habitats than they needed to know for utilitarian purposes, which means that knowledge for the sake of knowledge was a key feature of social existence.

From the picture they paint, it seems to me that these societies would hardly care about questions such as the 'decolonisation' of knowledge. Whatever its origins, knowledge was something to be captured, if necessary from outside, as long as it could be mobilised for action or for performance. They showed 'great receptivity to novelty', Guyer and Eno Belinga (1995: 94) argue. 'Personal abilities existed first, but they could be augmented and actualised within the person, making that person a real person, singular to themselves' (1995: 102) and recognised as such by others – the social process was about putting these singularities together. It is as if the Internet was speaking unmediated to this archaic unconscious or to these societies' deepest and hidden brain.

It is nowadays common sense to argue that the technological devices that saturate our lives have become extensions of ourselves. The novelty is that in the process, they have instituted a relationship between humans and other living or vital things African traditions had long anticipated.

Indeed, in old African traditions, human beings were never satisfied with simply being human beings. They were constantly in search of a supplement to their humanhood. Often, they added to their humanhood various attributes or properties taken from the worlds of animals, plants and various objects. Modernity rejected such ways of being and their compositional logics, confining them to the childhood of Man. Clear distinctions between ourselves and the objects with which we share our existence were established. A human being was not a thing or an object. Nor was he or she an animal or a machine. This is precisely what human emancipation was supposed to mean.

Our own relationship to ourselves and to what surrounds us has changed as a result of our increasing entanglement with objects, technologies or other animate things or beings. Today we want to capture for ourselves the forces and energies and vitalism of the objects that surround us, most of which we have invented. We think of ourselves as made up of various spare-parts. This convergence, and at times fusion, between the living human being and the objects, artefacts or the technologies that supplement or augment us is at the source of the emergence of an entirely different kind of human being we have not seen before.

With the advent of algorithmic thinking and various forms of automated reasoning, machines are increasingly endowed with decision-making capacities. The concretisation of reasoning in machines – in other words the automation of reasoning – has cast a shadow on deductive reasoning and on the uniqueness of human reasoning. 'Biologically bounded thought has been displaced by an abstract architecture of reasoning able to carry out tasks and make decisions by correlating data' (Parisi 2016).

In a global culture in which the footprints of social life are increasingly digitalised, software is becoming the engine of society and algorithmic reasoning a new form of thinking. To a large extent, software is remaking the human. The production of massive amounts of data at exponential rates has pushed us to the threshold of a different ontology of number. Numbers have become the engines not only of calculation and computation, but also of invention, imagination and speculation. We can no longer rely entirely on dominant epistemological and ontological assumptions about numbers. New ways of theorising measurement and quantification are more than ever required if we are to account for the ongoing computational reconfigurations of subjectivity and of the social (De Freitas, Dixon-Román and Lather 2016).

CONCLUSION

If, as Gerard Delanty and Aurea Mota (2017) argue, the emerging paradigm is that 'the human societies and the Earth have now forged a tenuous unity as well as a consciousness of that unity'; and 'the presuppositions of modernity are now once again called into question with the emergence of an entangled conception of nature and society, Earth and the world', then the question facing us is the following: What interpretive categories do we need for making sense of the world and of human societies, within a trajectory of time that encompasses planetary time?

Africa is a planetary laboratory at a time when history itself is being recast as an integrated history of the Earth system, technical systems and the human world. Here, a technological revolution is taking shape at a time when the continent is increasingly perceived as the last frontier of capitalism. Out of Africa, an incredible amount of wealth has been extracted over centuries. This wealth has flowed out to every corner of the globe. To be sure, the continent's natural assets are in danger of being depleted. Waste and pollution have increased exponentially. But Africa remains the last territory on Earth that has not yet been entirely subjected to the rule of capital.

It is the last repository of a vast body of untapped wealth – minerals underground, plants and animals, water and sun, all the forms of energy latent in the Earth's crust. Its biosphere is still more or less intact. Its hydrographic power, its solar energy, its territorial immensities are hardly touched. It is the last major chunk of our planet that has not yet been entirely connected to its many different parts. This single gargantuan landmass can still support a huge number of people. It is the only place on Earth where people can still come and begin anew and where the potential for the human species is still high. The times, therefore, are propitious for big questions concerning the relation of human life to planetary life in a context of geological recasting of historical time.

REFERENCES

Bar-On, Yinon M., Rob Phillips, and Ron Milo. 2018. 'The Biomass Distribution on Earth'. *Proceedings of the National Academy of Sciences* 115 (25): 6506–6511. https://doi.org/10.1073/pnas.1711842115.
Blackman, Lisa. 2016a. 'The Challenges of New Biopsychosocialities: Hearing Voices, Trauma, Epigenetics and Mediated Perception'. *Sociological Review Monographs* 64: 256–273. doi: 10.1002/2059-7932.12024.

Blackman, Lisa. 2016b. 'The New Biologies: Epigenetics, the Microbiome and Immunities'. *Body & Society* 22 (4): 3–18. doi: 10.1177/1357034X16662325.

Citton, Yves. 2016. 'Fictional Attachments and Literary Weavings in the Anthropocene'. *New Literary History* 47 (2): 309–329. doi: 10.1353/nlh.2016.0016.

Comaroff, John L. and Jean Comaroff. 2009. *Ethnicity, Inc.* Chicago: University of Chicago Press.

De Freitas, Elizabeth, Ezekiel Dixon-Román and Patti Lather. 2016. 'Alternative Ontologies of Number: Rethinking the Quantitative in Computational Culture'. *Cultural Studies ↔ Critical Methodologies* 16 (5): 431–434. doi: 10.1177/1532708616655759.

Delanty, Gerard, and Aurea Mota. 2017. 'Governing the Anthropocene: Agency, Governance, Knowledge'. *European Journal of Social Theory* 20 (1): 9–38. doi: 10.1177/1368431016668535.

Du Bois, W.E.B. 1903. *The Souls of Black Folk: Essays and Sketches*. Chicago: A.C. McClurg.

Feierman, Steven. 1990. *Peasant Intellectuals: Anthropology and History in Tanzania*. Madison: University of Wisconsin Press.

Fernandez, James W. 1982. *Bwiti: An Ethnography of the Religious Imagination in Africa*. Princeton: Princeton University Press.

Fitzgerald, Des and Felicity Callard. 2015. 'Social Science and Neuroscience beyond Interdisciplinarity: Experimental Entanglements'. *Theory, Culture & Society* 32 (1): 3–32. doi: 10.1177/0263276414537319.

Guyer, Jane I. and Samuel M. Eno Belinga. 1995. 'Wealth in People as Wealth in Knowledge: Accumulation and Composition in Equatorial Africa'. *The Journal of African History* 36 (1): 91–120. doi: 10.1017/S0021853700026992.

Hayles, N. Katherine. 2005. 'Computing the Human'. *Theory, Culture & Society* 22 (1): 131–151. https://doi.org/10.1177/0263276405048438.

Hayles, N. Katherine. 2016. 'The Cognitive Nonconscious: Enlarging the Mind of the Humanities'. *Critical Inquiry* 42 (4): 783–808. doi: 10.1086/686950.

Hountondji, Paulin. 1997. *Endogenous Knowledge: Research Trails*. Dakar: CODESRIA.

Hountondji, Paulin. 2008. 'Knowledge of Africa, Knowledge by Africans: Two Perspectives on African Studies'. *Revista Critica de Ciencias Sociais* 80: 149–160.

Letsekha, Tebello. 2013. 'Revisiting the Debate on the Africanisation of Higher Education: An Appeal for a Conceptual Shift'. *The Independent Journal of Teaching and Learning* 8: 5–18. https://www.iie.ac.za/Documents/HPG14077_PDF%20Article_2_Revisiting_2013.pdf.

Mavhunga, Clapperton Chakanetsa. 2014. *Transient Workspaces: Technologies of Everyday Innovation in Zimbabwe*. Cambridge, Massachusetts: MIT Press.

Mbembe, Achille. 2017. 'Difference and Repetition: Reflections on South Africa Today'. In *Being There: South Africa, a Contemporary Art Scene*, edited by Suzanne Pagé and Angeline Scherf. Paris: Éditions Dilecta.

Meloni, Maurizio. 2014. 'How Biology Became Social, and What It Means for Social Theory'. *The Sociological Review* 62 (3): 593–614. doi: 10.1111/1467-954X.12151.

Ndebele, Njabulo. 2016. 'They Are Burning Memory'. Tenth Annual Helen Joseph Lecture. University of Johannesburg, 14 September.

Ngũgĩ wa Thiong'o. 1986. *Decolonising The Mind: The Politics of Language in African Literature*. London: James Currey.

Parisi, Luciana. 2016. 'Automated Thinking and the Limits of Reason'. *Cultural Studies ↔ Critical Methodologies* 16 (5): 471–481. doi: 10.1177/1532708616655765.

Pötzsch, Holger and N. Katherine Hayles. 2014. 'Posthumanism, Technogenesis, and Digital Technologies: A Conversation with N. Katherine Hayles'. *The Fibreculture Journal* 23: 95–107. http://twentythree.fibreculturejournal.org/fcj-172-posthumanism-technogenesis-and-digital-technologies-a-conversation-with-katherine-n-hayles/.

Rose, Nikolas. 2016. 'Reading the Human Brain: How the Mind Became Legible'. *Body & Society* 22 (2): 140–177. doi: 10.1177/1357034X15623363.

Santos, Boaventura de Sousa. 2007. *Another Knowledge Is Possible: Beyond Northern Epistemologies*. London: Verso.

Santos, Boaventura de Sousa. 2010. 'The University in the Twenty-First Century'. *Eurozine*, 1 July. https://www.eurozine.com/the-university-in-the-twenty-first-century/.

Santos, Boaventura de Sousa. 2013. *Epistemologies of The South: Justice against Epistemicide*. Boulder: Paradigm Publishers.

St. Pierre, Elizabeth A., Alecia Y. Jackson and Lisa A. Mazzei. 2016. 'New Empiricisms and New Materialisms: Conditions for New Inquiry'. *Cultural Studies ↔ Critical Methodologies* 16 (2): 99–110. doi: 10.1177/1532708616638694.

Steiner, George and Emílio Rui Vilar. 2008. *Is Science Nearing Its Limits?* Manchester: Carcanet.

Stiegler, Bernard and Daniel Ross. 2017. 'The New Conflict of the Faculties and Functions: Quasi-causality and Serendipity in the Anthropocene'. *Qui Parle: Critical Humanities and Social Sciences* 26 (1): 79–99. doi: 10.1215/10418385-3822421.

Svensson, Patrik and David Theo Goldberg. 2015. *Between Humanities and the Digital*. Cambridge, Massachusetts: MIT Press.

Vansina, Jan. 1990. *Paths in the Rainforests: Toward a History of Political Tradition in Equatorial Africa*. Madison: University of Wisconsin Press.

Decolonising Minds via Curricula?

Grant Parker
Stanford University and Stellenbosch University

It may be useful to tease out some common threads that emerge from the foregoing chapters. In doing so it is impossible to avoid addressing the merits of the decolonisation movement itself, though that is not the intention. Rather, the emphasis will be on identifying some centres of gravity within the preceding discussions.

In the interests of full disclosure, I should first offer a word about my subject position. I offer these comments as an outsider to the field, yet no stranger to South Africa or to the broader issues at stake. A South African by birth and training, I was trained academically in ancient Greek and Roman studies. In keeping with recent trends, I have pursued ancient studies in a context of the comparative global humanities.[1] In fact the frequent resistance of my field to engaging with (South) Africa has provided an incentive and an urgent need to explore connections and contexts, including colonial histories, anew.[2] For this reason, while a classicist may seem uniquely unsuited to comment on the topic of decolonisation, I would argue that such a background encourages a broad and deep view of some of the issues at stake.

TIME FRAMES

First, a broader issue to emerge in the discussion around decolonisation is that of time frames. An oft-noted assumption of the Fallist protests was that university curricula are unreconstructed creations of colonialism: the existing reality is more complicated, as contributors here point out (see Sayed, Motala and De Kock, Chapter 8, and Jansen [2017]). This makes the 'Why now?' question disconcerting in several respects, in both a national and an international framework.

To be sure, the initial use of the term 'decolonisation' had a strictly political valence, denoting the process by which former colonies gained self-determination from mostly West European metropoles, most specifically in the period from 1947 (Partition) to 1962 (Algeria's independence from France), though those dates by no means encapsulate the entire process.[3]

In South Africa, by contrast, the call for decolonisation comes very belatedly in relation to twentieth-century world history, and even then somewhat belatedly compared to the establishment of democracy in the country. Measured from the final crisis of apartheid in the late 1980s, the protests of 2015–2016 took place nearly a generation after the fact. What is more, its leading proponents have been an emerging generation of university students rather than established political leaders, a distinction that has implications for the nature of historical consciousness and the salience of precedent in debates.[4]

In terms of slogans, it is not merely that the term 'decolonisation' has become a proxy for 'transformation' (Jansen 2017: 163). Rather, it occupies the uneasy middle ground between the 'liberation' touted by the African National Congress ANC and other groups in the middle decades of the twentieth century and 'transformation' that has taken on institutional significance, at universities and elsewhere, in the years since 1994. To put it bluntly, this is a difference between revolution and reform, in language that is less inflammatory. Thus, at the same time as the term 'liberation' wears thin for an (ANC) establishment that has been in power for some 25 years, the term 'transformation' marks the slow pace or indeed lack of substantive change, as viewed by its most vocal critics, such as the Economic Freedom Fighters (EFF). Decolonisation may be seen as bridging the gap between moderate and radical visions of change. Such tensions, I suggest, are substantially about the time frame of social and economic change.

One of the implications of the temporal distance between the accession of the ANC and the present time is that the matter of language has become harder to address: the window to implement language policy change in schools and universities was surely the 1990s, at a time when the goal of nation building was a focus of the Mandela government. On the matter of language I shall have more to say below, but for the present let us be aware of the complex temporalities, the difficult dynamics of continuity and change around language – and not least the fact that the matter of diversifying languages on university campuses has failed to progress significantly since 1994.

It is in this context of timscales that public art deserves special attention, as a medium that gives character to university campuses and indeed to other locations of the public domain. The debate around statues, which reached fever pitch in March and April 2015, is still not resolved, if the continued sequestering of public art at the University of Cape Town (UCT) and the official decision to move the statue of President Marthinus Theunis Steyn at the University of the Free State (UFS) in November 2018 are any indication of broader trends. As Brenda Schmahmann (Chapter 9) shows, public artworks, such as Cigem Aydemir's *Plastic Histories* (2014) at the self-same UFS and Willem Boshoff's *Kring van Kennis* (2000) at the University of Johannesburg, have a unique capacity to make viewers think about the relation of the present to the past and the future. By focusing on university campuses as physical locations and on the workings of space and place, it is tempting to see this scenario in terms of human geography: for many black students, so the argument goes, have taken offence at their continued presence on university campuses (Miller and Schmahmann 2017). That presence has been in relation to the supposed lack of transformation, and especially the paucity of black academic staff, in historically white universities (HWUs).[5]

While anyone interested in art may be pleased that public artworks actually do, in such settings, communicate with viewers, the question arises as to why statues and other symbols have been invested with so much power in public debate. This too has sometimes been seen as a question of timescale: Why now? The offending Rhodes statue at UCT famously received little notice for so many years.[6] It would appear that the protesters' decision to focus on the statue was a result of frustrations with lack of progress on other fronts, frustration with university administrations seemingly as proxies for the post-apartheid state. This has resulted in a general fixation with symbols or, as Pierre Nora would have it, with sites of memory (Nora 1989). In twenty-first-century South Africa, Nelson Mandela himself has become a site of memory, so that the many placards criticising him as a sell-out in the political transition of the 1990s are clearly of a kind with colonial- and apartheid-era statues. Via Facebook and other social media, symbols have a new capacity to circulate. In this model, the older generation of statues have become symbols of continuity, whether positively or negatively. It is all the more important to be alert to the discontinuities and ruptures that artistic interventions such as Boshoff's and Aydemir's have articulated, precisely because they have the capacity to make subtle points and to invite reflective discussion about continuity and change. As it is, amid the politics of spectacle, symbols are often viewed less subtly and sympathetically. Figurative statues may even be potential proxies for physical violence (see Miller and Schmahmann 2017).

Well may we ask what the net effect on such symbol-mindedness on university curricula may be (O'Connell 2015). It is possible that an overriding emphasis on symbolic significance of any object of learning limits and ultimately detracts from its pedagogic potential.

IDENTITIES AND ESSENCES

In the discourse around decolonising the curriculum, Africa has been one of the key recurring concepts; another has been race. To be sure, amid discussions around syllabi both explicit and implicit questions about the nature of Africa come to the fore. Who has the right to speak for Africa? How might we conceive of Africa, some 20 years after then President Thabo Mbeki launched his African Renaissance project?[7] Do some elements of (South) African pasts inform the country's character more than others?[8] The class-room experience of Auerbach, Dlamini and Anonymous (Chapter 6) shows that such discussions today inevitably take place within the shadow of a neoliberal world economy, impinging on both content and form, despite the intentions of curriculum designers.

South Africa's place in Africa continues to evolve: the Southern African Development Community (SADC) order is one manifestation and the recent xenophobic attacks another. Whereas many South African-based academics had taken up the question in practical terms for a considerable time, the landscape has evolved not only amid socio-political and demographic change but particularly as a number of academics with roots to the north of the Limpopo made their home in South Africa: Harry Garuba, Catherine Odora Hoppers, Mahmood Mamdani and Achille Mbembe are among those whose names recur in a number of chapters in this book, although the African continent is now more widely represented on the personnel of several university campuses. The impact of some of these scholars, not least those named above, has been substantial in proportion to the relatively small numbers involved. As the so-called Mamdani Affair at UCT in 1998 drastically exposed, the established frameworks for thinking about Africa have been sub-ject to question. The Mauritian initiative is a significant counter-example to the Mamdani Affair given that part of its newly designed intellectual content has been spearheaded by an emerging generation of scholars, pushing new agendas by virtue of both their youth-fulness and the newness of their institution(s) (see Auerbach, Dlamini and Anonymous Chapter 6). Such discussions would suggest that hard questions about teaching Africa considerably precede the recent protests – and that is without going back to the debate between Ali Mazrui of Makerere University and Walter Rodney of the University of Dar es Salaam (see Mamdani, Chapter 1) and acknowledging that the more recent protests are by no means necessarily richer and subtler in the arguments raised. Again, it would seem that in the politics of spectacle, identities are starkly conceived, and in the process dialogue and critical self-awareness are sidelined.

So too the matter of race: arguably this element of identity is more prone to essen-tialism than any in South Africa, as recent analyses show (including Lange's Chapter 4 and Naudé's Chapter 11). Gerhard Maré's timely contribution to the debate about race has gone so far as to claim that South Africans would be well served, as an experiment, to abandon the terms 'race' and 'racism' for an agreed period, so as to explain via peri-phrasis what they actually mean. So saturated has the terminology become, so differently have people used the terms for different ends. It is disgracefully true that apartheid-era definitions of race continue to inform official calibrations of the population, such as those produced by Statistics South Africa.[9] How, if at all, might South Africans escape the racial thinking of apartheid, as notoriously spelled out in the Population Registration Act, no. 30 of 1950? As Maré (2014) shows, there are many reasons for this lack of change around the conceptualisation of race. One of the most troubling aspects of the persist-ence of old-style racial thinking is that in the process inequality is overlooked. There may even be some intentionality behind this phenomenon – dare one say false conscious-ness? – insofar as beneficiaries of black economic empowerment are able to use race as a smokescreen to divert attention from the small numbers of those enriched through the initiative. This is merely one context in which race has been subject to essentialism, and in this case it is clear who is benefiting. The broader reality is that thinking about race in South Africa is in many ways remarkably regressive, and that the language of public discourse around it (about which more below) is but one factor that marks and reinforces this obstacle impeding more equitable futures.

If essentialism is the disease, what is the cure? Certainly, comparison is one way forward, though by no means a simple or contested one. When, for example, indigenous experiences are seen in an international framework, that is a start: to be sure, much of the theory about decolonisation comes out of Latin America, and of course other regional arenas of potential comparison. In *Citizen and Subject*, Mamdani forcefully argues against any supposedly exceptional status for South Africa; rather, apartheid is the 'generic form of the colonial state in Africa' (Mamdani [1996] 2018: 8).

In more general terms, the 'tired binaries' of decolonisation discourse are an enormous obstacle to the prospect of any real progress, including that between indigenous and coloniser, and the supposed equation of Europe: Africa = centre: periphery (see Jansen's Chapter 3). Indeed, the deleterious effects of such dichotomous or 'Manichaean' thinking were subject to strong critique from Frantz Fanon ([1952] 2008: 27). The claims made by Professor C.J. Raju during his South African visit in November 2017 may be considered a crude and essentialist attempt to valorise indigenous knowledge (see Hoadley and Galant's Chapter 5). There are more careful and useful ways of advancing the same general argument, and several scholars and units are already doing exactly that.[10]

LANGUAGE

The issue of language comes up in the preceding chapters in two different senses: the status of English in relation to other languages and especially indigenous ones, and also the use of slogans in political discourse. The second of these may be dealt with dispatch, since I have already touched on it. Put simply, #RhodesMustFall and #FeesMustFall as mass movements function via slogans, and these are of course more attuned to political impact than to fine-grained social analysis. Such linguistic use owes much to digital media: Twitter, in particular, requires brevity. There is much substance to Jonathan Jansen's comment that slogans 'have no substantive merit in a massively unequal society harbouring deep grievances in the present about an unresolved past' (Chapter 3). In its sloganeering form, we might say that contemporary political language has become a marker of deep difference and of the difficulty in engaging in debate at all. Nowhere is this truer than in the House of Assembly, where physical altercations have become a new if occasional norm inside the House since the EFF joined Parliament in 2014. Needless to say, in such an environment language is also subject to a kind of essentialist reduction of meaning, being put to aggressive more than reflective use. By this reckoning, dialogue, as a particular kind of (Western) academic language, is a canary in the coalmine. The experience of Auerbach, Dlamini and 'Anonymous' (Chapter 6) has much light to shed on the pedagogic challenges and opportunities around political language.

To take up the other linguistic matter: Ngũgĩ wa Thiong'o (1986) in his slim but land-mark book, *Decolonising the Mind*, was primarily interested in the power differential between colonial languages, including English, and indigenous languages, including Kikuyu (Gĩkũyũ) and Kiswahili. By arguing repeatedly for the centrality of indigenous languages, he offered a manifesto for decolonisation via novels, drama and other lit-erature. In his own 'farewell to English', his own much-publicised creative choices have added visibility to the matter and, speaking in South Africa, he maintained his emphasis on language (see Ngũgĩ 2017). Among the many developments that can be pointed out in the three decades or more since Ngũgĩ's initial publication, three stand out for their rele-vance: (1) the increased predominance of English via information technology, including social media; (2) China's increased influence on the continent, including a new Chinese government initiative to teach Mandarin at South African schools and universities, effect-ively a dynamic of recolonisation amid a debate about decolonisation (Shishenge 2018); and (3) the post-apartheid language policy, means of which 11 languages have official status, again with the effect of benefiting English as a lingua franca.

These points needs no elaboration in the current context, but it is nonetheless worth-while pointing to the road not taken: Neville Alexander (1936–2012) was one of the few activists to have insistently focused on language in policy discussions leading up to the 1994 election (Alexander 2014).[11] His arguments for a multilingual model received only limited uptake, and certainly the 11-language policy that was adopted has fallen into all the traps he foretold. Many of his proposals were aimed at heightening the opportunities for indigenous languages, both in education and other sectors. Whether the opportunity for linguistic liberation has evaporated is a moot point. In this respect universities have severely limited opportunities and resources to redress a situation in which the 'unassail-able position of English', as Chinua Achebe diagnosed a comparable situation in 1975, seems more entrenched than ever in South Africa (Jansen, Chapter 3).

DISCIPLINES

How does decolonisation look in relation to different academic disciplines, and what is its relation to interdisciplinarity? We may start with disciplinarity, defined as institutional and intellectual divisions of learning, which brings us to the very heart of the history of universities – in a Western frame going back to Alexandria's Museum and Library under the Ptolemies (third century BCE) – and to histories of learning even more broadly (Mamdani, Chapter 1). In the period since Second World War it is possible to identify two contradictory developments: on the one hand, a strong tendency towards interdis-ciplinary undertakings, especially in research; on the other, the increasing boundedness of particular kinds of knowledge, particularly in science, technology, engineering and mathematics but also in the social sciences and beyond. Some of this bounded kind of knowledge may be more commercially profitable in the contemporary world economy.

In an African context we come back again to the debate between Mazrui and Rodney, with divergent emphases placed on excellence and relevance (Mamdani, Chapter 1; Jansen [2017]). Mbembe, in this volume (Chapter 12) and in a famous lecture (2015), goes further and looks ahead. He develops the idea of the 'pluriversity', which he describes in terms of the 'process of knowledge production that is open to epistemic diversity'. He explains further: 'It is a process that does not necessarily abandon the notion of universal knowledge for humanity, but which embraces it via a horizontal strategy of openness to dialogue among different epistemic traditions' (Mbembe 2015; compare Tamdgidi 2012). This is Mbembe's utopian vision of a decolonised university in the future – a hypothetical construct of the future but nonetheless a vision with specific, identifiable features.

It is clear that decolonisation looks very different in different disciplines, a fact that emerges whenever practical applications are addressed. In this context it is telling that several of the chapters refer to disruption (including Hoadley and Galant, Chapter 5; Sayed, Motala and De Kock, Chapter 8; Keet, Chapter 10), which is at one point glossed as 'epistemic disobedience' (Le Grange, Chapter 2). What is less clear is what is being disrupted. The so-called Western canon has been an object of attack, even though it is by no means entirely Western (see Sayed, Motala and De Kock, Chapter 8 and Mbembe, Chapter 12), nor have attempts necessarily been undertaken to 'enlarge' it (in Soudien's sense) and thus create it anew (Chapter 7).[12] Aversion to the supposed hegemonic nature of canons seems to have foreclosed any possibility of potential pedagogic value in their more experimental forms: the notion of a decolonised canon does not have to be the oxymoron it might seem. To take a different case study, the private Mauritian university with its emerging institutional curriculum constitutes an explicit counterpoint to trad-itional brick-and-mortar institutions, and an implicit (and sometimes explicit) comment on them (Anonymous, Chapter 6). Such opportunities arise in part from new informa-tion technologies – a hypothetical rather than unalloyed blessing, given that the digital divide limits the extent of access.

Some other discrepancies are perhaps glossed over here: for example, in humanities research there are now strong incentives and attractive opportunities to pursue interdis-ciplinary projects, whereas institutional curricula with regard to teaching are less flexible or welcoming of innovation. What is more, compared to the 1960s, the humanities today have a less revered and less resourced status: though the traditional humanities now seem like an unnecessary luxury at best and Eurocentrically oppressive at worst, attempts to reconstitute African humanities leave much room for further work, including practical suggestions.[13] The Mamdani Affair is merely one reminder of the practical challenges facing the humanities in South Africa. The challenges around composing a syllabus are, if anything, even more fraught now than in 1998.

It is with this note of concern about the relation of curriculum theory and practice that I would like to end. One of the bigger unspoken questions in the background is simply: What are universities for? Or even, how practical does knowledge have to be in order to be socially beneficial? Contrast, for example, literary texts with Fluid Flow Mechanics as objects of learning. The divergent range of knowledge on university campuses firstly poses challenges to theory and secondly obscures the practical difficulties involved in creating, implementing and revising syllabi – indeed, an enriched sense of implementation gives more room for experimentation and evolution. Many of the examples given focus on research more than pedagogy.[14] At the time of writing, history was one area in which theory is in dialogue with practice (Motshekga 2015; Bam 2018).

None of this is intended to question the need decolonisation per se, rather it is to emphasise practical difficulties en route, and at the same time to recognise the progress that many universities have in fact already made – progress that has been drowned out or even wiped out by the adversarial character of debate on campus. Provided it effectively opens up, rather than forecloses, debate on key topics – including (South) African futures, the nature of identities, knowledge and community – the matter of decolonisation contains an invitation to reconsider existing practice and explore new alternatives.

NOTES

1   See, especially, Parker (2017): several of the essays collected in that volume explore the colonial foundations of classical studies, often in comparative vein. As Ngũgĩ (1986: 19) hints, Banda's creation of the Kamuzu Academy in Malawi comes across as an egregious example of the colonial complicities of ancient Greece and Rome. By contrast, several contributors in Parker (2017) show that 'classical antiquity' has also been part of histories of resistance and critique.

2   Given its many disciplines – including history, literary studies, archaeology, linguistics, reception studies – it is better to consider classics a field; in fact it fits well into an area studies paradigm, focusing on the Mediterranean.

3   Among recent historical outlines, see for example Shepard (2015).

4   See Jansen (2017: 104–125) on the 'leaderless revolution'. The launch of a History Ministerial Task Team in May 2018, with a view to reintroducing history in schools, is a potentially valuable measure towards strengthening the historical consciousness of young South Africans (Motshekga 2018).

5   See Lange (Chapter 5) on the 'phenomenology of presence'. For another inflection of the same issues, compare Ramoupi (2014).

6   Holiday (2005) is the exception that proves the rule.

7   Papers from the marquee event (September 1998 in Johannesburg) were published in Makgoba (1999). The concept draws explicitly on Cheikh Anta Diop's ideas from the immediate post-Second World War flush of decolonisation. The African Renaissance, despite some overlap with the decolonisation debate, receives no mention from any of the contributors, presumably a sign that it no longer commands widespread interest, and that Fallist student activists have not necessarily engaged with it.

8   Consider for example Motshekga's (2018) supposed quotation of Nkrumah, in a context of possibly reintroducing history into the school curriculum: 'I am not African because I was born in Africa, but because Africa was born in me'.

9   See, for example, Statistics South Africa (2016: 21).

10 See Chapter 6; cf. Bam (2018).

11 The Project for Alternative Education in South Africa (PRAESA) was Alexander's brainchild and continues to reflect his goals: http://www.praesa.org.za/our-history/.

12   The point needs to be made that the inclusion of an item in the canon should not be seen in itself as an endorsement but rather as an invitation to critique.

13   The many think tanks mentioned by Soudien (Chapter 7) notwithstanding: one issue is that many focus on research rather than pedagogy.

14   Jansen's (Chapter 3) three examples above contain an unexpectedly poignant note, in light of the untimely death of Professor Bongani Mayosi – itself a reminder of the extraordinary personal burdens involved.

REFERENCES

Alexander, Neville. 2014. *Interviews with Neville Alexander: The Power of Languages against the Language of Power*. Pietermaritzburg: University of KwaZulu-Natal Press.

Bam, June. 2018. 'Context Informs Schools History Report'. *Mail and Guardian*, 16 June. https://mg.co.za/article/2018-11-16-00-context-informs-schools-history-report.

Fanon, Frantz. [1952] 2008. *Black Skin, White Masks*. Translated by Richard Philcox. New York: Grove.

Holiday, Anthony. 2005. 'Rhodes Statue Insults the New Order'. *Cape Times*, 14 March.

Jansen, Jonathan D. 2017. *As by Fire: The End of the South African University*. Cape Town: Tafelberg.

Makgoba, Malegapuru William, ed. 1999. *African Renaissance: The New Struggle*. Cape Town: Mafube and Tafelberg.

Mamdani, Mahmood. [1996] 2018. *Citizen and Subject: Contemporary Africa and the Legacy of Late Colonialism*. Princeton: Princeton University Press.

Maré, Gerhard. 2014. *Declassified: Moving beyond the Dead End of Race in South Africa*. Auckland Park: Jacana.

Mbembe, Achille. 2015. 'Decolonizing Knowledge and the Question of the Archive'. Presentation at the University of the Witwatersrand, Johannesburg, 22 April. https://wiser.wits.ac.za/system/files/Achille%20Mbembe%20-%20Decolonizing%20Knowledge%20and%20the%20Question%20of%20the%20Archive.pdf.

Miller, Kim and Brenda Schahmann, eds. 2017. *Public Art in South Africa: Bronze Warriors and Plastic Presidents*. Bloomington: Indiana University Press.

Motshekga, Angie. 2018. 'Launch of History Ministerial Task Team Report'. Speech delivered at Freedom Park, Pretoria, 31 May. https://www.gov.za/speeches/minister-angie-motshekga-launch-history-ministerial-task-team-report-31-may-2018-0000.

Ngũgĩ wa Thiong'o. 1986. *Decolonising the Mind: The Politics of Language in African Literature*. Harare: Zimbabwe Publishing House.

Ngũgĩ wa Thiong'o. 2017. 'Language at the Centre of Decolonisation'. Lecture delivered at the University of the Witwatersrand, Johannesburg, 2 March. https://www.wits.ac.za/news/latest-news/general-news/2017/2017-03/language-at-the-centre-of-decolonisation-.html.

Nora, Pierre. 1989. 'Between Memory and History: *Les Lieux de Mémoire*'. *Representations* 26: 7–24. doi: 10.2307/2928520.

O'Connell, Siona. 2015. 'A Search for the Human in the Shadow of Rhodes'. *Ufahamu: A Journal of African Studies* 38 (3): 11–14.

Parker. Grant, ed. 2017. *South Africa, Greece, Rome: Classical Confrontations*. Cambridge: Cambridge University Press.

Ramoupi, Neo Lekgotla Laga. 2014. 'African Research and Scholarship: 20 Years of Lost Opportunities to Transform Higher Education in South Africa'. *Ufahamu: A Journal of African Studies* 38 (1): 269–86.

Shepard, Todd, ed. 2015. *Voices of Decolonization: A Brief History with Documents*. Boston: St. Martin's Press.

Shishenge, Enock. 2018. 'Africans Are for Sale Again, as Mandarin Takes Over'. *City Press*, 9 September. https://www.news24.com/Columnists/GuestColumn/africans-are-for-sale-again-as-mandarin-takes-over-20180907.

Soudien, Crain. 2016. 'Looking Backwards: How to Be a South African University'. *Educational Research for Social Change (ERSC)* 4 (2): 8–21.

Statistics South Africa. 2016. Statistical Release P0301, Community Survey 2016.

http://cs2016.statssa.gov.za/wp-content/uploads/2016/07/NT-30-06-2016-RELEASE-for-CS-2016-_Statistical-releas_1-July-2016.pdf.

Tamdgidi, Mohammad H., ed. 2012. 'Decolonizing the University: Practicing Pluriversity'. Special issue, *Human Architecture: Journal of the Sociology of Self-knowledge* 10 (1) https://scholarworks.umb.edu/humanarchitecture/vol10/iss1/.

Contributors

Jess Auerbach is a Visiting Researcher at the Open University of Mauritius. Her research interests include aesthetics and sensory studies, decolonial education and social mobility across Lusophone, Francophone, and Anglophone African contexts. Her first book, *From Water to Wine: A Sensory Ethnography of the Emergent Middle Class*, is forthcoming from the University of Toronto Press.

Tarryn de Kock is completing a PhD in Education at the University of Sussex, with a focus on privatisation in public schools. She has worked as a researcher for the Centre for International Teacher Education at the Cape Peninsula University of Technology and at the Human Sciences Research Council, focusing on teacher education, teacher governance, privatisation and decolonisation. She has also served as research officer for the Teachers' Commission of the 2017 National Education Collaboration Trust Policy Dialogues.

Mlungisi Dlamini is an independent researcher and consulting editor based in Mbabane, Eswatini. He has broad interests and work experience in political economy, legal anthropology, phenomenology, history and archaeology. This is his first publication; he is working on a second on how the financialisation of 'communal lands' affects practices of tributary land management and security of tenure.

Jaamia Galant is based in the Humanities Faculty Education Development Unit at the University of Cape Town, working on programme evaluation. She is completing a PhD at the Institute of Education, University College London, focusing on research practices in higher education. She has been extensively involved in national mathematics curriculum policy developments over the past 20 years and has worked as a mathematics educator in the Schools Development Unit at University of Cape Town and as a researcher at the Centre for Research in Science and Technology at the University of Stellenbosch, with a particular focus on research management in higher education.

Ursula Hoadley is an associate professor in the School of Education at the University of Cape Town. Her research interests focus on pedagogy, curriculum and school organisation at the primary level. She is currently engaged in research on early grade reading programmes in South Africa, Uganda and Liberia. Her most recent work, *Pedagogy in Poverty: Lessons from 20 Years of Curriculum Reform in South Africa*, was published by Routledge in 2018.

Jonathan Jansen is Distinguished Professor of Education at the University of Stellenbosch. He is president of the Academy of Science of South Africa and chairperson of the Jakes Gerwel Fellowship, as well as the author and co-editor of *Schooling in South Africa: The Enigma of Inequality* (Springer, 2019).

André Keet holds the chair of Critical Studies in Higher Education Transformation at Nelson Mandela University and is the chairperson of the Ministerial Oversight Committee on Transformation in South African Public Universities, a member of the Council on Higher Education and visiting professor at the Centre for Race, Education and Decoloniality at the Carnegie School of Education, Leeds Beckett University. He worked in national human rights institutions in post-1994 South Africa before joining the University of Fort Hare in October 2008. He also spent time at the University of the Free State as director of the Institute for Reconciliation and Social Justice, advisor to the vice-rector and acting deputy vice-rector for Student Affairs and External Relations.

Lis Lange is the deputy vice-chancellor: Teaching and Learning at the University of Cape Town. From 2014 to 2018, she was vice-rector (Academic) at the University of the Free State, where she had previously been senior director of the Directorate for Institutional Research and Academic Planning.

She has been involved in the development and implementation of science and technology and higher education policy in South Africa, working in different capacities at the Human Sciences Research Council, the National Research Foundation and the Council on Higher Education, where she was executive director of the Higher Education Quality Committee between 2006 and 2010. She has published in the fields of history, higher education and quality assurance and has served as a member of the board of the International Network of Quality Assurance Agencies in Higher Education.

Lesley Le Grange is distinguished professor in the Faculty of Education at the University of Stellenbosch. He is chairperson of the Accreditation Committee and a member of the Higher Education Quality Committee of the Council on Higher Education in South Africa, vice-president of the International Association for the Advancement of Curriculum Studies, and Fellow of the Royal Society of Biology (UK). His current research interests are exploring resonances and dissonances between African traditional values and (post)human theories, exploring implications of an immanent ethics for (environmental) education research and decolonising the curriculum.

Mahmood Mamdani is the Herbert Lehman Professor of Government at Columbia University in New York and executive director of the Makerere Institute of Social Research in Kampala, Uganda. He specialises in the study of African history, politics and society. Previously, he was professor at the University of Dar es Salaam in Tanzania (1973–1979), Makerere University in Uganda (1980–1993), and the University of Cape Town (1996–1999) and served as President of CODESRIA (Council for the Development of Social Research in Africa) (1998–2002). He is the author of award-winning books that include *Citizen and Subject*, *When Victims Become Killers* and *Good Muslim, Bad Muslim*.

Achille Mbembe is research professor of History and Politics at the Wits Institute for Social and Economic Research in Johannesburg and a visiting professor in the Department of Romance Studies at the Franklin Humanities Institute, Duke University. He has also held appointments at Columbia University, Yale University and the University of California, Berkeley. Mbembe's research interests concern the social sciences and African history and politics. His major book, *On the Postcolony*, was published in French in 2000 and the English translation was published by the University of California Press in 2001.

Shireen Motala is the senior director of the Postgraduate School at the University of Johannesburg and professor in the Faculty of Education. Prior to joining University of Johannesburg in 2010, she was the director of the Education Policy Unit at the University of the Witwatersrand. She is currently a trustee on the boards of the Centre for Education Development and the South African Institute for Distance Education. Her research interests are in the areas of education financing and school reform, access and equity, education quality and the internationalisation of higher education.

Piet Naudé is professor of Ethics and director of the University of Stellenbosch Business School. He is a member of the Alexander von Humboldt Foundation research group and holds life member-ship of the Centre for Theological Inquiry at Princeton University. His publication on the Belhar Confession, *Neither Calendar nor Clock* (Eerdmans, 2010) was awarded the Andrew Murray-Desmond Tutu Prize. His most recent book is *Pathways in Ethics* (Sun Press, 2016).

Grant Parker is an associate professor in the Department of Classics at Stanford University and extra-ordinary professor in the Department of Ancient Studies at Stellenbosch University. His research addresses various aspects of monuments and memory. He recently edited *South Africa, Greece, Rome: Classical Confrontations* (Cambridge University Press, 2017).

Yusuf Sayed is professor of International Education and Development Policy at the University of Sussex, the South African Research Chair in Teacher Education, the founding Director of the Centre for International Teacher Education at the Cape Peninsula University of Technology, and honorary professor at the Institute of Social and Economic Research at Rhodes University. He is currently engaged in several large-scale studies about teacher professionalism, teacher education and continuing professional development in South Africa and globally. He recently published *Engaging Teachers in Peacebuilding in Post-conflict Contexts: Evaluating Education Interventions in Rwanda and South Africa* (UK Department for International Development, 2017).

Brenda Schmahmann is a professor and the South African Research Chair in South African Art and Visual Culture at the University of Johannesburg. Her most recent books are *Picturing Change: Curating Visual Culture at Post-apartheid Universities*, *The Keiskamma Art Project: Restoring Hope and Livelihoods* and *Public Art in South Africa: Bronze Warriors and Plastic Presidents*.

Crain Soudien is the chief executive officer of the Human Sciences Research Council and formerly a deputy vice-chancellor at the University of Cape Town, where he remains an emeritus professor in Education and African Studies. He is the chairperson of the Independent Examinations Board and of the Ministerial Committee to Evaluate Textbooks for Discrimination and was formerly the chairperson of the District Six Museum Foundation, the president of the World Council of Comparative Education Societies and the chair of the Ministerial Committee on Transformation in Higher Education. His publications include *Nelson Mandela: Comparative Perspectives of His Significance for Education*; *The Making of Youth Identity in Contemporary South Africa: Race, Culture and Schooling*; *Realising the Dream: Unlearning the Logic of Race in the South African School*; and *Inclusion and Exclusion in South Africa and Indian Schools*.

Index

The first letters of movements with a hashtag (#) are used for alphabetical ordering. Prepositions are not used for alphabetical ordering.